PENGUIN BOOKS

THE AMERICAN MAGIC

Ronald Lewin, one of Britain's most distinguished
military historians, is the author of a number of books,
including studies of Field Marshal Erwin Rommel,
Field Marshal Sir Bernard Montgomery, and Winston
Churchill, as well as, of course, the best-selling *Ultra
Goes to War*. Mr. Lewin is married and has three
children. He lives in Surrey, England.

THE AMERICAN MAGIC
CODES, CIPHERS AND THE DEFEAT OF JAPAN

Ronald Lewin

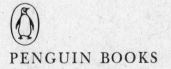

PENGUIN BOOKS

Penguin Books Ltd, Harmondsworth,
Middlesex, England
Penguin Books, 625 Madison Avenue,
New York, New York 10022, U.S.A.
Penguin Books Australia Ltd, Ringwood,
Victoria, Australia
Penguin Books Canada Limited, 2801 John Street,
Markham, Ontario, Canada L3R 1B4
Penguin Books (N.Z.) Ltd, 182–190 Wairau Road,
Auckland 10, New Zealand

First published in the United States of America by
Farrar, Straus and Giroux 1982
First published in Great Britain by Hutchinson and Co. Ltd 1982
Published in Penguin Books 1983
Copyright © Ronald Lewin, 1982
All rights reserved

LIBRARY OF CONGRESS CATALOGING IN PUBLICATION DATA
Lewin, Ronald.
    The American magic.
    Bibliography: p.
    Includes index.
    1. World War, 1939–1945—Cryptography.   2. World
War, 1939–1945—Secret service—United States.
3. World War, 1939–1945—Pacific Ocean.   4. World
War, 1939–1945—Japan.   5. Japan—History—1912–
1945.   I. Title.
[D810.C88L48   1983]   940.54'86'73   82-22266
ISBN 0 14 00.6471 0

Printed in the United States of America by
R. R. Donnelley & Sons Company, Harrisonburg, Virginia
Set in Baskerville

To
the Allied soldiers,
sailors and airmen
whom Magic and Ultra
guided to victory

If I ascend up into heaven, thou art there;
If I make my bed in hell, behold, thou art there.
If I take the wings of the morning
And dwell in the uttermost parts of the sea,
Even there shall thy hand lead me,
And thy right hand shall hold me.

PSALM 139

Acknowledgments

WITHOUT THE GENEROUS hospitality in Washington of Miss Kay Halle, OBE, who has done so much to further Anglo-American relations, my researches would have been more prolonged and far less agreeable.

Like all who have enjoyed their swift and friendly assistance, I cannot fully express my gratitude to William Cunliffe, John Taylor and their colleagues in the Modern Military Section of the National Archives in Washington and to Dr. Dean Allard and the staff of the Naval Archives.

I am also much indebted to the following, who either advised on passages of my text or helped me in other ways with information and encouragement: Professor Stephen Ambrose, Patrick Beesly, Walter Bell, Bennett Boskey, William P. Bundy, Admiral Arleigh Burke, USN, Captain Malcolm Burnett, RN, Professor Raymond Callahan, Aileen Clayton, Robin Denniston, Vera and William Filby, Professor M. R. D. Foot, Alfred Friendly, Edward Hitchcock, Captain W. J. Holmes, Harry Homewood, Major David Horner (Australian Army), Edwin Huddleson, Professor R. V. Jones, Professor Warren F. Kimball, Paul Kramer, Professor Walter Laqueur, Paul de Laszlo, Admiral Edwin Layton, USN, Bruce Lee, Jon Lellenberg, Walter Lord, the late Professor Arthur Marder, Dr. John Mason, Vice-Admiral Sir Ian McGeoch, Professor G. C. McVittie, Roger Nelson, Mary Pain, Colonel Walter Pforzheimer, Dr. Forrest Pogue, Justice Lewis Powell, Commander Francis Raven, Professor Dr. Jürgen Rohwer, Admiral Donald M. Showers, USN, Henry Schorreck, David Shulman, Justice John Paul Stevens, Brigadier John Tiltman, Dr. L. Tordella, Justice Byron White and Patrick Wilkinson.

It is conventional to thank one's wife for aid and comfort. In this case, the value of the editorial comment I have received transcends conventional language.

RONALD LEWIN

Contents

A Note on Sources   xiii

Of Codes and Ciphers   3

1   Don't You Dare, Mr. Dewey   5

2   The Path to Pearl   16

3   That Damn Cloud   49

4   A Plan Called MO and a Plan Called MI   81

5   The Stab in the Back   112

6   The Salt Mines   128

7   The Fork in the Road   155

8   "You Are the Hero"   176

9   A Broken Axis: The Blockade-Runners' Ruin   204

10   Massacre of the *Marus*   218

11   Overhearing Oshima   232

12   A Scent in the Morning Air   247

13   The Mastiffs and the Spaniel   274

Notes 293

Appendices

  I "America Deciphered Our Code"   301

 II Special Security Officer for the South West Pacific
     Theater: Memorandum from the Adjutant General to
     the Commander-in-Chief, South West Pacific Area   304

III Special Security Representatives and Special
     Security Officers, 15 February 1945   306

Bibliography   309

Index   313

Illustrations and Maps
[following page 154]

The American Sigaba Machine
An American version of "The Bombe"
Joseph Rochefort
William F. Friedman
Arlington Hall
Mt. Vernon
Admiral Layton
Portion of the machine constructed for reading Purple
Members and staff of the Congressional Inquiry
Admiral King
Henderson Field
Admiral Nimitz
The great base at Rabaul
Admiral Mitscher with his chief of staff, Arleigh Burke
The Great Marianas Turkey Shoot seen from USS *Lexington*
The Great Marianas Turkey Shoot seen from the air
Admiral Halsey
Seeadler Harbor
MacArthur, Roosevelt and Nimitz
Mitscher on *Lexington*
Halsey asks for more
MacArthur walks ashore at Morotai
Testimonial presented to William F. Friedman

Maps

The Pacific Theatre of Operations   101
The Solomons and Northern Australia   102

A Note on Sources

THE ORIGINAL DOCUMENTS on which this narrative is based are too voluminous for more than a representative selection to be quoted in the text. The following is a list of primary source material. All files, unless otherwise indicated, are held in the Modern Military Section of the National Archives in Washington. A bibliography of books consulted appears as an appendix.

Development and Organization of the U.S. Signal Intelligence

A Selection of Papers Pertaining to Herbert O. Yardley, 1918–1950.

Narrative of the Combat Intelligence Center, Joint Intelligence Center, Pacific Ocean Areas.

History of the Special Branch, MIS, War Department, 1942–1944.

History of the Operations of Special Security Officers attached to Field Commands, 1943–1945.

Marshall letter to MacArthur on the use of Ultra intelligence, 23 May 1944, and related correspondence.

Allocation of Special Security Officers to Special Branch, Military Intelligence Service, War Department, 1943–1945.

Instructions for Maintaining the Security of Special Intelligence in the Southwest Pacific Areas, issued by GHQ, SWPA, 15 June 1944.

War Department Regulations Governing the Dissemination and Security of Communications Intelligence, 1943–1945.

Reports by U.S. Army Ultra Representatives with Field Commands in the South West Pacific, Pacific Ocean and China/Burma/India Theaters of Operations, 1944–1945.

Use of CX/MSS Ultra by the United States War Department, 1943–1945.

Synthesis of Experiences in the Use of Ultra Intelligence by U.S. Field Commands in the European Theater of Operations.

Ultra and the U.S. Seventh Army, by Major Donald S. Bussey.

Reports Received by U.S. War Dept. on the use of Ultra in European Theater, W.W. II, October 1945.

Operations of the Military Intelligence Service, War Department, London (MIS WD London).

Six Lectures on Cryptology, by William F. Friedman, April 1963.

Problems of the SSO System in World War II: Dept. of Army.

MIS War Dept. Special Security and other correspondence relating to special intelligence in the Pacific Ocean Area.

The Need for New Legislation Against Unauthorized Disclosure of Communications Activities, 9 June 1944.

A Brief History of the Signal Intelligence Service, by William F. Friedman, 29 June 1942.

Procedures for handling Ultra Dexter Intelligence in the CBI, 22 March 1944.

Signal Intelligence Service—changes in Directive of September 27, 1939: memorandum from the Chief Signal Officer of the Army to the Adjutant General.

List of Special Security Representatives and Special Security Officers, 15 February 1945.

Reminiscences of Lieutenant Colonel Howard W. Brown, prepared under the direction of the Chief Signal Officer.

Operations

Statement for Record of Participation of Brigadier General Carter W. Clarke, GSC, in the Transmittal of Letters from General George C. Marshall to Gov. Thomas E. Dewey, the Latter Part of September 1944.

Hearings before the Joint Committee on the Investigation of the Pearl Harbor Attack (U.S. Government Printing Office, 39 volumes).

Incidental Exhibits re Pearl Harbor Investigation.

Interview with Mr. Ralph T. Briggs, by the Historian, Naval Security Group, 13 January 1977.

Information from George W. Linn, Capt. USNR (Ret.), 23 October 1980.

Papers of Field Marshal Sir William Blamey (archives of the Australian War Memorial).

The Role of Communications Intelligence in Submarine Warfare in the Pacific, Jan. 1943–Oct. 1943.

The Role of Radio Intelligence in the American-Japanese Naval War, August 1941–December 1942.

Radio Intelligence in World War Two: Tactical Operations in the Pacific Ocean Areas, January 1943.

Blockade-running Between Europe and the Far East by submarine, 1942–December 1944.

MIS Contribution to the War Effort.

Selected Examples of Commendations and Related Correspondence Highlighting the Achievements of U.S. Signal Intelligence During WW II, 10 January 1946.

Estimated Unit Locations of Japanese Navy and Army Air Forces, 20 July 1945.

Translations of Japanese Army Messages, sundry volumes, June 1943–1945.

Magic Summaries: Japanese Army Supplements, 1944–1945.

Oral histories of Admirals Layton, McCollum, Arleigh Burke, etc. (U.S. Naval Archives, Washington).

Allied Strategic Air Force Target Planning (August 1945).

Examples of Intelligence obtained from Cryptoanalysis, 1 August 1946.

Japanese Water Transport, 6 April 1943–17 June 1944.

Suicide Attack Squadron Organization, CINCPAC and CINCPOA, July 1945.

Army-Navy Committee on the Japanese Air Forces Estimate of the Japanese Situation, 23 June 1945.

Diplomatic

The "Magic" Background to Pearl Harbor (8 vols., U.S. Department of Defense, 1977).

Magic Diplomatic and Far Eastern Summaries, 1942–1945.

Magic Diplomatic Extracts, July 1945: selected items prepared by MIS, War Department, for the attention of General George C. Marshall.

Publications of the Pacific Strategic Intelligence Section, COMINCH/CNO: a series of invaluable summaries prepared in 1945 from current signal intelligence.

Magic Reports for the Attention of the President, 1943–1944.

The Naval Attaché Series (SRNA). Some 5,000 decrypts ranging from summer 1940 onward. Daunting for a British historian, as the first (from the Japanese Naval Attaché in Rome to Tokyo, 18 June 1940) reads: "England is reported to have surrendered. We are transmitting this information for what it may be worth!"

There's magic in the web of it.

WILLIAM SHAKESPEARE,
Othello

THE AMERICAN MAGIC

Of Codes and Ciphers

THE MEANING OF the words "code" and "cipher," and the difference between the two systems they represent, are not always understood. During the Hearings before the Joint Committee on the Investigation of the Pearl Harbor Attack, which opened in 1945, Owen Brewster, senator from Maine, sought clarification from one of the most distinguished code breakers of the U.S. Navy, Captain Joseph Rochefort. Their dialogue is relevant to the theme of this book.

SEN. BREWSTER: What is the difference, Captain, between a cipher and a code?

CAPT. ROCHEFORT: In the original understanding, sir, a code has a group of letters or numbers—sometimes the letters are pronounceable and sometimes not—which designate a letter or number, a phrase, perhaps a whole sentence or complete thought. That would be termed a code.

SEN. BREWSTER: And you would need a code book of some character in order to interpret it?

CAPT. ROCHEFORT: Yes, sir: you would require the book. That is, the original people would.

SEN. BREWSTER: Whoever would get it decoded would have to have a book indicating the significance of these letters and symbols?

CAPT. ROCHEFORT: Yes, sir.

SEN. BREWSTER: What about a cipher?

CAPT. ROCHEFORT: A pure cipher would interchange each letter of the original text so that rather than having a group of letters meaning a whole thought or sentence or phrase, each letter would be changed, or each numeral.

SEN. BREWSTER: You mean the letter "A" might mean "X," for example?

CAPT. ROCHEFORT: Yes, sir: and then the following letter "B" might mean "L." Where you interchange your letter by another letter, or a numeral by another numeral, that would be a pure cipher.

SEN. BREWSTER: Is that peculiar to the Japanese, or do other countries use somewhat similar systems, as far as you know?

CAPT. ROCHEFORT: Ciphers go back before the days of Julius Caesar.

CHAPTER ONE

Don't You Dare, Mr. Dewey

He is brought as a lamb to the slaughter, and as a sheep before her shearers is dumb, so he openeth not his mouth.
    Isaiah 53:7

LATE IN SEPTEMBER 1944 an officer of the United States Army, Colonel Carter Clarke, carried out a mission unparalleled in the history of his country or, indeed, in the annals of warfare.

On the personal order of the Army Chief of Staff, General George Marshall, and without the knowledge of his President, he set out to persuade the governor of New York, Thomas E. Dewey, not to betray to their enemies the Allies' most intimate and treasured possession— their ability to read the secret military and diplomatic messages of the Germans and the Japanese.

The circumstances were extraordinary and urgent. Dewey was the Republican candidate nominated to oppose Roosevelt in the forthcoming presidential election. General Marshall had received information that during his campaign Dewey intended to make use of evidence that before Pearl Harbor the Americans had already been able to decipher revealing Japanese signals. Marshall feared that Dewey would seek an electoral advantage by brandishing this evidence —partial and inaccurate though it might be—and by publicly accusing President Roosevelt of behaving with criminal negligence, at the time of the Pearl Harbor disaster, insofar as the code breakers had given him warning about what was coming and he had failed to act. On the political battlefield so explosive a charge might be decisive.

Marshall was caught in a trap. He knew that he must not consult the President or make any move on Roosevelt's authority, since this would certainly be interpreted by the opposing party as an electoral maneuver. As the head of the Army, on the other hand, he had a unique perception of the vital, the irreplaceable intelligence derived from those deciphered enemy signals. Every morning they lay on his desk—manna from heaven. One flamboyant speech from Dewey might destroy in a few seconds the work of years, by "blowing" the vast system of intelligence gathering which the Americans and the British had so painstakingly constructed. More to the point, Marshall well understood that many thousands of men would have to die unnecessarily as the price of Dewey's self-indulgence.

Like Eisenhower on the eve of D Day, Marshall was faced with a crucial question to which he alone could provide the answer. He saw all the implications. He bore the responsibility: the Army Chief of Staff was where the buck stopped. On the morning of September 25, therefore, he issued confidential instructions: Colonel Carter Clarke of the Military Intelligence Service was to fly to Tulsa, Oklahoma— where Dewey was stopping on his way back from the West Coast—and deliver to him a letter. Clarke was to travel in civilian clothes: he was to tell nobody about his mission, nor was he to hand the letter over to Dewey if a third party was present. So Clarke went home, took a peacetime suit out of storage and prudently sent it off to be pressed.[1]

That night he returned to the Pentagon for his final briefing, and very soon he was in Tulsa, having had a brief sleep, a haircut, a shave and some breakfast. (That pressed suit, that freshly clipped hair! In his recollection of those events Clarke had the true intelligence officer's eye for trivial but verifying detail.) His first contact was with William Skelly, president of the Skelly Oil Company, who as Dewey's campaign manager was handling all arrangements. Skelly was difficult. "You must write down the name of the man who has sent you," he said, "seal it and give it to Governor Dewey." Within minutes Clarke and Dewey were alone together. The Governor opened the outer envelope of Marshall's letter, remarked, "Well, Top Secret—that's really top, isn't it"—read the first two paragraphs—and stopped. He then said, Clarke recalled, that "he did not want his lips sealed on things that he already knew about Pearl Harbor, about facts already in his possession or about facts which might later come into his possession from other sources but which, if they were contained in General Marshall's letter, could not be used because he had given his word on this letter, thereby sealing his lips."

Moreover, Dewey added, he could not conceive that General Marshall and Admiral King* were the only ones who knew about the letter, or that Marshall was capable of approaching an "Opposition candidate" with a proposition such as the letter appeared to contain. "Marshall," he said, "does not do things like that. I am confident that Franklin Roosevelt is behind this whole thing." Then, after glancing at the opening paragraph again, he put the letter down, saying, "I have not reread them because my eye caught the word 'cryptograph.' Now if this letter merely tells me that we were reading certain Japanese codes before Pearl Harbor and that at least two of them are still in current use, there is no point in my reading the letter because I already know that." Instead of being re-elected, he observed, Roosevelt ought to be impeached.

Should he telephone General Marshall and repeat his statements? Clarke argued that these were matters which could not be discussed, or even mentioned, on the telephone under any consideration whatsoever. Dewey therefore handed back the letter, telling Clarke, "I shall be in Albany, Thursday, and I shall be glad to receive you or General Marshall or anyone General Marshall cares to send to discuss at length this cryptographic business or the whole Pearl Harbor mess."

And so it was that the second act of this drama was played out at Governor Dewey's Executive Mansion at Albany, New York. Here Clarke arrived at midday on the 28th, having reported back to the Pentagon and received from Marshall a new letter to be placed in the Governor's hands—as well as full authority to answer any questions of a technical nature that might arise. Dewey now took a different line. In view of the circumstances, he said, of his own personal position, of what he already knew and might subsequently learn, he refused to see Clarke or anyone else alone or to read a letter which he could neither retain nor discuss with a trusted associate. That associate, already present in Dewey's reception room, was one Elliott V. Bell, New York State Superintendent of Banks. The electric atmos-

---

* Marshall had wisely taken into his confidence the Chief of Naval Operations. The heads of the armed services thus presented a united front, since the Army Chief of Staff was equally responsible for the Air Force.

phere of a presidential election campaign is vividly illustrated by Dewey's further statement that he could not afford to read a letter which he could not keep, as he might later be charged with having seen a letter different from the one he had actually read.

An odd incident now followed. Clarke, said Dewey, might be curious to know whether or not he had a recording device in his room. The colonel replied, "No, Governor, I am not curious: I merely assume that you have one." "Well," Dewey answered, "I haven't, and I did not ever have one when I was District Attorney. I had one in my witness room, of course, but never in my own private office."

But there still remained the stumbling block of Mr. Elliott Bell. Clarke offered to go out to a public telephone box and call Marshall surreptitiously or, if he was not available, to fly back to Washington and deliver Dewey's ultimatum. "I have a direct line in here," Dewey pointed out, "and I have a line that goes through the switchboard and there is no tap on either unless O'Connor has just put one on. I have them checked several times in a week, so I feel that they are safe." Who, then, was O'Connor? When Clarke was told that he was the Democratic leader in Albany he indicated that he would prefer not to use the phone. "Oh, hell," said Dewey, "*I'll* phone Marshall. I've talked to him before and this will be all right." In a few minutes he was through to the Army Chief of Staff, who, after speaking to Dewey, authorized Colonel Clarke to hand over the letter to the Governor, to leave it with him and to discuss in the presence of Elliott Bell any points that might emerge.

As Clarke was opening the envelope Bell made a discouraging intervention. "Colonel," he said, "hundreds of people know all about the Midway affair and how most of our other successes in the Pacific have been due to our reading Jap naval codes. Everyone who has ever been out there knows about it and talks freely about it. Why, not long ago at a dinner where a large number of people were present, I talked to a naval commander who had been out there and had participated in nearly every engagement we have had. He said that they always knew where the Jap ships were, and that our people were told by radio where to station their own ships to meet the Japs, and that all this information came from reading Jap codes." Undeterred by this hearsay evidence of treasonable insecurity, Clarke handed over a letter whose significance is such that the complete text now follows.

TOP SECRET

For Mr. Dewey's eyes only.

27 September 1944

My Dear Governor:

Colonel Clarke, my messenger to you of yesterday, September 26th, has reported the result of his delivery of my letter dated September 25th. As I understand him you (a) were unwilling to commit yourself to any agreement regarding "not communicating its contents to any other person" in view of the fact that you felt you already knew certain of the things probably referred to in the letter, as suggested to you by seeing the word "cryptograph," and (b) you could not feel that such a letter as this to a presidential candidate could have been addressed to you by an officer in my position without the knowledge of the President.

As to (a) above I am quite willing to have you read what comes hereafter with the understanding that you are bound not to communicate to any other person any portions on which you do not now have or later receive factual knowledge from some other source than myself. As to (b) above you have my word that neither the Secretary of War nor the President has any intimation whatsoever that such a letter has been addressed to you or that the preparation or sending of such a communication was being considered. I assure you that the only persons who saw or know of the existence of either this letter or my letter to you dated September 25th are Admiral King, seven key officers responsible for security or military communications, and my secretary who typed these letters. I am trying my best to make plain to you that this letter is being addressed to you solely on my initiative, Admiral King having been consulted only after the letter was drafted, and I am persisting in the matter because the military hazards involved are so serious that I feel some action is necessary to protect the interests of our armed forces.

I should have much preferred to talk to you in person but I could not devise a method that would not be subject to press and radio reactions as to why the Chief of Staff of the Army would be seeking an interview with you at this particular moment. Therefore I have turned to the method of this letter, with which Admiral King concurs, to be delivered by hand to you by Colonel Clarke, who, incidentally, has charge of the most secret documents of the War and Navy Departments.

In brief, the military dilemma is this:

The most vital evidence in the Pearl Harbor matter consists of our intercepts of the Japanese diplomatic communications. Over a period of years our cryptograph people analyzed the character of the machine the Japanese were using for encoding their diplomatic messages. Based on this a corresponding machine was built by us which deciphers their messages. Therefore, we possessed a wealth of information regarding their moves in the Pacific, which in turn was furnished the State Department—rather than as is popularly supposed, the State Department providing us with the information—but which unfortunately made no reference whatever to intentions toward Hawaii until the last message before December 7th, which did not reach our hands until the following day, December 8th.

Now the point to the present dilemma is that we have gone ahead with this business of deciphering their codes until we possess other codes, German as well as Japanese, but our main basis of information regarding Hitler's intentions in Europe is obtained from Baron Oshima's messages from Berlin reporting his interviews with Hitler and other officials to the Japanese Government. These are still in the codes involved in the Pearl Harbor events.

To explain further the critical nature of this set-up which would be wiped out almost in an instant if the least suspicion were aroused regarding it, the battle of the Coral Sea was based on deciphered messages and therefore our few ships were in the right place at the right time. Further, we were able to concentrate our limited forces to meet their naval advance on Midway, when otherwise we almost certainly would have been some 3,000 miles out of place. We had full information of the strength of their forces in that advance and also of the smaller force directed against the Aleutians which finally landed troops on Attu and Kiska.

Operations in the Pacific are largely guided by the information we obtain of Japanese deployments. We know their strength in various garrisons, the rations and other stores continuing available to them, and what is of vast importance, we check their fleet movements and the movements of their convoys. The heavy losses reported from time to time which they sustain by reason of our submarine action, largely result from the fact that we know the sailing dates and routes of their convoys and can notify our submarines to lie in wait at the proper points.

The current raids by Admiral Halsey's carrier forces on Japanese shipping in Manila Bay and elsewhere were largely based in timing on the known movements of Japanese convoys, two of which were caught, as anticipated, in his destructive attacks.

You will understand from the foregoing the utterly tragic consequences if the present political debates regarding Pearl Harbor disclose to the enemy, German or Jap, any suspicion of the vital sources of information we possess.

The Roberts report on Pearl Harbor* had to have withdrawn from it all reference to this highly secret matter, therefore in portions it necessarily appeared incomplete. The same reason which dictated that course is even more important today because our sources have been greatly elaborated.

As another example of the delicacy of the situation, some of Donovan's people (the OSS) without telling us instituted a secret search of the Japanese Embassy offices in Portugal. As a result the entire military attaché Japanese code all over the world was changed, and though this occurred over a year ago, we have not yet been able to break the new code and have thus lost this invaluable source of information, particularly regarding the European situation.[2]

A further most serious embarrassment is the fact that the British government is involved concerning its most secret sources of information, regarding which only the Prime Minister, the Chiefs of Staff and a very limited number of other officials have knowledge.

A recent speech in Congress by Representative Harness would clearly suggest to the Japanese that we have been reading their codes, though Mr. Harness and the American public would probably not draw any such conclusion.

The conduct of General Eisenhower's campaign and of all operations in the Pacific are closely related in conception and timing to the information we secretly obtain through these intercepted codes. They contribute greatly to the victory and tremendously to the saving in American lives, both in the conduct of the current operations and in looking towards the early termination of the war.

I am presenting this matter to you in the hope that you will

---

* For details of this and other reports on Pearl Harbor, see Note at the end of this chapter.

see your way clear to avoid the tragic results with which we are
now threatened in the present political campaign.

Please return this letter by bearer. I will hold it in my most
secret file subject to your reference should you so desire.

Faithfully yours,

(signed) G. C. MARSHALL

Before Dewey had even finished reading this historic document
his instant reaction was: "Well, I'll be damned if I believe the Japs are
still using those two codes." Clarke immediately assured him that this
was indeed the case, and that "one of them was our life blood in intelligence." Moreover, he emphasized, their capability of reading the
enemy's codes and ciphers was a vital interest shared between the
Allies, so much so that Churchill considered this his secret weapon and
that it had really saved England. Dewey could not know, but Clarke
rammed home the point, that it had been very difficult to break down
British resistance over sharing this secret intelligence precisely because
of the American lack of security-consciousness. The message that he
and Marshall were conveying, in fact, was that Dewey must keep his
mouth shut not only because American lives were at stake, but also
because the Alliance itself might be put at risk in an area of the
greatest sensitivity.

That issue was clarified further when Dewey said, "There is little
in this letter that I did not already know. There is one point though,
what in hell do Jap codes have to do with Eisenhower?" Tactfully
Clarke explained the importance for the current campaign in Europe
of intelligence acquired through the British breaking of the German
Enigma cipher[3]—of what it meant to be able to decipher the signals
of the German armed forces, of the German secret service, and so on.
"He seemed," Clarke noted, "satisfied." And so Dewey should have
been, since this was a body blow. Any reader of this pregnant conversation will perceive that even in respect of the Americans' ability
to break Japanese signals the knowledge on which Dewey and Bell
founded their case was superficial: beneath the surface an immense
amount was going on about which they were unaware. On the German
side, however, Dewey's ignorance was absolute. By this revelation he
was poleaxed. Nor had he grasped—until it was explained to him—
that information gained from reading the Japanese diplomatic cipher
(the source of so much intelligence before Pearl Harbor) had become,

by 1944, of no less importance in respect of the German war.* This was the significance of Marshall's reference to "our main basis of information regarding Hitler's intentions in Europe."

The confrontation succeeded. Dewey and Bell had a brief private talk, and then Bell announced, "Well, Governor, we have pledged ourselves not to discuss this letter with anyone else, but just between ourselves, what about Colonel Clarke—who is he going to discuss it with?" Clarke promised that he would mention the matter to nobody but Marshall and his own immediate superior, Major General Clayton Bissell, the intelligence chief in the Pentagon. So Dewey summed up: "Colonel, I do not believe that there are any questions I want to ask you nor do I care to have any discussions about the contents of the letter. Will you give me your full name, serial number, office location and phone number, and your residence number and phone number?" They then shook hands, and Dewey's last words were: "Well, I hope we meet again under more auspicious circumstances."

It is a matter of record that throughout his unsuccessful election campaign Governor Dewey used to his advantage neither the speculative knowledge which he claimed to have acquired before Marshall's approach to him, nor the genuine and specific information supplied in the general's letter. And the relationship this established bred a mutual respect. When Marshall testified in 1945 before the great Congressional Inquiry into the Pearl Harbor Attack he revealed that the first time that he met Dewey personally was by chance at President Roosevelt's funeral, but that thereafter he had given him access in the Pentagon to conclusive documentary evidence about the code breakers' achievements and their full significance. Dewey, he declared, had behaved with great consideration. Honor had been satisfied—on both sides.

Dewey's main interest had been in the breaking of Japanese codes and ciphers. Nevertheless, though Marshall was able to persuade him about the need for silence and the overwhelming requirements of security, even in those delicate and desperate negotiations he could inevitably do no more than skim over the surface. But now that the contemporary documents are becoming available in very substantial quantities, it is at last possible to identify and assess the vast range

---

* See Chapter 11 for further details.

and battle-value of the intelligence acquired through cryptographic means during the war against Japan. What Marshall properly sought to conceal is now an open secret. Moreover, many of those who were involved in these clandestine affairs, and for decades considered it their duty to keep their peace, have more recently found it possible to supply information and advice in what is a more relaxed clin.ate of opinion about wartime security. The time is thus ripe for a broadly based review of the relationship between the breaking of codes and ciphers and the defeat of Japan.

Such is the purpose of this book. It is a story of an American triumph.

NOTE. The number and variety of the investigations into the circumstances preceding the disaster at Pearl Harbor are liable to cause confusion. It may therefore be helpful to have available, at the outset, this chronological table.

1. *The Roberts Commission* was set up by executive order of President Roosevelt, and an investigation conducted by Justice Owen J. Roberts was carried out between December 18, 1941, and January 23, 1942.

2. *The Hart Inquiry.* Admiral Thomas C. Hart, under instructions from Secretary of the Navy Frank Knox, held his inquiry between February 12 and June 15, 1944.

3. *The Army Pearl Harbor Board,* which was appointed by instruction of the Adjutant General, sat between July 20 and October 20, 1944.

4. *The Navy Court of Inquiry,* appointed by Secretary of the Navy James Forrestal, sat between July 24 and October 19, 1944.

5. *The Clarke Inquiry,* an investigation by Colonel Carter Clarke (under instructions from Major General Clayton Bissell, chief of the Military Intelligence Department) "regarding the manner in which certain Top Secret communications were handled."

6. *The Clausen Investigation,* a private investigation initiated on December 1, 1944, by Secretary of War Henry L. Stimson, to carry further the findings of the Army Pearl Harbor Board.

7. *The Hewitt Inquiry.* Under the instructions of Secretary of the Navy James Forrestal, Admiral Hewitt, between May 14 and

July 11, 1945, conducted an inquiry to carry further the findings of Admiral Hart.

8. *The Joint Committee on the Investigation of the Pearl Harbor
   Attack*. Ordained in 1945 by Resolution 27 of the 79th Congress, this committee sat for months under the chairmanship
   of Alben W. Barkley, senator from Kentucky. The hearings,
   whose record fills 39 volumes, constitute the fullest and probably the final official investigation. The board of inquiry was
   composed of senators from Kentucky, Georgia, Illinois, Maine
   and Michigan and of representatives from Tennessee, North
   Carolina, Pennsylvania, California and Wisconsin.

CHAPTER TWO

The Path to Pearl

The past is a prologue.
Inscription outside the National Archives,
Washington, D.C.

OSCAR WILDE ONCE said that until Dickens wrote his novels there were no fogs in London. The fogs were there of course, in quantity, but it needed a writer to quicken men's awareness so that their imagination could grasp a reality to which they had previously been indifferent. We are liable to see incorrectly until a shift of attention brings the object into focus. There is the well-known case of the chessboard. Seen from one angle, the white squares protrude and dominate: seen from another, the black squares stand out. Something like this has happened in the cloudy world of cryptanalysis.

The achievement of the British (preceded by the Poles) in breaking—from 1940 onward—thousands upon thousands of German signals enciphered on the Enigma machine, and thus obtaining the invaluable intelligence known as Ultra, was immense. Shrouded in secrecy for three decades, it has understandably excited historians and astonished the general public ever since, in 1974, the story which had been rigorously kept under cover, as if in a sealed box, was opened in Group Captain Winterbotham's best seller, *The Ultra Secret.**

Such an immediate fixation on the success of those brilliant men and women at Bletchley Park who broke the German ciphers was en-

---

* A Polish publication in 1967 opened the lid a little. The French General Bertrand's *Enigma* (1973) went rather further. But it was Winterbotham's book that first received universal attention and, more importantly, prepared the way for a steadily increasing release of Ultra documents by the British.

tirely reasonable. As more and more information was released by the authorities, and people who had taken part in the great operation began to speak out, it became clear that the whole conduct of the struggle against Hitler would have to be considered in a new light. This was a fascinating and compulsive event, for never in the history of warfare has it become so rapidly necessary to revise, in a radical fashion, the pre-existing ideas about how battles were fought and strategies devised.

Nevertheless, this concentration has been directed merely on one set of the squares on the board. If the angle of vision is altered, and attention focused on the Americans' penetration of the codes and ciphers of the Japanese, another pattern stands out and fixes one's eye: a new set of squares predominates. In its effect on the Pacific war (and in important respects on the war against Germany) this technical victory can then be seen to have had consequences often as remarkable as those that resulted—in Europe, in the Mediterranean, and in the Battle of the Atlantic—from the breaking of the Enigma ciphers. The cryptanalysts did not win the Second World War on their own. But in the Pacific as on the German fronts the end came years earlier, and many thousands of lives were saved, because of their ability to read the enemy's signals. In its particular field the American achievement was no less significant than the British, and it is high time that it was given the fullest emphasis.

The Americans themselves have been slow to grasp this truth.* One valid reason has been the lack of authoritative documents. Still, a great deal of essential material has in fact been made available in recent years. There is a more subtle cause: the wound of Pearl Harbor. The shock of that disaster and the heart-searching to discover what went wrong—or at least to identify satisfactory scapegoats—have given excessive prominence to the nature of the Japanese signals which were translated at the time and which, the critics argue, should have supplied a sufficient advance warning to avert catastrophe. These were Japan's *diplomatic* signals, protected by encipherment on the machine that came to be called Purple. All the information gathered from this source was known then, and throughout the war, as Magic.

---

* No slur is intended on certain writers who have published admirable work in this area. I refer more indiscriminately to the opinions and attitudes of the usually well-informed.

Right up to 1945 and VJ Day, Magic was indeed, as will be seen, a rich source of intelligence for the Allies about the thoughts, the plans, the resources and the actions of the men in Tokyo and Berlin—on a worldwide scale.

But neither the Japanese nor any other Foreign Office would include in the signals* passing to and from its embassies abroad the kind of military detail—the fine print of war—which General Marshall described to Governor Dewey as being so vital and so sacrosanct: "Operations in the Pacific are largely guided by the information we obtain of Japanese deployments. We know their strength in various garrisons, the rations and other stores continuing available to them, and what is of vast importance, we check their fleet movements and the movements of their convoys." Such gold must be drawn from a different mine.

The Pacific struggle was primarily a maritime war—a struggle fought on or over or under the sea itself, and including an almost endless series of amphibious assaults on the enemy's far-flung chain of islands. It is not surprising, therefore, that almost from the beginning the richest and, at times, the decisive source of information was the system of codes used by the Japanese Navy. Had these codes not been penetrated, the vast fleets of warships so swiftly constructed by the Americans would sometimes have been blind and fumbling monsters. And then, by 1943, the Japanese Army was also so deeply committed as a buttress for the collapsing Imperial domain that its codes too could be effectively broken. Marshall's desperate desire to protect these sources was simply realistic: if they had been compromised the war in the Pacific might not have been lost, but victory would have been incalculably more expensive in time, effort and blood.

It is not, however, generally realized—even in the United States—that the immense wealth of intelligence produced by the American code breakers from the naval and military signal traffic of the Japanese was also known, comprehensively, as Ultra. Apart from the information acquired from the German ciphers there was, in fact, this *other* Ultra, derived from the Japanese codes. Combined with Magic, the

---

* "High level diplomatic traffic had been available since 1941 but its value was strategic in nature and very seldom did anything of immediate tactical importance develop from this source." The U.S. History of the operations of Special Security Officers attached to Field Commands, 1943–1948.

scale and scope of the Ultra material obtained in the Pacific represents a formidable feat of intellect and ingenuity on the part of the American cryptanalysts. Both justice and historical truth, therefore, demand that it should be seen in proper perspective—that a fair balance should be struck between the American performance and the British, or, for that matter, the German and the Japanese.

One revealing perspective is that of time. If the quality of America's success in the field of signal intelligence *after* Pearl Harbor has not been fully recognized, still less has the length and the assiduity of preparation which preceded that success. To understand, we have to go back twenty years and start with an earlier confrontation between the United States and Japan.

Herbert Yardley was the man who, during the Washington Naval Conference of 1921–22, first penetrated the Japanese code system on a massive scale. Unfortunately, he lacked the first quality essential in code breakers who serve governments: loyalty. For loyalty in this secret world is not only desirable: it is possible. By 1944, it was officially estimated, at least 50,000 men and women were acquainted through their work with one or another aspect of the Americans' attack on the enemy's signal traffic—whether in cryptanalysis itself, or in translating, or in evaluating, distributing and applying in action the intelligence obtained.* (For the British the figures are less easy to establish, but at Bletchley Park and its outstations, in the processes of interception and distribution and in command headquarters at home and on the battlefronts, possibly a quarter of the American total was engaged.) It is a matter of record that except on authorized occasions, such as testifying for the Pearl Harbor Investigation, virtually none of this enormous company broke silence in a significant way for many years after the return to peace and, for the great majority, their demobilization to private life. Even now, many see it as their duty to be silent. But Yardley was a maverick.[1]

By the time of the 1921 Washington Conference (where his critical breakthrough occurred) the man who, as a young coding clerk in the State Department, privately cracked the President's own enciphered

---

* The official history of the U.S. Signal Corps records that, apart from the numerous personnel deployed in theaters of war abroad, the Signal Intelligence Service alone had 10,000 on its books at home.

telegrams had a considerable track record as a cryptanalyst. After the United States entered the war in 1917 he was made head of MI 8, the code-breaking section of the Military Intelligence Division, and then led a similar unit within the American delegation to the Peace Conference at Versailles. On his own initiative he next—in May 1919—persuaded the Departments of State and War to take the unprecedented step of funding "a permanent organization for code and cipher investigation and attack." Though Yardley's career ended in squalor, this was the act of a pioneer: from this point onward, right through the days of Pearl Harbor and the cryptanalytical triumphs in the Pacific, the story is like an unbroken thread. There would sometimes be contretemps and confusion, but henceforward the U.S. administration would always maintain, as an arm of government, some surreptitious group devoted to the penetration of other countries' signal traffic. Between Yardley and the NSA, in fact, the line of succession may meander, but it is continuous.

In his own case the key word is surreptitious. For absurd technical reasons the State Department was incapable of funding Yardley's operation in Washington, and the "permanent organization"—soon to be christened the Black Chamber—had to be privily established in the upper half of 22 East Thirty-sixth Street, New York City.* Its prime mission, moreover, was breaking Japan's diplomatic codes and ciphers. All salaries, house maintenance and similar expenses were covered by secret allocations at first from the State Department and then from the conniving War Department.

There is a marked contrast here with the British experience. If Yardley was indeed to behave later—as will be seen—like a masterless maverick, this was surely due, in part, to circumstances that set him outside the herd, a loner, committed to staking his reputation on the proof of a case which he himself had argued. In London, however, the core of that brilliant team in Room 40 of the Admiralty which, during the Great War, had dexterously read the German naval codes and the vital Zimmermann Telegram was quietly shifted, after 1918, under the protective wings of MI 6 and the Foreign Office.[2] Here, with an easy continuity, it continued to function during the twenties and thirties

---

* Later the bureau was moved into an office block under the cover name of the Code Compilation Company.

in the Broadway offices of MI 6 near Victoria Station, clumsily disguised as the Government Code and Cypher School. But the continuity
was personal as well as institutional. When GCCS moved out to
Bletchley Park at the outbreak of war in September 1939 one observes
that the founding fathers of B.P.—Commander Alastair Denniston,
Nigel de Grey, Dillwyn Knox and others—had all learned their trade
in the Room 40 of another war and kept their hand in at GCCS
through two decades of peace. The tradition of the British is tradition.

Thus the route to Bletchley's solution of the Enigma ciphers which
produced what might be called Ultra G—Ultra derived from German
signals—appears to advance with the directness and calculated purpose
of a highway. By contrast, the American journey which ended in the
terminal points of Magic and Ultra J—the Japanese-derived Ultra of
the Pacific war—followed a far more circuitous course which at times
was so devious and overgrown that it seemed to disappear. Nevertheless, anyone who draws a map of American cryptanalysis can see that
here, too, the track was continuous.

And the cartographer can take Washington in 1921 as his datum
line. Everything then conspired in Yardley's favor. The Naval Conference was convened by the United States for a variety of reasons,
mainly self-interest—to prevent the British and French from doing
the same thing, to break the long-standing treaty of alliance between
Britain and Japan and to advance a general desire among nations to
limit armaments by mutual agreement. The American administration
had the evident will. Yardley provided the secret weapon.

Even before the conference opened he and the bright minds in the
Black Chamber had broken the codes then used for Japan's diplomatic
signals: not easily, not swiftly, but decisively. When the State Department put him in commission he boasted that he would master the
codes within a year, and he was not too far out. The conference began
in November, but already—and for some time—daily couriers had
been carrying pouches from New York to Washington containing the
Chamber's translated texts of signals sent to and from the Foreign
Office in Tokyo. Indeed, it was a message of July 5 from the Japanese
ambassador in London which alerted President Harding and his colleagues to the danger—as they saw it—that a disarmament conference
might be assembled in Europe. Hence their pre-emptive strike.

The position of the Japanese was complicated. A sense of grievance over their meager pickings* from the Versailles Peace Conference, and vaulting ambition in the Pacific and China, were balanced by grave economic problems at home and a fear about pushing the United States too far. There was a bluff to be called if the cards could be accurately guessed, or even seen. The Black Chamber did the trick, by breaking a crucial signal from Tokyo to the Japanese ambassador of November 28. "It is necessary," he was told, "to avoid any clash with Great Britain and America, particularly America, in regard to the armament limitation question. You will do your best to maintain a middle attitude . . ." The cards in the Japanese hand were now nakedly exposed. The cable made it clear that far from fighting to the last ditch in defense of their claim to be allowed to build warships up to 70 percent of the British and American total, they were regretfully prepared—if pushed—to settle for 60 percent and an agreement "to reduce or at least to maintain the status quo of Pacific defenses."

The rest was easy. Charles Evans Hughes, the American Secretary of State, simply outstared the Japanese negotiators until, on December 10, another signal from Tokyo was decoded by the Black Chamber. The pouch carried it down from New York: "There is nothing to do but accept the ratio proposed by the United States." So a Four Power Pact was signed on December 13 which limited the building of capital ships in the ratio Britain 5, United States 5, Japan 3.† The British, in effect, had broken with Japan. The Americans were cock-a-hoop, feeling that they had achieved their first major diplomatic triumph on the international stage. A year later Yardley was awarded, via the War Department, the Distinguished Service Medal—theoretically for his work during the Great War, but the timing of the award was hardly coincidental.

This story of the Black Chamber and the Naval Conference has been told more than once, not least by Yardley himself, but certain of its features need stressing. The first is that the British delegation was hoodwinked as much as the Japanese. That acute and omniscient Secretary of the British Cabinet, Sir Maurice Hankey, the doyen of

* Or was it a form of racial resentment about "equality"? The Japanese contribution in the First World War was small-scale: the reward was not inconsiderable.
† The figures are usually expressed in this way. The full agreement was in the ratio of Britain 10, United States 10, Japan 6, France 3.3, Italy 3.3.

the international conference scene, was well versed in the wartime achievements of Room 40 and the value of code breaking in the game of diplomatic poker. But though he was acting as secretary to the British delegation, led by Lord Balfour, he never seems to have suspected the ace up the Americans' sleeve or to have understood the inner significance of Hughes's mulish obstinacy. Indeed he wrote to the Prime Minister, Lloyd George, on December 4 that "Mr. Hughes has deliberately slowed down the Conference; for, incredible as it may seem, he thinks that we are going too fast for those frightened hares of Orientals." He even told his wife that the pact was a great diplomatic triumph for Balfour and himself.[3]

But the real irony was this: though the Japanese once again claimed that they had been robbed and the Americans preened themselves, what happened in Washington that winter was a victory without a morrow. Pearl Harbor may have flashed off a war in the East, but its roots lie in the naval pact. The agreed building ratio meant that the British Navy, with its worldwide commitments, would never thereafter be able to match the Japanese in the Pacific while the Americans would find it difficult to engage on equal terms in a two-ocean struggle. In spite of their great naval expansion after December 1941 the strain of a double commitment, in the Pacific and the Atlantic, was exhausting: before Pearl Harbor it was impossible.* And the sop that completed the bargain, a joint agreement by London, Washington and Tokyo "to reduce or at least to maintain the status quo of the Pacific defenses," proved immensely favorable to Japan. How absurd it seems, looking back, to think that Australia and New Zealand pressed hard for a naval conference in 1921! It was a double con: the future allies had unintentionally strengthened their future enemy.

None of these harsh facts, of course, diminishes in the slightest the quality of Yardley's technical feat—and fortunately so, for it was the peak of his career. During the rest of the decade, as will be seen, he was first effaced and then disgraced. Meanwhile, the salient point is that the paymasters of the Black Chamber were the Departments of

---

* In October 1941 Admiral King wrote to a friend: "The Navy cannot do more than is now being done—we are still more than a year away from any marked accession of ships of the "2-ocean Navy" . . . So—if a war status comes about, what to do?"

State and War. Where was the Navy? The question opens up huge vistas. For the truth is that the route followed by American cryptanalysts was not a single road, but several.

The notion that the armed or secret services of a country work wholeheartedly for the interests of the nation has a very diminished credibility. In the limited field of cryptanalysis, for example, we now know that Nazi Germany's effort was dissipated and blunted because of internecine struggles between the Abwehr, Himmler's SD, Göring's Luftwaffe team, Foreign Office units and the Navy's brilliant but independent organization. And so—though fortunately to a less stultifying degree—it was in the United States: from the beginning to the end. American cryptanalysis traveled along separate roads because, in particular, there was not room on the same route for two powerful juggernauts, hostile, suspicious, proud, each convinced of its own primacy and a God-given entitlement to the right-of-way. Certainly there were times when the tracks converged and the Army and Navy can be observed working valuably in tandem. The historian is bound to note—as informed observers felt when it happened—that these were memorable exceptions which merely proved a rule.

This "apartheid," already visible in that datum year of 1921, was also foreign to the British experience. With GCCS as the acknowledged central authority any cryptanalysis by the services, particularly the Army and Navy, tended to be carried on at least in liaison with Broadway. By 1940, when Bletchley is beginning to fizz, men and women of every uniform (as well as civilians on the Foreign Office list) move in at increasing rates and work in a miraculous harmony—a harmony marred mainly by the natural clashes of temperament and ideas inevitable in so brilliant a caravanserai. But between the U.S. Navy and its airmen, and the Army with its Air Corps, a gulf yawned which it was difficult to bridge.

In 1921, as it happened, the Office of Naval Intelligence in Washington had just emerged from a long sleep. Blue-water admirals had so far dismissed it as a mere post office for passing on reports from elsewhere. The arrival in 1920 of Captain Andrew Long as director of ONI, a man of thrust, determination and daring, transformed the scene rather as, in January 1939, British Naval Intelligence was stimulated by the arrival of a new director, Rear Admiral John Godfrey, "exacting, inquisitive, energetic . . . like the driver of a sports car in a traffic queue, he saw no danger or discourtesy in acceleration."[4] Certainly ONI suddenly accelerated.

What happened, in fact, was that in the field of cryptanalysis the Navy suddenly began to enter the twentieth century. There were two notable events whose consequences carry right through into the Pacific war—setting the Navy, it might be said, on its private road. First, Long substantially increased the number of naval intelligence and language student officers at the U.S. Embassy in Tokyo—a theme to whose significance we must return. Secondly, we seem to be swept into a Watergate world, for on the testimony of a future rear admiral, then Lieutenant Commander Ellis Zacharias, we must accept that late in 1920 counterespionage experts (with the help of a professional safe-cracker) broke into the office of a Japanese consulate* and acquired a photocopy of the current "fleet code" of the Japanese Navy.[5]

Of course such little local disturbances occur. During the winter of 1928–29 a young intelligence officer called Foster was on duty in the Third Naval District in New York, working closely with the FBI, the Police Department, the Post Office and other agents in the surveillance of foreigners. He learned that Japanese tourists in New York, who traveled as civilians though they were identified as Army and Navy officers, had a habit of calling at the New York headquarters of the Japanese Imperial Railway, where they arrived with parcels but left empty-handed. The assumption was that they were handing in cameras or photographic material, particularly shots of the locks or other installations taken during their transit of the Panama Canal in Japanese shipping.

Further investigation indicated that the Imperial Railway establishment was in fact a central clearing house for Japanese espionage in North America. A clandestine operation was therefore mounted which, according to Foster's personal reminiscences in the Washington Naval Archives, "put our government in possession of a copy of the complete No. 1 Imperial Japanese Secret Code." Furthermore, he added, Zacharias later confirmed that this had "laid the basis for the penetration of Japanese signal traffic"—a claim that is demonstrably excessive.[6]

---

* Other sources suggest that this may have been the office of the Japanese Naval Inspector in New York—a more likely home for a code book, though the JNI's office may of course have been a part of the consulate.

How riveting such revelations are! Yet anyone wishing to understand the true story of Magic and Ultra—to understand, indeed, the real quality of the American achievement—must approach them with grave reservations and an acutely critical mind. For the effective and continuous operation of code breaking and cipher cracking, particularly in wartime, cannot conceivably depend on forays of this kind. It must be systematic, minutely organized, and based on an immense structure of theoretical perception, mathematical skills, machines of an extreme sophistication and, above all, sheer and unremitting hard work. "Snatches"—as the jargon has it—can be useful, at times even critically important, but they can never be more than spectacular episodes in a long, long struggle characterized more by sustained brainwork than by occasional burglary. This assertion is dogmatic, but sheathed in safety, for no reputable and experienced cryptanalyst would deny it.

A British example illustrates the point. On May 8, 1941, in the chill Greenland waters, an intact U-110 was captured with its Enigma machine and associated documents.* These obviously provided Naval Intelligence with the precious list of daily settings for the Enigma to cover what would have been the remainder of the U-boat's cruise. The German Navy's general-purpose cipher, Hydra, was soon penetrated although it had previously defied solution. But setting lists become rapidly out-of-date, while ciphers continue to change. In the long term, therefore, what mattered was not any immediate result of this dramatic snatch, but rather the understanding of the general principles on which this area of the German cipher system worked. As the months and years passed, and fresh problems were constantly posed, the Bletchley people thus acquired a *modus operandi*, guidelines and ultimately a feeling-in-the-fingers. Practice, the Official History of British Intelligence says, perfected their methods. "Without the assistance of further captures, they were able after the first week of August to decipher all but two days of the Home Waters traffic *down to the end of the war*."†

The significance, therefore, of the Americans' "snatch" of the

---

* The German U-boat Command was unaware, of course, of the precise fate of U-110, or that the machine and the vitally important papers were in British hands.
† Author's italics.

Japanese code book—the Red Book, as it was called—was not the journalistic overtones of its acquisition but the fact that, over the next few years, it caused the Navy to lay the foundations of a *system*—a system which would steadily expand and mature. The complex problem of translating the code book—a task taking several years—itself emphasized the need for language experts who were not simply literary scholars but could understand the technicalities of Japanese naval terminology and the implications of their telegraphese, as well as the personalities, doctrines, operational concepts and organizational structure of the Imperial Navy. In peace the problem of providing such people on a war scale was insoluble, but at least from now on it was recognized. It was not simply overlooked or ignored, so that when the demand for translators after 1941 became astronomical there was at least a background of foresight and preparation.

The true start of a system can perhaps be marked by the arrival in the Navy's Code and Signal Section of Lieutenant Laurence L. Safford, a man with proper Annapolis antecedents who nevertheless put a bomb under the old regime when, in January 1924, he took over a newly created Research Desk and, in effect, gave birth to the Navy's communications intelligence organization. Even by the date of Pearl Harbor this already comprised 700 officers and men, of whom a relatively small proportion, it is true, dealt with cryptanalysis and translation while the rest handled interception and direction finding. (By 1945 the Washington personnel alone of the Navy's communications security unit numbered 6,000.) And in December 1941 the Code and Signal Section in Washington, now christened Op-20-G, was headed by Commander L. F. Safford. In this sense, certainly, the advance from an antediluvian past into an efficient future had a definite continuity.

The system soon took an embryonic shape. First, Safford saw the need for a regular team of cryptanalysts, and got his way. Zacharias was attached to the unit for training in 1926, and his account of his experiences might well have been written about Bletchley Park:

My days were spent in study and work among people with whom security had become second nature. Hours went by without any of us saying a word, just sitting in front of piles of indexed sheets on which a mumbo jumbo of figures or letters was displayed in chaotic disorder, trying to solve the puzzle bit by bit like fitting together the pieces of a jigsaw puzzle. We were just a few then in Room 2646, young people who gave ourselves to cryptography with the same ascetic devotion with which young men enter a monastery.[7]

Room 2646 was the heavily protected room in a wing of the old Navy Building where work on translating the Red Book was first initiated. (Neither that work nor, indeed, the very existence of the Red Book was communicated to the Army!) But Safford was now in a classic dilemma. Code breakers are an expensive luxury unless they can actually be supplied with coded signals to break. And there is a more subtle point, familiar to the cryptanalysts on all sides during the Second World War. Unless you acquire a minimal number of signals in a particular code or cipher, it is often intolerably difficult—if not impossible—to identify the particular characteristics of the traffic. These things have their hallmarks, but they often become obvious only after intensive study of many signals. The answer is interception: picking the signals out of the air.*

In 1925, therefore, a radio surveillance post was set up on Guam. Next year two more were activated in the Philippines and a more obscure one, an echoing shell laid against the side of Asia, on the fourth floor of the American consulate in Shanghai. Mobile monitoring soon followed—for the Russian trawlers of today, bristling with more electronic gadgetry than fishing gear, are no innovation. In 1926 Commander Zacharias voyaged to Hong Kong on the destroyer *McCormick*, packed with technicians and technology, to test the potential: so effectively that in 1928 he was off again, this time on the U.S.S. *Marblehead*, to listen in to the signals of the huge Japanese Combined Fleet as it fought in mock battle its annual war game. Zacharias claimed that he had been able to put together "the complete and accurate plan of the entire operations." Certainly the Director of Naval Communications wrote in commendation of his subsequent report, "it covers a line of naval information which is very

---

* Not, of course, the *only* answer. A mass of Japanese Army signals, transmitted from many stations in Manchuria (before and after Pearl Harbor) as well as from the Pacific theater, was intercepted and available for the U.S. Army's cryptanalysts: and yet, as will be seen, the Japanese Army code was not broken until 1943.

important for us to get hold of, and the value of which we have so far failed to appreciate."[8]

The groundwork had thus been firmly laid. And when Safford had to depart for a formal stretch of duty at sea there were high-class alternatives to fill the gap: the brilliant Agnes Driscoll, for example, and Joseph Rochefort, in the view of his peers the most effective cryptanalyst in the Navy. Lieutenant Rochefort had been serving in the intelligence office of a battleship, a man who had made his way up from the ranks in the Naval Reserve, when in October 1925 he was posted to the Safford section. Outstanding as an operator, he was a nonpareil among the many good officers whom the American system produced to handle their signal intelligence during the Second World War.*

Nor was his or Safford's sea time a disqualification. It is doubtful whether the American Navy insisted on such officers serving a spell afloat for much more subtle reasons than that this was the right and proper thing for a sailor to do. Nevertheless, when war came it was of the highest importance that naval intelligence officers—even crypt-analysts—should know at first hand how things go on at sea: suitably amended, the same is true of the other two services. The huge concentration of brain and ability at Bletchley Park, unexampled in its product, could nevertheless be said to have been impaired, in however slight a degree, by the fact that so few of its members had heard a shot fired in anger, flown in an air raid or straddled a deck in a sea fight.

The point of real significance, however, is that Rochefort was soon sent to Japan for a three-year language course. We have come close to a vital nerve. The histories, biographies and memoirs relating to the Pacific war constantly but indifferently refer to this officer or that as "a language specialist," "a Japanese translator" and so on. What is overlooked, or certainly underemphasized, is that from the mid-twenties a small but constant annual flow of selected officers, Marine and Army as well as Navy, was given the opportunity for a thorough grounding in Japanese: a calculated policy, whose fruits were abundant. Without such a long-term capital investment naval intelligence in wartime would have been paralyzed.

---

* Yet the service he dignified sank him in the end. See p. 138.

As they crop up in the records the names of the pupils set bells ringing in the mind: names only too soon to become familiar, during the dark days of Pearl Harbor and the later lifting of the clouds. Apart from Rochefort and Zacharias, there were Edwin Layton (later Fleet Intelligence Officer to Admiral Nimitz and postwar director of the Naval Intelligence School), Kramer, McCollum,* Lasswell whose cryptanalytic skills stamped the death certificate for Admiral Yamamoto, Redfield "Rosey" Mason (a pillar of Op-20-G),† Eddie Pearce (one of the invaluable signal intelligence team that operated in Australia during the Pacific war), and Daniel McCallum who spent eight months on Guadalcanal listening to the voice communications of the Japanese Army and Navy. Well before Pearl Harbor the Office of Naval Intelligence fortunately recalled the nine language students then in Tokyo, partly as an insurance against capture in case of war and partly so that they could train with Radio Intelligence units at Pearl Harbor and in the Philippines: at least one of them, Rufus L. Taylor, became a Vice Admiral, Director of Naval Intelligence, and later Deputy Director of Central Intelligence.

Consider one case history, that of Captain Henri Smith-Hutton: a perfect example in that he was sent to Tokyo for training as a language officer in 1926, just about the time when the system was beginning to roll. He and his like would work under the Naval Attaché, with diplomatic privileges though not the sacred immunity of a true Embassy man. At any one time there would normally be about six from the Navy, eight from the Army, and one from the Marines. In these early days they had at least a limited freedom, visiting Japanese naval installations (though only by prior arrangement and under strict control) and making friends, however superficially, among their hosts. During his three years Smith-Hutton even translated with his instructor the *Japanese Coast Pilot*—with the knowledge and assistance of the Japanese Navy Department! In 1928 he and Zacharias got together in Nagasaki, and met again next year when he was posted

---

* At Pearl Harbor time, December 1941, Commander (later Admiral) McCollum and Lieutenant Commander Kramer were serving in the Far Eastern Section of the Office of Naval Intelligence in Washington.
† Throughout the war, Op-20-G was the Navy's central signal intelligence unit in Washington.

to ONI in Washington and found Zacharias running the Eastern Section.

Then Smith-Hutton was transferred to *Houston*, becoming Fleet Intelligence Officer of the Asiatic Fleet (where another officer, Joseph Wenger, was handling communications intelligence).* In November 1932 he is back at the Embassy in Tokyo, as an Assistant Naval Attaché for translation and intelligence. He commands a destroyer, and then becomes communications officer on the U.S.S. *Augusta* on the Eastern Station (with Wenger on the C. in C.'s staff). Finally, in the spring of 1939, he returned as Naval Attaché to Tokyo.† This interweaving of language study, sea time and understanding of signal intelligence is a good instance of the sensible interwar training and nursing-along of selected officers which, when Pearl Harbor exploded, left the U.S. Navy better equipped than has been realized—for reasons that have not been fully appreciated.[9]

Meanwhile, the Army too had been doing more than allowing a few young captains to exchange the cherry blossom of Washington for the cherry blossom of Tokyo in pursuit of the Japanese language. The Army, indeed, had a longer and more interesting record than the Navy in both main areas of secret communication—protecting your own signals and attacking the enemy's: a record that went back to the American Civil War. Very good work was done in France in 1918 by very good men. Yet, curiously enough, the Navy outdistanced the Army in the immediate postwar years. The millstone around the Army's neck was Herbert Yardley. At best a paramilitary figure, sustained by secret or slush funds, he and his Black Chamber prevented any organic development within the Army itself by their very existence and their undoubted cost. He had to go.

The Chamber was unaccountable. "No research whatsoever was conducted in cryptanalysis; there were no training activities, no intercepts, no code compilation, no secret ink work. The personnel consisted of six persons all told and 37½ percent of the total payroll went

* Joseph N. Wenger later ran the signal intelligence unit at Cavite in the Philippines, took a leading role at Op-20-G in Washington in 1936–38 and during the war, and after becoming Deputy Director of Naval Communications was a key figure in the young National Security Agency from 1949 to 1953.
† Smith-Hutton was repatriated in 1942. Thereafter he was not much involved in signal intelligence.

to one man, who had little interest other than to continue as long as possible to maintain himself in the sinecure into which he had been permitted to establish himself. . . . Yardley devoted most of his time to two or three private enterprises (commercial code compilation, real estate brokerage, consultant in code matters to commercial firms) and he was having a 'field day' at Government expense."[10] Yardley's principle was "let joy be unconfined": an obsession for poker, mistresses and the life of pleasure, combined with a flamboyant egocentricity, led to one of the most bizarre betrayals since the homosexual Colonel Redl, the Austrian staff officer, was discovered in 1913 to have been marketing military secrets to the Russians to "maintain his standard of life."[11]

Early in 1929 an investigation by the Signal Corps disclosed many of these deficiencies, and arrangements were soon in train to transfer to the Chief Signal Office entire responsibility, in peace and war, for interception, code breaking and all other aspects of signals intelligence. The bell had tolled for the Black Chamber. Then, like a devil jumping through the trapdoor in a pantomime, there appeared on the scene the wholly unexpected figure of Mr. Secretary Stimson.

Stimson came in as Secretary of State on the wings of Hoover's newly elected administration. For a trenchant playwright, Robert Sherwood made an astonishing understatement when, in *The White House Papers*, he called him "a stickler for form." A prissy conventionality was not Stimson's way: he was driven by fervor, and faith in the common decencies. So when, in due season, a few deciphered Japanese signals were laid on his desk his outrage was instantaneous and his reaction draconic. Announcing the famous dictum "Gentlemen do not read one another's mail,"* he ordered that these unethical activities of which he had been unaware should cease immediately, so far as his Department was concerned, and that all funding should stop.† The Black Chamber was out of business and its employees, lacking a civil service status, were left with a small gratuity but no

---

* The statement is part of American mythology. It is not *absolutely* certain that Stimson made it at the time. In his memoirs, *On Active Service in Peace and War*, prepared in collaboration with McGeorge Bundy, the relevant passage reads "as he later said." The statement itself seems to have crystallized out in several different versions.

† Closure of the intercept post in the Shanghai consulate inevitably followed. When the 4th Marines arrived in Shanghai in 1932, a communications center with intercept capabilities was established inside their headquarters.

pension. Everyone loyally and silently accepted an unfortunate fate—except Yardley.

His revenge was unique. We are sated, now, with "revelations," so that it is impossible to recapture the sense of shock—particularly among those still working devotedly in the field of signal intelligence —when in 1931 Yardley's book *The American Black Chamber* appeared, preceded by some outspoken articles in *The Saturday Evening Post.** There was a furor in Japan: the Foreign Minister, for example, looked back to the Naval Conference and accused the United States of "a breach of faith." When Yardley then sought to publish a successor, *Japanese Diplomatic Secrets*, the U.S. Government suppressed it. Yardley never recovered from an unpardonable breach of trust. The Canadians wanted to use him as a cryptanalyst in 1940, but the British banned him. He pushed hard to get into the OSS, but General Donovan's refusal was uncompromising—so his war work was that of an enforcement agent in the Office of Price Administration.[12]

But why were the Japanese so furious? There is very strong evidence, particularly in the Japanese files, to suggest that even before *The American Black Chamber* appeared Yardley had made approaches in Washington and, after some bartering, sold to the Japanese for the Judas price of $7,000 all his secret knowledge about the penetration of their codes. The real reason for the rage in Tokyo may have been pique at a double cross, for the fruits of their clandestine purchase were now available around the world in a notorious best seller.

And yet, as so often is the case, the really important consequences of this Hollywood-style melodrama took place far from the public gaze—consequences in both the United States and Japan so serious, indeed so revolutionary, that their effect was felt right up to the war. We are about to watch the birth pangs of Magic.

It would be a delusion to assume that because the Americans read the enemy's codes and ciphers during the Second World War with results that were often devastating, the logical conclusion must be that the Japanese were less than skillful in this complicated game. In that war, the cracking of their signals was often a laborious and even a stressful affair. Their fatal failure was more a matter of carelessness

---

* Students of bureaucracy might note that when in January 1932 the American Military Attaché in London purchased a review of the *Black Chamber* in the *Times Literary Supplement* he reported to the War Department that the cost was five cents, which was "chargeable to Procurement Authority MID 36 P 1-0222 A-062-Z."

and self-complacency than technical sterility. And during the interwar years the Japanese effort in the related fields of crypto-communication and signal intelligence was energetic, organized, integrated, well staffed and technically originative. The Americans had a very able adversary.

It is not surprising, therefore, that after Yardley had blown so many secrets sky-high the head of the Foreign Ministry's communications section in Tokyo, Shin Sakuma, and Captain Jinsaburo Ito of the naval branch, sought far and wide—at home and abroad—for men and means to improve the security of their signals. Compared with the Germans, the Japanese were slow to start their revolution— though swifter than anyone else. But the shift was radical. Out of this search for greater security there emerged, during the thirties, a decision to abandon code for their most confidential and secret messages: instead, they would encipher them on a machine, in a manner that seemed to be insoluble. By a supreme irony, this decision ultimately enabled the Americans to "read the Japanese mail" with absolute ease: that is to say, the *diplomatic* mail.

The concept of an enciphering machine was neither new nor unknown in the United States. Indeed, Edward Hebern of Illinois had developed such a device and demonstrated it to the Navy in Washington in 1921. Safford had interested himself in it. Agnes Driscoll of the Research Desk had previously worked for Hebern. But there was not enough mileage in his ideas and the Hebern invention was never firmly gripped and exploited. Other comparable machines, however, were on the world market during the twenties. The basic technology was thus an open secret. The question was, who could introduce the sophisticated variations that would produce an unbreakable cipher? It was like atomic energy. The world community of physicists understood the equations and the theories, but who could convert them into an effective weapon?

Characteristic of all these systems was the wheel or "rotor," around whose circumference would be a series of points or studs representing the letters of the alphabet and cross-linked, within the wheel, by an infinitely complicated arrangement of wires. Imagine, then, an instrument in the front of which there is an ordinary typewriter keyboard but, at the rear, a set of these wheels positioned side by side. Pressure on letter *A* of the keyboard initiates an electric current or impulse which passes to a letter point or stud on the first rotor, then through its inner wiring to *another* point, representing a different letter. The current then passes into and through the next rotor, and the next . . . The means of converting that current back into a letter might vary, but one thing was certain. The letter finally produced would not be *A* but—say—*X:* and for a cryptanalyst the problem of discovering the original letter which *X* had replaced would be incredibly difficult.[13]

Such—with subtle but critical additions and modifications—was the nature of the famous Enigma machine, manufactured and publicly marketed from 1923 onward by the Chiffriermaschinen Aktiengesellschaft of Berlin. Adopted and adapted by the German Navy in 1926, and then, in 1929, by the Army, it was used universally throughout the war by Hitler's High Command and all his armed and secret forces.

> Alas, regardless of their doom,
> The little victims play!

For the Poles at first, and Bletchley in 1940, broke into the ciphers and fished continuously in this rewarding sea.

Enigma was no stranger to the American cryptanalysts. In 1927 the Signal Corps had acquired in Germany, for $144, a model of the commercial version. By 1931 the Assistant Military Attaché in Berlin, Major Evans (also of the Signal Corps), had attended German army maneuvers and reported that "the German Signal Corps were using a typewriter type of enciphering device *in the field*."* Moreover, he had inspected—by permission—and reported fully on highly elaborate Enigmas established in the Reichswehrministerium at the communication centers of both the Army and the Navy.[14]

When the Japanese made their move, therefore, the Americans were not unprepared. They understood many of the technical and theoretical principles of Enigma, though they were far from knowing how to break any signals enciphered on it. So when, in 1931, the Japanese Navy introduced its own ciphering machine, Type No. 91 (since 1931 was 2591 in the Japanese calendar), they must have greeted

---

* Author's italics.

the first evidence of its existence without surprise, but with trepidation. In fact there were two varieties of the machine, the modified version supplied to the Foreign Office being named Type No. 91-A. This Foreign Office version—which came to be known as the Red Machine—was gradually mastered by a combination of cryptanalytical techniques and, it has been said, by a "snatch" (of relevant papers) arranged by Zacharias in Washington during the temporary seduction of a Japanese officer. This episode is described in Ladislas Farrago's *The Broken Seal*, but as the nature and content of the papers are not defined it is impossible to assess their significance. Such episodes make good stories, but what the historian wants to know is the nature and quality of the end-product.

And, in fact, the Red Machine was only an aperitif. As the advancing thirties drew Japan closer to the center of the impending storm, the special signals unit of the Navy, under Captain Ito, developed and perfected an entirely new instrument: the J machine, the Alphabetical Typewriter, *97-shiki O-bun In-ji-Ki*, Type 97, or, as the Americans called it, Purple. Of all the many enciphering systems used in the Second World War—the British Typex, the American Sigaba, the Hagelin products—only Purple and Enigma have attained "star quality": which is to say that they alone strike a chord in the minds of the layman as well as the specialist. And the reason is simple. To these two machines the Japanese and the Germans gave their total confidence throughout the war, convinced to the point of self-delusion that Purple and Enigma would protect even their most secret signals. But the machines failed their masters. Like the Enigma ciphers, those produced by Purple were cracked at a sufficiently early stage and were then broken consistently until defeat laid the machines to rest. Even a layman can grasp the drama of great expectations that so ruinously miscarry. As the Book of Isaiah puts it: "How art thou fallen from heaven, O Lucifer, son of the morning!"

Most books* and articles about Purple state that the Alphabetical Typewriter was a direct derivative from Enigma. But this was not so—as is confirmed by signal intelligence experts of the greatest authority in both Britain and the U.S.A. There are perhaps two

---

* Including, alas, the author's *Ultra Goes to War*.

sources of confusion. Certainly the Japanese (like other nations) acquired a commercial Enigma, and because Purple had some similar characteristics it seemed a legitimate assumption that one had spawned the other. And then, there is an area of darkness. In defeat, the Japanese meticulously destroyed their enciphering machines. How many—if any—survived, and if so where? Perhaps one hides like a hermit crab within the shell of the NSA or its British counterpart, GCHQ, but none is on public display nor do photographs of the original instrument appear: only approximate drawings.

The real complication, however, lay in the central area of Purple's mechanism. Ronald Clark put the situation well in *The Man Who Broke Purple*. "As Einstein said in describing his efforts to discover God's law, 'God is subtle but He is not malicious.' He may make it difficult for man to fathom the laws of the universe but will not be perverse in His manner of concealment. With cryptographers, the case is different."

And in 1937 (the Japanese year 2597: hence Purple's type number) the case did indeed seem different to the American specialists in signal intelligence when they received the first intimations that a new and formidable cipher had been introduced on the Japanese circuits. But war, and preparations for war, have their own rhythm, a wayward rhythm of challenge and response. Almost inevitably, improvement in a weapon stimulates improvement in its antibody. Better armor generates better antitank guns which generate better armor. Radar detects aircraft which are then fitted with devices that confuse radar.

So the central question is, how did the Americans produce the antibody enabling them to penetrate a cipher system which, as the Japanese thought, was absolutely impenetrable? Many books confidently assert that this antibody was a highly skilled cryptanalyst of great experience called William F. Friedman.

His personality cult has, indeed, dramatized him as "*the* man who broke Purple": and it can certainly be argued that without that man Purple would not have been broken. Nor is the cult surprising. Friedman was what the Statue of Liberty stands for. His father was a Russian Jew from Kishinev who, to avoid the pogroms, emigrated in 1892 and became a salesman for Singer sewing machines. The son, brought up in Pittsburgh, became the outstanding cryptanalyst of his generation—inventing, indeed, the word cryptanalysis—and for his work he would be awarded two of the highest American distinctions, the Medal for Merit and the National Security Medal: honors he received, as President Truman put it, "for exceptional technical ingenuity which ranks him among the world's foremost authorities." So it is not surprising that in 1937 Friedman looked like Purple's menacing antibody.

He came from far back because by 1918 his civilian reputation for code work, achieved at the famous Riverbank Laboratories of the bizarre Colonel Fabyan near Chicago, had already been tested and proved in the military field by his performance at General Pershing's headquarters in France. And then—once again, in the datum-line year of 1921—he was persuaded to rejoin the Signal Corps as Chief Cryptanalyst to the War Department on a six-month contract. He carried on for another thirty-four years.[15]

Until 1929 and the fall of Yardley, however, Friedman's title was more grandiose than his situation. His staff was minute, and his efforts were directed more toward cryptography—the development for the Army of new codes and ciphers and the relevant technology—than toward cryptanalysis. The Signal Corps history indeed points out that "in peacetime, naturally, Army cryptanalysts have no enemy-enciphered traffic to work on. There are no messages of a hostile army to intercept, analyze or decrypt." (An exaggeration, surely, and specious: for though no Japanese Army signals hostile to the U.S.A. may have been intercepted in peacetime, what about other Japanese Army traffic? Did they *never* use their radios?)

For the Army, however, the benefit of the Stimson showdown in 1929 was a clear breakaway from the State Department and from Yardley. Now all work on codes and ciphers was firmly lodged under the Chief Signal Officer, General Gibbs, who created an entirely new unit called the Signal Intelligence Service. Its director, with an enormous staff of six, was none other than William Friedman, charged with "preparation and revision of Army codes and ciphers and, in the goniometric* location of enemy radio stations, the solution of intercepted enemy code and cipher messages, and laboratory arrangements

---

* Goniometry: from the Greek = measurement of angles, i.e., direction finding.

for the employment and detection of secret inks." Faced with such a program the seven at SIS might well have quoted to themselves those lines from Lewis Carroll's "The Walrus and the Carpenter."

> "If seven maids with seven mops
>   Swept it for half a year,
> Do you suppose," the Walrus said,
>   "That they could get it clear?"
> "I doubt it," said the Carpenter,
>   And shed a bitter tear.

But in this case there were no grounds for weeping. SIS, which by Pearl Harbor had expanded to 331 (and by VJ Day to 10,000), triumphantly got clear the most complex of all the puzzles that came its way: Purple.[16]

Nevertheless, to understand the giant strides in cryptanalytical capability made by the American Army between the wars, it is important to dismiss the conventional image of Friedman as a brilliant little David who, single-handed, felled this new Goliath. When it happened, the cracking of Purple was the work of a team rather than a solo effort. Yet it was here, precisely, that Friedman's contribution was valuable. He had few equals in those early days at solving a cipher or designing a cryptographic device. But beyond that he was a lucid and invigorating expositor, pouring out papers some of which stand as landmarks in the history of his art, and inspiring disciples by the advice and example of a dominant, originative personality. He shrewdly perceived the dangers of the Yardley enterprise: a upas tree, under whose shade nobody else grew tall.* In other words, he identified the essential need for a training program. Friedman may have been something of a monomaniac, but that mania was invaluable, and the way he infected others was constructive and farsighted. "Oh! He is mad, is he?" said King George II of General Wolfe. "Then, I wish he would *bite* some other of my generals."

There is indeed no British analogue of the Signal Intelligence School for the U.S. Regular Army which was established in 1931, or,

---

* Some critics have suggested that Friedman himself cast a shadow within which his associates found it difficult to attain full stature. As he was a man who provoked adverse and even jealous comment, such judgments are not easily assessed.

perhaps, of the training manuals prepared by Friedman.* If it was a matter of quality rather than quantity—nine graduates emerged before Pearl Harbor—the investment was good: Lieutenant Preston Corderman, for example, the school's second student in 1932, took over SIS as a colonel in February 1943 and ended the war as a general. But even more impressive are the pains taken to bring on officers in the Reserve. From 1929 onward small groups of such officers were given brief introductory courses, a system gradually expanded to include civilians and other ranks, so that by the outbreak of the Second World War over 280 had taken part. No one becomes an instant cryptanalyst. Still, this sowing of seed compares well with the more lethargic husbandry of the British.

The Poles' successful penetration of the Enigma cipher from 1932 onward was largely the work of a hand-picked trio of brilliant young mathematicians, Rejewski, Rózycki and Zygalski.[17] In similar fashion Friedman drew into SIS three rising doctors of mathematics with a high potential, Rowlett, Kullback and Sinkov. Rowlett in 1964 would receive a congressional award of $100,000 for his work and, in 1966, the presidential gift of a National Security Medal. Kullback became head of the Office of Research and Development in the early days of the NSA, after controlling during the war the cryptanalytical branch of SIS with over 2,500 on his staff. By 1945 Colonel Sinkov, with a Legion of Merit award, was Cryptanalytic Officer, U.S. Army Forces, Far East, and later a leading figure in the communications division of the NSA. These were men of the highest quality. So, for that matter, was the Chief Signal Officer, General Joseph Mauborgne, whose experience spanned the whole range of developments described in this chapter: before peace came in 1918 he had already been trained as a military cryptanalyst and headed the Engineering and Research Division of his corps in Washington. When the staff of SIS began their assault on Purple, therefore, they were hardly a group of virginal innocents.

There is great virtue (as well as sometimes a dangerous weakness) in the basic American military doctrine that one should first very

---

* In April 1945 the Americans captured Burgscheidungen Castle in Germany, a signal intelligence headquarters. Here they found copies of the lecture series on Military Codes and Ciphers which Friedman had used for officer training in the thirties, and which the Germans had similiarly employed. Clark, *The Man Who Broke Purple*, p. 158.

carefully identify the essential objective and then drive straight for it with the maximum force available: no finesse of indirect approach, no "peripheral strategy." And something like this happened early in 1939. As Friedman himself wrote:

> After work by my associates when we were making very slow progress, the Chief Signal Officer asked me personally to take a hand ... at his request I dropped everything else that I could and began to work with the group.

Moreover, interchanges between Safford and Friedman were now formalized by an unprecedented official sanction which enabled the Army and Navy teams to pool much of their know-how and, by mutual agreement, to peg out the areas which each group would explore. So Friedman with an enlarged staff concentrated on the central crux, Purple, while the Navy combined its fundamental work on the Japanese naval codes with attacks on Tokyo's other diplomatic systems: helping SIS, at the same time, by sharing what it had learned about the Red Machine and passing on any signals in the Purple cipher intercepted by its own surveillance stations. This was a laudable example of how to maximize effort by concentrating force—even though there was still not enough extra effort available for a decisive attack on the Japanese Army codes.

The battle, nevertheless, was harsh and prolonged. It broke Friedman himself: a man who, in any case, had a high degree of neurosis and was liable, not infrequently, to intense depression and even suicidal urges. Most accounts of the penetration of Purple dwell, quite rightly, on the price that Friedman paid, without, however, assessing the comparable strain undergone by the men he was leading. And this should be recorded, for, as he himself wrote, after victory had been achieved: "Naturally this was a collaborative, cooperative effort on the part of all the people concerned. No one person is responsible for the solution, nor is there any single person to whom the major share of the credit should go."

Indeed, to outline in even the most simplistic terms the nature of the technical challenge involved is sufficient to indicate that while a single genius might conceivably have done the job, cooperative effort was far more likely to have succeeded.

One of those who were able to speak with the authority of experience recalled:

The Purple machine first appeared, I believe, on 20 February 1939, working between Tokyo and Washington. It spread gradually to other posts in order of their importance and traffic volumes. It took nearly four years to replace Red with Purple. Posts equipped with Purple kept their Red machines for communications with posts that had not yet received new machines.

Let me state categorically that the Purple was not an Enigma— though statements that Purple was an Enigma have appeared widely in the public domain. There were no Enigma type wheels involved. The basic ingredient was telephone selectors/wipers (*waipaa* in Japanese) such as could be found in any dial telephone system of that date. Their obvious advantage was that they were commercially available and were reliable in operation.

A wiper unit was six levels wide and twenty-five steps long. Normally one level was used for the stepping control and the other five for the substitution matrix. A number of these units could be tied together to create a matrix of any desired size and the matrix did not have to be square.

For some reason completely incomprehensible to me they borrowed from the Red to the Purple the division of the alphabet into 20/6. Whatever 6 letters were plugged in the plugboard to the "vowel" positions enciphered only amongst themselves, and similarly for the "consonant" positions. This was the Achilles' heel of the machine.

The matrix used to encipher the 6 stepped once for each step of the machine and was 25 steps long—on the 1st, 26th, 51st, 76th, etc., steps letters on the six wheel ciphered identically. The ciphering of the 20 was far more complex. There were three 20-wide 25-long matrices. The current went successively through each of the three in a fixed order, in so doing passing through three successive monoalphabetic substitutions. The advancement of these three matrices was regular meter with a minor eccentricity to avoid all three advancing simultaneously.

Abbreviated by the author (and almost certainly rendered inaccurate by abbreviation!), this summary is quoted as evidence, for the inexpert, of Purple's complexity, and for those at home in cryptanalysis as proof that the mechanical processes involved were inherently different from those of Enigma. Yet this at least the two systems had in common: for all their sophistication, they were not immune to the attack of patient, brilliant minds; and the theoretical attack on Purple by the Americans was clearly at the highest intellectual level.

But the Japanese also committed a fundamental error—one of the worst in the book, it might be said, since whenever they or the Germans committed it during the war it tended to provide the laboring cryptanalysts of the Allies with much aid and comfort. Long after the Americans had broken the Red Machine the Japanese would transmit the same signal in both the Red and the Purple cipher. To be able to compare a text you can decipher with one you are still seeking to decipher is an immense advantage—even though the puzzle may still be very difficult to resolve. As the authority already quoted recalled, "The basic attack was by cribbing . . . the Japanese sent an incredible number of messages on the Red Machine to more than one post, or relayed messages from one post to another. Consequently mountains of cribs became available in the exact form in which the message was enciphered under the Purple."

The lack of familiarity with the Enigma on the part of the Japanese can be confirmed, incidentally, from their own lips. Immediately after Pearl Harbor it became evident to the German and Japanese navies that they must take steps to coordinate their communications systems if they were to function as allies in war. On January 21, 1942, however, the Japanese Naval Attaché in Berlin signaled to the Vice-Chief of the Naval General Staff in Tokyo: "Large numbers of cipher machines (such as the Enigma) have been made ready by the German Navy, and it is our feeling that they should be set up on the ships of the Japanese Navy. As regards this, even though it will be to our distinct advantage to have these cipher machines, the fact of the matter is that no preparations have been made to take care of them, and even before these preparations are made, the necessity of mutual communications will certainly arise. In view of that, even if we make the use of cipher machines a fundamental principle, there will be a need to establish joint use codes, and I have already requested the Germans to conduct serious research along these lines."

Such, anyway, is the background—however generalized and opaque —to an incontrovertible fact: after some eighteen months of herculean struggle the principles and structure of the Purple machines were sufficiently diagnosed for a working replica or analogue to be constructed.* The first break seems to have occurred in August 1940 and the first complete text of a message was established on September 25. Indeed the eight-volume *The "Magic" Background of Pearl Harbor*, which was released by the U.S. Department of Defense in 1977, begins uncompromisingly: "By the fall of 1940 United States Government cryptanalysts had solved some of the Japanese Foreign Office's highest grade cryptographic systems. The interception, decryption and translation on a current basis of secret Japanese worldwide diplomatic messages then began." It never stopped, until well after the bombs burst above Hiroshima and Nagasaki.

By the fall of 1940, of course, the European war was in full flood. The Battle of France had been fought and lost: the Battle of Britain was still unresolved. And on September 27 the sinister ten-year pact was signed in Berlin by Germany, Italy and Japan which promulgated their mutual recognition of the Nazis' "New Order" in Europe and committed the three signatories to undertaking war in common against any intervening nation—a commitment with immense consequences, since it precipitated Hitler into war with the United States after Pearl Harbor. This, therefore, is a natural point at which two questions may properly be asked. What progress had the British themselves made in penetrating the Japanese signal traffic; and to what extent had the British and Americans, even before they became belligerent allies, cooperated in this particular respect? The answer must be that the distance traveled was far greater than is generally realized.

During the thirties three signal systems were obvious targets for British cryptanalysts—the German, the Italian and the Japanese. (There was indeed a fourth, the Russian, but from 1927 onward this proved to be impregnable.† After June 22, 1941, and the German invasion all attacks on Russian codes and ciphers ceased—or so it is claimed!) By an odd chance, success was in inverse proportion to the identifiable threat from the country concerned. The Italians repre-

---

* A replica more efficient in at least one respect than the original. Certain contact points in the Purple machine were made of copper, which wore with use and tended to produce garbled texts. In the American analogue brass was employed, not copper, and the malfunction was avoided.

† Apart from some low-grade codes.

sented more of a nuisance than a major menace, and yet—partly as a result of the Abyssinian crisis and Italian intervention in the Spanish Civil War—very considerable penetration of their signal traffic was achieved. The major menace was Hitler's Germany, but for a variety of technical reasons all the high-level German traffic, particularly that in the Enigma cipher, remained impenetrable. Only the farsighted recognized during these years the grave threat from an increasingly aggressive Japan: nevertheless, on this front the British cryptanalysts were both active and effective. It is relevant to remember, moreover, that the peacetime resources of GCCS were smaller than those of the combined American agencies, while the range of potential enemies against whom precautions had to be taken, in Europe and the Far East, was very much greater.

By the mid-thirties the little Japanese section in GCCS was already expanding, and the main Japanese military and naval codes and ciphers had been solved. The introduction in 1937 of the Purple machine, however, presented a baffling problem which the British were unable to overcome: just as Polish aid was invaluable in their conquest of Enigma, so American know-how was needed before Purple could be vanquished. Still, by September 1939 and the outbreak of the European war, definite progress was being made in the attack on the Japanese naval code, JN25, and long experience of the Japanese signal traffic made it possible to keep roughly abreast of the composition and movements of the Japanese Navy.

After September 1939, and the transference of GCCS from London to Bletchley Park, it was inevitable that the main weight of effort, of manpower and of equipment should be thrown into a nonstop assault on the German and (after Mussolini entered the war) the Italian communications systems. Here were actual and belligerent enemies. Nevertheless, work on the Japanese traffic continued steadily, both in England and at bases in the Far East. The main center was the Combined Bureau in Singapore.

This effort was of central importance. Such Anglo-American cooperation as the Tizard Mission to the United States in the autumn of 1940 (which disclosed to the Americans most of Britain's most treasured military secrets, including the famous cavity magnetron), and such common enterprises as shared development of the hush-hush proximity fuse,[18] created a climate of opinion within which the most clandestine of all activities, cryptanalysis, could be mutually discussed. By early 1941 the British were way ahead in their command of the Enigma cipher, while the American command of Purple was absolute. It was obviously important that in any pooling of information the British should not appear as ill-educated about Japanese communications.

And such a pooling did occur. In the spring of 1941 four American representatives, two from the Navy and two from the Army, arrived at Bletchley Park. Friedman should have been part of the team, but he had collapsed into a hospital. Like the Three Wise Men, the quartet brought gifts of a rare quality: a model of the Purple machine (equivalent, in its way, to the Polish gift of an Enigma machine to British and French officers in Warsaw in 1939) and information about their work on the Japanese code systems.* It seemed natural to respond to this gesture by sharing Bletchley's knowledge of how to break the Enigma cipher and by explaining the quality of the Ultra intelligence derived from it. But the fact is that much reluctance had to be overcome: perhaps understandably, since in early 1941 the British were fighting for their lives—were, indeed, still actually expecting an invasion—while the Americans were (at least theoretically) peaceful neutrals. Better counsels prevailed. Even so, the conditions were strict: the number to be let into the secret was severely limited and the names of all those indoctrinated must be reported to GCCS.[19]

About the same time as the Bletchley visit, another small American mission arrived at the Combined Bureau in Singapore, with the similar purpose of exchanging—in absolute secrecy—information about Japan's signal traffic and the means of penetrating it. As a fruitful consequence of these clandestine discussions one British naval officer, trained in Japanese and experienced in cryptanalysis, was introduced into the American signal intelligence station on Corregidor in the Philippines.[20] Since the British were, in important respects, ahead of the Americans in their attack on the Japanese naval code, he came not merely to learn but actually to contribute. Perhaps more importantly,

---

* It was agreed that the British would break Tokyo/London traffic and the Americans Tokyo/Washington. The Americans honored this to the extent of reading Tokyo/London for familiarization, to obtain cribs, etc., but without passing on the contents. The limited information about Ultra led the Americans, particularly the Navy for the Atlantic battle, to develop their own technology—the "bombes"—and in the end they became the major contributor in this field, according to American sources.

a secret channel of communication was now established between Corregidor and Singapore which enabled each side to pass cryptanalytical information to the other directly, thus bypassing the slow, cumbrous and perhaps less secure official channels.

This was an extraordinary coming together. Months before Pearl Harbor, a basis had been laid for Anglo-American collaboration in the most intimate and sensitive areas of signal intelligence. The collaboration would expand and intensify, from 1942 onward, until American officers and men would work at Bletchley alongside the British: all American commands in the Mediterranean and European theaters would receive a stream of German Ultra intelligence on equal terms with their British counterparts: and throughout the peak period of the Battle of the Atlantic the Admiralty's Operational Intelligence Center, which lived on Ultra, would be in close and virtually daily communication with the U.S. Navy's Atlantic Section, Operational Intelligence, under Commander Knowles in Washington.[21] Long before America went to war, however, the collaboration found potential expression in a variety of ways.* Through the British ambassador in Washington, for example, intelligence from the Magic intercepts that might be of use in the struggle with Germany was secretly forwarded to London. There was a growing sense of confident unity.

The path to Pearl had certainly meandered across many years. But if we sum up the credit balance for American signal intelligence on the very eve of Pearl Harbor we see much that is laudable. War would reveal weaknesses, but the pressure of war would soon rectify many of them. There were deficiencies in manpower, an organization still inadequate and among senior officers an almost universal fear, distrust or misunderstanding of this strange phenomenon called Sigint. Nevertheless, the track record was promising. The cryptanalytical groups and associated intelligence officers in Washington, Hawaii and elsewhere were the end-product of two decades of experience. The vital diplomatic cipher of the Japanese had long been broken, and though the current naval code was still elusive the men working on it had overcome similar difficulties in the past. Intercept stations were in

---

* Statements made by authorities like Safford and Layton before the Congressional Inquiry into the Pearl Harbor Attack amply confirm the extent of Anglo-American cooperation in this field before December 1941. Fabian testified that "we had an established liaison with the British at Singapore" in evidence at the Hewitt Inquiry.

action; though they were far too few for wartime, and though the means for passing intercepted signals to the decrypting and translating centers were often antediluvian, broadly speaking the system was viable and would not take long to improve. The huge volume of Magic signals intercepted and deciphered during 1941 speaks for itself.

So far as Sigint was concerned, therefore, an optimistic observer might have commented, in Roosevelt's famous words, that the only thing to be feared was fear itself. The test came on December 7, 1941.

CHAPTER THREE

That Damn Cloud

*Why, with some of the finest intelligence available in our history,
with the almost certain knowledge that war was at hand, with
plans that contemplated the precise type of attack that was
executed by Japan on the morning of December 7th—why was it
possible for Pearl Harbor to occur?*
  Report of the Congressional Inquiry, 1946

*History is not merely what happened: it is what happened in the
context of what might have happened.*
  Hugh Trevor-Roper, valedictory lecture as Regius
  Professor of Modern History, Oxford University,
  May 20, 1980

*There has never been an American tragedy. There have only
been great failures.*
  F. Scott Fitzgerald, 1927

IN 1937, DURING the Japanese assault on China, the U.S.S.
Mindanao was held at anchor off Canton by blockade. Here, for six
months, the daily weather conditions were logged and forwarded to
Washington—unknown to the crew, who had lightheartedly put on
record each day that the sky was clear except for a single cloud above
the ship! But at last a sealed order reached the captain from Naval
Headquarters: "Proceed 500 yards upriver and get out from under
that damn cloud."[1]

In a sense the United States has distinctly failed, even after forty
years, to get out from under the "damn cloud" of frustration, suspicion,
backbiting, national shame and distorted fact which has continued,
ever since Pearl Harbor, to hover over the American conscience like
that cloud above *Mindanao*. There is still, for example, a persistent

lobby promoting the "conspiracy theory" that President Roosevelt, eager to involve the United States in war, was personally responsible for ensuring that available evidence about an imminent Japanese attack (evidence which, the argument assumes, pointed directly at what was about to happen) somehow got manipulated and withheld from those who "needed to know."

The conspiracy theory is moonshine.* There is a simple test. To achieve so malign a purpose Roosevelt would have been unavoidably compelled to carry with him General Marshall, the Army Chief of Staff, and Admiral Stark, the Chief of Naval Operations—each of whom, incidentally, was desperately concerned to avoid or at least postpone hostilities in view of the currently feeble state of the U.S. armed forces.† The main point, however, is that anybody who thinks that George Marshall, upright, honorable and incorruptible, could have been persuaded even by a President to mislead his subordinate commanders, by the devious suppression or distortion of vital information, in order to precipitate a war with Japan—the last thing he wanted—is living in a dream world.

Years of controversial debate on this issue have shown that those committed to the "conspiracy theory" are no more susceptible to rational argument than medieval theologians scuffling about the number of angels capable of balancing on the head of a pin. It is startling, nevertheless, to compare this realm of fantasy with the harsh realities of life as disclosed in the remarkable document entitled Magic Summary 609, of November 25, 1943. (Though declassified in October 1979, this seems to have escaped attention in the National Archives.) The Summary prints the complete text of a circular sent out by the Japanese War Ministry on the day after Pearl Harbor to Japan's

---

* Hostile to Roosevelt though the Congressional Inquiry may have been—Marshall told his biographer Forrest Pogue in 1956 that it was "intended to crucify Roosevelt"—the basic conclusion was that there was no evidence to support a claim that American officials had "tricked, provoked, incited, cajoled or coerced Japan into attacking the Nation in order that a declaration of war might be easily obtained from the Congress."
† "Our state of mind . . . I am referring now to both Stark and myself—was to do all in our power here at home, with the State Department or otherwise, to try to delay this break to the last moment, because of our state of unpreparedness, and because of our involvement in other parts of the world." Hearings, Part 32, p. 560. Marshall is testifying about the situation at the end of July but it summarizes a persisting attitude. On November 27, as the crisis approached, Marshall and Stark sent a joint memorandum to Roosevelt pleading for time and avoidance of war in the Pacific.

Military Attachés throughout the world, giving the Army's explanation about why Japan went to war.

The circular states *explicitly* that after the occupation of Indochina, Japan decided "to complete her war preparations by the end of September at the very latest, and at the same time to exert every effort through diplomatic channels to see her demands fulfilled. If her demands were not met by early October, an Imperial Decree would be issued deciding upon war against England and the United States." After the establishment of Tojo's Cabinet in October, the decision was made, on November 5, to open hostilities early in December. "Thereafter, Japan went ahead with plans for war." Finally, after receipt of the U.S. proposals of November 20, "the Supreme War Command immediately decided upon war, and on December 1 the Imperial Decree was issued."

Conspiracy is a more convenient explanation than the true reasons for the disaster of December 7, 1941. But it is the very complexity of those reasons which has made it difficult to heal the wound in the American psyche. One cause of such a deep-seated trauma is often shock—and as the radio announcements of the Japanese attack blared over the United States shock would be an understatement of the general reaction. On the morning of December 7 the Institute of Pacific Relations met in conference at the Country Club in Cleveland, Ohio. The director divided this body of Far Eastern experts into two groups which then, independently, assessed the possibility that Japan might take military action against the United States. About two o'clock the groups reassembled. Each announced the same conclusion: *the Japanese would make no move for a year, or more.* As discussion continued Kay Halle, who was covering the conference for a local radio network, was handed a slip of paper to pass on to the director. It was the announcement, just released by Roosevelt's press secretary, that the Japanese had bombed Pearl Harbor. If professional Orient-watchers could be taken so humiliatingly by surprise, how much greater the impact on millions of ordinary citizens![2]

Neither the man in the street nor the members of the Institute of Pacific Relations had any knowledge of the really relevant information—the intelligence which, because of the achievement of the men who had already broken the Purple diplomatic cipher, was available to the Roosevelt administration and to its senior military advisers in abundant detail. Here is the point of pressure. It generates a set of questions, still not entirely resolved, which were not even answered satisfactorily during the massive interrogations contained in the 39 volumes, published in 1946, of the Congressional Hearings on Pearl Harbor. The questions bear painfully on such matters as the degree of awareness, within the Administration, of impending hostilities: the specific issue of Pearl Harbor itself and why, both in Washington and on the spot, men responsible for its safety were staggered by the actual event: and—more technically, but of fundamental importance—why the handling and dissemination of secret intelligence within the armed services in and before December 1941 was so desultory.

Such questions have been asked, on the whole, with reference to the intelligence, and the staff arrangements, which existed during the last few hectic weeks that preceded Pearl Harbor. This was the central thrust of the Hearings themselves, in their formal but intensive hunt for scapegoats, and it has dominated most subsequent discussion. But we now know of an earlier event which, had its implications been properly grasped, might have kept the American fleet and shore installations at Hawaii on the alert and produced, for the Japanese, a very different reception. Ironically, it was ignored by those directly concerned with American security. But war, like life in general, is full of irony. That able pilot Captain Fuchida, who led the attack on Pearl Harbor, survived long enough to be flying above Hiroshima on another fatal day and to wonder what had caused so curious a cloud.

During the summer of 1941, B1A, the section of the British counter-intelligence department MI 5 which handled double agents, had a particularly dexterous specimen in play, code-named Tricycle.[3] (So effective was Tricycle that in 1944 he was cast for a central role in the great deception program which preceded the D Day landings.) Tricycle was in fact a Yugoslav named Dusko Popov, personable, worldly-wise and possessing a good cover story of business activities which, together with the apparent efficiency of his reporting from Britain, commended him to the Abwehr headquarters in Lisbon, for whom he was theoretically working as a spy—though his every action and every message were in practice controlled by his masters at B1A. Around midsummer the Lisbon Abwehr asked Tricycle to go to the United States.

The task proposed was to establish a new German espionage network on a large scale, as the previous organization had been penetrated and pulverized. The British, after carefully weighing a project of considerable risk, decided to let Tricycle carry on: and so, on August 10, 1941, he set out for the States, taking with him in microdot form a substantial questionnaire supplied by the Abwehr. This, of course, was already British property. Meanwhile the intelligence authorities properly and naturally warned J. Edgar Hoover about Tricycle's real character. On his arrival, therefore, he inevitably came into the hands of the FBI, who, by photographic enlargement, also acquired a copy of the questionnaire.

It is on the three quarto sheets of this remarkable document that the case for a great might-have-been can be erected. For amid the routine questions such as would predictably have been given to a German agent in the United States to answer—queries about rates of aircraft production, the operation of Lend-Lease, shipbuilding, convoy organization, etc.—the extraordinary feature was this: no less than *one third* of the questionnaire was concerned with Hawaii in general and Pearl Harbor in particular. Why, it might reasonably be asked, should an Abwehr agent concern himself about exact details (sketches are requested) of the hangars, depots and fuel supplies on Hawaii's airfields, or the location of the military and naval ammunition dumps? Why should he be asked to obtain, in respect of Pearl Harbor, "exact details and sketch about the situation of the state wharf, of the pier installations, workshops, petrol installations, situations of dry dock No. 1 and the new dry dock which is being built," or "how far has the dredger work progressed at the entrance and in the east and southeast lock?"

The Germans had no conceivable strategic interest in Hawaii during 1941 or, for that matter, at any time during the war: no interest which would have required so meticulous an investigation. There was only one possible conclusion: the inquiries were to be made on behalf of Germany's ally, Japan, and Japan was seeking the sort of information which normally implies an aggressive intent.* It should be remembered that though the final decision had not yet been taken in Tokyo, by August 1941 Admiral Yamamoto had already made great progress in planning and training for the Pearl Harbor attack. And

---

* Detailed evidence about the interconnections between German and Japanese intelligence services during the war is presented in Chapter 11.

Magic itself had provided a background against which the question-naire might have been interpreted. In a deciphered signal of January 30, 1941, from the Foreign Office in Tokyo to the Embassy in Wash-ington, detailed instructions were issued for coordinating Japanese intelligence activities in the U.S.A. Paragraph 8 reads: "We shall cooperate with the German and Italian intelligence organs in the U.S. This phase has been discussed with the Germans and Italians in Tokyo, and it has been approved." Knowledge of such Axis integra-tion should have made Tricycle more meaningful.

Unfortunately that idiosyncratic personality, the head of the FBI, felt a deep and puritanical distrust for dubious figures like agents: more so in the case of double agents. In spite of his briefing from the British, therefore, Hoover treated Tricycle so high-handedly and dis-missively that the questionnaire seems to have been inadequately evaluated—if it was assessed at all. Its immense significance was never reported to the American High Command—nor produced later as testimony during the Pearl Harbor Inquiry. It has been suggested—after the revelations about the mole Anthony Blunt—that another alleged British mole in MI 5, Guy Liddell, maliciously warned Hoover against Tricycle. But this was entirely unnecessary. If Liddell had the kind of relationship with Hoover which is implied, he would have realized that he need take no personal risk: Hoover's temperament would do the job on its own.*

Yet how enormous is the might-have-been! Unmistakable intelli-gence, in the hands of the right authorities, about a major Japanese interest in the defenses, docks and airfields of Hawaii might well, if received as early as August, have created an alertness of mind and suggested a new slant on Japanese planning which, if followed by sensible preparations, could greatly have diminished, even if they could not avert, the disaster of December. There is nothing involving signal intelligence in the abortive story of Tricycle, but as one ex-amines the character of the Sigint that preceded Pearl Harbor, and reflects on the way that it was handled, it is impossible not to feel that if the people involved—the command staffs and the various in-telligence units—had been aware of the Hawaii section of the ques-

---

* Senior officers in MI 5 and MI 6—as well as in the CIA—who knew and worked with Liddell all rebut the charge that he was a mole. (Private information.)

tionnaire some of the Magic intercepts ought to have appeared to them in a different and far more menacing light.

The operative word is "ought." For skepticism is the function of the historian, and though the questionnaire cries its message aloud a residual doubt still lingers as to whether the cry would in fact have been heard. If we now turn to the sequence of Magic intercepts which flowed in during 1941, and examine some of the pictures formed on the basis of this rich intelligence, we are bound to ask whether even the indisputable evidence of the Tricycle questionnaire would have been powerful enough to shatter assumptions which consistently led the Americans to look elsewhere, and not at Pearl Harbor. One must remember also the series of messages from Tokyo[4] (sent not in Purple cipher but in the codes called J19 and PA-K2) which from early September onward instructed the Japanese agent in Honolulu precisely what and how he was to report—a prescription not unlike Tricycle's.* These decodes were seen by all the senior naval intelligence officers in Washington, but they were universally discounted as routine procedure. Admiral Stark does not appear to have been informed; Admiral Kimmel, commanding the Pacific Fleet at Pearl, was certainly not. No alarm bells rang.

Perhaps the most remarkable feature of the thousands of intercepted diplomatic signals which were deciphered before Pearl Harbor is that if certain events had taken a different course there might have been no more Magic. On May 5 Tokyo sent to the Embassy in Washington: "According to a fairly reliable source of information it appears almost certain that the United States government is reading your code messages. Please let me know whether you have any suspicion of above." The source was, in fact, the Germans, who had told the Japanese ambassador in Berlin, Baron Oshima, that their agents in America had made this awkward discovery. But though the Washington ambassador, Nomura, held an investigation, and though on May 20 he actually informed Tokyo that he had established that some of Japan's codes were being broken by the Americans, no more action was taken other than to increase security in the handling of codes. On March 20 the Tokyo Foreign Office had signaled to Oshima in Berlin, in plain terms: "I feel that we need not worry about our code messages

---

* See below, p. 63.

being deciphered." And even now, nobody saw any real reason for worry.

This characteristic complacency, revealed in so many other aspects of the Japanese conduct of the war, was fatal. Until the end, the Americans were able to continue—within the limits of their ingenuity —the rewarding game of breaking the enemy's codes and ciphers without arousing more than a fleeting suspicion. In the field of cryptography, above all, the superior attitudes struck by aggressive dictatorships tend to be counterproductive. For the Germans suffered from the same myopia. Whenever doubts were raised about the impregnability of the Enigma cipher the answer was always the same: any suspected leak was probably due to a coup by the British secret service or, alternatively, breaks might have occurred by chance on a particular day but as the cipher was constantly changed it would inevitably, in the longer term, defeat the British cryptanalysts. When Admiral Doenitz, still head of U-boat Command, was driven by concern over the security of his ciphers in the spring of 1943 to set up an elaborate court of inquiry into the matter, the end result was very much the same as that reached by the Japanese two years earlier— business, in fact, more or less as usual.

And yet, and yet: suppose the suspicions aroused in Tokyo by the Germans' warning had led the Japanese to a radical review of their codes and cipher systems.* There were options open to them, and a considerable background of cryptographic skill. It is not inconceivable, therefore, that a determined effort on their part to make their signal traffic more secure might have blanketed off large areas just when the Americans were enjoying their reward for so many years of cryptanalytical effort.† Eighteen months later, at the time of the Solomons campaign, a routine alteration of the Japanese naval code denied Admiral Nimitz and his people access to vital information for week after critical week.‡

---

* It is ironical that a number of the Magic intercepts for March and April 1941 disclose that the Japanese, believing that both the Germans and the Italians were breaking their codes, took careful precautions against their Axis friends.
† The flurry of messages about Japanese suspicions related to their *codes,* and was transmitted in Purple encipherment. The implication is, therefore, that even at this time they still believed Purple to be secure. But if the Japanese had really taken fright and radically modified their codes, they might well, as a precaution, have undertaken a further sophistication of Purple itself. Here lay the potential danger for the Americans.
‡ See Chapter 5.

Which raises the central question. By a happy chance, the Americans were thus allowed to continue with their deciphering of Japan's diplomatic signals, whether in the Purple cipher or in the associated high-grade codes, all through the months of 1941. Of what value were the thousands of signals deciphered? What profit was there from the information gained? And—the most delicate question of all—were indicators and warnings overlooked that ought to have been recognized?

The Japanese network of diplomatic communications was, of course, worldwide. The Americans were able to tap into the network over the whole range: in consequence, the intercepts deciphered were not merely between the Tokyo Foreign Office and the Washington Embassy (signals on which the greatest emphasis has been laid) but also between the Foreign Office and its representatives (to pick a few names at random from the intercepts) in Mexico City, Moscow, Lima, Rome, Bangkok, Berlin, Vichy, London, Shanghai, Singapore, Buenos Aires, Batavia. The cumulative effect of the evidence provided by this sustained dialogue between the Japanese Foreign Office and its outposts is staggering, for what the dialogue is saying—with many nuances and shifts of tone—it that here is a nation preparing itself meticulously to undertake the act of war: and not defensive war. From this point of view there is a consonance between the attitude of Roosevelt's administration toward Japan in 1941 and the content of the Magic decrypts. Whatever its vagueness and sometimes its obscurities—the usual aspects of a Rooseveltian policy—the summer freezing of Japan's assets, the oil embargo, the refusal to buy peace by significant concession, the hard line followed in the final negotiations are all consistent with the picture of Japan painted by Magic: a country engaged with ruthless and devouring energy in pursuing its own interests, and not to be deflected from that pursuit.

What caused the shock in Washington on December 7 (though this is not true of the American people in general) was the attack on Pearl Harbor, not the fact that Japan had gone to war. That had already been elevated from a possibility to a likelihood. The ability of the Americans to read so copiously the Japanese diplomatic mail—to listen to what they were *actually* saying to one another—confirmed the sinister significance of Tokyo's more openly aggressive moves. Once again, therefore, the "conspiracy theory" seems irrelevant. A close study of Japanese preparations, as revealed by Magic, suggests that the Americans' real problem was even to attempt to keep pace with their rapid development, with this beaver-like activity on every front, rather than to precipitate events.

In particular, Magic made it clear that Japan spoke with two voices. The emollient tones of Ambassador Nomura, as he engaged month by month in his secret conversations with Secretary of State Cordell Hull (and with the President) were in a very different key from the harsh, discordant note sounded by many of the Magic intercepts: the note of reality. Just as, during the Washington Naval Treaty negotiations, Yardley's mastery of the Japanese code had provided the American representatives with invaluable insight, so Magic's gift supplied an important alternative perspective which qualified the gentler propositions of diplomacy.

Magic began the process of diminishing Nomura's credibility even before he was *en poste*. He formally presented his credentials to President Roosevelt at noon on February 14. But on December 25, 1940, a translation was made of an intercepted signal dispatched on the 10th from Tokyo to the Washington Embassy: "With the appointment of Ambassador Nomura we wish to formulate a definite plan for our propaganda and information-gathering work by seeking cooperation of Japanese bank and business officials in the U.S." During the next few weeks the New York office listed eighteen different Japanese agencies suitable for intelligence collecting, and Washington reported on a meeting with businessmen and newspaper representatives at which they had agreed both to gather intelligence and to cable "their opinions and manipulations" secretly through diplomatic channels. These developments were formalized on January 30 by another decrypt in the Magic files, this time to Washington from Matsuoka himself, the Foreign Minister, in which he gave instructions for the intelligence setup to be recognized "in view of the critical situation in the recent relations between the two countries, and *for the purpose of being prepared for the worst*."* He laid down, moreover, that copies of his message should be sent, "as Minister's orders," to Canada, Mexico, San Francisco (copies from San Francisco to Honolulu, Los Angeles, Portland, Seattle and Vancouver), New York, New Orleans and Chicago. Nomura arrived like a dove, but he had been preceded by a hawk.

---

* Author's italics.

This impression was intensified during the spring and summer by a long series of Magic messages which threw a bright light on the clandestine maneuvers of the Japanese. From South American capitals came a wealth of evidence about the hasty organization (as in the U.S.A.) of Japanese civilian agencies for espionage, of new courier services and of a searching investigation into the capacity and reliability of local radio transmitters. Cooperation on the spot with Germans and Italians was mandatory. The activities of the Germans themselves had caused Roosevelt so much concern that in August 1940, long before the birth of the OSS, he had authorized by his own private executive act the formation of a small undercover group, headed by Nelson Rockefeller, to sabotage the efforts of Nazis and their sympathizers in South America.[5] Magic's revelation of hectic Japanese preparations in this area during 1941 told its own tale—with the implication that a fallback position was being organized in South America for the Japanese intelligence services as an insurance against the possibility—or presumption—that war might expel them from the United States.

And as for that country, what were the recipients of Magic to think of the two intercepts of May 9 and 11, one sent to Tokyo from Los Angeles and the other from Seattle, in which the Japanese representatives reported fully on the recruitment of spies, the surveillance of aircraft plants and their output, the "maintenance of connection" with "second generation" Japanese-Americans in the Army, the study of shipping, the penetration of the labor movement and so on?

The dual voice of Japan was particularly well disclosed by Magic during Foreign Minister Matsuoka's visit to Europe in April. While Nomura continued his pacific discussions with Hull in Washington, the Magic intercepts of Matsuoka's own reports back to Tokyo showed how firmly and comfortably he had consolidated relationships with Hitler and Mussolini. More than that, they included his triumphant signal to the Washington Embassy of April 13 in which he announced his conclusion, in Moscow, of a pact of neutrality with the Russians. This was of vital significance for the Americans, since—at least on paper—it relieved pressure on Japan from the north and cleared the way for a shift of her forces southward. That strategic fact remained even though the fiery Matsuoka had resigned on July 16. His successor, Admiral Toyoda, was thought to be more amenable but at the same time Magic threw up a signal of July 14 from Canton to Tokyo, which mentioned that "next on our schedule [after Indochina] is sending ultimatum to Netherlands Indies . . . in the seizing of Singapore the Navy will play the principal part . . . Army will need only one division to seize Singapore and two divisions to seize Netherlands Indies . . . with air forces based on Canton, Spratly Islands, Palau, Singora in Thailand, Portuguese Timor and Indochina and with submarine fleet in Mandates, Hainan and Indochina we will crush British-American military power . . ."

This Canton signal was dismissed by the U.S. Office of Naval Operations as wishful thinking rather than a directive. Nevertheless—and bearing in mind the increasing amount of evidence supplied by Magic as the months slipped by toward December 7—it seems reasonable to accept the verdict in the introduction to Volume I of *The "Magic" Background**: "Thus, the American State Department was kept fully aware of the real feelings of Japanese authorities, which were much at odds with the seemingly sincere statements of Ambassador Nomura." Remembering that Nomura himself was kept in the dark by the war party in Tokyo as to the true nature of their intentions, we may go further and ask how much weaker the negotiating position of Roosevelt and his Secretary of State would have been without the extraordinary range of information that came into the Administration's hands by grace of the men who broke Purple. If Magic did nothing else, it never ceased to warn about Japan's hard, incessant and (for all her cosmetic tricks of diplomacy) inflexible drive toward an act of aggression . . . somewhere.

It is a natural consequence of military disaster that the nation concerned should search its heart for decades to find out precisely what went wrong, and who were the guilty parties. Dunkirk, the fall of Crete and of Singapore, the early defeats in the North African desert are all matters of continuing scrutiny by the British. It is therefore not surprising that the American inclination has been to seek proofs that the Magic material, if properly handled, should have revealed Pearl Harbor as the "somewhere," the main objective in the Japanese war plan. Two quite separate issues, however, tend to be confused in this search. The first relates to the use of intelligence: did Magic in fact clearly reveal that Pearl Harbor was a target? The second is a

---

* *The "Magic" Background of Pearl Harbor*, 8 vols., U.S. Department of Defense, 1977.

specifically operational question: irrespective of whether Pearl Harbor was definitely known to be a target, why in early December 1941 were its defenses so inadequately organized that they were taken by surprise? For it is not unrealistic to presume that even if an attack on Pearl had not been definitely forecast, a greater degree of alert readiness—at a time when war seemed imminent—might have substantially mitigated the tragedy.

Before answering the first question we must clear the ground. Brutally successful operations suggest that they are the implementation of long-prepared plans, solidly supported by the military hierarchy of the aggressor. So it seemed when the German panzers poured through the Ardennes in their 1940 *Blitzkrieg* against France. But now we know (a) that this was a substitute plan formulated by General Manstein and forced through by Hitler to replace the German General Staff's earlier plan for a less concentrated assault farther north, and (b) that even when the offensive through the Ardennes and across the Meuse was carried out, the more conservative senior generals—and, to a degree, Hitler himself—were terrified at the danger to the German flanks as Guderian and Rommel thrust the *Blitzkrieg* onward. They tried to check it. The panzers' *Blitz* was, in fact, not solidly supported by professional military opinion. This is equally true of the attack on Pearl Harbor.

Yamamoto himself had certainly identified and demanded the surprise destruction of the American fleet at Pearl as the essential precondition for Japan's survival in a war with the United States. But by the summer of 1941 the right torpedo for use in shallow waters was still being sought, and even in the first fortnight of September an elaborate war game at the Naval War College in Tokyo suggested that the air cover available for an assault on Pearl was insufficient and that an unacceptable loss, up to 50 percent of the aircraft carriers, would be incurred. As late as early November, Yamamoto found that though the tactical problems were now resolved he could not win over Admiral Nagano, the Chief of the Naval General Staff, and his colleagues. This opposition from the top continued to the last: Nagano only allowed the actual operation to proceed on the understanding that it could be called off, even at the last minute.

This is not to suggest that the broader aspects of the Japanese plan—a bomb-burst into Southeast Asia, the Dutch possessions and the

Philippines—were not endorsed or that Japan's basic determination was weakened. It is a reminder that the attack on Pearl was essentially a child of Yamamoto's foresight: but though he grasped that destruction of the U.S. Pacific Fleet was the critical factor on which all Japan's hopes of ultimate victory depended, a hard core of his country's senior naval officers was not convinced that the risk was worth taking. Thus while to Americans, then and afterward, the attack on Pearl seemed like a carefully calculated outrage, the nodal point of a far-flung offensive, to an important element of the Japanese war staff it appeared dubious, a project that was accepted grudgingly, skeptically, and at the last possible moment.

Since it was only late in the day that an attack on Pearl Harbor was written into the overall plan for a breakout into a Greater East Asia Co-Prosperity Sphere, there were no valid military reasons for filling the air with signals about Hawaii. On rational grounds, therefore, one would only expect to find a few amid the many Magic intercepts—and a few is what we find. The witch-hunters have concentrated on these. But though a particular signal, isolated from its context, may seem to be full of meaning, that meaning—in hindsight so evident—can dissolve when the signal is placed in its contemporary setting. Consider one of the most controversial of Magic's references to Pearl.

A signal of September 24 from Tokyo to the consul in Honolulu (deciphered and translated on October 10) instructed him to report in the future by dividing the waters of Pearl Harbor, for reference purposes, into five areas. "With regard to warships and aircraft carriers, we would like to have you report on those at anchor (these are not so important), tied up at wharves, buoys and in docks. (Designate types and classes briefly. If possible we would like to have you make mention of the fact when there are two or more vessels alongside the same wharf.)" On the 29th another signal (translated on October 10) contained a number of code signs for designating the location of vessels at Pearl: KS for the main dock in the Navy Yard, FV for the moorings at Ford Island and so on. Seen in isolation, such signals seem like a flash of light. Indeed, during the Congressional Hearings both Admiral Kimmel and General Short (the Army commander at Pearl Harbor) claimed that they would have grasped their significance had the signals been brought to their attention.

This is extremely doubtful. If we turn to Volume III of *The*

"Magic" Background, we see that this little cluster of signals is embedded in a large collection of Magic intercepts about Japanese intelligence gathering deciphered at that time: decrypts of messages to Tokyo from the United States, from Panama, from the Philippines, from South America, from South Africa and from Vladivostok. Set against this background, the signals of September 24 and 29 merge into a wider pattern: their significance no longer seems clear-cut and startling. No wonder that Commander Kramer (the chief translator in Naval Intelligence, who was also responsible for distributing the Magic decrypts) testified that he did not believe it was interpreted by the recipients of Magic "as being materially different than other messages concerning ship movements being reported by the Japanese diplomatic service."[6] The image which Magic had built up for months in the minds of the Americans was of Japanese agents swarming like ants over many countries and picking up bits of intelligence, both important and useless, with an industrious lack of discrimination. It is difficult to fault the assessors in Washington for failing to see anything alarming in the September messages about Pearl Harbor: nor can it be easily believed that on receipt of them Kimmel and Short would have smelled a strong scent of danger. One signal, in isolation, radiates significance: but when it is seen as one among very many, the strength of the radiation wanes. (The Tricycle questionnaire was potentially significant precisely because it was unique: a *German* initiative on Japan's behalf about Pearl. And if Hoover had handled Tricycle properly, so that the significance of his questionnaire was brought to the notice of the appropriate authorities, then these September signals to the Honolulu consulate might have been seen in a very different light.)

This problem of interpretation, because it haunts all who have to form judgments and initiate action on the basis of Sigint or any other intelligence, would often recur during the Pacific war. It is particularly well defined by Roberta Wohlstetter in her brilliant study of the Pearl Harbor story.[7] To illuminate it she borrowed a powerful aid from communication theory, the concept of "noise." Whether in terms of cybernetics or of intelligence perception, noise is the buzz set up by competing information signals which prevents the essential message from being heard loud and clear. For the military commander or his staff, that noise can have many origins: inflowing intelligence of conflicting character, existing preconceptions and set patterns of thought or behavior, political and psychological fixations, and false impressions formed through lack of access to relevant intelligence withheld by others.

At no time was this noise more strident than in Washington during 1941: after war began, in December, there was an immense simplification and never, until Hiroshima, was uncertainty so supreme. It was not, as has been seen, that Magic disguised Japan's aggressive intent. On the contrary: but the decrypts indicated that Tokyo had a puzzling variety of options. After the Germans invaded Russia, one favorite and widely accepted theory suggested that the Japanese would stab Russia in the back—Admiral Turner, the head of U.S. Navy War Plans, believed this until the end of November.* Then there was the good indication that the Japanese might act logically, and attack British and Dutch possessions without involving the United States— which would certainly have presented Roosevelt with a fearsome problem. Above all, there was the perfectly justifiable strategic appreciation of the war staffs in Washington, that if Japan launched an all-out war her targets would be Malaysia, Indonesia and the Philippines. Rainbow Five, the current U.S. war plan for the Pacific, predicated an advance by the American fleet across the central Pacific toward the Japanese-mandated Marshall Islands, and a Japanese counterstroke against the Philippines looked like a predictable riposte.

For each of these possibilities and propositions the Magic decrypts provided substantial and persuasive support. The "noise" generated by so copious an intake of first-grade but often incompatible intelligence was formidably distracting. In particular, it distracted attention from Pearl Harbor: so much evidence pointed elsewhere, so little at Pearl. There is an apt analogy. During the early months of that same doomed year, 1941, the British Chiefs of Staff and their advisers had a mass of intelligence from German Ultra and other sources which revealed a German buildup in Eastern Europe, but the "noise" of their concern about the Middle East, the Suez Canal and the vital oilfields prevented them, for far too long, from appreciating that the buildup was aimed at Russia and not for a drive southward.[8] General Wolfe in the eighteenth century observed that "war is an option of

---

* For a time, the movement of Japanese troops toward the Manchurian border increased the theory's credibility.

difficulties." In the twentieth century, one of the difficulties created by
the very efficiency of modern Sigint is its ability to expose the variety
of the enemy's options. Magic often clarified, but now it confused.

Signal intelligence also led the American command to make false
but pardonable deductions in another area and for different reasons.
The radio transmissions of the Japanese fleet were carefully and continuously monitored, particularly by Commander Rochefort's unit at
Pearl Harbor, since even though the naval code had not yet been
broken a meticulous study of call signs and of the changing volume of
signals—the process called traffic analysis—provided a wealth of
reliable information. A comparison between American estimates and
Japanese records shows that at least up to October 1941 the picture
formed of the Japanese naval order of battle was exact and comprehensive. The final movement of formations southward from home
waters toward Malaysia and the Philippines was detected—and it
conformed, of course, with the Americans' own strategic assumptions.
But a fatal gap appeared in the evidence when the carrier group of
the Pearl Harbor strike force not only slipped away to its secret
assembly area but also went on radio silence. Perplexed partly by a
recent change in the Japanese Navy's call signs and partly by spurious
radio transmissions intended to mimic the carriers' signal traffic, the
Americans assumed that the carriers were back in their home waters.

The scapegoat seekers have asked, retrospectively, why it was not
realized that the disappearance of the carriers off the map indicated a
threat to Pearl Harbor. But it was known that on previous occasions
the carriers had retired to home waters and gone on radio silence. The
southward movement of the bulk of the fleet, identified over and over
again, fitted in with what had been reasonably anticipated. There was
no specific indicator available—and nothing convincing has been dis-
interred by subsequent researchers—to pinpoint Pearl Harbor as a
target for the carriers. The weeks and months preceding their ultimate
attack represent a phase which, for the historian, makes the most
stringent demands on his duty to recall how things looked *at the time*.
This is the criterion to apply, and when one does so one sees that,
given all the existing circumstances and the extraordinary crackle
of "noise," no intelligence officer from any other country would probably have reached conclusions different from the Americans'—without
the crystal ball of a fortune-teller.

The Fleet Intelligence Officer of the Pacific Fleet, Captain (now

Admiral) Layton, exposed the contemporary problem most lucidly in his testimony before the Hewitt Inquiry, when he said:

> I would like to invite your attention at the present time to one phenomenon of this whole campaign. All those units that moved to the south, air, submarines, carriers, cruisers, battleships, destroyers, auxiliaries, plus those commands concerned thereto, appeared in traffic, appeared in substantial traffic. They were addressed in intelligence dispatches. There were no other commands so addressed so constantly as a rule. There may be one exception. The commander of the Carrier Fleet, who became the commander of the Pearl Harbor task force, was not so addressed and hadn't been so addressed and hadn't appeared in the traffic since mid-November.
>
> I would like to point out another fact, that in the previous Japanese naval activities in the Far East in connection with Thailand and French Indochina, we had received substantiating information from OpNav from most secret sources which outlined exactly what was taking place. The radio intelligence picture of the fleet activities was confirmed also from newspaper accounts later published as the presence by name of various units there. In the time of which we now speak, the time of this estimate of 1 December 1941, we had what we called the framework of an intelligence picture. There are in intelligence many pieces like a jigsaw. The intelligence officer attempts to find the framework or border to find the scope of the intelligence picture and therefore to fit pieces together and form a part of the pattern or all of it if possible. In this, since we had no other source of information, we had received no dispatches that would indicate to us the possibility of the framework being larger than it was. The framework fitting into this pattern neatly, my attention was focused toward the south.

What is being argued is that all this evidence, though marvelously informative about the general drift of Japan's preparations for war, about her aggressive intentions and her other objectives, had little convincing to offer, even under the microscope, about an imminent attack on Pearl Harbor. But it is an argument which, so far, has had nothing to say about how that evidence was actually handled.

In 1941 the most important intelligence of all, Magic, was like some rare and precious object carried on a fragile conveyance that has been tied together by frayed pieces of string. The structure contains large holes, and seems liable to collapse at any moment.

An obsessive regard for security, stemming from General Marshall, restricted the distribution of Magic intelligence to the Secretary of War, the Army Chief of Staff, the Director of Military Intelligence, the Secretary of the Navy, the Chief of Naval Operations, the Chief of the Navy's War Plans Division, the Director of Naval Intelligence, the Secretary of State and the President. At Pearl Harbor the Commander in Chief of the Pacific Fleet, Admiral Kimmel, was fed some Magic until July: thereafter it was withheld from him, and his Army counterpart, General Short, was largely in the dark. MacArthur in the Philippines was a recipient theoretically, though he claimed at the Congressional Hearings that he remembered seeing none of the Magic documents laid before the investigators. At the same time there was a prevailing vagueness about who was getting what. Naval officers in Washington, including Admiral Stark, worked under the impression that Kimmel was still receiving Magic. The Army intelligence staff believed, incorrectly, that Rochefort's unit at Pearl was breaking Purple and that the Magic decrypts produced were reaching General Short. A joint Army-Navy Intelligence Committee was authorized on October 11, but did not meet until *after* December 7. When the attack occurred, on that day, the intelligence staffs of both the Army and the Navy in Washington took it for granted that the fleet would already have left harbor, on its way to implement Rainbow Five.

Hypersensitivity about security, rigid restrictions as to who "needed to know," false assumptions about who actually knew . . . these were not the bases for a strong structure. And not only was an interservice intelligence staff lacking to evaluate Magic and correlate it with other information: the individual recipients were not always supported in this regard by their own staffs. Since the Magic decrypts were not retained after delivery, it was difficult if not impossible for any individual to carry in his head the kaleidoscopic scenario produced by the constant stream of deciphered Japanese signals.

All these and a number of other valid criticisms may be laid against the American system in 1941. But two fundamental points are often overlooked. First, however rickety the structure for evaluating and disseminating Magic, it did not prevent the Administration from getting a broadly accurate picture of Japanese intentions—if it be granted that it was not possible to establish the specific intention to attack Pearl Harbor.

Secondly, it is essential to recall that December 7, 1941, was for the Americans the equivalent of September 3, 1939, for the British. Up to each of those dates, neither country had faced the stern necessities of war: like all armed services in peacetime, theirs had not yet got into gear. Yet a comparison does no discredit to the United States. In September 1939 Britain had no Ultra—the first tentative breaks into the Enigma cipher would not occur until the spring of 1940. Thus there was no system for evaluation and dissemination, and no one who "needed to know"—for there was nothing to know. And, thinking of the starved commanders at Pearl Harbor, one remembers that although after Dunkirk the eastern Mediterranean was the epicenter of action for the British, it was not until August 1941 that a smooth and efficient organization was established for feeding the commanders in chief in Cairo, through a Special Liaison Unit, with Ultra intelligence direct from Bletchley Park.[9] Before December 1941 the Americans, by contrast, already had in Magic a long-tested method of acquiring intelligence from Japanese communications at the highest level: their cryptanalytical teams were able and experienced: and though they had only taken the first and timorous steps toward designating the right recipients and evolving effective means of evaluation and distribution, at least they had taken some steps, and were able to move forward, under the pressure of war, with a more confident stride. Midway is the proof.

But though, on a charitable view, it is possible to exonerate Roosevelt's administration and the military staffs in Washington for failing to perceive the precise threat to Pearl, it is less easy to excuse the fact that when the bombs fell and the torpedoes struck both the fleet and the shore installations on Hawaii were caught off guard. Kimmel and Short did not emerge unscathed from the Congressional Hearings. Were they alone at fault?

As the war rolled on, all experience in the handling of intelligence acquired through breaking the enemy's code and cipher systems showed that the paramount need was to get into the hands of the commander in the field, as quickly as possible, any information which would assist him in fighting the battle. This was war's lesson. But it is impossible not to feel that during those long peacetime months of 1941 the tendency in Washington was to look at the Magic material far more as a guide in diplomatic negotiation, or in the formulation of broad national policy, than as operational intelligence on which decisions about action—or at least readiness for action—could be based.

Certainly the real action, at this time, seemed to lie in the Atlantic, where the American Navy's involvement in the protection of convoys against U-boats was steadily increasing—to a point at which, well before Pearl Harbor and the outbreak of war with Germany, one American warship actually took over control in a battle of convoy escorts against the Germans. It is true, also, that wild hopes were aroused about the probable efficacy of American air power, particularly as the group of B-17 Fortress bombers on the Philippines was gradually expanded. But when all is said, the U.S. Pacific Fleet at Pearl was, and had to be, the main counter to Japanese aggression: indeed the counterattack plan, Rainbow Five, depended on the fleet.

And so, while it is understandable that during Magic's early phase there was an obsessive degree of concern about security, it is difficult to condone the fact that the commanders at Pearl were not kept on their toes by constant and up-to-date information as the skies darkened. In the final stage, it may be said, there were the notorious "war warnings."[10] But there had been other alerts which had come to nothing: "Wolf" can be cried too often. It seems extraordinary that more pains were not taken to capitalize on the invaluable Sigint available. That Kimmel should have been denied access to Magic from the summer onward, and that Short should have received it casually, if at all, suggests something fundamentally amateur in the system, particularly when one recalls that in Washington officers as elevated as Admiral Stark still continued to assume that the information was getting through. A war was necessary to tighten up the slack. Both Kimmel and Short were, in this respect, the victims of a failure in high places to think things through and to set up a *realistic* organization for putting Magic to the best possible use.*

---

* The first Commission of Inquiry, set up under Justice Owen J. Roberts on December 16, 1941, started the long crucifixion of Kimmel and Short: but it is significant that no Magic material was permitted to be laid before the Commission. Subsequently retired under threat of court-martial, the two commanders never recovered from a judgment based on inadequate evidence—for the responsibility of Washington was not, at this time, called in question.

Certainly both the admiral and the general felt that they had been assessed professionally, and presented publicly, as scapegoats* and sin-eaters for the guilt of others. Sometimes, however, the case for their defense is not well founded. One example, often quoted, is that of the notorious "Winds" signals. On November 19 Tokyo transmitted to Washington two important messages, not in Purple but in the high-grade J19 code, which, for the American cryptanalysts, had a slightly lower priority: as a result, the Navy did not break the two signals and make them available until November 26 (for one) and November 28 (for the other). Nevertheless, there they were. They were also picked up on other circuits: Tokyo–Singapore and in the Indonesian traffic. Evidently they were matters of substance. But what was their weight? Here are the actual texts.

Circular 2353

Regarding the broadcast of a special message in an emergency.
In case of emergency (danger of cutting off our diplomatic relations), and the cutting off of international communications, the following warning will be added in the middle of the daily Japanese-language shortwave news broadcast.

(1) In case of Japan-U.S. relations in danger: HIGASHI NO KAZEAME (east wind rain).
(2) Japan-U.S.S.R. relations: KITANOKAZE KUMORI (north wind cloudy).
(3) Japan-British relations: NISHI NO KAZE HARE (west wind clear).

This signal will be given in the middle and at the end as a weather forecast and each sentence will be repeated twice. When this is heard please destroy all code papers, etc. This is as yet to be a completely secret arrangement.
Forward as urgent intelligence. [Translated November 28.]

Circular 2354

When our diplomatic relations are becoming dangerous, we will add the following at the beginning and end of our general intelligence broadcasts:

---

* Short actually applied this word to himself when testifying before the Inquiry.

(1) If it is Japan-U.S. relations, "HIGASHI."
(2) Japan-Russia relations, "KITA."
(3) Japan-British relations (including Thai, Malaya and N.E.I.), "NISHI."

The above will be repeated five times and included at beginning and end.

Relay to Rio de Janeiro, Buenos Aires, Mexico City, San Francisco. [Translated November 26.]

Of the two circulars the former was evidently the more sinister and it was taken very seriously, but its full import could only be assessed if a weather forecast containing the name of one of the three winds (what became known as the "execute" signal) could be intercepted. An immense effort was therefore made—both the Army and the Navy putting a number of their monitoring stations on round-the-clock listening for this specific purpose, while the senior intelligence officers of both services were fully alerted. (A warning was also sent to the British in the Far East and to the Dutch.) The naval watch officers responsible for monitoring were even furnished with cards which read:

> East wind rain: Japan-U.S.
> North wind cloudy: Japan-U.S.S.R.
> West wind clear: Japan-British

The intention was for them to telephone immediately if they identified any of these signals, thus avoiding the slower channels of distribution. But was anything in fact heard?

Commander Safford was convinced that an "execute" *had* been intercepted. Commander Kramer made the same claim at first, but later shifted his ground and is not a solid witness. At the Congressional Hearings General Marshall denied having seen one. Rochefort was certain that no "execute" had been overheard—either by his people on Hawaii or, presumably, by anyone else. So two questions arise. The first is whether a signal was in fact received but (if so) apparently not distributed. The second is whether, even if a "real execute" had been intercepted, and processed, and circulated it would have been of much help to Kimmel and Short down at Pearl Harbor or, indeed, have given any warning to the men in Washington that Pearl was a target.

An East Wind doth blow!

CARTOON BY DON MOORE

At first sight, it would seem that Commander Safford's testimony was conclusive: a signal intelligence officer of vast experience who, at the time, was at the heart of the business in Washington. But under inspection (and when set against the authority of Marshall and Rochefort) his assertion about the receipt of an "execute" appears less reliable—particularly as, after forty years, no such signal has ever been produced.

What did emerge, however, in November 1980—after declassification by the National Security Agency—was a remarkable memorandum entitled: Information from George W. Linn, Capt. USNR (Ret.). The significant fact about Linn is that he had been a protégé of Safford's from the time in 1926 when he enlisted in the Reserve as a radioman. He was one of those enthusiastic amateurs whom the farsighted Safford encouraged by setting them to solve simple ciphers, and so on: "Captain Safford used this as a means of stimulating cryptanalysis and earmarking likely personnel, regular and reserve, for duty in that field." Safford so approved of Linn that he had him commissioned in the Reserve in 1932, and in January 1941 he was summoned to service in Op-20-G. On the eve of Pearl Harbor, December 6, Linn was the officer on duty for the 1601–2400 hrs. watch: the man who, in the most practical sense, was there "at five minutes to midnight."

His memorandum has two salient features. In spite of his profound loyalty to Safford, he saw that he had been "completely floored by the Pearl Harbor attack. He felt that a wealth of intelligence had been provided and yet the result had been a disaster." In Linn's view Safford's obsession with the idea that an "execute" had been received and suppressed had caused him to go "out on a limb."* For there had been no "execute."

This is the second feature of the memorandum. The earlier hours of that fatal evening had been taken up with processing the thirteen parts of Japan's final signal to its ambassador in Washington (to which we must return). The signal was intercepted by the Navy's station near Seattle and teletyped to Washington during the morning and afternoon: there was not much processing work to be done on it, however, since the text came out clean and the residual problem that evening

---

* "Although he never conceded that he was mistaken about the receipt of the message, he did admit later that nothing in the intercepts specified an attack on Pearl Harbor." Pogue, *George C. Marshall*; p. 432.

did not concern the cryptanalysts, but those responsible for distributing the intercept. By about ten o'clock, therefore, Linn was no
longer preoccupied. In fact, he recorded that he felt "free to start
scanning the mass of wind intercepts which had accumulated." There
had been one on December 4 which was at first thought to contain the
"execute," and here, possibly, is the origin of the persistent legend
that a real "execute" had been identified. But this signal, like all the
other weather signals that piled up, in fact contained no executive
order. Linn's final opinion conforms with all the other trustworthy
evidence: "I found nothing, and therefore concluded that an execute
had not been received prior to 2400 hrs. on Dec. 6."

Were it not for this explicit statement, another recent testimony
might seem to carry more weight. File SRH-051 in the National
Archives—Interview with Mr. Ralph T. Briggs, by the Historian,
Naval Security Group, 13 January 1977—is certainly startling, for
Briggs was a naval radio intercept operator in the Communication
Station at Cheltenham, Maryland, from September 1941 to August
1942. He claimed that on December 4 he "picked up on schedule the
Orange weather BAMS broadcast circuit," discovered that the text
contained the words "HIGASHI NO KAZEAME" and forwarded it
to Op-20-G in Washington. (In his interview he stated that "east wind
rain" meant "a break with the United States"—though the true meaning was "Japan-U.S. relations in danger.") Yet no copies of this message
could later be found in the files. An affidavit from Briggs signed
December 5, 1960, states: "I . . . duly note that all transmissions intercepted by me between 0500 thru 1300 on the above date [i.e., December 4] are missing from these files and that these intercepts contained the 'winds message' warning-codes."

Moreover, Briggs not only asserted that Safford informed him that
the message had gone right up the line, to the Director of Naval Communications, the Director of War Plans, the Acting Chief Signal
Officer for the War Department and Admiral Stark himself. This information, he said, had been given to him secretly *after* the C.O. of
his station had specifically and peremptorily forbidden him to assist
Safford with evidence during the post-Pearl investigations or even to
talk to him.

Was this a testimony of fact? Even supposing, as is alleged, that
Briggs's message was subsequently removed from the files for some

malign reason, it could scarcely have disappeared by the evening of December 6 when Linn "concluded that an execute had not been received"—and Linn was scarcely antipathetic to Safford. If the alleged "winds execute" was passed right up the line, are we to assume that serried ranks of senior officers lied about it as a cover-up, when so many errors of far greater magnitude were already in the public domain? Or are we to assess Briggs's claim either as a falsification of memory or as a by-product of partisan loyalty? It is difficult, at this distance, to feel that it matters very much.

For even if one had been received—even if it had been the HIGASHI NO KAZEAME code words, "east wind rain," which meant that the relations of Japan and the United States were in danger— and even if there had been an immaculate distribution of the intelligence so that Kimmel and Short, as well as all others concerned, had been informed, how can it be claimed that this would have added a jot or a tittle or an iota to what was already known? The possibility of diplomatic relations being severed was already very real. After receipt of the "execute," codes were to be destroyed in Japanese offices abroad: but there had been many similar instructions in the past, and war had not followed. At best, Kimmel and Short were entitled to plead no more than that if an "execute" had been intercepted and they had been informed, it would have provided yet another reason for their maintaining "conditions of alert," which they should, in any case, have already adopted.

Before considering their specific responsibility, however, it is worth recalling the verdict of the Congressional Inquiry: "Beyond serious question Army and Navy officials both in Hawaii and in Washington were beset by a lassitude born of 20 years of peace." That this "peace psychology" was in the air right up to the last minute, in the capital city itself as well as down in Hawaii, can be clearly illustrated if we return to that long and final Japanese signal with which Linn was concerned during the early evening of December 6, and examine what happened to it.

The first question is, what were the superiors of Kimmel and Short doing during those critical hours? (Kimmel himself was dining with a fellow officer, and Short was at an Army benefit dinner.) Stark was at Washington's National Theater for a performance of *The Student Prince*. The Naval Chief of Intelligence, Admiral Wilkinson, had a private dinner party. General Marshall, looking back in after years during which many other great considerations and crises had filled his mind, was as sure as an honest man could be that he himself was at home, and that his wife had spent most of the day involved in "an old-clothes sale." At the White House, the Roosevelts were having a small dinner party. Not much sign here of men standing to their guns with the ammunition stacked ready for use![11]

It is perhaps to be doubted, however, whether it would have made much difference if, on that evening, they had all been more immediately accessible. The gist of the thirteen-part signal to the Japanese ambassador in Washington consisted of old complaints against the Americans and the British, a renewed declamation of Japan's desire for peace and a rejection of the negotiating points recently put forward by Washington, which, in truth, had never had much chance of acceptance. The two men responsible for distributing the intercept to the high officials on the Magic restricted list (Kramer for the Navy and Colonel Bratton for the Army) managed to get it to virtually everybody before midnight—except Marshall, to whom Bratton decided to hand it over early next morning. But a comprehensive amount of evidence shows that this latest gift from Magic aroused not a single person to action on the night of December 6. When Roosevelt read it in his study, in the presence of Harry Hopkins, it is said that the President remarked, "This means war." However, his only definite response seems to have been to telephone Admiral Stark.

Early next morning the fourteenth and final part of the text came to hand. This, numbered Tokyo No. 907, simply said:

> Will the Ambassador please submit to the United States Government (if possible to the Secretary of State) our reply to the United States at 1:00 p.m. on the 7th, your time.

1:00 p.m. Washington time: *but that was dawn in Hawaii and early morning in the Far East*. Surely Part 14 implied that the Ambassador was to hand over the reply from the Japanese Government just before an attack was launched . . . somewhere. Bratton, who received the text at 9 a.m., immediately saw the implications and tried to telephone Marshall. But the general, unaware even of the previous evening's signal, was out on his usual morning ride—just about where the Pentagon now stands. By the time that he reached his office, as his biographer points out, the intercepts had been "seen and discussed by the President, the Secretaries of State, Army, Navy, the Chiefs of Army and Navy Intelligence, the Chiefs of Army and Navy War Plan Divisions, and the Chief of Naval Operations." Yet *nobody*, as yet, had sent a warning signal to Pearl Harbor. It is absurd, Dr. Pogue observed, to suggest that history had to stand still until Marshall turned his horse's head back to Fort Myer or took a quick shower.

The tragic futility of Marshall's own attempt to pass the word to Pearl has often been described, and there is no need to repeat the record of blind inefficiency on the part of all concerned. Its upshot is conveyed in a sentence. "The Japanese had carried out their work of destruction and General Marshall was in touch with Short's headquarters by telephone before a copy of his warning message finally reached its destination." MacArthur at Manila in the Philippines also heard of the Pearl Harbor attack on the commercial radio, well over two hours before Marshall's warning signal reached him.[12] But the particular point about reviving the whole sad story about the way that Washington handled the last major Magic intercept before the outbreak of war is to indicate that both Kimmel and Short had good grounds for maintaining, in self-defense, that their masters had unnecessarily kept them in the dark.

Unfortunately, however, the lamentable surprise achieved by the Japanese was not merely due to errors in Washington. For, Magic or no Magic, Pearl Harbor had long been seen to be a possible target. Admiral McCollum recalled in his Oral History:

> We actually carried out a daylight attack, a dawn attack, on Pearl Harbor in 1937. Carriers moved in at dawn and delivered a surprise attack on the Army and Navy installations and so on. Of course, sham stuff, but there it was, backed up by the battleships and cruisers which came streaming in under cover of aircraft and went through the motions of bombarding places like Diamond Head and Fort de Russy and so forth. *So, it was in our minds all the time.**

It may well have been in McCollum's mind all the time, for he was an intelligence officer with years of service in the Far East, including two as Assistant Naval Attaché in Tokyo. (From 1939 onward he was

---

* Author's italics.

back in Washington as head of the Far Eastern Branch in the Office of Naval Intelligence.) But what was a permanent possibility in the thoughts of a highly skilled specialist does not seem to have haunted Kimmel with the same degree of menace. Theoretically, he kept his fleet at readiness: in fact, there is a wealth of evidence to indicate that though practice operations were carried out neither his ships, r.or the antiaircraft units ashore, nor the vital radar stations were in that condition of alertness which imminent war demands. While Kimmel surely ought to have been kept in the picture by a supply of Magic, it is equally reasonable to maintain that an officer of his seniority and responsibility ought to have deduced, from the way the Japanese were openly behaving in view of the whole world, that he had better be prepared at all times to cope with "the worst case": war.

This, however, does not square with the recollections of the future Vice-Admiral George C. Dyer, who was executive officer of *Indianapolis* at Pearl Harbor. Sometime in August 1941 he got the heads of the ship's departments together and told them that a proper state of readiness was not being maintained against a surprise attack. The manning of a watch at that time only produced teams for half the antiaircraft guns aboard: only half the ammunition supply and communications systems could operate, and only a quarter of the fire control for the A.A. batteries. Men were on duty one day out of four. Dyer therefore went to "modified conditions two," with crews on duty two days out of four, which gave full fire control and service to the guns, and a tolerable ammunition supply. But two days later his wife telephoned to say, "All the wives have been calling me, asking, 'What's *Indianapolis* trying to do? Fight the war by itself?' Their husbands aren't coming home and they're upset." When the attack on Pearl occurred—and *Indianapolis* fortunately survived—Dyer's captain breathed, in effect, a sigh of relief. "In another week," he said, "the crew would have thrown us overboard." Testimony like this turns a searchlight on the prevailing mental atmosphere at Pearl Harbor. It is supported by too many other instances.[13]

In the December 1980 issue of the *Proceedings* of the U.S. Naval Institute, for example, Commander Ted Hechler, Jr., published his recollections of the Pearl Harbor attack. They began:

> The customary prewar ways lasted right up to the time war started. I remember December 6, the day before the Japanese

attacked. Saturday morning inspections were an institution in the Navy before the war. On that particular day the inspector was Rear Admiral H. Fairfax Leary, Commander Cruiser Division Nine and Commander Cruisers Battle Force. Leary had been in the job since early in 1941 when he relieved Admiral Husband Kimmel. I was then an ensign, serving on the new light cruiser *Phoenix*. The men were in their whites, lined up in rows for personal inspection. When it came to the inspection of the ship herself, Leary had on his white gloves so he could check for dust. How irrelevant it would all seem twenty-four hours later. The end of Saturday inspection was the traditional signal for liberty call, and I went ashore for the day with two fellow ensigns.

Phoenix was moored in open water about 1,000 yards from Battle-ship Row, alongside Ford Island, and survived the attack on the 7th unscathed—except for one bullet hole. But as the enemy's planes flashed by, Hechler recalled, the awnings above the antiaircraft guns had to be removed before they could be brought to bear, and locks on the ammunition boxes had to be *hacked* off. Even then, the fuses on the shells had a minimum peacetime setting designed to prevent them from exploding before they had reached a safe distance from the ship: in any case, many of the fuses were defective, and unexploded shells rained down on shore. The sophisticated automatic artillery proved useless at close quarters, and *Phoenix*'s best defense was her machine guns. In the end she streaked for the sea, at 30 knots, and lived to fight another day.

It is true that the result of the attack on December 7 was a strategic success for the Americans rather than the Japanese. Yamamoto's coup, the desperate throw of the gambler that he was, failed because by a miracle the American aircraft carriers were at sea, and because his attack plan left out the fuel stocks and workshops, so that in spite of terrible damage Pearl Harbor continued an unbroken record as a great fleet anchorage and naval base. And because the carriers sur-vived, the incredible became possible in the Coral Sea and at Midway. Yet the story, like that of the fall of Singapore, is full of might-have-beens. Suppose the long debates about the fortification of Singapore had led to the installation of artillery pointing inland as well as out to sea. Suppose that the aircraft carrier which was intended to ac-company *Prince of Wales* and *Repulse* had arrived with them instead of being grounded in the West Indies. Suppose the men in command at this vital bastion had been of a different caliber. Like the loss of Britain's pivot in the Far East, that disastrous day at Pearl Harbor illustrates vividly the statement by Professor Trevor-Roper that history "is what happened in the context of what might have happened."

Yet the most difficult thing to predict, so they say, is the past.

CHAPTER FOUR

A Plan Called MO and a Plan Called MI

A conference was held by the Admiral to discuss the measures to counter the expected Jap offensive in the Hawaiian area and Alaska. It is generally believed that a serious attempt will be made to capture Midway and raid Oahu.
> Command Summary, Headquarters of Admiral
> Nimitz, May 18, 1941

After a battle is over, people talk a lot about how the decisions were methodically reached, but actually there's a hell of a lot of groping about.
> Admiral Frank Fletcher, USN

ONE OF THE greatest challenges ever presented to cryptanalysts is that of the Voynich manuscript, a small illustrated book discovered in 1912 at a villa near Rome by William Voynich, a dealer in literary rarities. An accompanying letter is dated about 1665, but scholars concur in placing the manuscript itself between 1450 and 1550. Its illustrations, hand-painted on vellum, are a bizarre mixture of astronomical figures, plants and bulbous human figures—mainly female. The associated text, inked in on most of the pages, has consistently intrigued and defeated some of the world's best cryptanalysts ever since Voynich made his discovery, which now rests in the Beinecke Rare Book and Manuscript Library at Yale University.

Here is a classic problem: a manuscript, containing something like a quarter of a million characters in its text, which stubbornly refuses to reveal its meaning. Is it actually a form of sophisticated cipher? Friedman and others of comparable skill have tended to think of it rather as a code: a "synthetic language like Esperanto, using an invented alphabet for further concealment." Brigadier Tiltman, a peer of Friedman's from Bletchley and the prewar days of GCCS, has taken this line. Many universities on both sides of the Atlantic, the Vatican Archives and the Bibliothèque Nationale in Paris have contributed their resources toward a solution. More than one seminar on the Voynich manuscript has been held at the NSA. And the upshot is—nothing.[1] After more than half a century of intensive work by some of the most acute minds in the business those Rubensesque ladies and the brownish ink of the text remain inscrutable, enigmatic, invincible.

The Voynich manuscript is worth a mention because it provides a perfect paradigm, a deeply instructive example, of everything that is unacceptable for the wartime cryptanalyst. Scholars studying it have moved at their own pace—over a decade, or even more—before daring to publish their conclusions: others at their leisure have been able to devise their devastating refutations. But in war the master is time. Almost always an enemy's signal ceases to be of value in operations unless it can be deciphered or decoded very shortly—certainly within a tolerable number of hours—after it has first been transmitted. During the chase of the battleship *Bismarck* every relevant German signal, whether from the ship herself or from various headquarters in Europe, was intercepted and then deciphered at Bletchley. But the cryptanalysts were only just learning how to unravel the German naval cipher, and there was usually something like a delay of forty-eight hours in breaking the signals. In effect, therefore, the decrypts were interesting historical documents but, as it turned out, useless in the delicate—and finally victorious—process of bringing *Bismarck* to bay.[2] So speed in combat deciphering is essential, combined with results that can be *practically* applied in battle. War does not allow for fifty years of research which end in negative, contentious confusion.

In the spring of 1942 the cryptanalysts of the United States Navy were manifestly not in a position to act like men of leisure. Though much had been preserved at Pearl Harbor—warships recoverable, oil stocks intact, installations undamaged—and though Yamamoto had failed to destroy those precious aircraft carriers, the American Navy was in disarray while its new allies, the British and the Dutch, were predictably on their way to losing what they had not already lost. Meanwhile the Japanese tide surged forward like the implacable rollers on a surf riders' beach. The predicament of the Americans, lonely and exposed, was nakedly defined on two March days. The 9th saw Roosevelt signaling to Churchill: "the Pacific situation is now very grave," and a week later, on the 17th, it was agreed between President and Prime Minister that the United States would be responsible for defending the whole of the Pacific area—including Australia and New Zealand. The failing hand of the British Empire was passing on the torch to an inexperienced and wounded successor.

Since the theater was so vast, since the Japanese already occupied so many territories and since the Americans were thus denied virtually all the conventional means of intelligence, an immense burden was thrown on their intercept stations and the cryptanalytical units in Washington and Hawaii.* Information would have to be plucked out of the air. But two decades of preparation were eminently justified in the event: what looked, on paper, like unavoidable disaster was turned into a triumph. In this reversal the major role was played by the Fleet Radio Unit, Pacific—or FRUPac—at Pearl Harbor. "FRUPac," as Captain Holmes wrote, "was under the gun."†

But in those tense spring days the question for everyone, from the President downward, was . . . intelligence about what? The Japanese now had so many options. Australia? California? It is true that as Tokyo expanded with proprietary presumption into the Greater East Asia Co-Prosperity Sphere the broad response of the United States was that of Francis I, the sixteenth-century king of France, to the claim of the Spaniards that an edict of the Pope had declared everything a hundred leagues west of the Azores to be their property. "We fail," said Francis, "to find this clause in Adam's will." But defiance is one thing: effective action based on accurate information is another. Here lay the challenge to FRUPac.

What could scarcely be guessed was that the Japanese were already infected by what they themselves called Victory Disease: a cosmetic name for excessive arrogance, or the Greeks' *hubris*. "Pride," as the Psalms said, "goeth before destruction, and an haughty spirit before a fall." An empire had been gained for so little! By May 1, 1942, the Japanese had lost only a couple of dozen small ships of war, a few

---

* In the Philippines the third signal intelligence center, Cast, was also still functioning, though it was doomed.
† The Hypo signal intelligence unit at Pearl was not rechristened FRUPac until later in the war, but it will not be confusing to use as appropriate the later title, under which the unit is more generally known.

hundred aircraft, a few thousand men, and something over 300,000 tons of merchant shipping and transports: a bargain price.

Still less was it understood by the Americans that the prewar rivalries within the Japanese armed services were unquenched. One faction saw profit in a strike westward, to the Bay of Bengal and Ceylon, with ahead the dancing mirage of German allies advancing through North Africa and the Caucasus. The naval staff in Tokyo wished to drive far to the south, cutting off Australia by the capture of Samoa, Fiji and New Caledonia. The Army, for its part, dreaded an Australasian involvement, fearing a dangerous diversion of its troops. Only Admiral Yamamoto, commanding the great Combined Fleet, grasped the essential point: American naval power in the Pacific must be obliterated, and quickly—in 1942. The rest would then follow.

Territorial ambition, compounded by service rivalries, produced plans that spring which in fact differed little from the definition of those "areas which are to be rapidly occupied or destroyed, as soon as the war situation permits," the objectives contained in Combined Fleet Operation Order No. 1. This was issued on November 1, 1941 —*before* Pearl Harbor. The plans were threefold. (1) The bases of Tulagi in the Solomons and Port Moresby on the southern flank of New Guinea would be occupied to secure domination of the Coral Sea and northern Australia. (2) The minute atoll of Midway, in the open Pacific to the northwest of Hawaii, would be assaulted by an amphibious operation primarily—and this was Yamamoto's thinking —because the American Pacific Fleet would have to intervene and risk destruction by a superior Combined Fleet. At the same time a diversionary strike would be made on the Aleutians, far to the north on the rim of the Bering Sea. (3) As a convenient sequence, the Fiji-Samoa-New Caledonia line would be secured, thus severing a direct channel of communication between the United States and Australia. Plan 1 was code-named MO: Plan 2 was called MI. Since both failed, Plan 3 was aborted.

Set out this way, the Japanese intentions have all the linear clarity and visible pattern of a jigsaw after it has been completed. For the Americans at the time, however, there was at first nothing but a miscellany of bits and pieces—and even those were difficult to lay hands on.

The fundamental problem was technical: at Op-20-G in Washington and FRUPac in Hawaii there was a dangerously long period after Pearl Harbor when they were simply unable to read enough of the enemy's mail. Already, before Pearl, the current code for concealing important Japanese naval signals, JN25, had been under attack. But it was replaced by a version called by the Americans JN25b—which rates a place in history alongside Purple and Enigma. (JN25, because after the initial break in the twenties the basic types of naval codes, as one succeeded another, were numbered serially from JN1 onward.) In its earlier form JN25, which was expressed in messages of five-digit groups, was still yielding little if anything to the cryptanalysts, but under a new and concentrated assault it might well have surrendered. Then, as was the Japanese custom before any major operation, early in December 1941 the character of the code was changed. At first JN25b was impenetrable. It was all to do again.

People usually think of a code as a list of words or sets of numbers, the code groups, that can be directly substituted in a signal for their nominated equivalents in the original text. Many codes were as simple as that, and the analyst's problem, therefore, was merely to establish exact correlations between the individual code group and the original word or phrase which it represented. The JN system, at least as exemplified in JN25, was more complicated. A message would first be encoded by the Japanese: then, drawing on a stock of 100,000 five-digit numbers mixed at random (an "enciphering table"), the clerk would convert into a ciphered text the already encoded message. Thus the Americans had to "strip" the cipher before the coded signal could be bared and broken. And there were other tricks. The objectives of specific operations, for example, would be covered by the use of symbolic letters—MO for Moresby, MI for Midway, AL for Aleutians. In the JN25 system combinations of two or three letters were also used as "geographic designators"—i.e., to identify places rather than plans. (As we approach Midway, the significance of this practice becomes increasingly critical.)

The responsibility for finding a path through this maze fell mainly on the Pearl Harbor station, FRUPac (or Hypo), under Commander Joseph Rochefort. There was, of course, collaboration with Op-20-G, with Fabian's unit on Corregidor until it was evacuated to Australia (and then—in due course—with the reconstituted Belconnen group) and with the British at Singapore until, shortly before its fall, that signal intelligence team was evacuated to Colombo. But Hypo bore the brunt.

Eyewitnesses describe the intensity and dedication with which Rochefort and his small command mounted their prolonged but successful assault on JN25. Their accounts match those which tell of the strains undergone at Bletchley during critical periods, and not surprisingly, for the personalities involved were of the same timbre. Utterly different in background, training and experience, they were all people of quick intelligence, absolute devotion to their task and—almost always—of highly idiosyncratic temperaments. In another sense, one may say that they were like fine-drawn wires capable of sustaining over long periods the tensions of precise tuning.

Jasper Holmes watched it all from his observation post within the Combat Intelligence Unit.[3] "Had I not witnessed it," he wrote, "I never would have believed that any group of men was capable of such sustained mental effort under such constant pressure for such a length of time." Like troglodytes, they inhabited a kind of underworld cellar, approached only by two locked doors and in a permanent state of shabby disorder amid which heaped files and the ejections of IBM machines struggled—as the occupants were indeed doing—for survival. Rochefort presided, in his ancient red smoking jacket and carpet slippers: a man driving himself to the limit on two or three hours of sleep and a diet of coffee and sandwiches. He slept on a cot among the squalor and had to be expelled to take a bath. A perfectionist, he allowed no message to leave Hypo until he himself had checked the translation—for even when the code was being broken, the nuances of the Japanese language could lead men astray. (A fine instance occurred before Midway. When the name of the light carrier *Shoho* first appeared in the signal traffic, Hypo misinterpreted the Japanese text and thought it was a new, larger carrier with the name of *Ryukaku*. As such it was misleadingly given a place in the Japanese Order of Battle, until, several months later, the truth was established from captured documents.)

But, as Holmes pointed out, it was of course a team effort. His vignette of two of its members vividly recaptures their style.

Lasswell approached cryptanalysis like a chess-player manoeuvring relentlessly to untangle his problem. His desk was usually clear of everything but his current puzzle. He worked sitting upright at his desk, wearing a carefully pressed Marine Corps uniform of the day, his sole deviation being a green eyeshade for protection against the hours under fluorescent lights. Finnegan barricaded himself behind a desk with two flanking tables, all piled high with IBM printouts, newspapers, messages, crumpled cigarette packs, coffee cups, apple cores, and sundry material, through which he searched intently, usually with success, for some stray bit of corroborative evidence he remembered having seen days or weeks before. He paid little attention to the hours of the day, or days of the week, and not infrequently he worked himself into such a state of exhaustion that his head dropped into the rat's nest on his desk and he reluctantly fell asleep. Rochefort was a master at matching the talents of these two translators. A Finnegan hunch checked out by Lasswell's siege tactics made a firm foundation on which to build.

At Op-20-G, still lodged within the Office of Naval Communications in Washington, the engine ran hot. Edward Van Der Rhoer recalled the spring day on which he reported for duty.[4] " 'Christ in the foothills!' shouted the balding, cherubic-faced man seated at one end of the room with his back to the rest of us . . . The effect was electrifying. Much scurrying about until someone found the missing volume; the volume itself, however inanimate, managed to look guilty." Commander Rosey Mason, Annapolis-trained and one of those selected to learn Japanese in Tokyo, was an abrasive rough diamond whose career had not smoothed his edges: "a driving leader," Van Der Rhoer thought, "who did not spare himself or others. I often had the feeling that he was a candidate for an early ulcer." (By the end of the war, in fact, Mason had been promoted to captain and obtained his heart's desire, a command at sea.)

But for all the stations working on the JN25 problem—Op-20-G in Washington, Hypo at Pearl, Cast in the Philippines and Belconnen in Australia—there were in fact several advantages which helped to ease their burden: advantages presented by a variety of inherent weaknesses in the enemy's signal procedure. Since the classic mode of penetrating a code or cipher system is to detect and exploit the careless slips of operators or structural defects within the system itself, this meant, in practice, that the Americans' situation was difficult but not hopeless—so long as JN25 could be broken before another disaster occurred. But in the springtime of '42 the sands in the hourglass were running out fast.

Occasionally, for example (though perhaps more often in diplomatic ciphers), the Japanese would start a message with the word for "begin" and finish with OWARI, or "end." Since these would normally appear in a text, it was a useful means of discovering the disguised opening and conclusion of a signal. In the early days, again, they were negligent about Australian place names, failing to conceal them by a symbol, so that repetition of particular places could provide valuable hints. Similar guidance was given by the Japanese handling of dates and proper names. Then there was the beautiful art evolved and applied by the British and the Germans as much as by the Americans. Practiced crews at an intercept station could learn to "read the handwriting" of individual enemy signalers, for just as we each have our unique fingerprints, so each operator tapping out the Morse code has his specific, identifiable touch and rhythm. (The British gave their method a name, TINA. It played a significant part in keeping track of the hunted *Bismarck*.*)

Thus the Americans could often identify the source of an encoded signal: indeed, certain Japanese signalers were so familiar that they were like old friends, followed in their posting from ship to ship. In cryptanalysis, it is obvious that if you are sure of the source of a signal you have already got a number of indicators about the possible or probable shape and nature of its contents, since messages on a particular circuit—say between a fleet commander and his subordinate units—tend to have various characteristics. Few of these and other flaws in the Japanese system may have led directly to the complete cracking of a signal, still less to a complete comprehension of the structure of a code. But cryptanalysis is not romantic, a matter of instant and total revelation, so much as infinitely patient pattern-making from a multitude of apparently disconnected pieces. And you have first to find the pieces.

Above all, the arrogant certainty of the Japanese that their initial victories were absolute committed them to a tremendous and, as it turned out, fatal assumption. No fighting nation dares to use for too

---

* This technique was, of course, only applicable in a valuable way to a transmission from the ship or submarine originating the message rather than to rebroadcasts of the signal by shore-based repeater stations within the local communications zone: as might often occur.

long any particular code or cipher, since all experience has proved that your enemy, as he grows accustomed to your signal security, will find it progressively easier to break. But a change of code involves the distribution of new code books to every regular recipient of your signals. The early bomb-burst of the Japanese far and wide into the southern Pacific produced a vast profusion of bases, fleet headquarters, task forces and air commands often separated by many hundreds or thousands of miles from home, or indeed from one another. Thus the problem of distributing the latest version of a code was staggering and at times insuperable.* There were two critical benefits for the Americans. First, if a Japanese unit or headquarters had not received the new code book, a message which had been signaled to other recipients in the new code might, in this case, be transmitted in the old one: and if the Americans had penetrated the old one, by laying the two texts side by side it was possible to learn a good deal about the code just recently introduced. More to the point, the sheer logistic difficulty of circulating the new code books might persuade the Japanese to postpone a code change which, for good precautionary reasons, they actually desired to make. Very soon we shall see that this is the sort of dilemma that causes battles to be lost—and won.

So the breaks began to happen, though for an apparent eternity the pace was slow and agonizing. Looking back after the war, Rochefort reckoned that the best average was a reading of 12 to 15 percent of a message.[5] The gaps had to be filled in by intuition, back-reference to other signals, a general awareness of what was going on. To a very important degree this depended on exact knowledge of the Japanese Order of Battle—what warships existed, how they were grouped, where they were based, their movements, changes in their command. For this understanding the well-established American drills for direction finding and traffic analysis paid high dividends.† By direction finding, individual units, command headquarters or task forces could

---

* A great hindrance to the orderly distribution of new codes, ciphers or lists of call signs was the sinking of ships which happened to be carrying them. In the spring of 1942, for example, a Japanese *auxiliary* vessel was lost in convoy: the news was radioed to many command headquarters which would not normally have been informed—with obvious implications.

† Summarizing the situation on the eve of the Coral Sea battle, the report on the Role of Radio Intelligence in the American-Japanese War states: "Traffic analysis continued to play an extremely important role as the month of April ended. Even without success in decryption of Japanese messages, sufficient warning could have been given our battle forces." (Ch. 2, "The Battle of the Coral Sea," Appendix II, Part II, p. 234, Item No. 56.)

be located—with varying precision.* Analysis of the Japanese Navy's radio traffic was particularly instructive, since the Americans became adept at identifying the various call signs included in signals (so that even if you could not read the signal's contents, you at least knew who had sent it to whom—an obvious benefit). Moreover, study of the increase or decrease in volume of the radio signals in a particular area could tell much about fleet movements, regroupings, impending operations. There were, indeed, characteristic patterns for the Japanese signal traffic that preceded—for example—an action by a strike force of aircraft carriers or an amphibious assault. Here was a powerful backup for FRUPac.

Admiral Layton wrote to the author in 1980: "I agree with you that traffic analysis plus direction finding has been little understood and undervalued by many who should know better. . . . Traffic analysis was sharpened in 1941 and thereafter by the many years of careful study and analysis, application and watching the machine in action in peacetime, and observing its changes. Those engaged in traffic analysis were unsung heroes in my opinion; of course, when decrypts were available, they helped the traffic analysis to arrive at conclusions that were almost 'Magic,' if you can excuse the correlation." From the signal intelligence people at Bletchley Park to the army, naval and air commanders and their staffs, all who during the Second World War profited from the British equivalent, "Y Service," would concur in that verdict. We shall never fully understand the Allied conduct of the war until this vital aspect has been most meticulously explored.[6]

The point when the pieces really came together and enabled FRUPac to pass its first major test can be easily indicated: it was a day in early April 1942. But the severity of that test can only be gauged by understanding how the disaster at Pearl had left its mark. The very validity of signal intelligence was called into question by the Magic that failed. Top echelons of the armed services were filled, moreover, with senior officers who still looked on the mysteries of decoding like a Doubting Thomas for whom the old ways were best. Nor should this attitude be ridiculed. In the British forces there was a fair sprinkling of admirals and generals who only cautiously, or even contemptuously, accommodated themselves to the newfangled notion

---

* Postwar investigations suggested that neither the U.S. radio-direction-finding equipment nor the superior British R.D.F. reached Japanese standards.

of Ultra. What FRUPac urgently needed, therefore, was a manifest and credible success.

When the opportunity arrived it was wholly unexpected. The Commander in Chief of the United States Fleet, COMINCH (who had been so designated by the President on December 20, 1941), was Admiral Ernest King, an officer of austere rigidity and quarterdeck style whose description, "the bald eagle," is belied neither by his photographs nor by his performance. It was thus entirely out of character when Rochefort received from this cautious conservative (in his first and only message from King) an instruction to produce a long-range estimate of Japanese intentions on the basis of existing signal intelligence. This was a make-or-break situation.[7]

Rochefort replied: (1) that the recent sortie of a Japanese carrier force into the Indian Ocean had been called off and that the fleet was withdrawing eastward; (2) that Australia was not a Japanese objective;* (3) that an operation was being prepared, based on the great harbor of Rabaul in New Britain, for which units had already been assigned; and (4) that further indications foreshadowed some other major development in the Pacific which could not, as yet, be pinpointed. Since (1) was in fact already happening, (2) was correct insofar as the Japanese never decided to *invade* Australia, (3) presaged the move against Port Moresby, Operation MO, which precipitated the Coral Sea battle and (4) referred to the birth pangs of Midway, Rochefort's forecast was not only remarkable in its accuracy: as its truth unfolded in the weeks that followed, it strengthened the credibility of FRUPac and, by association, the other signal intelligence agencies. King himself was perhaps slow to succumb, but King was King. What is more important to watch is the growing trust of Admiral Nimitz. As Commander of the Pacific Fleet, Nimitz was the man who issued operational orders and, like Jellicoe a generation earlier, could lose the war in an afternoon.

Since the force most liable to cause such a catastrophe was Admiral Nagumo's First Air Fleet (which had carried out the attack on Pearl Harbor) knowledge of its movements was mandatory, and the first item in Rochefort's estimate—increasingly confirmed as the days went

---

* Relatively, rather than absolutely, true. From the Japanese Official History it is evident that a strong naval pressure for the invasion of northeastern Australia was balked by the Army, which refused to supply the necessary divisions on the ground that the need was greater elsewhere.

by—had a sinister weight. For Nagumo, at the end of March, had sailed off into the Indian Ocean with his five heavy aircraft carriers and an accompanying battle fleet, aiming—successfully—to savage Ceylon and the bases of the British Eastern Fleet. (The British signal intelligence unit shifted, just in time, from Singapore to Colombo was able to give valuable advance warning of Nagumo's approach.[8]) This diversion of the Japanese carriers, when American naval weakness in the Pacific was so grave, offered an obvious relief for Nimitz: but now they were coming back. By the end of April a combination of traffic analysis and decoded signals had absolutely established that two of the heavy carriers, *Zuikaku* and *Shokaku*, were to move southward, staging through the great base and forwarding center of Truk in the Carolines to link with the Japanese Fourth Fleet, which Vice-Admiral Inouye commanded from Rabaul.

As well as the presence of Cardiv 5 (the Americans' name for the carrier group) that other carrier still thought of as *Ryukaku* (but henceforth referred to under her true colors as *Shoho*) was revealed by the intercepts as due to operate in southern waters. Simultaneously FRUPac extracted from intercepted signals mounting evidence of a buildup of aviation units in the South Pacific: the detected transfer thither, for example, of the Tainan Air Group. All those indicators— sometimes substantial, sometimes but straws in the wind—fitted with the growing perception that an operation called MO was looming, aimed at Port Moresby.

A decoded signal of April 24 from the Fourth Fleet, issuing new call signs, quite specifically referred to the MO Fleet, the MO Attack Force and the MO Occupation Force, while an associated signal to Cardiv 5 clearly connected the heavy carriers with the operation. This meant mischief: but FRUPac had long ceased to have doubts about what was in train. Had any existed, they would have been blown away by a decoded instruction radioed by Admiral Inouye at Rabaul on May 4 to Cardiv 5 and his heavy cruiser group, Crudiv 5: ". . . the MO Striking Force will launch an attack from a southeasterly direction on bases in Moresby area on X—3 day and X—2 day. This order is in effect until its successful completion. Commence preparations." FRUPac's calculation, based on existing intelligence, was that X day was May 10. The main actions in the Coral Sea battle were, in fact, fought on May 7 and 8. Rochefort's original *ballon d'essai* had landed right in the target area.

For Admiral Nimitz intelligence of this quality—even though it was necessarily sometimes imprecise and speculative—must have seemed like manna from a suddenly generous heaven. But his own mental attitude at this time should be sympathetically understood. Midway had not yet happened—Midway, the battle before which, as will soon be told, FRUPac enabled him to make his preparatory command decisions on the basis of indisputable evidence and thereby win a conclusive victory. During the run-up to the Coral Sea battle, which shattered Operation MO, the case for signal intelligence and its credibility was still to be proved. The attack on JN25 was, at this stage, producing intelligence which was of inestimable value. Nevertheless, not infrequently, support came from "informed deductions" from signals only partially broken. One must therefore recognize Nimitz's nerve, and his good sense, in allowing Rochefort's assessments and indicators to guide his dispositions. Clearly much credit must also be given to the sound judgment of his Fleet Intelligence Officer, Edwin Layton.[9] Even then, as Samuel Eliot Morison observes in his rousing account of the battle, "to know your enemy's intentions is fine, but such knowledge does not always mean that you can stop him."

And that, indeed, was the problem. The Americans' relatively brief experience of fighting the Japanese had taught them the lesson which the British were learning from the Luftwaffe and which the destruction of *Prince of Wales* and *Repulse* off Singapore had driven home. The battleship was no longer queen of the waves. There would never be another Jutland in which serried ranks of sea monsters pounded each other to death. The aircraft carrier had taken over as successor-queen. Throughout the Pacific war the urgent first question—on both sides—would always be, where are the enemy's carriers? In April 1942 signal intelligence had produced the answer, for sure. *Zuikaku*, *Shokaku* and *Shoho* were converging for Operation MO.

It was impossible for Nimitz to balance the equation. Of the four carriers then available for action in the Pacific, *Hornet* and *Enterprise*, under Admiral Halsey, did not reach Pearl Harbor until April 25 on their return from launching the famous Doolittle raid on Tokyo. Refueling, reprovisioning, reorganizing the air units and rearming them with a new type of bomb took five days. Halsey sailed for the Coral Sea, with 3,500 miles to go, on April 30. Next day the Japanese heavy carriers set out from Truk—with the same objective but with a third of the distance to cover. And this was known to Nimitz. The port controller at Truk reported their departure, and his decoded signal made it evident that Halsey could hardly arrive in time for the impending action. Thus Nimitz was left with *Yorktown* and *Lexington*: two against three.

It is true that sundry bases in Australia held about 300 American and Australian aircraft, but by a Chiefs of Staff order control of these rested in the hands of MacArthur, not Nimitz. In any case their crews were untrained for work over the sea, and in practice such Army bombers as took part in the Coral Sea battle (and, later, at Midway) were unsuccessful. Nimitz and the Navy were on their own. Since the possible area of operations was so vast, it was evident that if he put his two carriers in the wrong place, with the wrong instructions, the Japanese might easily slip the Port Moresby Occupation Force through to its destination unimpeded. And that spelled disaster, for it was at Moresby that MacArthur intended to establish the first base for his cherished return drive, and from airfields at Moresby the Japanese could ravage northern Australia.

But Nimitz, with the aid of the cryptanalysts, got it right. On May 1 *Lexington* and *Yorktown* linked up at Point Buttercup, an attractive cover name for a patch of bare ocean at 16°S, 161°45′E or, more intelligibly, on the wide eastern flank of the Coral Sea: on the flank, that is, of the waters through which it was known that the Japanese intended to move. Aboard *Lexington* Admiral Fletcher, in command of the carriers and cruiser groups that together formed Task Force 17, declared in his operation order that his mission was to "destroy enemy ships, shipping and aircraft at favorable opportunities in order to assist in checking further advance by enemy in the New Guinea-Solomons Area." Within a week it was all over, and the Coral Sea had entered its niche in history: not the turning point in the Pacific war—another month was needed for that—but the discernible point when the turn began. *Shoho* sunk, *Shokaku* temporarily out of action, *Zuikaku* diverted elsewhere, the transports of the Moresby Occupation Force withdrawn (for a while, the Japanese thought, but in fact forever): this was a fair return for the loss of *Lexington* and a damaged *Yorktown*.[10] Each side made so many tactical mistakes during the conflict that Morison has suggested an alternative title for it, the Battle of Naval Errors. But, he adds, "there is no teacher of combat that can even remotely approach the value of combat itself: call Coral Sea what you will, it was an indispensable preliminary to the great victory of Midway."

At FRUPac they had the extraordinary experience of receiving from the Japanese themselves confirmation of a defeat which signal intelligence had done so much to bring about. "In the basement," Holmes wrote, "we watched all intercepted messages for news. The Japanese used the word *gekichin* to report the destruction of an enemy ship, and *chimbotsu* to describe the sinking of one of their own ships. The traffic-analysis desk flagged every important message and rushed it to Holtwick* in the machine room. As each printout rolled off the machines, hungry eyes searched for the code group for *chimbotsu*."[11] The availability of those messages in the U.S. Naval Archives now makes it possible to taste the precise savor of such moments. Here is an excerpt from the relevant after-action report by the Fourth Fleet at Rabaul, as it was almost completely decoded at the time.

> . . . Part 3. Our losses: SHOHO, sunk (hit by 7 torpedoes and 13 bombs), 22 aviation personnel made forced landings; 80 of these were injured, 16 seriously, 64 minor; others went down with the ship.
>
> SHOKAKU . . . hits, 3 and 8; damage to gasoline storage, engine rooms, etc. (some blanks here); 94 killed, including 5 officers; 96 seriously injured—number of minor injuries.

Unlike the airmen who died above—and often in—the Coral Sea, the staff at FRUPac had not pushed themselves to the ultimate. They had simply done their best. Signals like this were their reward.

In this account of the impact of signal intelligence on the Pacific war the battle of the Coral Sea can be precisely placed. It was the equivalent of the British victory in the Mediterranean on March 28, 1941, when Admiral Andrew Cunningham, sallying from Alexandria, overwhelmed the Italians in the battle of Matapan. By breaking into an Italian naval cipher shortly beforehand Bletchley was able to supply Cunningham in advance with the two essential clues: the Italian fleet would be making a thrust into the Aegean or the eastern Mediterranean, and this would happen on March 27. So warned,

---

* Lieutenant Commander Holtwick had worked on cryptanalysis in the Navy Department and the Asiatic Fleet between 1934 and 1939. He joined Hypo in the summer of 1940.

Cunningham had his own ships at the right place and at the right time. The experience of Nimitz is parallel. Neither admiral was provided with exact, up-to-the-minute, point-by-point information during the action, as happened later, for example, in the sinking of *Scharnhorst*.[12] Bletchley can then be observed supplying her pursuers with immediate, and critically relevant, Ultra intelligence throughout the hunt. But for an action at sea the vital question for a commander has always been, where should he position himself in relation to the enemy, and what are the enemy's broad intentions? The British Intelligence History says of Matapan that "it was the first important operation in the Mediterranean to be based on Sigint." The same may be said of the Coral Sea battle in relation to the Pacific.

The sight of Doolittle's bombers buzzing over Tokyo hardened the Japanese resolve to proceed with Yamamoto's Midway plan, called MI, and what was truly a strategic reverse in the Coral Sea looked to the Imperial High Command like a heartening victory. MO, therefore, was simply postponed. During the operations they had picked up the invaluable base on Tulagi, off Guadalcanal in the Solomons: they could surely build on this. And the immensely superior Combined Fleet was still intact—particularly the heavy carrier groups, Cardiv 1 and Cardiv 2, with *Akagi, Kaga, Hiryu* and *Soryu*. Indeed the 1st and 2nd Air Squadrons working from these craft considered that the 5th Air Squadron, which flew in the Coral Sea action, had leveled it with America's best, the pilots of *Lexington* and *Yorktown*, although 5th Air was in their view the least competent unit in the fleet. The word went round, therefore: "son of concubine gained a victory so sons of legal wives should find no rival in the world."[13] The "Victory Disease," in fact, was still endemic, and preparations for Operation MI went steadily ahead.

Unfortunately for Tokyo those preparations were being monitored by American signal intelligence even before the events in the Coral Sea. At first the evidence came in piecemeal, without any obvious connection between one fragment and another. But shapes and patterns gradually emerged, to be confirmed in the end by intercepts so specific in detail and so conclusive in their significance that Nimitz, on the eve of his next great battle, had a more intimate knowledge of his enemy's strength and intentions than any other admiral in the whole previous history of sea warfare. The difference between his situation and that which preceded the Pearl Harbor catastrophe is like the passage of light-years.

The "geographic designator" which the Japanese employed for Midway was AF. Two months before Operation MI began to appear above the horizon in a meaningful way, as early as March 4, 1942, the decoding of an intercept caused the Naval Operations Division, Op Nav, to report to Admiral King as Commander in Chief: "this dispatch seems to indicate that areas AF and AFH are in the vicinity of Hawaiian Islands." Well, Admiral Nagumo himself described the barren six-mile atoll of Midway, 1,135 miles to the northwest of Pearl Harbor, as "a sentry for Hawaii." After the loss of Wake Island during the first Japanese surge forward, Midway became the most westerly American holding in the Pacific. Later on that little clue, first spotted in early March, would click into place.

During the night of March 3–4, moreover, Pearl Harbor was bombed for a second time: nothing dramatic, just an attack by two four-engined flying boats which missed their target because of thick cloud and dropped their loads on the hills behind Honolulu.* But how could laden seaplanes reach Hawaii? Holmes and Layton swiftly and simultaneously deduced the answer. They must have flown in from the distant Marshall Islands and refueled en route. Later their guess was confirmed: the Japanese had positioned three tanker submarines, as well as one to provide a navigational beacon and another to furnish weather reports, in a cluster of islets about 500 miles from Pearl Harbor, French Frigate Shoals. (The name recalls *Boussole* and *Astrolabe*, the frigates whose commander La Pérouse discovered the islands in 1786. Before the war the Americans themselves had started to use the sheltered anchorage for seaplane landings.)

All this made sense. Traffic analysis and some driblets of decoding had already identified an air group on the Marshalls, and direction finding had revealed the presence of submarines in the waters off Hawaii. Indeed, Nimitz was warned during the afternoon of the 3rd that something was in the wind. But the Fleet Intelligence Officer's pointer to French Frigate Shoals had a deeper significance. It was soon established that the Japanese cover word for these events was the

---

* Appropriately, the bombs fell on the slopes of Mount Tantalus. For a minutely detailed account of this K Operation, see Admiral Layton's article "Rendezvous in Reverse," in the *Proceedings* of the U.S. Naval Institute, May 1953.

K campaign, K standing for Hawaii, and steps were sensibly taken to deny the Shoals by mining and visits from patrol craft. Three months later, however, the results of this signal intelligence had a more rewarding consequence for Nimitz.

For the complex Operation MI the Japanese intended to use French Frigate Shoals as a base for seaplane reconnaissance over Pearl Harbor. But the move was anticipated. On May 6 a signal went out to a list of high-level addresses, King, Nimitz, Op Nav, the Belconnen unit, etc., quoting a decoded message from the enemy's Fourth Air Attack Force. "Request we be supplied 10 crystals for frequencies 4990 and 8990 kilocycles for use in aircraft *in the second K campaign.* Above to reach this headquarters (Kwajalein) prior to 17th." A reply, on the 10th, announced that the crystals required *"for use in K operations"* would be sent out by air from Japan to Kwajalein on the 12th.[14]

The implications of a second K campaign were obvious. Two seaplane tenders, *Thornton* and *Ballard,* were therefore sent off to take post at the Shoals. Not long afterward the 1,400-ton submarines I-121 and I-123 arrived there from Japan with a large load of fuel and lubricating oils, to serve as milch cows for an air-reconnaissance unit, but the American presence drove them off.* After four days of careful periscope-watch Commander Toshitake Ueno of I-123 signaled to Kwajalein on May 30 that the Shoals were under surveillance, and the second K campaign was suspended. This deterrence, founded on accurate signal intelligence, was of critical value to Nimitz in the battle that followed a few days later, since the absence of Japanese reconnaissance meant that his main force reached the scene of action undetected. As Nimitz was playing his cards from a weak hand, this was equal to the present of another aircraft carrier.

To bring such a battle about—to force the Americans to commit themselves in that cataclysmic "fleet action" which has been the dream of all naval officers since capital ships came into being—Yamamoto's plans were indeed complex. Characteristically so, for the general trend of Japanese strategical thinking was to count on achieving surprise by bringing together widely separated forces at the critical point, on programs of precise timing which prevented flexibility and made small contingent allowance for things going wrong.

---

* Two four-engined flying boats were scheduled to refuel from the submarines and then investigate the strength of the fleet at Pearl Harbor.

(Their moves before the mammoth conflict at Leyte Gulf in 1944 provide an extreme example.) Before Midway cryptanalysis would rob them of that surprise, but the very complexity of the enemy's design made it difficult at all levels, from FRUPac and Op-20-G up to Nimitz and King, to decide exactly what Yamamoto had in mind.

Nevertheless, there was a fatal flaw in the Japanese facade, a crack through which FRUPac and its associates could do what Admiral Fletcher called "a hell of a lot of groping about." For safety, routine changes in the JN25b code should have been carried out by the Japanese, but because of overwhelming difficulties in the distribution of new code books the change was deferred, first from April 1 and then from May 1. It was not finally effected until May 28, which, in terms of the impending battle, was equivalent to "the last minute before midnight." This miraculous breathing space gave the cryptanalysts the chance to perfect their penetration of JN25. By the month of May they understood about a third of the code structure, which in turn meant that up to 90 percent of a routine signal could frequently be translated: the point being that the code groups most frequently used were the first to be broken. In addition, by "working back" over the large body of signals intercepted during the Coral Sea action but not decoded at the time, the cryptanalysts could garner many clues and insights.*

And this was a benign gift. The variety and deceptive intent of the Japanese maneuvers might otherwise have led Nimitz to misread Yamamoto's mind. In essence, the enemy High Command saw Midway and its surrounding seas as the remaining gap in their perimeter—a gap through which, as they assumed, Halsey had slipped on his way to raid Tokyo. By seizing the atoll and eliminating the American fleet that must rush to its defense, they would mend their fences and prepare the way for a final return visit to Pearl Harbor.

The Carrier Striking Force (the four heavy craft of Cardivs 1 and 2) was to take up a position off Midway, and soften up its defenses before the arrival of an Occupation Force with its transports and escort of battleships and cruisers. Meanwhile the Main Body of the Combined Fleet under Yamamoto himself would stand off at a distance, ready

---

* This type of retrospective analysis could be done more easily by Op-20-G in Washington than by FRUPac or the Belconnen unit in Australia, for shortage of personnel meant that these stations were hard-pressed, and compelled to concentrate resources on the search for vital clues in current traffic.

to administer the *coup de grâce* on the American Pacific Fleet after it had entered the fray and been worked over by the dive bombers and torpedo planes of the Striking Force. The Main Body was to be split, Yamamoto retaining his three most modern battleships while a detached force of four older battleships would hover between Midway and the Aleutians, a backup for the fleet in the south and a cover for the Second Mobile Force. This, with its light carriers, cruisers and troop transports, was to set Operation MI rolling on June 3 by bombing Dutch Harbor and then supporting landings at Kiska, Attu and Adak, far away in the Aleutians. The stab was essentially diversionary. It was intended to detach Nimitz's attention—and his ships—from Midway, but there would be a further advantage: if the Aleutians were firmly gripped, any future attack on Japan by the most northerly route would be blocked.

The Aleutian diversion can be disposed of summarily, since it was detected even before it started. As early as March 9 a decoded signal, passed between the Japanese First Air Attack Force and the Fifth Fleet, suggested that these units were "arranging as yet unknown operations in northern sector," on which Radio Intelligence commented: "If this impression is correct it may indicate possible operations against Aleutian Islands with air and sea forces." During May the designator AO began to appear in the Japanese traffic, and this was soon identified as representing the Aleutians. That something was stirring in the north—but subsidiary to Midway—was suggested about May 18, when an earlier radio instruction to a submarine unit (which one was unknown) was belatedly evaluated: "Please change the directive of the movements of the *AF (Midway) and AO (Aleutian) Occupation Forces* and related forces in the following manner . . ." Sundry specific demands for weather reports from the Aleutian area also had more than a casual significance.

Nevertheless, conclusive evidence was accumulating that the main target was Midway. On May 17, after much pondering, Nimitz began grouping a North Pacific Force under Admiral Theobald. He gave the admiral, however, only five cruisers escorted by ten destroyers: the precious carriers he kept in hand for the great action that now seemed imminent. Japan's deception plan failed, in fact, to deceive.

The unfortunate Theobald, however, miscalculated. Even though Nimitz sent him a warning on May 28 that the Japanese objectives were Kiska and probably Attu (at the western end of the Aleutian

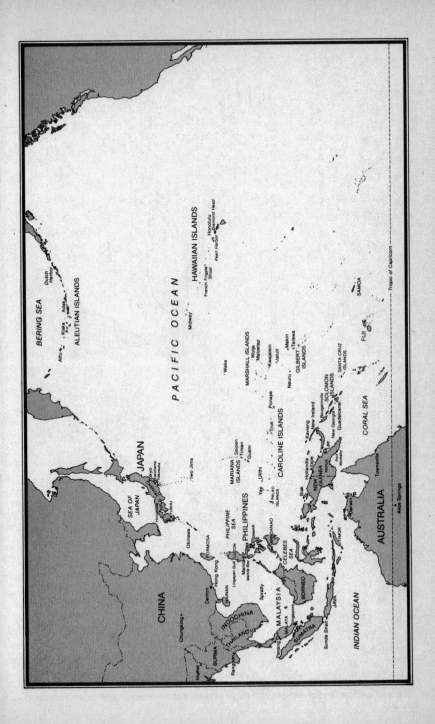

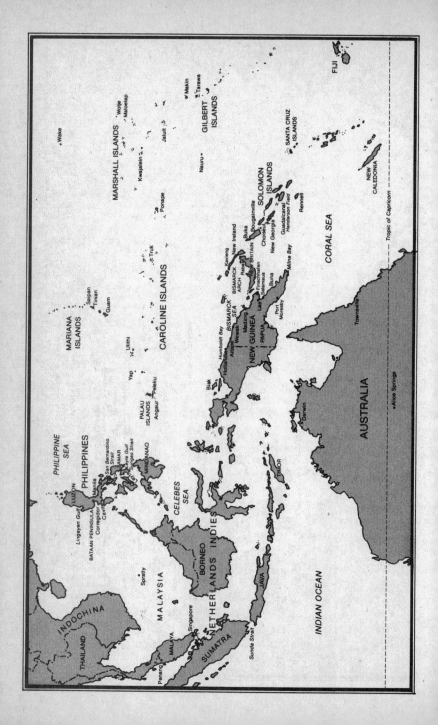

chain) he was worried that this was a feint to draw him away from the distant Dutch Harbor, just off the tip of Alaska—in his view the more likely target. In sum, Theobald's ships were in the wrong place when the Second Mobile Force under Admiral Kakuta moved in on June 3. It mattered little. The Japanese gained two irrelevant islands in the northern mists—and Theobald's professional reputation waned.[15] What did matter was the advance information provided by signal intelligence, for if on the very eve of Midway Nimitz and King had suddenly discovered, out of the blue, that a Japanese occupation force was assaulting the Aleutians, the news would certainly have thrown them "off balance."

But there was nothing unexpected about Midway. The night before the action, "The Battle of the Fourth of June," Admiral Fletcher with his carriers was at exactly the right point on the surface of the Pacific —his presence unknown to the enemy. It is fascinating to follow the steps that led up to this tactical surprise. To change the metaphor, there is something compulsive about observing how Yamamoto's intentions gradually took shape in the Americans' minds just as one watches a dried Japanese flower, when immersed in water, slowly unfold until its true shape and dimensions are revealed.

The first clear indicators came at the beginning of May. On May 2 a signal from the Chief of Staff, Second Fleet (which in fact, under Admiral Kondo, controlled the Midway Occupation Force), referred to an A Force and a *Striking Force* for which anchorages would be required at Truk—already recognized as the assembly area for major operations. Two days later a signal from an unidentified ship (addressed to C. in C., First Fleet, Yamamoto's own command) reported that it would be undergoing repairs "during the time of *the said campaign*." "The date of completion being [near May 21, the cryptanalysts estimated], will be unable to accompany you in the campaign." Next day a signal from Yamamoto himself to Tokyo revealed that he was requesting "for current scheduled operations" a speed-up in delivery of fueling hoses for two cruiser divisions (4 and 7, part of the Occupation Force) and two destroyer detachments. "Expedite," "current scheduled operations," "fueling at sea": the implications were obvious. Something big, and something soon.

But where? The exchange of signals on May 6 and 11 about supplies of special radio crystals for "the second K campaign," already quoted, pointed directly at the Hawaiian area. That the operation in train would be substantial was proved by another signal, on May 7, setting up a commanders' conference. This, an elaborate affair, was followed by a number of other signs that exercises and war games were being held—and the Japanese always ran training programs before any major act of war. Why did a signal from the commander of the Japanese Second Fleet, on May 11, order Air Landing and Attack Forces, and an Occupation Force, to move to the Saipan-Guam area and *wait for a forthcoming campaign?* It was not likely, FRUPac commented, that "the Japanese were merely carrying out a drill." Why on the 12th did Yamamoto signal to the Fourth and Second Fleets: "we are now arranging for the military equipment, shells and bombs which you will require at Truk during the forthcoming campaign"? And why, on the 13th, did another decode reveal that specific charts were being demanded for the armada assembling at Saipan—including a variety of charts for the waters around Hawaii and its western approaches?

As the famous broadcast put it when Japanese planes first roared over Pearl Harbor, this was evidently "not a drill." The hardening evidence crystallized. A broken signal of May 15, ordering a stock of equipment and stores for AF, preceded this comment on May 22: "All indications are that the Japanese are making very detailed plans for the occupation of Midway, and also for equipment and use of the island after its occupation." (It is sometimes argued that this had already been demonstrated by the intercept of an Imperial General Headquarters order to Yamamoto of May 5 instructing him to occupy Midway and the western Aleutians. But the official Japanese History shows that this was an order delivered by hand, and not by radio.) On the 16th the small print was readable. The staff of the First Air Fleet was found to be signaling: "As we plan to make attacks from a generally northwesterly direction from N—2 to N day inclusive, please send weather three hours prior to takeoff on said day . . . on the day of the attack we will endeavor to [unintelligible] at a point 51 miles NW of AF and move pilots off as quickly as possible."

Before the estimate of the 22nd, in fact, a steady flow of decodes was suggesting that the Japanese were already taking the capture of Midway for granted, and even planning ahead for "a second campaign." First Air Corps on the 21st, for example, was requesting "delivery during May of the replacement planes for use in the second phase." On the 24th, deliveries of Zero fighters were noted to all four of the

Cardivs' carriers, *Akagi, Hiryu, Kaga* and *Soryu*. But that, too, was the day when another signal, referring to "the effective date of the new Combined Fleet communication organization list," made it clear that the inevitable replacement of JN25b by a new code system was close at hand.

The change was too late. Before it happened, both the place and the date of Operation MI had been established beyond doubt. Yet doubts had existed. Though it seemed already certain at Pearl Harbor that AF represented Midway, so much hung on this assumption that something irrefutable was still needed—particularly as Admiral King, kept up-to-date by Op-20-G in Washington, feared that it might all be a feint and that the South Pacific might be the real objective, while the Army was haunted by the possibility of an invasion of California. (Once again, the reminder is necessary that the credibility of signal intelligence—in spite of the Coral Sea—had still to be validated,* and that the traditional training of American staff officers had been to estimate as precisely as possible an enemy's capabilities and then take guard against the most *dangerous* course open to him. It was not unreasonable to believe that a fresh assault on Pearl Harbor or— perhaps in a more hysterical mood—on the west coast of the continent represented the gravest danger.) A new move, however, dispelled all dubieties.

According to his memoirs the idea came first to Jasper Holmes. It was not unlike another device, evolved by the British: the basic notion being that, when in doubt, you compel the enemy himself to produce the conclusive evidence you seek. The British would select known gaps in German naval minefields and then arrange for mines to be dropped in them, knowing that this would have to be reported to local units in a lower-grade code which the British could read, but also, at a higher level, in a naval cipher they were seeking to break. A decoded low-grade signal could thus provide a pathway into an unbroken higher-grade system.

Before the war Holmes was head of the Materials Testing Laboratory at the University of Hawaii, where he had been involved in a project for using a mixture of coral and salt water for concrete-making

---

* Not, of course, for Nimitz, who had accepted the evidence that the assumption was a certainty: but for senior officers who had not shared the process of evaluation, were further from the scene, and had to weigh the alternatives.

on Midway. He knew, therefore, that fresh water was in short supply on the atoll. Now, one of Midway's advantages was that the undersea telegraphic cable to Hawaii was still operating and untapped by the Japanese. So he suggested to Rochefort that the Midway command should be secretly instructed by cable to send out, uncoded, a radio signal that the fresh-water distilling plant had broken down. When this was heard at Pearl Harbor a reply was sent, also uncoded, that a water barge was on its way. All the intercept stations were alerted to listen out, and sure enough on May 21 Naval Intelligence at Imperial General Headquarters in Tokyo broadcast a signal that Wake Island had reported a shortage of fresh water on AF and a request that it should be supplied immediately.* Belconnen in Australia picked this up, broke the text and transmitted a translation the same day (the 21st) to OPNAV, CINCPAC, COM 14 at Hawaii, COM S.W. PAC-FORCE and COMINCH, adding: "This will confirm the identity of AF." The meaning of the AF symbol first noticed in March, and the objective of Operation MI, were now evident. Nimitz knew exactly what was in the wind.

But when? The difficulty over that 10 percent of the signals which could not be decoded arose because these stubborn passages contained references to times and dates, protected by the Japanese with yet another layer of cipher which had so far defeated the "stripping" of the cryptanalysts. Shrewd calculation had by now reduced the likely period for the attack to somewhere between the 1st and 10th of June. But "somewhere" is insufficient for an admiral who has to position his fleet in the right place at the right time to deal with an undoubtedly superior force. By a superhuman effort FRUPac achieved a last-minute breakthrough, and when he was satisfied Rochefort slipped off his smoking jacket, made himself shipshape, and took the news to Nimitz: the last step in a prolonged and nerve-racking feat of detection, the knowledge that June 3 was deadline for the Aleutians, and June 4 for Midway.[16]

Holmes went out for a breath of air and found himself talking to one of *Yorktown*'s officers. Just then one of the FRUPac team, Thomas

---

* By chance, the ground was already prepared—by the Japanese themselves. In November 1941 their Naval Attaché in Washington took a flight around Hawaii, Midway, Wake and Guam, and filed a report to Tokyo on "State of American Alert." Paragraph 4c of his report reads: "We noticed the lack of pure water on Wake and Midway. For drinking water filtered fresh water was used; for miscellaneous purposes sea water was used."

Dyer,* emerged from the underground chamber where he had been slaving on the time-date problem.

> Under his arm was his old lunch box. His uniform looked as though he had slept in it for three days. He had. He was unshaven and his hair looked as though it had not been cut for a month. It had not. His eyes were bloodshot from lack of sleep, and his gait betrayed how close he was to utter exhaustion. With a seaman's contempt for a landlubber, my carrier friend remarked, "Now there goes a bird who should be sent to sea to get straightened out."

In fact, it was the *Yorktown* man who would soon be under sailing orders, the climax to a series of brilliant dispositions which Nimitz was able to make because, and entirely because, of the Early Warning System supplied by signal intelligence. Even a random glance through the war diary maintained at his command headquarters discloses their logical, remorseless process.

For the intimate and confidential relationship within which that process occurred there is no more authoritative witness than Admiral Layton. The following account, from a letter to the author, vividly recaptures the atmosphere and the sense of urgency.

> Joe Rochefort and I were old and close friends both professionally and socially. We conferred many times daily—via a secure (no switchboard) sound-powered telephone he was at one end at "his shop" and I at my end—about material arriving in the COMINT (Command Intelligence) channel. He would always call me when they came across a "hot" item, and would ask my views about problems as they arose—blanks in the text, garbles and the like— to see if we could guess a meaning or value for the benefit of the cryptanalysts and translators. On around May 12 he phoned me to say that he had some fragments that were so hot that they were practically burning the table, and suggested that I come over to his shop right away. I did.
>
> They were only fragments, with many unrecovered values, but they were HOT. One recovered value that had been proven during the MO campaign was for "Occupation Force," and an

---

* Lieutenant Commander Thomas Dyer, USN, was actually one of the most expert cryptographers in the Navy—at or even above Rochefort's level, some would claim.

internal date cipher we hadn't previously been able to crack was
there too—as was AF, which we *knew* was in the Hawaii region,
somewhere: we were both almost positive it was Midway, but had
no proof. While I was there, fragments of another signal came in
which carried the already proven value for "Occupation Force,"
referred to the 11th and 12th Air Forces and an Army "detachment," and contained the phrase "forthcoming campaign." After
analyzing the various implications, Joe and I were convinced that
an occupation of Midway was being planned.

I went to Admiral Nimitz on my return, reported to him on my
opinions and conclusions, and urged him to see for himself the
piecemeal evidences. I told him I was confident that it would
convince him that an assault on Midway, involving an amphibious
operation, was being planned for the near future. We reviewed the
fact that the great part of the Combined Fleet, which had returned from the Indian Ocean and operations off Malaya, the
Philippines, etc., was now back in the home waters of Japan—
some vessels had been freshly dry-docked, and were clearly being
prepared for some big operation.

Admiral Nimitz quizzed me closely. He wanted to know all the
whys and wherefores on which Joe and I based our belief that AF
was Midway. He then said that I was to tell Joe that he, Chester
Nimitz, considered that the *positive* identification of AF should
receive the highest priority, as that was the key to the Japs' future
thrust. I reported this to Joe, and every day we talked over the
puzzle and exchanged ideas. You know the rest.

"The rest," as has been seen, involved a hard grind and some brilliant
ideas. But before "the rest" could produce a result at sea, Nimitz
would need to dispose his forces with the utmost care: he would need,
also, that kind of luck which Napoleon believed to be the attribute of
a successful commander.

Sometimes in battle God seems to be on the side not so much of the
big battalions as of the commander with the better judgment. Which
is to say that such planning sometimes produces, by chance, not only
the calculated consequences but also happy by-products which could
not have been predicted. When Halsey arrived too late for the Coral
Sea action, for example, he was retained in those southern waters with
his Task Force 16, *Enterprise* and *Hornet*. But Nimitz, seeing the
urgent need to concentrate against Cardivs 1 and 2, summoned Halsey

back to Pearl Harbor, where his Task Force arrived on May 26.* Before he left station, however, a Japanese patrol plane had spotted him and reported the presence of hostile carriers 450 miles to the east of the Solomons.† And Yamamoto, who already believed that two American carriers had been sunk in the Coral Sea, continued to assume that Halsey's force was still far away, as impotent to aid at Midway as during the earlier battle. So it looked as though the enfeebled Americans would be very weak indeed.

Moreover, when Halsey did reach Pearl Harbor he was suffering from an acute skin infection, so Nimitz relieved him, appointing in his place a man with ice in his veins, Admiral Raymond Spruance. After his subsequent destruction of the Japanese carriers at Midway, Spruance coolly refused to pursue an apparently demoralized enemy. Had he done so, he might have lost his own ships beneath the huge armament of Yamamoto's lurking Main Body, whose existence neither he nor, for that matter, FRUPac or Nimitz realized. Remembering Halsey's notorious and ill-considered dash after the Japanese decoy ships at Leyte Gulf in 1944, who can be sure that "The Bull" might not have charged another red flag at Midway? But Nimitz was on a lucky streak. It was certainly luck, as well as good planning, that made the Japanese swallow whole the bait sown by a radio-deception scheme which, from May 25 onward, simulated the traffic of an American carrier force in the southwestern Pacific—as if Halsey had never departed. In Tokyo the Naval Staff deduced that the threat to Midway had escaped notice.

The day after Halsey's Task Force 16 reached Pearl *Yorktown* also crept in, desperately wounded in the last engagement. They said it would take some ninety days to mend her. But the writing was clear

---

* Ordering him, on the 15th: "Consider it important that you not be sighted by the enemy." (If the proposition in the following footnote is correct, this implies that Nimitz wished Halsey to avoid being seen by the search aircraft the Japanese would send out after he had *intentionally* disclosed his presence. In fact, as Halsey withdrew to the north, the Fifth Air Attack Force lost contact with Task Force 16 at 1500 hrs. on May 15 and never regained it.)

† Task Force 16 was so observed at 1015 on May 15. A cogent passage in John B. Lundstrom's *The First South Pacific Campaign* (pp. 154 ff.) argues on information supplied by Admiral Layton that Halsey was possibly acting under secret orders from Nimitz to arrange deliberately for the sighting to occur. Not surprisingly, such a message is not in Halsey's war diary, or his memoirs, or the CINCPAC file. Speculative but unconfirmed, it remains an interesting proposition.

on the wall—a fleet action imminent. By one of those technical tours de force which so dramatically express the American genius for improvisation, a swarm of worker-ants in the shape of over 1,400 welders, fitters, electricians and shipwrights restored her in two days: at 0900 on May 31 *Yorktown* was ready to sail again. And because of FRUPac's warning about French Frigate Shoals, no aircraft detected her departure under Admiral Fletcher (in overall command), preceded on the 28th by Spruance with the other two carriers. Nor were they sighted by submarines. Yamamoto was convinced that the American main fleet would only sortie from Pearl Harbor *after* he had attacked Midway. Because of his advance information Nimitz dispatched his ships beforehand, and thus they eluded the string of submarines which were not deployed along their lines of surveillance until June 3, and saw nothing.*

Surprise resulted in success. Walter Lord's sparkling account of that success is entitled *Incredible Victory*, but in retrospect—and in the light of an intelligence story which at last can be told in detail— the sinking of *Akagi, Kaga, Soryu* and *Hiryu* for the loss of *Yorktown* looks as logical as it once seemed unbelievable. Every move during that glorious 4th of June has been charted and analyzed by the naval historians of both sides. Here it is enough to say that the Japanese stretched their bow to its uttermost limit, and it cracked. Losing that tensile strength, the Combined Fleet became a force without a future. Indeed, within a few months the output of American shipyards had not only replaced all losses: it was producing extra armadas in an abundance which the Japanese could not hope to equal.

Many thousands—perhaps millions—of words have been written about Midway. Two impressions persist. The first is of sacrifice: of instant and dedicated self-annihilation by the airmen who consummated the victory.† Their losses are heartrending. Out of 51 torpedo planes

---

* What happened on the Midway atoll is usually overshadowed by the drama of the sea fight. But it should be remembered that, stimulated by his advance intelligence, Nimitz in spite of his other preoccupations acted with hectic energy, manning, arming and stocking the islets of the atoll so vigorously that its garrison comfortably withstood all attacks from the air and, had the Japanese actually attempted to land, might have made Midway's resistance as imperishable as the enemy's on Tarawa.
† In a book written from an American viewpoint by an author who soldiered as an ally such a reaction is not unnatural. A more dispassionate observer would note that at Midway the Japanese themselves lost 250 aircraft and the cream of their crews, some of whom flew to their targets in the certain knowledge that insufficient fuel could only carry them one way.

launched by the Americans 42 failed to return: out of one unit of 15, none. A photograph survives of that extinguished squadron, Torpedo 8. The serious but relaxed demeanor of these young men recalls inescapably those later photographs of kamikaze pilots, ceremonially sipping their farewell saki before racing to an inevitable doom. But in the cemeteries of courage, it is said, the crosses have the same color.

Yet there is another and, historically, a more significant truth. The anonymous author of the U.S. Naval Intelligence's after-action report completed his assessment with a proud but justified assertion. "Claims made ever since the last World War by Combat Intelligence experts in every nation of the world, as to the usefulness of cryptanalysis and the traffic analysis during the course of a sea battle, were proved beyond further doubt at Midway."

CHAPTER FIVE

The Stab in the Back

American boys will die, Mr. Speaker, because of the help furnished our enemies.
> Representative Elmer J. Holland of Pennsylvania,
> speech in Congress, August 31, 1942

America is a terribly public society.
> Kingman Brewster, U.S. Ambassador to the United
> Kingdom, BBC TV interview, March 11, 1980

DURING THE PACIFIC war the American nation was like a warrior in mortal combat whose front is protected by his shield but who is liable, at any moment, to be felled by an unexpected blow from behind. The Navy, the Army and their air forces provided that shield, but American society itself made room for stiletto thrusts which, more than once, might have nullified the sacrifice of its youth. When General Marshall wrote his desperate but uncompromising letter to Governor Dewey, this was the danger he had in mind. There is a real sense in which the epitaph for those wartime years might be: "We are betrayed by what is false within."

The danger arose from the irresponsibility, and sometimes the extreme animosity, of certain elements in the press and among the politicians. At a deeper level, the activity of those who imperiled their country in print or on the platform was only possible because of a permissiveness on the part of the whole society within which they uttered—a permissiveness which, pushing constitutional rights to the limit, is prepared to accept that "anything goes" and of which the Freedom of Information Act is the most recent expression. But in wartime "a terribly public society" can suffer terribly from self-inflicted wounds.

Since the essence of signal intelligence is secrecy and security, it was in this area that damage was most likely to be done—and most liable to prove fatal. The trouble was that neither the Founding Fathers themselves nor any subsequent amendments to their admirable Constitution had provided sufficient legal safeguards against the risks inherent in sophisticated modern warfare. A sudden leak, whether calculated or thoughtless, can now destroy instantaneously an intelligence system which may have taken years to construct: a system, moreover, on which the actual safety of the nation may depend. To prevent or at least to block and mop up such leaks requires swift and ruthless action authorized and initiated by incontrovertible laws. For too long after Pearl Harbor the United States lacked the effective powers.

Nothing more clearly illustrates this impotence than the aftermath of Midway. On June 8, as a disconsolate Yamamoto was withdrawing the eleven battleships and eight heavy cruisers of his Main Body which, with their attendant destroyers and light carriers, had remained *hors de combat* throughout the decisive conflict, Admiral King sent a signal to Admiral Nimitz.

> COMINCH to CINCPAC. Contents of your 31/1221 May were published almost verbatim in several newspapers yesterday. Article originated with Stanley Johnston embarked in BARNETT until June 2nd. While your dispatch was addressed Task Force Commanders it was sent in channel available to nearly all ships which emphasizes need of care in using channels. Para. COMINCH investigating on BARNETT and at San Diego.

All this was true. On June 7 a report appeared on the front page of the Chicago *Tribune* headlined "Navy Had Word of Jap Plan to Strike at Sea." "The strength of the Japanese forces," it said, "with which the American Navy is battling somewhere west of Midway Island in what is believed to be the greatest naval battle of the war was well known in American naval circles several days before the battle began, reliable sources in the naval intelligence disclosed here tonight." This information was stated to be so accurate that "a feint at some American base, to be accompanied by a serious effort to invade and occupy another base, was predicted." The names and armament of the relevant enemy warships were registered in exact detail. The article was anonymous, and the dateline was Washington, D.C. In other words, the *Tribune* was telling the world that Nimitz knew in advance not only the Japanese Order of Battle but also the plan for an Aleutian diversion. Such knowledge could only have been derived from signal intelligence.[1]

It was no coincidence that the owner of the *Tribune* was Colonel Robert McCormick, the rabid isolationist and committed censor of the Roosevelt administration, or that the Midway article was also published in the New York *Daily News* (owned by his cousin Joe Patterson) and the Washington *Times-Herald* (owned by Patterson's sister Eleanor). Nor, indeed, was it a coincidence that on December 4, 1941, three days before Pearl Harbor, the *Tribune* had published details of Roosevelt's "war plans."

Admiral King's fury was justified in every respect. The article's author, Stanley Johnston, was a war correspondent of courage and initiative. On *Lexington,* during the Coral Sea battle, he had distinguished himself by helping to rescue men trapped inside the burning carrier. But the ship on which he was returning from the action, *Barnett,* was merely a transport: yet because of the injudicious and wide dissemination of Nimitz's signal described in King's message it seems certain that Johnston had a look at it while on *Barnett*—perhaps in the hands of one of *Lexington*'s survivors also on board. *Barnett* reached San Diego on June 3. The article appeared on the 7th, and Arthur McCollum of the Naval Intelligence Department describes in his oral history how, when he got to the office that day, "my goodness, the place was shaking."[2]

King complained that the *Tribune* had published Nimitz's signal "almost verbatim." Well, the text is now available in the Midway file amid Nimitz's papers in the Naval Archives in Washington. That 31/1221 of May 31, 1942, reads: CINC PACIFIC FLEET ESTIMATE MIDWAY FORCE ORGANIZATION X STRIKING FORCE 4 CARRIERS (AKAGI KAGA HIRYU SORYU) 2 KIRISHIMAS 2 TONE CLASS CRUISERS 12 DESTROYERS SCREEN AND PLANE GUARD X SUPPORT FORCE 1 DV OR XCV 2 KIRISHIMAS 4 MOGAMIS 1 ATAGO 1 ? BD SCREEN XX OCCUPATION FORCE 1 TAKAO 1–2 MYOKOS (QUESTION) 1 CHITOSE 1 CHITOYODA 2–4 KAMIKAWA MARU 4–6 AK 8–12 AP 12 DESTROYERS X APPROXIMATELY 16 SS ON RECONNAISSANCE AND SCOUTING MISSION MID PACIFIC-HAWAIIAN ISLANDS AREA. Issued on May 31— several days, in other words, before the Midway engagement occurred

—this appreciation dramatically illustrates the quality and accuracy of the signal intelligence with which Nimitz was furnished.

But it also proves beyond argument how false the *Tribune*'s assertion was that Johnston wrote the article "from his own knowledge of the situation with the aid of reference books on the Jap navy, from his knowledge of the Jap Coral Sea losses, and from discussions with the naval men of all countries and his battle comrades of the remaining ships available to the Japs." In fact, if Johnston's article is laid beside the original text of Nimitz's signal, it becomes evident even to an ignoramus in these matters that his layout of the Japanese forces and the precise reference to individual warships follow the same form and, revealingly, contain some of the same errors as the admiral's signal. (The supporting detail which Johnston provided, of tonnage, gun strength, etc., was clearly drawn from one of the "reference books" which he confessed to know intimately, *Jane's Fighting Ships.**) Since the impeccable source of the article was so demonstrable and its drift so dangerous for American security, the question for the authorities was . . . what to do next?

For Johnston was not the first in the field. Consider the case of the future Vice-Admiral Paul Frederick Foster, a remarkable man who before 1939 was the only U.S. officer, apart from Admiral Byrd, to receive the Medal of Honor, the Navy Cross and the Distinguished Service Medal, and who by 1958 had been appointed General Manager of the Atomic Energy Commission. (Foster died in 1971.)

During the spring of 1942 Roosevelt was greatly concerned about the quality of the defense installations—and of the local commanders—in the Panama Canal Zone and in the Aleutians. As to Panama, the President had received a long message from Chiang Kai-shek warning him that Japanese aircraft carriers would be arriving in the Galápagos archipelago in March to launch a "Pearl Harbor" raid on the Canal Zone, and other reports indicated that the Japanese were intending to seize the Aleutians. That Chiang's warning was unsubstantiated

---

* In one interesting respect *Jane's* and Johnston revealed their joint ignorance. Johnston's article stated that the *Mogami*-class cruisers had guns of 6.1-inch caliber. But in his oral history Captain Smith-Hutton records that while he was Naval Attaché in Tokyo in 1939 he filed a report that the *Mogami* class actually had 8-inch guns, information which was disregarded in the Naval Department in Washington and was only confirmed at Midway (where *Mogami* herself was put out of action for two years, and her partner *Mikuma* sunk).

and the other reports premature is irrelevant. The point is that privately, and on his own executive authority, the President ordered Foster to carry out clandestine investigations in each area, giving him the highest priority for the execution of his delicate mission. And what happened? On March 7, 1942, the Washington *Post* published this paragraph.

> Mystery . . . from time to time an unidentified person keeps popping up on the White House appointment schedule, giving rise to plain and fancy rumors as to who and why he is. Commander Paul Foster, USN, identified no more specifically than as a naval officer, has been coming around for chats with the President frequently of late. Yesterday he came in again and had a lengthy session in the Executive inner sanctum. Best guesses bet that the Commander is about to be sent on a special assignment . . . which remains a secret.

In England in 1942, one might assume, the editor responsible for a passage like this would soon have found himself on the way to the Tower of London![3]

But it is one thing to peach on a President and perhaps put a confidential enterprise at risk. It is another to blow the fact that your countrymen are breaking their enemy's codes. And here, in the summer of 1942, was the rub. The Navy at first favored revenge. On June 9 the Secretary of the Navy, Frank Knox, ruled that "immediate action be taken . . . to obtain indictments under the Espionage Act (50 USC 31) against Mr. Stanley Johnston . . . and such other individuals as are implicated in the unauthorized publication of a newspaper article . . ." Early in August the convening of a grand jury in Chicago was announced. In a sense the Navy had little to lose by roasting the *Tribune*, for since the Japanese introduced JN25c on May 28 they had, in any case, been unable to break any signals and presumably when the next change occurred the enemy, alerted by the *Tribune*'s criminal indiscretion, would shift into an entirely new system, leaving the cryptanalysts with another labor of Hercules.

In August the Japanese did indeed change their codes—earlier than was usual, which looked sinister. For long, in fact, it was assumed that the alteration really had occurred as a result of the *Tribune* article. But the most intensive investigations on the Japanese side since 1945 have produced no evidence whatsoever that this was the case or that the change was more than normally prudential. Still, the Navy now knew that at least it was not faced with having to deal with an entirely different system. Though modified, the new code retained the characteristics of the broad JN25 formula. It therefore seemed to be unprofitable to fight the *Tribune* case in open court, with all that was entailed by way of producing classified evidence, the Nimitz signal, the fruits of FRUPac and Op-20-G: all the hard stuff, in fact, which would be mandatory if the case against the *Tribune* could be made to stick. So the indictment was waived and the grand jury faded.

More was involved, anyway, than a private war between Roosevelt's administration, an infuriated Navy and the egregious Colonel McCormick. The United States had allies, who were also successfully working on the Japanese and other signal traffic. On August 15, in fact, the head of the British Naval Delegation in Washington, Admiral Cunningham, warned King in writing about "the danger that details of our special intelligence methods may be compromised during the course of the trial." Fortunately that fear was unfounded: otherwise, the relationship of the alliance over military secrets might have been gravely strained. Fortunately, too, the frightening experience of those August days triggered off another sequence of events whose results were wholly beneficial.

But the British concern reflected more than an immediate fear. Behind it lay a deep and continuing suspicion about the Americans' ability to preserve security—almost a mirror image of the Americans' postwar suspicion about British laxity. By mid-1942, it should be remembered, a system for processing and distributing the intelligence acquired at Bletchley Park had been refined to such an extent that until the end of the war the Germans never discovered any valid grounds for believing that their own Enigma ciphers had been compromised—nor, for that matter, the Japanese. Thus the contrast between the *Tribune* leak and the rigid precautions of the British system was painful and, indeed, petrifying.*

It could at least be hoped that the armed services of the United States might, sooner or later, put their own house in order. Yet even

---

* One reason, for example, why the *Tribune* had felt free to publish Johnston's detailed description of the Japanese fleet as estimated by the Americans before Midway was that, at that date, the censorship code did not bar newspapers from revealing the names, or the positions, or the movements of *enemy* warships.

such good housekeeping would only be effective, particularly in regard to the protection of signal intelligence, within a wider context of public understanding and legal enforcement. In *The American Democracy* Harold Laski wrote: "There is something in the psychological climate of America which resists any ultimate regimentation of behaviour or opinion. Something always escapes the net which is thrown about the people. Non-conformity is an element in American life which is always called into being by the spectacle of conformity. There is what Emerson called 'this din of opinion and debate.' "[4] What this meant, during the war years, was that the Roosevelt administration was never able to introduce a structure of legal control capable of stifling effectively those "scoops" by journalists or outbursts by politicians which, as in the *Tribune* case, thoughtlessly or even intentionally endangered the republic. In spite of all the pressures from courts and legislators, in the face of all propaganda appeals for discretion, from time to time a terribly public society continued to go its own way.

Here, it might be said, was an extreme example of the principle of freedom of information—a principle whose perils had been forecast a century earlier by the Marquis de Custine in his remarkably prophetic account of the Tsarist regime, *La Russie en 1839*. When he asked himself why Russian diplomacy seemed to be based on more accurate information than that of Western nations he answered: "It is because our papers warn them of everything that happens and everything that is contemplated in our countries. Instead of disguising our weaknesses with prudence, we reveal them with vehemence every morning; whereas the Russians' Byzantine policy, working in the shadow, carefully conceals from us all that is thought, done and feared in their country. We proceed in broad daylight; they advance under cover: the game is one-sided."[5] As a compatriot of Custine's remarked, *plus ça change, plus c'est la même chose*.

For this gap in the American security system there is an explanation, if not a justification. During the thirties the society and indeed the government of the United States had been primarily inward-looking. The Depression's savage consequences were a sufficient cause. But one significant effect was on the general attitude toward national security: it became introspective, so that more eyes were turned on actual threats at home than on potential threats from abroad. It is indicative that during these years recruitment for the FBI—which, like MI 5, had internal security as its main responsibility—was on a far more lavish scale, and its prestige greater, than was enjoyed by the agencies concerned with intelligence about other countries and their possible menace. There was in fact no perceived need—certainly before 1939—to take counterintelligence precautions in a meaningful way. J. Edgar Hoover might keep his tabs on the Commies, but there were no stringent laws against leaks capable of endangering the nation's safety.

And so, compared with the draconian restrictions imposed on the British in the Second World War, even then American security was vitiated in two debilitating respects. First, such protective legislation as was attempted always contained loopholes through which, with the aid of a skillful attorney, the miscreant could too frequently manage to crawl. Secondly, there was *and still is* within the American legal edifice no room where cases involving the security of the state can be examined *in camera*, without the presence of the public or the media and with no possibility that the proceedings will be reported. Here was the difficulty that haunted the Navy and the high men of Washington during the *Tribune* affair, for if trial by grand jury had been pushed to its limit there was no way that the cryptanalysts' penetration of JN25 could have been shrouded. That was how it would have to be. Since the British had the capability of resorting to secret trials, and the backing of stern laws vigorously applied "in defence of realm," their amazed concern was well founded.

However, at least the soldiers and sailors could try to plug some of the holes in the dike. As early as June 13, 1942, the Chairman of the Joint Intelligence Committee reported to the Joint Chiefs of Staff on an urgent review by the heads of the FBI, ONI and the Military Intelligence Service "of present and prospective cryptanalytical activities, in order to assure the maximum security and efficiency in the conduct of this essential work."

The gist of their findings was that too many cooks were stirring the broth: in effect, that too many people "in the know" maximized the risk of leaks. They recommended, therefore, that all agencies engaged in cryptanalytical activities other than the ONI, MIS and FBI should be stopped in their tracks. The Joint Chiefs took the point and recommended to Roosevelt accordingly. As a result, on July 8 the President issued a diktat.

MEMORANDUM FOR THE
DIRECTOR OF THE BUDGET

I am enclosing a copy of a memorandum received today from the Chief of Staff and the Commander-in-Chief of the U.S. Fleet. I agree with them. Will you please have the proper instructions issued discontinuing the cryptanalytical units in the offices of the Director of Censorship, the Federal Communications Commission and the Strategic Services. If you are aware of any other agencies having services of this character, will you please have them discontinued also.

F.D.R.

In one brief paragraph, the President had committed to the intelligence directors of his armed forces and the national security services something approaching that centralized control over cryptanalysis which had existed in England since the outbreak of war. Imperfections still remained, but a notable advance had been achieved—thanks in no small degree to the self-righteous Colonel McCormick, hoist by his own petard.

Since naval security was most at risk during this stage of the Pacific war, Admiral King moved fast—even anticipating the President. On June 20 he issued to the commanders in chief of the Pacific, Southwest Pacific and Atlantic fleets a long instruction entitled "control of dissemination and use of radio intelligence." The first important directive of its kind to American *operational* commanders, its imperious authority and broad scope made it an admirable forerunner of those historic memoranda sent by General Marshall to Eisenhower and MacArthur in 1944 after a comprehensive procedure for handling "special intelligence" had been agreed upon by the British and the Americans before the invasion of Europe.

The *Tribune* was evidently on King's mind, for in an opening broadside about the unique value of radio intelligence he stated that "any disclosures in the past with regard to the source of radio intelligence have invariably resulted in an immediate change in the enemy's communications and the consequent loss of weeks or months of painstaking effort on the part of our radio intelligence personnel." He therefore laid down strict regulations about avoiding the disclosure of such intelligence in its pure state, or of its sources, to subordinate commanders; about care over using such intelligence to gain a tactical advantage in battle if by so doing the source of information would be compromised; and about scrupulous security—all copies of sensitive signals should be burned as soon as possible after reading, and on ships at sea, particularly in action, all telltale documents should be destroyed if there was the least risk of their falling into enemy hands.*

At least the Navy now had a lucid rule book, issued by a commander whose notorious passion for discipline was once defined by his daughter: "He is the most even-tempered man in the Navy. He is always in a rage." By mid-1942 the Americans, often so swiftly educated by error, were adopting *at least in principle* some of the long-established procedures of the British. On June 30, in fact, a standing joint committee was set up between the War Department, the Navy and the FBI (including names now well known to the reader, like Friedman, Carter Clarke, Wenger and Kramer) to coordinate and exercise surveillance over all work in the field of radio interception and cryptanalysis.†

King's directive, paragraph (c), laid down specifically that all special intelligence "should be passed without reference to its secret source and should contain, somewhere near the beginning of the message, the word ULTRA or the word ZEAL." In practice Ultra, hereafter, was generally used as the denominator of material derived from breaking the Japanese naval and, later, military codes (in distinction from Magic, which covered material obtained via the Japanese diplomatic ciphers), much as Ultra was used by the British to denote the special intelligence obtained at Bletchley from penetration of the German Enigma and other cryptographic sources. It would be pleasant to be

---

* In this context the name of Captain John P. Cromwell, commander of the submarine *Sculpin*, demands an honorable mention. On November 19, 1942, *Sculpin* attacked a convoy, was depth-charged to the surface and sunk by gunfire. Though forty-two survivors were collected and interrogated, Cromwell refused to abandon ship, preferring to drown rather than to risk revealing what he knew about the link between "special intelligence" and submarine operations. His epitaph is: "He chose to die to protect the Ultra secret." For this he was posthumously awarded the Congressional Medal of Honor.

† In the spring of 1940 the British set up the "Y Subcommittee" to "cover all types of wireless activity" (Hinsley, p. 91). In 1942 the level of overall surveillance was raised by the creation of the Signals Intelligence Board, presided over by "C" (the head of MI 6 and the Secret Service) and attended by the Directors of Intelligence of the Army, the Navy and the RAF as well as Commander Travis, in charge at Bletchley Park. Under the Board the "Y Subcommittee" continued as a technical branch reviewing and coordinating "all types of wireless activity." The office of its secretary was in the headquarters of MI 6 on Broadway, near to that of "C," with whom he was in regular contact. The Americans never achieved so integrated a system for controlling signal intelligence.

able to assert that the admiral's instructions and authority provided final and absolute protection for the Americans' signal intelligence system.

But it was not as simple as that. Many factors, some innocent and some malign, continued to threaten the compromising of Ultra and Magic throughout the war years—certainly up to the point when American forces had achieved such an ascendancy over the Japanese that the loss of signal intelligence, though still damaging, would no longer have been disastrous. And these were factors quite separate from anything *inherent* in the use of information obtained by cryptanalysis. Every belligerent nation, the Japanese no less than the British and the Americans, the Germans and the Italians, monitored their enemy's radio traffic to catch the slightest evidence in its contents that their own codes or ciphers had been broken. Such a possibility was always a concern at Op-20-G, FRUPac and the other agencies, though we now know that the Japanese, like the Germans, never discovered that their "secret" signals were wide open. The real threats, in fact, were of a different order.

The first order was that of magnitude. As early as the summer of 1944 it was officially estimated that at least 50,000 members of the Army and Navy had handled cryptographic material and several thousand—exclusive of those involved in interception—had been specifically concerned with cryptanalysis. It is fair to say that in spite of an intense awareness of the problem, and careful precautions, and the stern instructions stemming from King and Marshall, it was not until that same summer that the embryo appeared of a satisfactory means of surveillance. This was the introduction in both the European and Pacific theaters of "Ultra advisers," evolved along the lines of Bletchley's Special Liaison Units after consultation with the British: the advisers being handpicked men of keen intelligence, attached to all command headquarters, who had the dual responsibility of passing on Ultra information and also keeping a constant check on security. Their strength lay in the fact that their allegiance was directed to, and their authority derived from, the High Command in Washington and not the individual headquarters to which they were posted. Even so, it was only the Army and the Army Air Force that, under Marshall's aegis, adopted the Ultra advisers.

The problem of security was increased by the factor of mass multiplied by distance. The Pacific theater was so enormous. The units of all three services were so scattered, so separated by hundreds or thousands of miles, so often switched from one area or command to another, that such common-sense precautions as the prevention of loose talk, or the thoughtless issuing of orders which disclosed an Ultra source, were extraordinarily—and understandably—difficult to make watertight. And then, sometimes, the services themselves were wantonly naïve.

It was an absolute rule among the British, broken very rarely indeed, that those who had been involved in Ultra must never be allowed to risk capture by the enemy.* Without repeating this rule precisely, Admiral King broadly made the same point in both his original set of instructions and the revised, expanded version which he issued to all commanders in chief on March 25, 1943. Nevertheless, we meet such indefensible episodes as the case of Lieutenant Ralph Cory of the U.S. Marines.

Before the war Cory had been a civilian engaged in consular work in Japan. By a natural process he found himself drafted to Op-20-G in Washington, and fully involved in the cryptanalytical operations at the Navy Department's offices on Constitution Avenue. During the Congressional Inquiry, in fact, Commander Kramer testified (Part 9, p. 3951) that Cory was the officer who translated the disputed "winds executive" message of December 4, 1941. But he got sick of what he called pencil-pushing, and joined the Marines. (That he was allowed to enlist seems sufficiently reprehensible.) On August 12, 1942, he was a member of a fighting patrol of the 5th Marines on Guadalcanal, included as a Japanese linguist because the patrol's mission was to round up disorganized enemy groups thought to be starving in the jungle. The official history of the Marine Corps describes how the patrol landed on the wrong beach, came under heavy machine-gun fire and lost all but three survivors who swam to safety. Cory's friend in Washington, Edward Van Der Rhoer, who dined with him on his last night at home, recalls that "one of the swimmers thought he saw a soldier thrust his bayonet into Cory's body, stretched out on the sand where he had first fallen." But suppose Cory had been taken alive, tortured in the exquisite Japanese way, and talked![6]

At times there was certainly too much talking. Take the famous

---

* But the author has personal knowledge of two officers who, in different theaters, worked behind the enemy lines after they had handled Ultra intelligence. One, it is true, later discovered that one of his men had orders to shoot him if capture seemed imminent.

occasion when Admiral Yamamoto's aircraft was intercepted in April 1943 and shot down by American long-range fighters over Bougainville, as a result of a decoded signal which betrayed his route.* It was impossible to conceal so startling a success or, as it turned out, to prevent speculation about how it had been devised. Once again Captain Holmes was a witness of the consequences.

> The apprehensions of the cryptographers were amply justified, because security for handling Ultra information on Guadalcanal was woefully inadequate, and too many people learned about it. It became an item of widespread interservice gossip that the dramatic interception of Yamamoto's plane had been contrived through broken Japanese codes. It was a miracle that the story did not break in American newspapers.[7]

A miracle indeed, particularly as General MacArthur, with no justification, was more than eager to lay public claim to the laurels for his own command: fancying, as he put it, that he could "almost hear the rising crescendo of sound from the thousands of glistening white skeletons at the bottom of Pearl Harbor." (The casualties at Pearl, as a matter of interest, were 2,403 killed *from all causes*.) However, MacArthur also noted regretfully that "Washington lauded the action as one of the most important bags of the war, but labeled it top secret and forbade its publication, fearing it would jeopardize the work of the cryptanalytic division."

But the press was not always so repressible. There was at least one leak about Guadalcanal. On November 11, 1942, the Washington *Post* reported that the Marines under General Vandegrift "captured the Japanese landing code, and he knew when and where they were coming in." Five days later a far more delicate issue was raised by a paragraph in *Time* magazine. Referring to the radio communications from a certain clandestine station in South America, it stated:

> Its complicated coded and transposed messages were intercepted and turned over to the U.S. experts, who broke the code. From then on, officials in Washington followed carefully the work of Nazi spies in Argentina, Chile, Peru, Colombia, Mexico and even in the U.S.

---

* For details of this episode, see p. 187.

One has to stretch the imagination to visualize the *Times* in London, at that particular date, announcing—as was the case—that MI 5 was feeding misinformation to Germany through double agents, assisted by knowledge supplied from Bletchley Park as a result of the breaking of the Abwehr's Enigma cipher and the British ability to read the Abwehr's secret signals interchanged between its stations in Germany, Spain, Portugal and elsewhere! Commenting on *Time* magazine's disclosure, Wenger in a formal protest from Op-20-G observed sourly that a Magic intercept, in the same week, of a Japanese message from Madrid to Tokyo declared: "From my experience of the past three years, all leakage of the war plans of the United Nations can be laid at the door of the United States." Though this was a wild and unsupportable exaggeration, it contained just enough truth to hurt. As Wenger said, "The unfortunate Chicago *Tribune* affair should have taught us a good lesson but it apparently did not, for the publicity continues."

In fact, the South American revelations were intolerable. That the whole continent was riddled with Nazi (and Japanese) agents and sympathizers, and had been since long before Pearl Harbor, was well known to the U.S. security authorities and particularly to the FBI—since J. Edgar Hoover had managed to retain Latin America as part of his bailiwick, even after the establishment of the Office of Strategic Services. That clandestine radio signals were being intercepted and broken was also true. But what could not be explained publicly, or used to stifle the press, was the practical fact that in certain instances it was actually rewarding to allow a hostile station to continue to transmit even after its existence had been detected, partly because further useful intelligence might be obtained from its transmissions. But there was another good reason, indicated in a memorandum from Op-20-G of December 17, 1942. "It should be pointed out that although certain exposures have already been made concerning these clandestine operations, nevertheless the cryptographic systems employed are still being used on at least two other circuits, and it would be inimical to our further cryptanalytical operations should further disclosures result."

In other words, if the geese are laying golden eggs, why kill them? Yet months afterward, in July 1943, the Pan-American Union in Washington published an English translation of the *Annual Report Submitted to the Governments of the American Republics* by the so-called Emergency Advisory Committee for Political Defense in Monte-video. This translation not only described in full the interception of clandestine radio messages but actually added documented appendices which printed the deciphered signals of Axis agents. For Chile alone, seventy-one deciphered signals were quoted. The record of four Axis groups in the Argentine, each with its own secret radio transmitter, was also supplied. Moreover, these appendices appeared only in the *English* version, not in the Spanish original.

It is no wonder that, as an ending to the war seemed to be visible—if only at a distance—in June 1944 a confidential paper on the Need for New Legislation Against Unauthorized Disclosure of Communications Activities reviewed the whole sad story of a terribly public society from before the publication of Yardley's *Black Chamber* right down to the latest wartime leak, and ended on a despondent note. The construction of codes and ciphers, it pointed out, had now become so sophisticated that "solutions which once could be achieved by relatively few experts and by simple means in a short period of time, now require complex machinery, large forces of personnel and extensive time-consuming research." The ballooning of Bletchley Park from the modest establishment of GCCS in 1939 to a vast organization, relying on intricate technologies and a staff of thousands, made this truth as obvious in England as it was in Washington. "The problem of obtaining intelligence in time to be of operational value," the report asserted, "may soon be almost insurmountable." If that was the case even if security was kept tight, in wartime conditions, and nevertheless the sieve still sometimes leaked, what would be the situation in peacetime when emergency restrictions were lifted but national safety would still have to be assured?

The answer to that question is written into the postwar history of the United States.* It must not be further pursued in a chapter which, already, has made a large chronological leap ahead. Nevertheless, the evidence it contains—only a part of a bulging portfolio—provides an essential background for the continuing story of signal intelligence in the Pacific. As the author wrote of Bletchley Park in his *Ultra Goes to War*, "like the intellectuals and technologists who struggled at Los Alamos to perfect the atom bomb before the enemy stole a march,

---

* And, of course, of Great Britain—Philby, Burgess, Maclean, Blunt and Blake are but a few names in the catalogue of treason.

the cryptanalysts and their colleagues were daily haunted by *to-morrow*," by the fear that some failure of security might put the enemy on the alert and cause him to protect his secret signals by some new, and perhaps impenetrable, system of code or cipher. This was equally true of FRUPac, or Op-20-G, or the Army's experts at Arlington Hall. They lived on a razor's edge.

And it is ironical that this chapter should have opened with the affair of the Chicago *Tribune*'s article in June 1942 and the ripples of concern which ran, as a result, from the cryptanalysts right up to the Joint Chiefs of Staff and across the Atlantic to London. For it was at this very moment that the Japanese altered their JN25 code and left the Americans without what, at Midway, had proved to be their most powerful weapon.

Does the road wind up-hill all the way?
Yes, to the very end.

CHAPTER SIX

The Salt Mines

*True wisdom is shown by those who make careful use of their
advantages in the knowledge that things will change.*
    Thucydides, *The Peloponnesian War*

A COMMENT MADE over two thousand years earlier by the historian of the Peloponnesian War might well have been taken as a motto by all those who worked on signal intelligence during the war in the Pacific. For things *would* change: the alteration of the JN25 code system by the Japanese in August 1942 was merely an instance of routine changes in their codes and ciphers which all combatant countries prudently make from time to time, thus producing a constant challenge to the cryptanalysts of their opponents. But the record of the Pacific war amply demonstrates that such challenges, of a routine character, presented no fundamental problems for the Americans. The graver danger, as described in the previous chapter, was that some unfortunate breach of security—whether in the press, in public statements or through laxity in the armed services—might put the Japanese on the alert and cause them to introduce radical rather than routine alterations in their cryptographic systems. This was the permanent nightmare.

It was intensified by the enormous expansion of the American signal intelligence agencies from 1942 onward—virtually a nonstop process until the end of the war. The larger the numbers of men and women recruited, the more elaborate the technology involved, the more complicated and comprehensive the organizational structure, the wider the range of penetration into signals not simply of the Japanese diplomats but also of their Army, Navy and Air Force—the greater the need for a thick cloak of security to cover these secret and manifold activities.

That expansion cannot be easily seen as a whole. Sometimes it occurred spasmodically. Sometimes developments were happening independently but simultaneously in both the U.S. Army and the U.S. Navy. And all the time that the expansion was proceeding, a fighting war was ablaze in several Pacific theaters. It would thus be difficult, and indeed confusing, to attempt to show how the Magic and Ultra intelligence actually affected operations in that war while, at the same time, describing in a piecemeal fashion how agencies for producing, processing and distributing the intelligence were created and extended. This chapter, therefore, steps aside from the chronological sequence of the whole book and contains, as a background for what is to follow, a survey of the main developments in American signal intelligence, from the point of view of its organization and expanding structure, between 1942 and 1945.

The breaking of the Purple cipher and the brilliant entry, before Midway, into the Japanese naval code were proof enough that the intellectual base of American cryptanalysis was strong. Yet once the nation was plunged into war several weaknesses were immediately apparent—apparent, indeed, from the very day of the Pearl Harbor attack. In spite of prewar recruitment and farsighted training there was still a critical shortage of personnel in all areas of signal intelligence. Procedures, techniques and suitable staff for evaluating and processing that intelligence were scarce or nonexistent. No system was even on the drawing board for disseminating it to commands in the field, or for ensuring that it was securely handled there. Many senior officers in all services—very significantly, many regular *intelligence* officers in all services—either knew nothing of this secret source or tended to ridicule what little they knew. There was much to learn, and much to be done.

Indeed, a revolution was necessary, as may be gauged from the experience of a single lieutenant in the Signal Corps, Howard W. Brown. During the summer of 1941 Brown was Operations Officer in the Army's little Sigint unit in the Philippines, which, headed by the able Major Joe Sherr, consisted of no more than six sergeants, three corporals and six privates. By an agreement between the Army and the Navy, reached at a conference in Manila in May 1941, the Navy's own Sigint unit, Cast, was concentrating (in its tunnel on Corregidor) on breaking Japanese diplomatic traffic, since it alone possessed a Purple machine. Sheer's team did the interception. What is astonishing is the slowness—and therefore the inefficiency—of the routine as Howard's own account reveals.[1] He is describing the method for passing over intercepted signals and their translations between his own unit and Cast.

> The normal procedure for handling exchange information was as follows: Major Sherr or I would take the sealed bag into Manila in time to meet the harbor boat arriving from Corregidor at 1000; hand our bag to the code room at Fort Santiago, Manila (a large vault built in one of the old Spanish dungeons); open the bag and extract the decoded messages; arrange decoded messages in a folder, by points of origin, attaching any message from previous days which had bearing on, or reference to, the current messages; take the folder to G-2 (or in his absence to his assistant), and let him read the file; return to the code room and file the translations by point of origin and date.
>
> When Headquarters, United States Armed Forces in the Far East, was established in July 1941, the above procedure was altered in that the file was first taken to General Sutherland, Chief of Staff to General MacArthur, and if it contained anything which he thought might be of interest to General MacArthur (which it frequently did) he would ask us to take it in to the General. Some of the General's off-the-record comments were classic.
>
> From a security standpoint this system was perfect. . . . The serious drawback was the time delay. For instance, a message intercepted on the first day would be sent to Corregidor on the second day and the translation received from the Navy on the third day if in a readable system. Sundays and holidays usually delayed delivery another day because the Navy usually took these days off.

And so the system continued until the Japanese attacked. It may have been secure, but if it be considered as a means of operating in wartime one might be forgiven for judging that they did things quicker in the days of the Pony Express.

During the weeks after the war began, Brown strove hectically to improvise, from bits and pieces of the sparse equipment available, any means of interception which would enable him to listen in to the radio traffic of the Japanese Air Force. Though he could not translate what he heard, by identifying individual call signs he could often

calculate when a raid was imminent and warn a threatened airfield—
only to discover, too often, that in these early days the U.S. Air Force
had a blithe contempt for Sigint and disregarded his prophetic voice,
with the result that precious planes were destroyed on the ground.
It was war on a do-it-yourself basis. Still, he became so expert at
predicting the appearance of the reconnaissance aircraft which regularly visited Corregidor, and so won the confidence of the antiaircraft
gunners, that "we were often able to tell them what 'Foto Joe' was up
to, and at times could tell them at what time, and from where, he was
likely to appear. The AA batteries would load and cock their guns, and
pull the triggers as 'Foto Joe' came by trying to gain altitude. This information and action accounted for about six planes." Before the end,
a capture of Japanese code books on Bataan made it possible to set
up a small radio intelligence office in Malinta Tunnel on Corregidor
which, with four receivers and the occasional use of a naval direction
finder, spent a profitable time monitoring the signal circuits of the
enemy's army and air units in the Philippines, providing early warning
about incoming raids, and even registering Japanese losses. "We were
able to confirm 'probables,' or reports of safe arrival, and the extent of
damage, by such messages as: 'Ikamura is landing in the water, looks
like he won't be home,' or 'Taji landed at Nichols with one motor
burning.' "

On the day that MacArthur departed, leaving General Wainwright
to make the final stand, the general summoned Brown to his office
shortly before midnight, shook his hand and said, "I want to con-
gratulate you. Captain Hart tells me that you have discovered a
system to solve Japanese messages. I am proud of you, and want to
thank you." But, unlike Wainwright, Brown too left the Philippines.
After an abortive attempt to establish an intercept station on Mindanao, on April 14 he was flown off to Darwin in Australia, a passenger
in a moribund B-17, one of whose engines was dead while another was
spouting oil. "When we landed, more than one big strong man kissed
the ground."

These experiences of Lieutenant Brown (who ultimately became a
colonel handling radio intelligence on the staff of MacArthur's Chief
Signal Officer) serve as vivid evidence of the low base from which the
Americans set about building up a comprehensive Sigint system in
the Pacific theater whose tentacles, in their ultimate expansion, would

reach out to—and indeed over—the threshold of Japan. In the United States, meanwhile, the backup force of those working in the Army's cryptographic services had a similar mushroom growth. On Pearl Harbor day 181 people were working in the Washington headquarters of the Signal Intelligence Service: at the end, 7,000. On that day, 21 people were operating 13 IBM tabulating machines: in 1945, 1,275 operators controlled 407 machines.[2]

What happened in Washington—for the Navy's installations there expanded to a similar degree—was characteristic of the American response in wartime. Sometimes the reaction might be slow, but once a genuine need was perceived the whole resources of a nation rich in manpower and technology would be ruthlessly and efficiently applied in the search for an answer. A country whose ingenuity was capable of launching a new Liberty ship every few days tackled the problem of codes and ciphers with the same constructive energy. The British at Bletchley Park, the Germans with their B-Dienst, evolved tools for signal intelligence of the highest quality, but in sheer quantitative application the Americans were pre-eminent.*

After Pearl Harbor the Army's Signal Intelligence Service† took over the entire responsibility for producing and handling Magic, the intelligence acquired from reading the Purple diplomatic cipher— thus terminating the cumbrous system which had split this vital work between the Army and the Navy. Such a task, together with a con- tinuing attack on the Japanese Army's code systems and other targets, involved an immense amplification of Section B—which contained the cryptanalysts and intelligence assessors. With many other ac- cumulating responsibilities—training, research and development of new equipment, monitoring the security of the Army's own radio transmissions—SIS's quarters in the old Munitions Building in Wash- ington became cramped and inadequate. By August 1942 a new home had been found, for the Signal Corps "purchased the commodious and at that time sequestered domain of a private school for girls, Arlington

---

* In due course the Americans were actually producing for Bletchley Park the "bombe," or machines for automatically processing cryptanalytical data.
† In mid-1942 SIS was renamed Signal Security Service, and a year later it became the Signal Security Agency. For convenience, the original title of SIS is retained throughout the text.

Hall, in the Virginia suburbs across the Potomac." Like Bletchley Park, "the Hall" put a great strain on the mental stamina of its work force. They christened it "The Salt Mines." With some sardonic relevance the old tag was applied, "You don't have to be crazy to work here, but it helps."[3]

Not to be outdone, the Navy's Op-20-G also found itself a girls' school. For the first eight months of the war it continued to be housed in the Navy Department building on Constitution Avenue, that vast temporary structure erected in 1918 whose added excrescences still left it too small for its new population. Walter Whitehill, a historian in the Office of Naval Records, recalled: "In few places short of the palace of Versailles before 1789 could such widely divergent characters have jostled elbow in corridors. In most parts of the building, flag officers en route to vital conferences collided with whistling messengers delivering mail by tricycle, ensigns' wives bringing babies to the dispensary, plumbers with tools, civil servants in search of a cup of coffee, and laborers engaged in the perennial task of shifting somebody's desk and filing case from one place to another." And so, for peace, quiet and more elbow room, Op-20-G moved farther out of town, to the ivy-clad Mount Vernon Academy* by Nebraska Avenue where, in classrooms and newly built annexes, the code breakers continued until the end of the war.

One who shared this migration was Edward Van Der Rhoer, whose evocative memoirs, *Deadly Magic,* capture the bizarre atmosphere of a world where, as at Bletchley Park, hundreds of civilian intellectuals found themselves penned up, under a novel discipline, with the residue of the old regular system. For this, Van Der Rhoer noted, was "the time when the big wartime expansion of Op-20-G really began."

As at Arlington Hall—and at Bletchley—the background of the newcomers was varied. Van Der Rhoer himself had studied Japanese privately and in a special course at Harvard before joining Op-20-G. Many of those assigned, he noticed, "had been drawn intellectually and aesthetically toward the Japanese language, culture and history; many had spent years off and on in Japan, which had also become involved in their personal lives through the accident of birth or by

---

* Where, by an appropriate coincidence, the daughter of one of the father figures of American communications, Alexander Graham Bell, was educated.

marriage." And perhaps he defined a discovery shared by many of his colleagues and co-workers on both sides of the Atlantic when he wrote:

> It seemed to me as if, without knowing it, I had been preparing all my life for this work. I had always been fond of higher mathematics as well as all sorts of problem solving. I enjoyed the most sophisticated riddles, crossword puzzles and acrostics. I also liked the intricate calculations that went into chess. And in foreign language I had sought, in reality, to break a kind of code, to get at an inner meaning represented by symbols that were unknown to me in the beginning. Now I realized that my mind and personality had a special affinity with codebreaking.

Language skills were at a premium. The prewar arrangements for training officers to read and speak Japanese (described in Chapter 2) had produced a small, invaluable crop: but by 1942 what was required was a huge and instant harvest. And the same was as pressingly true in all the other fields of signal intelligence. The Army's major response was to open, in October 1942, a Cryptographic School at Vint Hill Farms in Virginia, where men and women were trained in cryptanalysis, traffic analysis and equipment maintenance. (The Signal Corps Unit Training Centers at Fort Monmouth and Camp Crowder developed similar programs.) The Navy, hungry for officers with all these specialties, was particularly short of Japanese-speakers, not simply for its shore-based signal intelligence units, but also because its ships were at sea and in action: aboard them, in steadily increasing numbers, went intelligence officers trained to handle Ultra material or—of high importance in many operations—either to translate immediately Japanese tactical signals intercepted by the fleet's own service or actually to listen in to voice exchanges between Japanese airmen as they flew in to the attack. At Boulder, Colorado, able young men by the hundred—mainly from the universities—took an intensive course crammed into eleven months. The crash course in Japanese for Bletchley Park was even shorter—six months—but was perhaps more basic. "For the Boulder Boys . . . much of the material that would have to be translated in the future was bound to be highly specialized. In addition to a general knowledge of the language, Navy translators had to become familiar with Japanese place names, Japanese ship names, the Japanese naval order of battle, and with the *Kanji* peculiar to naval technology. Available dictionaries were general, and most of them were obsolete."[4]

The normal presence at Boulder of about ten student-officers from the Royal Navy was but a small instance of the steadily enlarged relationship between the Allies throughout this secret realm. In *Very Special Intelligence* Patrick Beesly has described how (to a large degree through British persistence) the Admiralty's Operational Intelligence Center gradually formed the most intimate links with the signal intelligence service set up in Washington (and in Canada) for the purpose of defeating the U-boats in the Atlantic. But similar interconnections occurred in many spheres. GCCS representatives worked beside their colleagues at Arlington and Mount Vernon Academy. Others would fly in from England to exchange views, both learning and introducing new ideas. The ultimate Anglo-American cooperation and, indeed, integration over a worldwide system for handling Ultra intelligence was—as will be indicated later in this chapter—so phenomenally successful that an impression might be derived of absolute harmony. But here, as in other respects, right up to the level of planning Grand Strategy, though the end was usually reached the Allies' journey was frequently rugged. On both sides there were fixed ideas, suspicions, fears about security and inevitable beliefs that "we do it best" to be overcome.

An illuminating example is provided by Professor G. C. McVittie.* At Bletchley Park throughout the war McVittie was the chief expert in the deciphering and assessing of the enemy's meteorological signals. For obvious reasons, in war as in peace—only with more urgent reasons, usually, in war—great numbers of weather reports are made daily by radio from many sources and circulated, frequently by radio, from the meteorological stations responsible for collecting and synthesizing the relevant information. In war such intercepts have two particular values. In the European theater, for example, German, Italian—and Russian—Met. signals supplied essential information otherwise unobtainable about the continental weather systems: in the Pacific it is evident that similar information from Japanese sources was beyond price for the U.S. Navy and Air Force. But since

* After the war McVittie was, successively, professor of mathematics at the University of London (1948–52), professor of astronomy at the University of Illinois (1952–72) and honorary professor of theoretical astronomy at the University of Kent.

meteorological information, by its nature, had to be distributed quickly and widely, it was often passed simultaneously in lower-grade codes which had been broken and, to other recipients, in higher-grade codes or ciphers which were resisting attack. Thus if the cryptanalysts could identify in a code as yet unbroken some passage of meteorological information which had already been decoded from a lowei grade system, they had in their hands a lever to prize open signals in the higher code by which they had so far been defeated.

At Bletchley Park they were expert and experienced in both these practices. The German, Italian and Russian meteorological codes had all been broken at an early stage in the war. In the summer of 1942 Professor McVittie crossed the Atlantic to share the expertise so gained, but his record of what happened shows that it was not a case of roses, roses all the way.

During my visit to Washington in the summer of 1942 I found that Japanese Met. ciphers were the preserve of the cryptographic organization of the U.S. Navy. There were two main ciphers. The first had been named JN36, the second JN37. In January 1943, Tiltman* reported after a visit to Washington that the U.S. Navy was ignoring JN37 because they claimed to be getting all they wanted by reading JN36. Our experience of Met. ciphers in the European theatre was that a continuous flow of deciphered synoptics [i.e., relevant data] could be provided only by reading as many different ciphers as possible and even then the service might occasionally be interrupted by a simultaneous change of key. It was therefore decided that Philip Howse and J. Gillis should start work on JN37.

By May 1943 they had progressed sufficiently for us to contemplate the distribution of deciphered synoptics to forecasters in the Japanese war area. Enough material on which to work could not be intercepted in Europe and therefore we concluded that the west coast of Canada would be the best location for a production unit. Negotiations continued during 1943 with, finally, a visit from Canadian Defence Minister Ralston in December 1943, when I pressed strongly for the setting up of a unit similar to the BP Met.

---

* Among his many contributions to the work at Bletchley Park, and to Anglo-American cooperation, Brigadier Tiltman was notably responsible for the expansion of the Japanese Section at Bletchley.

group to deal with JN37. In January 1944, the Canadian Government agreed to this plan. During January 1944 the attitude of the Americans, as reported by GCCS's mission in Washington, remained unclear. The U.S. Army and Navy were at first reported to be going to make a concerted attack on JN37 but later we heard that they had agreed "in principle" to our doing it in Canada.

Howse and I left on February 9, 1944, by the *Queen Elizabeth* to New York. On arrival in Washington we entered into a period of confused negotiation with the Canadians and with the U.S. Navy cryptographic organization. By the latter part of March Sir Edward Travis (head of GCCS) and John Tiltman had also come to Washington and we finally discovered that General Marshall and Admiral King had decided "a long time ago" that the U.S. Navy was to break JN37 and that they would go ahead whatever we and the Canadians did. I felt that we had to retire as gracefully as possible from the competition and this was also Sir Edward Travis' conclusion. However, it was agreed that Howse should stay in Washington and work with the U.S. Navy cryptographers using the method which he and Gillis had devised for breaking JN37. Howse remained in Washington until the early part of 1946. On my return to BP in April 1944 I found that Gillis and seven members of the BP Met. group who had formed the nucleus of the subgroup working on JN37, refused to work on any aspect of Japanese Met. Gillis left the BP Met. group to work elsewhere in BP.[5]

In the Anglo-American alliance there were indeed many such rough edges. Yet had this particular episode been characteristic of the partnership forged by the Allies in the matter of signal intelligence, or had the U.S. Navy's cryptanalysts always behaved in the somewhat cumbrous fashion it suggests, the end-product would have been very different from what was so effectively achieved. As to the Navy, one has but to think of Midway, and of the remarkable—and rapid—breakthrough into JN25 by the staff of Op-20-G's outstation on Hawaii, to reassure oneself that Professor McVittie's recollection of an apparently uncertain and fumbling organization may represent a part but cannot stand for the whole of the manifest truth.

Yet the Navy itself suffered from internecine conflict. Writing to Walter Lord about Midway in 1966, Rochefort affirmed: "Generally I accept the 'War College Theory' that Intelligence does not provide estimates of the enemy intentions, but in the case of Hypo at that time—due to the individuals concerned and their long experience and unique abilities—in my opinion they were capable of producing (and on the only occasion when asked to did produce) a very good estimate of Japanese intentions." The claim is undeniable: in any case, War College Theories are not tables of absolute law handed down from Sinai. But in Washington in 1942 there was a different perception.

Some in high quarters, as has been seen, had identified other objectives for Yamamoto: California, perhaps, or the southern Pacific. Some even believed, uneasily, that Hypo might have been hoodwinked by an elaborate game of radio deception on the part of the Japanese. But there was no balm for the doubters when they were proved wrong: their reaction was rather to feel chagrin, and even jealousy. More to the point was the presence in Washington of the two brothers Redman —Joseph, the Director of Naval Communications, and John, who worked in the Office of Chief of Naval Operations. During the spring and summer of 1942 the Redmans, and others of like mind, effectively conducted a power struggle as a result of which the Navy's central cryptanalytical unit in Washington, and its outposts Hypo and Cast (now in Australia), were transferred with Admiral King's approval from a loose relationship with the Office of Naval Intelligence to the firm control of Redman's Office of Naval Communications.

Rochefort became the sacrificial victim. He was quirky, touchy, a difficult customer, manifestly brilliant but "temperamental." The relationship between Hypo and Washington became overheated, and the atmosphere was not improved by a proposal, endorsed by Nimitz himself, that Rochefort should be awarded the Navy's highest award for a noncombatant, the Distinguished Service Medal. So Rochefort was summoned back to Washington and put in the icebox. Somehow the recommendation for an award "got lost," and after he applied for sea duty this idiosyncratic but scintillating cryptanalyst was *limogé*: that is, removed from the scene by a posting to the Floating Drydock Training Center at Tiburon, California.

After the war Captain Holmes acquainted Nimitz with the facts, and the admiral responded immediately by recommending Rochefort for the Distinguished Service Medal—a request rejected by the Assistant Secretary of the Navy on the ground that the time had passed for considering such proposals. When Rochefort himself collaborated in the preparation of his "oral history" for the invaluable series recorded by the Oral History Department of the Naval Institute at Annapolis, he presumably supplied circumstantial evidence about his side of the story. Unfortunately, his history was impounded by the National Security Agency and, at the time of writing, is still held by the NSA as a classified document. Perhaps it is best that a veil remains drawn. Captain Holmes ended his recollection of the affair with a suitable epitaph: "It was not the individual for whom the bell tolled but the Navy died a little."[6]

When Holmes compiled at the war's end his official and—at that time—confidential Narrative of the Combat Intelligence Center, Joint Intelligence Center, Pacific Ocean Areas, it was suitably "forwarded for information" by Nimitz as CINCPAC to Admiral King as the head of the Navy, with a covering note which declared that "Captain Holmes had an unequalled opportunity to observe and take part in the development throughout the war of Intelligence for High Command. He played an able part in this development and his recorded observations and opinions are therefore of unusual value." That endorsement still stands. Indeed, the value of this document and of Captain Holmes's more personal narrative, *Double-Edged Secrets,* is unique, for nowhere else is there to be found a more authoritative account of how the signal intelligence outstation at Hawaii, diminutive at the time of Pearl Harbor, grew into an enormous tri-service intelligence factory capable of feeding the Americans' combat forces as they too expanded, advanced and splayed out over the Pacific Ocean Areas.

The first extension occurred in July 1942 when the Intelligence Center, Pacific Ocean Area (ICPOA), was established at Pearl Harbor: primarily a naval unit servicing the fleet, but with liaison to the Army and Marine Corps. Under its wing nestled the radio intelligence team, Hypo, and the Combat Intelligence Unit headed by Holmes himself— with the function of screening and passing on to appropriate users intelligence of operational value. Holmes was in intimate touch with Hypo: his provision of Ultra intelligence to ComSubPac, the officer commanding the U.S. submarines working out of Pearl Harbor, was of particular value during the opening phase of submarine operations when Ultra was treated like some delicate and fragile object, and a confidential relationship between the senior officers in intelligence and in fighting units was of critical importance.* Until September 1942 Rochefort was left in charge of ICPOA as well as Hypo—one of the sources, doubtless, of friction with Washington—until in September he was replaced in the larger command.

Then, on September 7, 1943, and just in time for the effective reassertion of American military power in the Central and South West Pacific, ICPOA became JICPOA: the significance being the change to a *Joint* Intelligence Center. Its head, indeed, was a colonel, Joseph Twitty, one of the prewar Japanese-language students in Tokyo: he acted, at the same time, as Nimitz's Assistant Chief of Staff for Intelligence while Captain Layton continued as Fleet Intelligence Officer. Holmes's Combat Intelligence Center also remained within JICPOA, but was now formally detached from the old Hypo, which was placed directly under the Pacific Fleet: it was at this point, in fact, that its new title emerged: FRUPac, or Fleet Radio Unit, Pacific. However, the CIC stayed inside FRUPac's building until the end of the war and contiguity bridged the organizational gap.

On paper this setup looked logical, sound and well integrated, since the intelligence complex at Hawaii was by now in steady connection by radio link, the Copec channel, with Op-20-G in Washington, with the radio intelligence unit in Delhi and with the other chief outstation, which had been operational in Australia since soon after the loss of the Philippines. In practice, however, the system was still far from perfect. The cryptanalysts, by their increasing domination of the Japanese army and navy codes, might be pumping out Ultra intelligence in full measure, but as regards the American Army— particularly throughout MacArthur's South West Pacific theater— there was as yet no efficient means of distributing that intelligence from the producing source and getting it, by a routine procedure, into the hands of the right people at the front—nor of ensuring that security was preserved once it got there.

And there was still a fundamental flaw. The old antagonism and suspicion between Army and Navy persisted in a manner that may at times seem infantile, until it be remembered that tribal loyalty, narrowness of vision and sheer egocentricity can make even the most

---

* For the early provision of Ultra to the submarine force, see Chapter 10.

senior and hardened officers occasionally enter a second childhood. Even as late as 1944 a proper dialogue between the two services in regard to intelligence matters, and a mutual trust, had still to be established. Holmes in his confidential postwar report pulled no punches. "It must frankly be admitted," he wrote, "that during the early years of the war, the Naval Communications organization had no confidence in Army security measures. This lack of confidence was firmly based on past experience." Probably the Army had a similar self-defeating self-justification. To see how this impasse was, in large degree, overcome it is necessary to look back to the disaster at Pearl Harbor in December 1941.

In the aftermath of that catastrophe Secretary of War Stimson, whose mind had traveled far from the days when he winced at the thought of "reading other people's mail," realized that a major cause had been the haphazard, unsophisticated handling of signal intelligence. As Chapter 3 disclosed, there was no real system. So Stimson decided that there must be a total review of the situation, and that this would best be carried out by a highly qualified lawyer, thoroughly equipped to assess and expound large cases involving complicated facts. On January 19, 1942, therefore, he appointed one of the outstanding leaders of the New York bar, Mr. (and later Colonel) Alfred McCormack, as his Special Assistant briefed to perform this essential task. The brief was, in fact, simple: to determine what had to be done in order to make signal intelligence operations meet the requirements of war and to ensure that all possible information was sucked from that source. The result of McCormack's investigations, as described in the History of the Special Branch, MIS, was so definitive—and in its consequences so fruitful—that it is worth quoting in full:

> At the end of some two months, he had arrived at several funda-
> mental decisions: first, that there was a very large job to be done
> all along the line; second, that a major effort should be made to
> expand and improve the operations of the Signal Corps in the
> radio intelligence fields; third, that the whole radio intelligence
> process, from the intercept operation down through the issuance
> of a finished intelligence report, presented so many interrelated
> priority problems that it could be carried out more effectively if
> considered as an intelligence operation throughout and placed
> under the operational control of G-2; fourth, that the individual

messages arriving at G-2 were far from finished intelligence, and that to exploit the source properly it was necessary to consider the individual messages together with related messages and all available information from other sources, to run down clues appearing in the messages in order to dig out information which was not apparent on first reading, to check back on obscure points with the Signal Corps, to determine then whether the item added anything of real significance, and to report any significant intelligence derived from the message in clear, simple English and in a manner which would bring out its significance, together with any necessary evaluation; and finally, that the intelligence job on the messages could be done effectively only by imaginative persons of absolutely first-class ability and suitable training, and not simply by any reserve officer or college graduate who happened to be available.

It is impossible to overstress the importance of McCormack's recommendations. They provided the birth certificate and the charter for what now became the Special Branch of the Military Intelligence Service, which, uniquely in the American military organization, enjoyed that independence and freedom from hierarchical control which characterized the British operation at Bletchley Park—a freedom whose absence was so ruinously evident in German signal intelligence. Like the staff of GCCS, Special Branch owed its allegiance to none of the regular military establishments, but, through McCormack, was responsible directly to the Secretary of War and to the Army Chief of Staff, General Marshall, on whose iron support it could consistently rely. Moreover, like Bletchley Park, it was very largely composed of able, handpicked civilians whose devotion was to the job in hand—those "imaginative persons of absolutely first-class ability and suitable training" whom McCormack's foresight had predicated as the necessary members of his team.

Even so, Special Branch was a long time a-growing. Civil service obscurantism and obstruction about manning levels were the more difficult to overcome because the unit was secret and, as it were, paramilitary in character.[7] Only experience could prove that the Army itself would not be an adequate hunting ground for recruits, and that a clandestine net would have to be cast over many civilian institutions. The lawyer McCormack turned to the law, whose bright young men soon shone in Special Branch as, in later years, they would

gleam in their own profession: a subsequent Justice of the Supreme
Court, a variety of judges at other levels and a galaxy of leading
lawyers on Wall Street and elsewhere learned the hard way, in Special
Branch, how to evaluate evidence and articulate their conclusions.
University professors, Japanese experts, a curator from the Boston
Museum of Fine Arts, a future managing editor of the Washington
Post and an ultimate prosecutor in the Nuremberg Trials represent,
with their varying skills and temperaments, the class of man who was
inducted. It is often said that Bletchley Park had the atmosphere of
an Oxford or Cambridge college: *mutatis mutandis,* the same might
be said of Special Branch. Each was the fine flower of a democracy:
neither the German, nor the Japanese, nor the Russian regimes bred
anything of comparable quality.

All the same, by March 1943 "despite continuous efforts to get relief
from the various restrictive orders and to find qualified people who
could be obtained notwithstanding those orders, the total had risen
to only 28 officers and 55 civilians." Still, much progress had been
made in understanding how to assess and coordinate intelligence, and,
as at Bletchley, a basis had been laid for a mammoth reference index
of informational data about the enemy—biographical, technical, economic, etc. In particular, reporting of intelligence to the highest authorities was ceasing to be jerky and *ad hoc:* it became routine and
regular, in the form of the "Magic Summary," a daily synopsis of
significant intelligence garnered from all sources but, to a considerable
degree, from the Magic intercepts of the Japanese diplomatic traffic
which the Army had taken over from the Navy as a full-time responsibility in June 1942. (These later became the "Diplomatic Summaries" and were accompanied by specific supplements relating to the
Japanese Army.*) Then, in April 1943, what can only be described
as a "quantum jump" occurred.

In that month McCormack visited England, accompanied by Friedman and Colonel Telford Taylor of MIS.† He spent two months

---

* From early 1944 a Japanese Naval Supplement was also issued to provide the Army
with the more important and relevant material obtained from Naval Ultra.
† Colonel (later General) Telford Taylor later became one of the U.S. prosecutors at
Nuremberg and, in due course, professor of law at Columbia University. During the
latter half of the war he was the chief Special Branch representative in the European
theater.

surveying the work of British signal intelligence, with profoundly important consequences. For the first time, the American MIS became fully aware of the extraordinary successes being achieved by the British in reading the Germans' Enigma-ciphered signals, and of the smooth, secure way in which that intelligence was processed and distributed to headquarters at home and to commands in the field. "It was learned," the History of the Special Branch records, "that the British had developed security principles and methods well beyond the point that had been reached by the U.S. Army."

Specifically, the team was impressed by the organization of Special Liaison Units which, attached to the staffs of commanders abroad, received Ultra intelligence from Bletchley by radio in a secure cipher, passed it on to the headquarters they served and were thereafter responsible for ensuring that it was handled with extreme and necessary circumspection. The Americans had nothing like this in their armory. It was rapidly decided to adopt the system both for Europe,* where invasion now seemed imminent and huge U.S. forces must be deployed, and—as appropriate—in the Pacific. Simultaneously arrangements were made for Special Branch officers to be trained and even to work full-time at Bletchley Park, while the information acquired by the British from German Ultra started to pass through Special Branch channels in a steady stream to Washington. The Special Branch History is explicit: "It was only through the adoption of such principles and methods that the U.S. Army was able to get full access to the results of the British signal intelligence operations; and adherence to those principles and methods had a great deal to do with persuading the U.S. Navy to make available in full the traffic turned out by it."

Which swings us right back to the Pacific, and to a consideration of some pertinent facts. First, as has been seen (and as the last sentence in the preceding paragraph confirms), in that theater liaison between the Army and the Navy over signal intelligence was often indifferent. Second, the Special Branch was a section of the Military Intelligence Service, an agency of the Army. But in the Central Pacific the com-

---

* For the performance of Special Branch "Ultra advisers" in the European theater, and their relationship with Bletchley Park, see Ronald Lewin, *Ultra Goes to War*, Ch. 9., "The American Involvement."

mander in chief and the dominant strength were *naval,* though in the South West Pacific General MacArthur held sway. These dissonant elements had somehow to be brought into harmony. What it amounted to was that Nimitz and MacArthur presented, in regard to signal intelligence, two quite different problems, and it is fascinating to observe how their resolution required two totally different procedures. In the South West Pacific Area (SWPA) the Special Branch had to be imposed from above; in Nimitz's command, arrangements were worked out between the Special Branch representative and the CINCPAC staff, and then ratified in Washington.

Edwin E. Huddleson, Jr., had emerged from Harvard Law School and was working in the Department of Justice (for the Solicitor General) in Washington when, in February 1941, he was drafted and later posted into the Counter-Intelligence Corps.[8] But he was "present at the creation," for in the very early days of 1942, prior to the formation of Special Branch, McCormack had already recruited him. Then, after sharing in Washington those first two formative years of the Branch, he was sent to Pearl Harbor in December 1943 as MIS's Special Security Representative, attached for rations and quarters to the local military commander, General Richardson, but under the operational command of MIS Washington, with the twin missions of keeping General Richardson fully informed from Ultra sources while building a liaison with the Navy—which meant, for example, establishing relations with JICPOA, with Captain Layton as Fleet Intelligence Officer, with Holmes at the Combat Intelligence Center, with FRUPac, and so on. It is fair to say that he found the situation rather complicated! But in dealing with it Huddleson had the invaluable assets of being under the operational control of the War Department, and of being able to communicate directly and confidentially with Washington by the Special Branch's own signal link, instead of having to make use of the Army's normal channels. With Special Branch as the focus, an area of mutual trust with the Navy staff gradually emerged.

This process of coming together was described to the author by Huddleson as involving these principal features: (a) the assignment to the Combat Intelligence Center of three additional Special Branch officers who were stationed for rations and quarters with the Navy but remained under operational command of MIS Washington (as did

Huddleson); (b) the assignment to each major Army and Army Air Force operational command in the Central Pacific of an MIS Special Security Officer, under similar orders, who could use both the Special Branch communications and the Navy's own channel, employed by CINCPAC to transmit Ultra intelligence to Halsey and Spruance and other fleet commanders; and (c) the subsequent placing of a Special Branch link at FRUPac, to permit direct Ultra communications between Special Branch Washington and the Special Branch group working in the Combat Intelligence Center.

The value of Special Branch had, however, already been warmly and objectively endorsed in 1945 by Captain Holmes's official narrative of the Combat Intelligence Center—and this, it should be noted, was a report by a *naval* officer to the *naval* authorities about the wartime work of a *naval* agency. Nevertheless, Holmes affirmed that "the Army Special Branch system of primary distribution of radio intelligence is a model for the Navy to follow." It is often observed that the British have a gift for evolving creative ideas while the Americans are masters at the practical application and exploitation of such ideas. Here, surely, is a classic example, for the concept of the Special Liaison Unit was wholly British, but once its value had been comprehended by the Americans it was seized and developed by them until it became a central strand of their intelligence network in Europe, in the remote theaters of China/Burma/India, and on every front in the Pacific where American forces were engaged.

For evidence of the transformation achieved at Hawaii we may turn, once again, to Captain Holmes. His Combat Intelligence Center, it will be recalled, was essentially a naval agency. Yet, as he recorded:

> Through the Special Branch system of communication, CIC was in touch with all Special Branch intelligence agencies throughout the world. An Army message center was finally set up at FRUPac to handle Special Branch communications. CIC could, and frequently did, call on Special Branch in Washington to check, verify, or amplify intelligence required for estimates, or to conduct special research for its benefit. Through the Special Security Officer, material could be distributed to Army forces as required with complete confidence in its proper handling and security. Much background material and many analyses were received from Special Branch by officer messenger. Army Communication Intelli-

gence service to CIC was thus fully on a par with Naval Communication Intelligence.

The importance of this combination, in one room, and under a unified direction, of all the varied requisite sources of intelligence, backed by two worldwide communication services, and able to draw on the multitudinous sources of JICPOA can hardly be overestimated. When estimation of enemy strength was made it could be done with the assurance that all of the best information was available. Moreover, it was found that Army and Navy information supplemented each other in many ways and that the result was frequently much greater than the sum of its parts.

But the scenario so far has covered intelligence activities at the base. It was in the battles of the Central Pacific, however, that the most practical benefits came. For when Nimitz's great armadas and air power began, in 1944, their irresistible thrust toward Japan, and the operational headquarters of army and air commands spread out far and wide, each was accompanied by a liaison unit from Special Branch —headed by a Special Security Officer—which held both the Navy and Special Branch crypto-channels for communicating Ultra intelligence, and performed in the field the function of receiving Ultra intelligence on these circuits, passing that information on to appropriate people, safeguarding Ultra security and acting as a vital and trustworthy link between Army and Navy. Broadly speaking, this healthy extension of Special Branch into operational areas in the Central Pacific was not carried out against the grain, but as a natural development, with the full backing and cooperation of the CINCPAC staff.

In the South West Pacific the pattern was strikingly and significantly different. A system was indeed enforced, but until the end a genuine harmony never emerged. In the records of the Pearl Harbor Inquiry there is an affidavit filed as late as May 8, 1945, by General Willoughby, MacArthur's Chief of Intelligence, whose tone of bitter frustration speaks volumes—though whether that frustration was in fact self-generated is a question for further consideration. Willoughby declared:

The Navy has shrouded the whole enterprise in mystery, excluding other services, and rigidly centralizing the whole enterprise. At this date, for example, this same system is still in vogue: as far as SWPA is concerned, the crypto-analysis is made in Melbourne. . . . The Melbourne station is under direct orders of Washington, is not bound by any local responsibilities, forwards what they select and when it suits them. The possibility of erroneous or incomplete selection is as evident now as it was in 1941. The only excuse the Navy has is that its field is primarily naval intercepts, but there is a lot of Army traffic or other incidental traffic. This collateral traffic is not always understood or correctly interpreted by the Navy, in my opinion.[9]

If that picture of disintegration is an accurate image of the intelligence service in SWPA only a few months before the end of the war in the Pacific, the natural reaction is to ask why—in view of the effective synthesis of those services in Washington and, to a substantial degree, in the Central Pacific—so lamentable a disarray still persisted. An old Army maxim lays down that the colonel is responsible for the failures of his regiment: Supreme Commanders also have their responsibilities, among which the creation of a sound intelligence structure should have a high priority. Willoughby's lament is merely an indictment of MacArthur.

The situation in SWPA was divisive from the start. When Commander Fabian and seventy-five men of the naval Cast unit were evacuated by submarine from Corregidor and located in Melbourne alongside the Intelligence Division of the Australian Navy, it was sensible and indeed inevitable that they should continue to work on the Japanese diplomatic traffic, Magic, for it was the old story of: "We have got/The Maxim gun, and they have not." Which is to say that Cast, in its new setting, possessed the only Purple machine in SWPA. It was natural, too, that as the Japanese Naval Ultra became more and more accessible, Fabian's team should handle it, maintaining and increasing its links with FRUPac in Hawaii and Op-20-G in Washington.

A prudent assessment of the realities would have appreciated at an early stage that, if this was the case, any Army signal intelligence agencies were bound to be secondary—particularly since the Japanese Army code was not effectively penetrated until well into 1943. Harmonious collaboration, one would have thought, was vital. But MacArthur always craved centralized institutions responsive to the pressure of his imperious thumb. It was not surprising, therefore, that he had hardly been in Australia for more than a week when, on April 1, 1942, he signaled to Washington:

> Investigation discloses that a central Allied signal intelligence section is required for the interception and cryptanalyzing of Japanese intelligence. The time delay and transmission uncertainties incident to sending intercepted material to Washington and elsewhere dictate that this work be handled locally. Allied forces here are organizing such a bureau.[10]

In a sense he got what he wanted, for on April 15, by agreement with the Australian authorities, a combined organization was created —the Central Bureau, which by the end of the war had ballooned to a scale of some 4,000 men and whose main headquarters* was always close to MacArthur's own, first in Australia and then, as he advanced, at Hollandia in New Guinea and at Leyte in the Philippines.

> The Australian Army component of Central Bureau came from the Australian Special Wireless group which had seen considerable service in the Middle East and Singapore, and also included some British personnel who had escaped from Singapore. The Royal Australian Air Force component consisted of personnel assigned from Victoria Barracks, Melbourne. There were three assistant directors, Lieutenant Colonel Abraham Sinkov of the American Army who had joined Friedman in the SIS in the early 1930s, Major (later Lieutenant Colonel) A. W. Sandford, who had served with the Special Wireless Section Type B at the Headquarters of 1 Australian Corps in the Middle East, and Wing Commander Roy Booth of the RAAF.[11]

Nevertheless, the name "Central Bureau" was a mere play on words. That increasing integration of signal intelligence activities which we have observed on Hawaii and over the Central Pacific (reflecting similar integrations and interconnections in Washington) was never achieved to anything like an equivalent degree in SWPA. It is ludicrous to pretend, as Willoughby implied in his affidavit, that naval

---

* The Bureau acquired a direct radio link with Arlington Hall and was thus tied in to the *Army's* signal intelligence base.

incompetence or ill will sabotaged the supply to MacArthur of relevant intelligence available from naval sources, for the record—as later chapters will sufficiently indicate—is unarguable. But it is certainly the case that a proper centralization of intelligence staffs, commonplace in British theaters such as the Middle or Far East, under Eisenhower in his great commands and even elsewhere in the Pacific, was singularly absent in SWPA.

Special Branch was first inserted into this checkered scene during the summer of 1943. But MacArthur kicked at the idea of accepting a Special Security Officer who would be attached to his command merely "for administration and discipline," who would "disseminate Ultra in accord with rules announced in security regulations issued by the War Department," and whose personal responsibility would be to MIS rather than to SWPA.* When the proposal to attach such Special Branch representatives was canvassed with the various American theater commanders during the summer of 1943 their response, as tactfully summarized in the History of the Operations of Special Security Officers attached to Field Commands, 1943–1945, was as follows:

> The commanding generals of the Pacific Ocean Areas and the China-Burma-India Theater readily concurred, but the Commander in Chief, South West Pacific, raised certain objections to the proposal on the ground that the SSO should be assigned outright to the command rather than remain under control of the War Department. Col. Carter W. Clarke, then Chief of Special Branch, was sent to Brisbane to confer personally with CINC, SWPA on this difference of opinion. As a result of this conference, General MacArthur concurred in the original plan.

In other words, a system for handling Ultra securely which was accepted without demur by his fellow Supremos, Eisenhower and Mountbatten (as it was by a prima donna like Stilwell, or Patton, or Montgomery) had to be forcibly imposed on General Douglas MacArthur.

---

* See Appendix II for the full instructions from the Adjutant General to MacArthur about the SSO's functions and responsibilities.

For there can be no doubt that the weight of pressure on MacArthur came not from Carter Clarke but from the Army Chief of Staff himself, George Marshall, for whom the sanctity of signal intelligence, with all its global implications, was infinitely more important than the predilections of a general whose wayward egocentricity he understood all too well but could not unconditionally support. Certainly it was Marshall who, when the next crunch came, intervened with undeniable authority.

As in the Central Pacific, so in SWPA, it became clear that as the American battle line rolled forward it would be necessary to attach further Special Branch officers to individual army and air commands in the battle areas. At the same time, as was noted earlier, the Americans and the British in the spring of 1944 reached agreement about a uniform policy for handling Ultra in all parts of the world and for adopting the British practice, in regard to their Special Liaison Units, as essentially the standard, universal procedure. It was Marshall, therefore, who wrote personally to MacArthur on May 23, 1944 (as he had already done to Eisenhower in respect of the European theater) to explain that "uniform regulations and centralized control over the handling of all Japanese Ultra wherever produced are essential to the adequate safeguarding of this vital source of intelligence."[12] He then attached an immensely detailed and stringent set of instructions for the handling of Ultra in all its aspects.*

And thus it was that in a properly coordinated manner the Special Branch officers gradually spread, and made their healing influence felt throughout the Pacific, as they did so constructively from D Day onward in Northwestern Europe. For reasons which will be already obvious—stemming, as they did, essentially from the idiosyncratic attitudes of MacArthur and his staff—the officers in SWPA trod the stoniest roads. This will become more evident at a later stage in the

---

* In the NA file containing the Marshall letter and related correspondence, there is an interesting communication from General Bissell (Head of Intelligence in the War Department) to "C" in London: Major General Stewart Menzies, the head of MI 6 or the Secret Service, who was also organizationally responsible for GCCS at Bletchley Park, the Special Liaison Units, and the whole question of distributing and protecting Ultra. Bissell sends "C" a copy of the regulations so that he can note the modifications deemed necessary for the special circumstances of the Pacific war. At Marshall's level, there was an absolute determination that in this vital matter the Americans and the British preserved a full accord.

book. Meanwhile, it happens that in the National Archives there is a list of Special Branch officers and their locations as of February 15, 1945.[13] To summarize this will give a useful indication of how, in a sense, they became nerve centers throughout the American system.

In the Philippines, where MacArthur's HQ is now at Leyte, there are seven officers at headquarters—one specifically for liaison with the Seventh Fleet, SWPA's navy—and one on Luzon. There is one at Eighth Army HQ in the islands, one at I and one at XXIV Corps. Seven are with the Air Force. Four are still working in the rear headquarters in Brisbane. In Nimitz's Pacific Ocean Areas there are twelve more officers, including one at 21st Bomber Command and another at USAF headquarters, while others have Army attachments. And away in the China/Burma/India theater we find eight at Delhi, one in Chungking, one with Mountbatten's Supreme HQ in Ceylon, one at Stilwell's old Northern Combat Command, and others at various Air Force headquarters, including Claire Chennault's 14th Air Force. Colonel McCormack's "imaginative persons of first-class ability" had come into their own.

The qualities of these Special Branch officers, and of the Ultra intelligence they provided, were generously recognized at the end of the war by commanders whom they had assisted. From Nimitz and many others (though not, apparently, from MacArthur) signals of commendation arrived at the headquarters of the Military Intelligence Service. The following example, dated October 1, 1945, happened to be sent by the Commander General, U.S. Forces, India-Burma Theater: it is quoted because it so felicitously registers what everyone wanted to say.

> I wish to express at this time my appreciation for the splendid contribution made by the War Department special security organization.
>
> Those officers in the theater, both on my staff and at forward commands, who have been familiar with this Military Intelligence Service activity, have found it of extraordinary value.
>
> I am fully aware that the success of this undertaking depended upon the quiet perseverance of many personnel, both civilian and military, who have performed their tasks in the United States and overseas under such conditions that the merit of their services could not be generally recognized, even within the Army. Those

of us in the India-Burma Theater who are familiar with this activity wish to commend all those who have played a part in this highly successful undertaking.

A century or so earlier the historian Thomas Carlyle, communing with himself in the reminiscences he never intended for publication, might have had in mind both these officers, and all who were unostentatiously involved in the work of Ultra and Magic, when he wrote of "the noble, silent men, scattered here and there, each in his department; silently thinking, silently working; whom no Morning Newspaper makes mention of! They are the salt of the earth. A country that has few or none of these is in a bad way."

To have organized on so huge a scale and over such vast distances a system for acquiring from the Japanese signals and effectively distributing what, literally, amounted to tons of intelligence—usually valuable, and often decisive—amounted to a major military victory, impossible to quantify but palpable in its magnitude. But there was another victory. The Japanese never grasped what was happening.

The same was true of the Germans, who never realized until the end of the war that their Enigma cipher had been regularly broken. When one considers the colossal volume of radio signals sent out during that war from Bletchley Park, from Arlington Hall, from FRUPac or Op-20-G in Washington, or crisscross over the theaters of war, and when one considers that the intercept stations of the Japanese and the Germans must certainly have picked up these myriad transmissions, it seems astonishing that over the years their cryptanalysts—many of high quality—never achieved a breakthrough. We must ascribe this not merely to security—though certainly the Special Liaison Unit/Special Branch organization was critical—but also to the high technology of the Allies which produced those enciphering machines—the Typex, the Sigaba—to whose protection, as it turned out, millions of Ultra signals could be entrusted with perfect security.

To end thus would be to end on a high note. But it will be remembered that when, in Bunyan's *Pilgrim's Progress*, Mr. Valiant-for-truth crosses the ultimate river into the land of peace, his final observation is: "With great difficulty am I got hither." And so, in the years before Hiroshima, the Americans had many a Slough of Despond and Hill Difficulty to overcome. It is not inappropriate, therefore, to turn back at this point to the days immediately after Midway, when the men and women in the Salt Mines had scarcely started their travail, when the Special Branch had yet to be born and when, for the Marines about to land on Guadalcanal, all was still to play for.

Sigaba, the American machine whose ciphers the Japanese never broke

An American version of "The Bombe," first used at Bletchley Park for processing the German Enigma cipher

Joseph Rochefort

William F. Friedman

Arlington Hall   NATIONAL SECURITY AGENCY

Mt. Vernon

Admiral Layton

Discovered in the National Archives by chance in *1981*, this appears to be the only available photograph of a portion of the machine constructed for reading Purple in *1940*

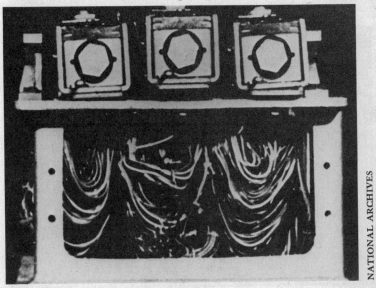

Members and staff of the Congressional Inquiry (courtesy Bennett Boskey, one of the staff present)

A phenomenon: Admiral King relaxes

Henderson Field, Guadalcanal, August 1942 NATIONAL ARCHIVES

Nimitz: the Neptune of the Pacific

NATIONAL ARCHIVES

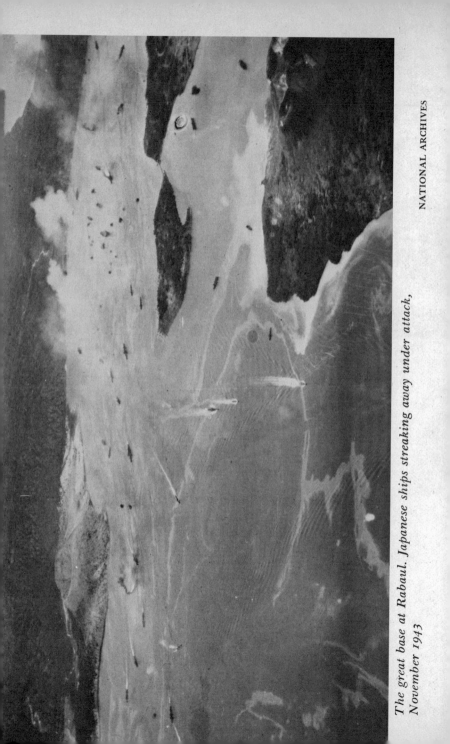

The great base at Rabaul. Japanese ships streaking away under attack, November 1943

NATIONAL ARCHIVES

Mitscher with Arleigh Burke, his Chief of Staff, off Okinawa, June 1945   U.S. NAVAL HISTORICAL CENTER

The Great Marianas Turkey Shoot: patterns in the sky seen from U.S.S. Lexington   NATIONAL ARCHIVES

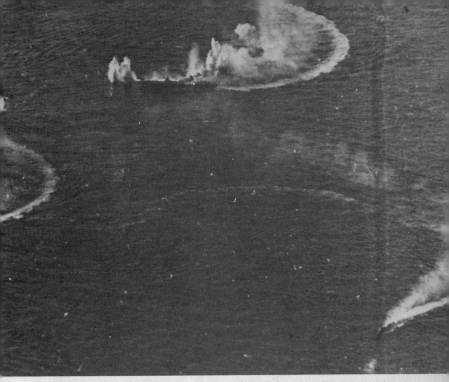

The Great Marianas Turkey Shoot: destroyers and the carrier
Ryukaku *weave patterns in the sea*   NATIONAL ARCHIVES

Halsey in command of the
Third Fleet

Seeadler Harbor.

The supreme trio: MacArthur, Roosevelt, and Nimitz meet at
Pearl Harbor, July 26, 1944   NAVY HISTORY DIVISION

Mitscher on Lexington   NATIONAL ARCHIVES

HIT FAST

HIT HARD!

W.F. HALSEY
ADMIRAL U.S. NAVY

HIT OFTEN

Produce for Your Navy

VICTORY BEGINS AT HOME

Halsey asks for more

MacArthur walks ashore at Morotai   U.S. NAVAL HISTORICAL CENTER
(COLLECTION OF ADMIRAL THOMAS KINKAID)

Testimonial presented to William F. Friedman on the occasion
of his retirement   NATIONAL SECURITY AGENCY

CHAPTER SEVEN

The Fork in the Road

It must be said that success or failure in recapturing Guadalcanal, and the results of the final naval battle relating to it, is the fork in the road that leads to victory for them or for us.
    Japanese after-action report

We are no longer reading the enemy mail and today [August 1] we must depend almost entirely on traffic analysis to deduce enemy deployment...
    Estimate of Enemy Intentions, August 1942,
    U.S. Pacific Fleet Command Summary

ALMOST THIRTY YEARS earlier, on August 3, 1914, the British Foreign Secretary, Sir Edward Grey, watched a continent slide into war and remarked, "The lamps are going out all over Europe." Such must have been Nimitz's midsummer sentiment about the Pacific, as the May 28 code change of JN25 was followed by a second alteration only two months later. FRUPac and Op-20-G were entering the dark. That marvelous illumination cast by the cryptanalysts no longer played over the Japanese battle array and Yamamoto's intentions, sometimes fitfully but sometimes, as at Midway, with the energy of a laser beam. And the lamps would not be easily or quickly relit.

This blackout was the more unfortunate because plans were already in train on both sides which, by the strange convergence of war, would make a small strip of ground and a stretch of water seem so vital in the opposing strategies that a death struggle, combat *à outrance*, would be undertaken to acquire control of them.

The strip was a landing ground scratched off the surface of Guadalcanal, immortalized as Henderson Field. The stretch was "the Slot": the narrow channel bisecting that 600-mile straggle called the Solomons, of which Guadalcanal and its offshore island Tulagi form part of the southern group while away to the northward New Georgia, Choiseul and Bougainville lie like steppingstones on the path to a majestic crescent, the Bismarck Archipelago. Here, on the far tip of the Bismarcks' northern element, New Ireland, was the Japanese base of Kavieng. Across the sea, on New Britain, the enemy had grasped and developed at Rabaul one of the most superb natural harbors in the Pacific. At Rabaul the Japanese had a launching pad for major operations, whether along the chain of the Solomons or southward, over and around New Britain, against the huge no-man's-land of New Guinea where the coastal points of Lae, Salamaua and Finschhafen were already in their hands. But at Guadalcanal and the Solomons, for month after month, two nations tested each other's will in a slugging match as the Germans and French had weighed one another up at Verdun.

The British people, their attention distracted by German successes in Russia, North Africa and the Battle of the Atlantic, little realized that summer how yet another corner of the old Empire would become the scene of such a trial of strength. But so it was. Bougainville belonged to the Australian Mandated Territory of New Guinea, and most of the other surroundings of the Slot formed the British Solomon Islands Protectorate.* Moreover, in the coming conflict their own kin would play a vital part, for the service of coast watchers set up by the Australians after the First World War became the eyes and ears of the Americans. But it was the U.S. Marines who supplied the spearhead. It took them "only forty-eight hours to get a footing on Guadalcanal. It was to take six months and cost the lives of thousands of American soldiers, sailors and airmen and the loss of many fine ships before the island was finally rescued."[1]

The Japanese High Command, for its part, was disturbed but not dispirited by a defeat at Midway whose true strategic consequences it failed to comprehend. As for their fellow countrymen, the veil of propaganda descended immediately. The press and the radio announced a massive naval victory: war correspondents were clamped in a sort of quarantine: even the surviving wounded were secreted, as Walter Lord put it, "like a victim of some medieval plague." Con-

---

* Tulagi was the headquarters of the British Solomon Islands Government. After its capture, the British Residency became an American command post.

fident, therefore, of a persisting superiority and the immense promise offered by the forward bases which they had already secured, Japan's warlords faced their Pacific problems in the spirit of General de Gaulle on the eve of a flight to the Middle East: "I am setting off for the complicated Orient with a few simple ideas."

The Japanese plan was threefold, logical and orderly. First the area around Tulagi—which had been seized on May 1 during Operation MO—would be firmly secured: then the whole chain of the Solomons: then the mass of New Guinea. Yet as Clausewitz said, "everything in war is simple, but the simplest thing is the most difficult." In this case the difficulty was created by the Americans, for the Joint Chiefs of Staff, anxious but alert, evolved their own triple scheme: in parallel, as it happened, to the enemy's. Their directive to Nimitz and Mac-Arthur of July 2 targeted them, too, onto Tulagi and the neighboring islands, next through the Solomons to Rabaul, and finally to the full recovery of New Guinea—the central purpose being to clear the lines of communication between the United States, Australia and New Zealand.[2]

The initial phase was code-named Pestilence (an indelicacy which Churchill, so sensitive about unsuitable titles for operations, would certainly have rejected) and the actual assault landing was more chastely christened Watchtower. What precipitated events and made Guadalcanal (code-named Cactus) the cockpit for a long and bitter conflict was the discovery, early in July, that the Japanese had moved over there and on the north side of the island, opposite Tulagi, were starting to create an airstrip.* This threat to Watchtower was unmistakable.

The determination of the Chiefs of Staff to counterattack was sustained by more than those general deductions which any good military man might have made from the dispositions of the enemy in the southern Pacific. For though cryptanalysis, the most penetrative organ of signal intelligence or Sigint, was at least temporarily blind, illumination now came from that other productive source, traffic analysis. The confidential assessment of Sigint's contribution to the Solomons campaign (which carries the dateline June 1943 and was

---

* The preparation of the airfield was noted on July 13 and by July 15 there was evidence that it was ready for use. The Role of Radio Intelligence in the American-Japanese Naval War, Vol. III, pp. 61 and 63.

thus written while all was fresh in the mind) sets out the matter
lucidly.

> Ten years before war broke out in the Pacific, American com-
> munication intelligence experts had foreseen that cryptanalysis
> would be of little use during periods which immediately followed
> a major change in an enemy's cryptographic systems. Conse-
> quently a method had been devised which derived intelligence
> from various external characteristics of the enemy's communica-
> tion system. . . . This method, called traffic analysis, was not ex-
> pected to be as accurate in its forecasts of enemy plans as
> cryptanalysis would be, but the experts hoped that it would have
> great potential value in time of war. These hopes were fully
> realized in the months of July and August 1942. . . . Traffic
> analysis was able to reveal the presence of the enemy in the
> Solomons, which occasioned the landing of the Marines there.

Though the assessment is scrupulous in pointing out that there were
no magical solutions, leading to estimates about the enemy's intentions "which could be made as confidently as was done at Midway,"
and though the product of traffic analysis was often more of a hy-
pothesis than an indisputable fact, nevertheless a crutch transforms
the life of a one-legged man and here was a strong crutch at a time
of desperate need. No better confirmation can be offered of the
history of how during the years before Pearl Harbor foresight, training and technical preparation—however restricted, however inadequate—equipped the Americans for the tasks ahead. The siting and
building of listening posts in the right places and in just sufficient
numbers, the readying of signalers and analytical staffs, the evolution
of techniques for understanding the pattern and significance of Japanese radio traffic—the sources of its transmission, the meaning of call
signs—all suddenly started to pay comforting dividends in that summer of 1942.

But traffic analysis, essentially a cumulative and cogitative process,
was not always able to produce the quick and certain intelligence so
necessary for commanders. Direction finding was thus an important
ally during the period when code breaking ran dry—"D.F.," the
method of establishing not the contents or the originator of a radio
signal so much as the physical location of the transmitter, whether

ship, aircraft or ground headquarters, by taking cross-bearings from at least two points sufficiently wide apart to produce an accurate cut. Here too the Americans were energetic, but there were scarcely enough surveillance posts to cover the vast Pacific theater and, of course, sheer distance often made it difficult or impossible to pick up the waning flicker of an enemy's signal. Too frequently, therefore, either intersections were not made at all or they were geometrically imperfect, suggesting false locations. In this situation the human eye was beyond price. At just the right time Australian forethought came to the Americans' aid, in the shape of the coast watchers.

A plain statement is possible. During the whole extent of the long-drawn-out Solomons campaign the coast watchers, combined with traffic analysis, supplied far more than the minimum of intelligence about the Japanese which the Americans required until the skills of their cryptanalysts reasserted themselves, the JN25 code was penetrated again, and operations could be based on a new and solid platform of information. Nor was it a coincidence that the native scouts of a coast watcher helped to save a future President of the United States. Cast away after the sinking in the Slot of his torpedo boat PT-109, a young officer was discovered by Biuku Gasa and Eroni Kumana. With his knife he scraped on a coconut shell his message, which, carried back by the scouts, helped to guide a canoe to his rescue: NAURO ISL . . . NATIVE KNOWS POSIT . . . HE CAN PILOT . . . 11 ALIVE NEED SMALL BOAT . . . KENNEDY.[3]

By 1941 Australian Naval Intelligence had organized over 100 coast-watching stations along a vast 2,500-mile perimeter stretching from New Guinea to the New Hebrides in the east. At its heart lay the Solomons. During the first onrush of the Japanese into the Pacific many vanished or were withdrawn, but in the Solomons a hard core of posts was retained and then expanded, providing, in the end, observation at key points along the Slot all the way from Guadalcanal to Bougainville. The watchers were of many types—from the Regular Navy, former District officers, planters. Equipped with durable and efficient radios, they could operate behind the Japanese lines under the shield of their own local knowledge and the loyalty, beyond praise or imagination, of the islanders. In its appendix "Native Help during the Guadalcanal Campaign," the official history of the Marine Corps singles out a retired member of the local constabulary, Sergeant Major

Jacob Vouza, who may serve as a symbol.* Captured by the Japanese on Guadalcanal, the brave man was bound to a stake, stabbed by swords in the throat and chest, and left for dead after stubbornly refusing to inform on the Americans. But he survived, extricated himself, and after being picked up by the Marines was saved by blood transfusion. Persistent in reconnaissance throughout the campaign, he was awarded the British George Medal and the U.S. Silver Star. Later, when the Solomons achieved independence, he was awarded a well-earned knighthood.

Japanese observers were far less frequently on enemy territory. They had not the same "feel" of the country as an ex-policeman or former planter, and the native population—the sea in which they swam—was predominantly hostile or indifferent. They were never as fully integrated into the overall intelligence system and conduct of operations as were the Allied units. As to the latter, it would be wrong to suggest that the Solomons network was unique, for both the Americans and the Australians inserted their men into many other areas—the Philippines being a notable example. For the coast watchers the Battle of the Slot was their finest hour; that time when Nimitz's staff noted in the war diary: "We are no longer reading the enemy mail and today we must depend *almost entirely*† on traffic analysis . . ."

Nevertheless, by any standards the contribution of that analysis was formidable. Based as it was on many hundreds of signals overheard and—when possible—traced to the transmitting source, it is difficult to describe in full detail, for so much depended on patient, gradual evaluation. July is an instructive month, since it was at this time that final decisions were taken and the last hurried preparations made for the Marines' amphibious assault on Tulagi and Guadalcanal. A selection of some of the most significant intelligence produced by traffic analysis during these weeks will therefore serve as a useful illustration of its capability.[4]

Already, by the beginning of the month, Sigint was reporting a marked increase of Japanese activity in the Solomons. On the 2nd, fifteen enemy warships and a dozen transports were identified in the Rabaul-Tulagi sector. On the 3rd, orders were picked up for a Special

---

* See also, as a model example, the patrol report of Constable Saku quoted in full on p. 114 of Zimmerman, *The Guadalcanal Campaign.*
† Author's italics.

Landing Force to proceed to Rabaul, where two cruiser divisions and two air tenders were noted. On the 7th, signals disclosing considerable convoy movement around New Britain and submarine reconnaissance in the Marshalls were suggestive, while on the 8th the arrival of the Yokohama Flying Boat Squadron at Tulagi and a decoded dispatch,* directing air personnel as replacements for the Fifth Air Attack Force in the Truk-Rabaul area, told their own story. The warning conveyed by these and other indications that the Japanese intended to consolidate their hold on the Solomons was confirmed on the 11th, when documents captured in New Guinea showed that the 11th and 13th *Billeting* Detachments were going to Guadalcanal.

The presence of the commanders in chief of both the Fourth and Eighth Fleets in southern waters, and an apparent division of the South Seas into an "Inside" and an "Outside" Zone, were painstakingly but correctly identified, and interpreted as indicating that at Rabaul Admiral Mikawa of the Eighth Fleet, on the heavy cruiser *Chokai*, would be in charge of operations while the Fourth Fleet, based on Truk, would cover the Outside Zone. By the 24th three cruiser divisions were known to be in the local order of battle. Some comfort came from a meticulous study of the signal traffic from the Japanese carrier divisions, which strongly suggested that they, at least, were being held back in home waters for training and refitting. On the 25th, moreover, an assessment of the enemy's own radio intelligence indicated very positively that "there appeared to be no sign of an enemy decipherment of our cipher systems, or of their compromise through capture." By the end of the month, nevertheless, it was clear that the Japanese were about to alter the JN25 code once again. (On the 30th, incidentally, the important two-letter designators in the enemy's current signal traffic had been worked out—RX for the Solomons, RK for New Britain, RZ for western New Guinea, RY for the Gilberts.) Both sides were all set to go.

But the Americans arrived first. Indeed, the swelling evidence of Japanese intentions drove preparations forward at such a pace that corners had to be cut and risks taken which, had the assault force met the resistance encountered later on Tarawa and other islands, might have resulted in disaster on the beaches. The force itself was created from the 1st Marine Division, which, in June, was en route from the

---

* Though JN25 resisted attack, some minor codes were being read, at least intermittently.

States to New Zealand, mainly in passenger ships, and only docked at Wellington during the first fortnight of July: neither the division nor its commander, General Vandegrift, anticipated that instead of the expected months of training they were to go straight into action. So hectic days and nights followed, during which stores and equipment were hauled ashore and repacked according to the priorities of "combat loading"—in the rain, on open quays, unaided by the local stevedores, for whom the union rule book mattered more than patriotism. In spite of the fact that Guadalcanal had been a British protectorate in past years, maps and hydrographic charts were in desperately short supply and photo reconnaissance was inevitably meager.

All the same, by July 31 about 19,000 Marines were on their way, in nineteen transports and four destroyers, under the close cover of Admiral Kelly Turner's Task Force 62 and the more distant protection of Admiral Fletcher's Carrier Force, including *Enterprise, Saratoga* and *Wasp*. To the astonishment of everybody—not least, of the Japanese—early on August 7 this considerable armada started its landings unobserved and virtually unopposed. A vicious struggle followed for Tulagi and its neighboring islets, but here, after three days, the area was secured—and never disputed thereafter. The story of Guadalcanal would be very different. Certain patches of ground seem hallowed by what happened there—the Hougoumont farm at Waterloo, the peach orchard and Round Tops at Gettysburg, the little airfield at Sidi-Rezegh by Tobruk, the tennis court at Kohima, the houses held by the airborne men beside the bridge at Arnhem. Guadalcanal was about to join the list, and in a unique way, for what characterized the next six months was the savage intensity of the struggle *in all three dimensions:* at sea it was worst of all.

The naval conflict that now followed, in the waters around or within the Solomons island chain, has no parallel in the history of warfare—for its duration (there were actions almost daily over a period of some six months); for its ferocity, intensified by the fact that so many battles were fought by night, at very close quarters, in areas where lack of sea room left little space for maneuver; and for the almost continuous slaughter of ships and men. Soon after midnight on November 13, 1942, two American admirals were killed at their stations on the bridges of their cruisers—Scott on *Atlanta* and Callaghan on *San Francisco:* during two world wars the Royal Navy in all its engagements only once experienced a similar loss, at Jutland in 1915. Moreover, as each side stubbornly attempted to reinforce its troops on Guadalcanal every possible permutation available in modern sea warfare was employed: strikes by land-based or carrier aircraft, swift jabs by destroyer flotillas, submarine attacks, venomous spurts by the P.T. boats, cruisers clashing together in the old-style line of battle, light and heavy aircraft carriers working on the fringes and even great capital ships firing their monster guns at almost point-blank range in the dark, like heavyweight boxers battering each other in the narrow confines of the ring.[5]

In the Mediterranean, in the Atlantic and in support of the Russian convoys many bitter, and occasionally even more murderous, engagements were fought by the Royal Navy. It is the *nonstop* violence, sustained over so many months, that characterizes the Solomons campaign, and it should be remembered that as both sides raised the stakes, and the Americans fed into the struggle more and more vessels scarcely out of their teeming construction yards, it was maintained by ships, officers and men often new to the rigor and variety of war at sea. Like Waterloo, this was "hard pounding": often literally so, for during a single night the Japanese would hurl over a thousand heavy shells onto Henderson Field.

Both the severity and the scale of sacrifice may be illustrated by a single instance—in mid-November it cost the Japanese the sinking of 77,606 tons of warships (two battleships, one heavy cruiser, three destroyers and eleven transports) to land on Guadalcanal a miserable 1,500 bags of rice, 260 howitzer shells and, out of 10,000 troops, the 2,000 who had survived the destruction of their convoy. Yet until the end neither the Americans nor their enemy considered the price too high, and in spite of all those ships on the bottom of the sea, the soldiers—those who lived—somehow got ashore. Between August 7 and November 12 the figures of the troops committed on Guadalcanal rose, in the American case, from 10,000 to 29,000. From an initial 2,200 the Japanese force—at 30,000—reached a similar level.

Virtually every night the Japanese tried to rush new troops down the Slot (because Henderson Field was never taken by land, or sufficiently damaged in numerous bombardments from the air or from the sea, the Americans normally commanded the *daytime* skies). As "the Tokyo Express," this constantly renewed effort has been immortalized. Less generally is it realized that between August and December 1942 no less than six major naval engagements took place. Like many battles on sea or land, these are known by different names in different records. The American roll of honor lists them as follows: Battle of Savo Island (surface action by night, August 8–9); Battle of the Eastern Solomons (air and surface actions, August 23–25); Battle of Cape Esperance (night surface action, October 11–12); Battle of Santa Cruz Islands (air and surface actions, October 26); Battle of Guadalcanal (air and surface actions by day and night, November 13–15); Battle of Lunga Point (night surface action, November 30–December 1). In the New Year the sands were running out for the Japanese. Nevertheless, by the beginning of February 1943—when "the fork in the road" was reached—there had been seven further considerable clashes: Rennell Island, the Northern Solomons, south of Savo Island, Cape Esperance again, Kolombangara Island, south of Choiseul, and off Rendova.

With experience, the Americans not only matched the enemy in courage and persistence; as their seamanship improved, their tactics matured, and sailors and airmen were welded into a harmonious co-operation, they also came to equal the Japanese in efficiency, where, at first, they had certainly been inferior. But neither increased skills nor a growing weight of weaponry would have been sufficient for victory, had the extra arm of intelligence been lacking.

Here the Americans were superior from the start, and the graph of that superiority rose steadily. In all aspects of the long conflict, at virtually every stage, one observes them enjoying a measure of prevision. Air reconnaissance naturally played a large part. The eyes of the coast watchers often supplied immediate and critically valuable intelligence: but inevitably this was spasmodic and unpredictable, since it depended on the position of a man's observation post, on whether he was changing ground or even being hunted by the enemy, on the effect of disease and strain on alertness, and on whether an intervening mountain or patch of jungle happened to conceal from him the passing-by of Japanese ships or aircraft. It was once again signal intelligence that truly dominated: Sigint in many forms—primarily traffic analysis, aided intermittently by direction finding and the breaking of lower-grade codes. Like the ground bass in a musical composition, it supplied the sustaining theme.

Within forty-eight hours of the Marines' landing on Guadalcanal both the value of applying, and the danger of misusing, good intelligence were made dramatically—and then disastrously—plain, as was the initial limitation of American tactics and, it must be said, a certain deficiency in the attitude of their sea commanders. The focal point, of course, was the beachhead, for during the early days of an assault landing the men ashore are short of heavy weapons and supplies, transport vessels clutter the waters close to land, and the protecting warships are inevitably restricted in their freedom of maneuver. If the Japanese reacted swiftly from their adjacent air and naval bases, Vandegrift's Marines and their supporting armada would be sitting ducks.

And Admiral Mikawa did react. At 11:30 a.m. on the 7th a coast watcher named Paul Mason,* perched on a hilltop on Bougainville at the northern head of the Slot, heard aircraft engines overhead, made a count, and broadcast on his teleradio: FROM STO 27 BOMBERS HEADED SOUTHEAST. "Some of the Allied ships caught the message direct from Paul Mason—they knew about X frequency and were tuned in. Most got it by a complicated but highly effective relay. Port Moresby, the control station for the Bougainville Coastwatchers, flashed it to Townsville, which sent it to Canberra, which shot it back to Pearl Harbor, where CINCPAC's big transmitter broadcast it over the whole Pacific. One way or another, every ship in the invasion fleet got the word within 25 minutes." Considering the distances involved, and the complications of communication, it might be maintained that neither the British early-warning systems in 1940, nor the later German network in Europe, did better than that. The value of such forewarning may be expressed mathematically: a bomber speed of 160 knots allowed just under two hours before the attackers could cover the 300 miles from Bougainville, and thus (as proved to be the case) effective fighter patrols had time to get airborne and reach the right height before they arrived.

Next morning it happened again. From northern Bougainville another watcher, Jack Read, signaled: 45 BOMBERS NOW GOING SOUTHEAST.† The news enabled Admiral Turner to get the Americans' transports, destroyers and cruisers on the move, so that when the planes appeared most ships were circling at speed and the antiaircraft teams were trigger-ready. Only one destroyer and one transport were lost,

---

* Mason, an Australian, had worked in the Solomons since 1915 and was a plantation manager on Bougainville: he was also adept at operating and repairing radios. (STO was his private call sign, the first three letters of Stokie, the planter on New Britain who had married his sister.)

† Similar signals were transmitted so frequently and helpfully during the campaign that "Forty bombers heading yours" became a catchphrase on Guadalcanal.

and the Japanese, as the fighter pilots say, were clobbered. But all that application of skill and judgment was merely a prelude to what Nimitz's biographer has called "the severest defeat in battle ever suffered by the U.S. Navy," and deep at the heart of that defeat was a failure to profit from signal intelligence.

By the early afternoon of the 7th Admiral Mikawa had assembled east of Bougainville an impressive strike force—his flagship *Chokai* and two light cruisers from Rabaul, and four heavy cruisers from Kavieng. Down the Slot they swept, intending to shatter the American transports during the following night, after eliminating their guard ships. Admiral Turner had been compelled to divide his Support Force into three to cover the separate transport groups. Just after midnight the Japanese column plunged in from the west, down the strait between Savo Island and Cape Esperance (the most northerly tip of Guadalcanal), and completely surprised their enemy: on two American cruisers the captains were actually asleep! It was a bull-in-a-china-shop situation. Far superior in their training and equipment for night fighting, in less than an hour the Japanese dealt with the opposition piecemeal, sinking three American heavy cruisers, and one Australian, and seriously damaging another, *Chicago,* as well as two destroyers. In killed their losses were 34: the Americans lost 1,023 killed and 709 wounded.

The transports were now at Mikawa's mercy, but he lost his nerve —uncertain about the true American strength and fearing that dawn might expose him to an air attack in difficult waters. Too much attention to the rule book, or some lack of Nelsonic élan, seemed to inhibit the Japanese from ruthless exploitation of unexpected opportunities. A few months earlier, in March, they had let General Alexander's army slip away when they had it bottled up in Rangoon.[6] In 1944, at Leyte Gulf, their battle fleet would have an American beachhead and its support craft naked before it—and it would turn away. But if this lack of thrust prevented an immediate disaster for Vandegrift's Marines, what can account for the sinking of Turner's ships in the night battle of Savo Island?

Traffic analysis had given ample warning that there was a threat from Mikawa's cruisers. It was known that they were at sea. On the 6th CINCPAC's bulletin had placed Crudiv 6 in the Rabaul area, Crudiv 18 in the Solomons, and *Chokai* off New Britain. While the Signal Intelligence History reasonably points out that "maintenance of radio silence by these units made it impossible to estimate their every move"—and certainly silence must have been total as the task force raced down the Slot—there was every ground for assuming that the Japanese would hit hard and hit quickly. A condition of extreme alertness was surely mandatory at Guadalcanal. Though Nimitz was merciful, this episode is difficult to excuse.[7]

Moreover, Mikawa's ships were actually spotted at least twice during the morning of the 8th, coming down from Bougainville. But the air-reconnaissance reports that reached Turner were either delayed or inaccurate, suggesting that the task force contained two seaplane tenders—which did not imply an attack by night.

However, the key to the whole catastrophe was the current inability to read the JN25 code. We now know that at 0800 on August 7 Mikawa sent out a general signal to his force commanders: "Today at 1300 Chokai and Crudiv 18 will depart RR [Rabaul] and rendezvous with Crudiv 6 off RXC." The combined divisions would then proceed to "RX–RX1 area": RX was the denominator for the Solomons, and RX1 for Guadalcanal! It was not until long after the battle that the cryptanalysts could decode this message, yet if it had been possible to pick up this crucial intelligence at the time the case might have been altered. The Battle of Savo Island is, in fact, a classic instance of how a combination of partial and mishandled information, and an incapacity to grasp intelligence waiting to be garnered, can result in a defeat more ignoble, in some ways, than Pearl Harbor—for this time the U.S. Navy was at sea, in action with the enemy.*

Nor was there much nobility in what followed. Admiral Fletcher, whose carriers in the Air Support Force, 120 miles away, were scheduled to provide air cover for an initial forty-eight hours, decided that the danger of a counterpunch was too great and withdrew his ships after a mere thirty-six hours. Turner and Vandegrift were horrified: the carriers were still in good shape, comfortably fueled and well stocked with aircraft. But Fletcher decamped, unmoved by protest. There was a domino effect: Turner then pulled out all the transports and their escorts, leaving the Marines literally "on the beach," high,

---

* After a subsequent investigation by a former Commander in Chief of the U.S. Navy, Admiral Hepburn, it was decided that responsibility for what had happened was so evenly divided that action against individuals would not be justified.

dry, alone and desperately short of many essential supplies and pieces of equipment—for the off-loading had been reckoned to need a minimum of four days, and there had inevitably been a good deal of chaos in the early stages.

Something was lacking. No such abandonment of a beachhead ever occurred in the European or Mediterranean theaters: off Norway, at Dunkirk, in the evacuation from Crete, at Salerno and Anzio, the navies, whether British or Allied, stood resolutely by the troops on shore. Admiral Cunningham's words come to mind when, after appalling losses of ships and men, General Wavell offered to free him from any further duty to extricate the men on Crete. Cunningham "said that the Navy had never failed the Army in such a situation, and was not going to do so now; he was going in again that night with everything he had which would float and could bring off troops."[8] More relevantly, one recalls the Battle of Samar on October 25, 1944, when Admiral Kurita with four battleships and six cruisers bore down on the American beachheads at Leyte Gulf, with only the thin line of Kinkaid's destroyers and light carriers between the Japanese and a catastrophe. Kinkaid's craft stayed, fought and made Kurita turn tail.* It could be done—and by the U.S. Navy.

The present lack was in inspiration from the top. The Guadalcanal operation fell under the control of Admiral Ghormley, ComSoPac, or Commander, South Pacific. He was a man defeated in mind before the battle started: indecisive, unaggressive. "The regiment is as good as its colonel" is a true old Army saying. Nimitz, fortunately, soon realized that Ghormley was a man of straw and replaced him, in October, with "Bull" Halsey—after which a gale blew steadily toward the enemy. (It is indicative that Ghormley never visited Guadalcanal to see for himself. Nimitz and Halsey, at considerable risk, both made the effort.) But before the wind changed there would still be much to do.

For now two major developments occurred. Not surprisingly, the Japanese realized that a larger conflict was looming. On August 15 four American destroyers dashed into Guadalcanal with a load of fuel and ammunition, and there was hectic activity as fighters and dive bombers were flown in to work from Henderson Field. The Japanese, for their part, landed reinforcements under heavy attack—

---

* In this action, by coincidence, *Chokai* met her end.

and precipitately charged the Marines, at the Battle of the Tenaru River, only to lose 800 dead and wounded when the unit of Colonel Ikki (who was notionally to have led the landings on Midway) was obliterated along with its commander.

So Yamamoto himself began to take over, from his Combined Fleet headquarters at Truk. And then, at midnight on August 17, the American cryptanalysts received the body blow they had long anticipated: all the important Japanese call signs were changed. As the signal intelligence record puts it, "this security precaution delayed the prompt identification of many enemy units in the heavy operational traffic." On two fronts, therefore, the stakes had risen. Nevertheless FRUPac and Op-20-G were not without resources. Study of the mere *volume* of the traffic, with such aid as direction finding could supply, provided many indications. More to the point, the port director at Truk used for his signals a minor code which the Americans were still reading, and thus monitoring of the buildup that Yamamoto set in train could still continue.

By August 22, in fact, it was evident that a considerable Japanese striking force was ready for action, with quantities of cruisers and destroyers and, probably, a cover of battleships, since the presence of the vast *Yamato, Kirishima* and other capital craft in southern waters had been clearly identified. For Nimitz and his subordinates the baffling question was, where were the heavy carriers? Even one would provide a focus for a powerful task force. The "big cats" were still thought to be somewhere far to the north: but there was no certainty, for the change in call signs had blanketed them off. Nor was the knowledge that they had been exercising many hundreds of miles away of much comfort, since it was recalled that before Midway the carriers had been put through a similar training. In fact Yamamoto had already summoned those old friends the heavy carriers *Zuikaku* and *Shokaku*, as well as the light carrier *Ryujo*. He now had a fleet of 58 ships, with 177 carrier-borne aircraft. (The Americans could have mustered 259, but *Wasp* with 83 planes on board had been detached to refuel.) All doubt ended when, on August 23, the Pacific Fleet Intelligence Summary recorded that heavy enemy landings would occur within the next twelve hours.

And this time, thanks to their intelligence, the Americans were not taken by surprise. As the Japanese bore down on the Solomons during the early morning of the 23rd Fletcher's own Task Forces, with the carriers *Saratoga* and *Enterprise,* were heading toward them on a roughly parallel course. The scene was set for the Battle of the Eastern Solomons.

Within forty-eight hours all of Yamamoto's designs had been foiled. His intention was to hamstring the Americans by destroying their carriers and then, having finished off the rest of the enemy warships, to pulverize Henderson Field into useless dust by air bombardment and the shells of his battle fleet: from *Yamato,* for example, with her 18-inch guns. Having cleared the seas and the skies, he then planned to run down the Slot to Guadalcanal a convoy of troop reinforcements from the Shortland Islands base, just south of Bougainville.

Instead, his *Ryujo* was sunk while *Enterprise,* though badly damaged, survived the day and, by flying off her aircraft to Henderson, actually added strength at the critical point: in any case, *Wasp* rejoined, and replaced her. The powerful advance force of the Japanese Main Body, under Admiral Kondo, was roughly handled and, by nightfall, had broken away to the north and safety. The Combined Fleet never got within bombarding distance of Guadalcanal. To crown all, when on the 25th Yamamoto persisted in running the troop convoy, its escorts were sunk or so damaged by American bombs that it was switched back ignominiously to the Shortlands. Paul Dull in *The Imperial Japanese Navy* (a source of constant enlightenment on the sea war in the Pacific) rightly observes that "it is difficult to understand Yamamoto's thinking in this battle."[9] Once again, as at Midway, he divided his forces instead of concentrating for the annihilating blow. And though it is certain that, had the Japanese fought to the limit, they must have won a vital victory, we see again that curious failure to press the advantage decisively home. But the most significant lesson of the Eastern Solomons battle was that if the Americans met the Japanese on the alert, and not asleep, and if they fought tenaciously instead of losing grip, then in spite of tactical errors, under-training and other limitations (of which there were many instances during those savage August days) they could survive a great fleet action and thwart the Japanese will. A spirit of determined aggression was quickening, even before Halsey's arrival.

The Tokyo Express now went into high gear—and stayed there until the end of 1942—as the Japanese determination to recover Guadalcanal hardened into desperation. Those nightly sallies down the Slot, shrouded in darkness, might well have been impossible to detect, executed as they so often were by destroyers racing at full speed. Nor, of course, were they *all* detected, still less obstructed, as the figures for the Japanese buildup indicate. But the significant question is, how much larger and more rapid might that buildup have been had the Americans not possessed two priceless advantages—the eyes of the coast watchers, who from time to time could observe an "Express train" forming up in daylight in the safe waters of the northern Slot, or during the early stage of its passage; and traffic analysis, which, in spite of all its current limitations, often provided just sufficient warning to enable the Americans to "prepare to receive boarders." By August 31 the Japanese Army had marked down Guadalcanal as its prime objective, giving only a second priority to the operations in New Guinea. On September 18 (as the massive War History of the Japanese Defense Agency records) the decision was taken to concentrate everything on Guadalcanal. Such was the measure of escalation since Vandegrift's Marines first scrambled ashore. The Solomons were now like one of those cornfields or peach orchards on a Civil War battlefield: neither side was going to relax its grip, whatever the cost in blood.

The coast-watcher service in the Solomons was directed from a station on Guadalcanal itself. The controller was a lieutenant commander from the Australian Navy, Hugh Mackenzie. Since he was in immediate constant contact with Vandegrift's command post, and since the U.S. Navy's warships offshore could monitor signals broadcast even by the most distant coast watchers on their X frequency, a simple but highly efficient early-warning system was developed. The extent to which it was valued—and built into the whole Allied intelligence network—may be judged by what happened after August 28, when Read on Bougainville reported to KEN (the code name for Mackenzie's control point on Guadalcanal) that the Japanese had constructed and were now operating from an airstrip at Buka, on the northern end of the island. This was followed by another report early in September from Paul Mason, whose lookout was on Malabita Hill at the southern end of Bougainville: he too noticed Japanese preparations for a landing field, on the plain beneath him. The implications were stark and obvious. That northern strip would save Japanese aircraft some 300 miles on missions against Henderson Field: the southern one would cut off another 200 miles. And early warning would be that much more difficult.

Mackenzie correctly decided that observation must be improved on the flank of the corridor down the Slot, along which the Tokyo Express and the raiding aircraft traveled. The answer was to plant watchers on Choiseul and Vella Lavella, the two big islands southward of Bougainville which actually formed the two sides of the mouth of the Slot: but how to get them there? With the aid of an assistant to the Australian Director of Naval Intelligence and Vandegrift's intelligence officer, plus a personal appeal to Admiral Ghormley himself at ComSoPac, four new watchers embarked on the U.S. submarine *Grampus* at Brisbane in Queensland on October 6, supervised by the head of the Allied Intelligence Bureau in Australia. By the third week of October two men were on Choiseul and another two on Vella Lavella (though the latter had prolonged difficulty in making radio contact with KEN).

Precise details about the coast-watching network and its efficient intelligence service (which included the rescue of many U.S. airmen shot down over the Slot, and aid for amphibious landings as the Americans began to feel their way northward) may be found in Walter Lord's brilliant evocation of their achievement, *Lonely Vigil*. The importance of the contribution, in enabling the Americans to contain if not wholly to counter the Tokyo Express, is self-evident. Certainly it was to Admiral Halsey, who declared that "the coast watchers saved Guadalcanal, and Guadalcanal saved the Pacific." A generous overstatement, since their efforts should be seen as part of a triple-pronged probe into Japanese intentions, of which air reconnaissance was—at least occasionally—another arm, the third being traffic analysis and the breaking of low-level codes.

So constant and varied were the nightly intrusions of the Tokyo Express during the remaining months of 1942 that it is difficult to illustrate the overall contribution of traffic analysis in this vital area. Sometimes a hint, sometimes a more specific warning: it was a continuous and complicated process. For simplicity, therefore, it seems better to select a "test tube" example—the case of January 1943. During this month the Japanese were already hedging their bets and cutting down on reinforcements for Guadalcanal, in secret preparation for the final evacuation. There are, in fact, only four identifiable sorties of the Tokyo Express during this period, and it is instructive to examine what happened to them.[10]

The first was during the night of January 2, by ten destroyers. Undetected by signal intelligence, they were spotted coincidentally by passing American bombers. Two were sunk and others damaged, but supplies and men got through to Guadalcanal. On the 10th a coast watcher's warning that destroyers had left the Shortlands, on course to the southeast, was supported by advice from ComSoPac that radio intelligence suggested an imminent Tokyo Express. P.T. boats intercepted, and Sigint subsequently confirmed damage to at least one destroyer. On the 13th things were more definite. This time ComSoPac at 1650 hours gave warning that an Express run was likely that night: ninety minutes later this was corrected to confirm that a destroyer dash was probable on the night of the 14th. All this was based on signal intelligence. And so it happened. Nine destroyers left the Shortlands during the late afternoon of the 14th (as a coast watcher reported). They were tracked in to Savo Island by a night-search aircraft and caught between Savo and Cape Esperance, in the middle of an electrical storm, by thirteen P.T. boats. In this action four Japanese destroyers were damaged (confirmed by Sigint) and 30 aircraft were lost as against 8 American. Finally, a sequence of warnings from CINCPAC, all derived from traffic analysis, indicated that another run was due on January 26. Late that night a search aircraft spotted seven destroyers and a cruiser some ninety-five miles from Guadalcanal. A few bombs seem to have persuaded the Japanese either to put in at a safe island or to return on their tracks, for the enemy vanished. These usefully isolated examples show very clearly how signal intelligence, coast watching and air reconnaissance were combined, with fruitful results. Of the preceding months, it may be said that the greater the frequency of the Expresses, the more potent was that combination.

Indeed, this frustration of the Japanese ability to maintain a force on Guadalcanal—not to speak of retaking Henderson Field—was a major factor in their ultimate collapse. The Express runs were made at a punishing cost in destroyers sunk and damaged, and the Japanese simply lacked squadrons sufficient to work with the Combined Fleet, to protect their carriers and to engage nightly in these expensive expeditions. Moreover, though they could still feed men into Guadalcanal—at a price—to supply them adequately proved impossible. There is a ghastly record of the misery endured by their troops—of starved, emaciated soldiers seeking a castaway's sustenance in the jungle instead of fighting their enemy; of units, debilitated by every form of tropical disease, too frail to hold out against the remorseless climate. The Marines, and the Army battalions which took over from them, had their many private agonies on Guadalcanal, but it may be supposed that for the ordinary Japanese soldier-of-the-line it was infinitely worse.

The clinching factor, however, was this: if any prolonged and hard-fought amphibious operation is to succeed it is necessary, sooner or later, to get superiority in the air and on the surrounding seas. Here the Japanese failed abysmally in all those air/surface actions, listed earlier, which from time to time punctuate the story of the Solomons campaign with shattering violence. The significant point is that, after their humiliating defeat in the Battle of Savo Island, the Americans were never again taken by surprise—in any important sense—at the start of a major fleet action: in consequence the Japanese, though they sank many fine ships, never achieved by their tactics that crushing victory which would have had a decisive, strategic importance. Yet though the quality of their airmen was steadily eroded, as the losses of Midway were compounded and the Americans swiftly increased the sophistication and quantity of their antiaircraft armament, the Japanese at critical times often had a marked superiority in weight of metal, mustering more battleships, more cruisers or more heavy carriers than their opponents. On paper, they ought to have won. The extraordinary achievement of the Americans in converting themselves—almost overnight, as it seemed—into a great and efficient naval power is not diminished by the judgment that, in the Solomons, it was Sigint and other forms of intelligence that gave them the edge.

Which makes the last chapter of the Solomons story all the more extraordinary. The damaging interception of those nine destroyers on January 14 was misinterpreted by the Americans, who thought that this and other Express operations during that month were merely a continuation of the effort to reinforce, sustained by the Japanese over so many weary months. In fact, the Japanese command had already accepted defeat. The run on January 14 was the opening move in Operation KE, the evacuation of Guadalcanal, whose careful planning, extreme secrecy and effective execution make it comparable with the evacuation of Gallipoli. On the 14th a group of 600 men, the special Matsuda unit, was set ashore to act as a rearguard for the coming withdrawal.

The job was done during three nights in early February. A succession of rescue vessels—as many as twenty destroyers at a time—removed by February 8 no less than 10,652 men for the loss of a single destroyer; nor were the Americans on Guadalcanal aware, until the afternoon of the 9th, that their enemy had departed. The question is inevitable—how was this possible? And the answer is presumably that —as the Germans were to prove in the Ardennes Battle of the Bulge— if meticulous security cloaks an operation, and if its planning is conducted with thoughtful care, and if you are given a streak of luck, then even the best of warning systems may be cheated. The Japanese themselves certainly expected trouble, for they held in the offing a considerable Strike Force of cruisers and carriers, ready to pounce on a predictable counterattack. It never came.

Still, this was not an evacuation about which it could be maintained with any degree of plausibility—as happened after Dunkirk—that it was "a victory within a defeat." For the Japanese defeat was absolute. Those ten thousand evacuees, after all, were only a third of the total force which had been so painfully landed on Guadalcanal. With Henderson Field and the anchorages in their hands, the Americans now had a firm base from which to begin to exploit northward. The "fork in the road" had been reached. During those early weeks of 1943 the Japanese made an irreversible move back along the route to Tokyo. And it was no coincidence that just about the same time, on January 21, the Japanese in New Guinea finally accepted that their invasion had been stemmed by Australian and American units under the command of General Douglas MacArthur.

CHAPTER EIGHT

"You Are the Hero"

*The prescience with which he may at times seem to have been
endowed was generally the outcome of the cracking of the
Japanese naval code.*
    Gavin Long, *MacArthur as Military Commander*

ONE RESULT OF the Second World War was that General Mac-
Arthur became the virtual Emperor of Japan. During the earliest
phase of the Pacific campaign, however, his progress was far from
imperial. Yet his arrival in Australia seemed at first like a sort of
salvation. After he had slipped out of besieged Corregidor—on the
clear instructions of the President—the general, his wife, his small
son and his most trusted staff officers were transferred by motorboat
and aircraft to Darwin, where he touched down on the morning of
March 17, 1942. Next he entrained for Alice Springs, in the stark
Australian outback.* Here he was met by Patrick J. Hurley, the
Republican from Oklahoma who later became Roosevelt's personal
representative with Chiang Kai-shek. Hurley cheered a defeated commander by telling him that the American people, always eager to pay
homage to a knight in shining armor, had taken him to their hearts.
Once it was Pershing, then Lindbergh. "Now," said Hurley, "you
are the hero."[1]

The Australian Government, which had not known that he was on
his way, felt a similar exhilaration. Those clouds of glory that surrounded MacArthur had not been darkened by his loss of the Philip-

---

* On February 19 others had moved southward from Darwin. On that day, the first time
that Australia had been attacked by an enemy, Darwin was bombed by Japanese aircraft.
The panic-stricken exodus that followed, reminiscent of James Thurber's *The Day the
Dam Burst*, came to be known as "The Alice Springs Stakes."

pines, and his presence seemed a guarantee of the American support without which a Japanese invasion appeared to be inevitable. This mood was universal. A few days later MacArthur met in Melbourne the Australian Commander in Chief, General Blamey, whose biographer recalls the charisma of the man from Corregidor. "Tall and graceful, lean, handsome and photogenic as a film star, he radiated belief in himself and in the sacred character of his mission. 'We shall win or we shall die,' he said with messianic simplicity, and a *frisson* of excitement ran through the continent." On the 26th he attended a lunch in Canberra, the capital, where it was announced that Roosevelt had awarded him the Congressional Medal of Honor. "I have come," MacArthur responded, "as a soldier in a great crusade of personal liberty."[2]

There are many reasons why the achievements of his South West Pacific Command, SWPA, were relatively meager during the months that followed this euphoria. The maelstrom in the Slot and the savage contest for Guadalcanal sucked in the best and the most of whatever ships and troops could be spared for the Pacific, while MacArthur's impassioned demands for reinforcements shifted neither Roosevelt nor General Marshall from their agreed priority, Bolero, the buildup of American forces in the United Kingdom for the invasion of Europe. In effect the South West Pacific Area was at the end of a limb. So long as Australia could be held securely—which soon became evident—neither heaven nor earth was going to be moved by the Washington administration, as MacArthur pleaded, to set him back on the road to the Philippines. It is only just to observe that he had to make do with what he could get, and that he was deficient in everything.

All the same, not every deficiency was inevitable, and in a book concerned with the impact of intelligence on the war with Japan it is mandatory to consider whether, in this vital field, MacArthur and his staff did in fact make the most of what they could get. The answer is, certainly not, and the basic explanation is simple.

At the heart of it all was MacArthur's own posture. Driven by the egomania of a potential dictator, he had all a dictator's ambivalence about advice—and what is intelligence but advice? Hitler too often preferred the voice of his own daemon to the warnings of his intelligence community. Stalin for obscure private reasons disregarded over seventy warnings, several of the utmost precision, that the Germans were about to invade Russia. And so there were times when Mac-

Arthur, though shrewd enough on occasion to act on good intelligence, spurned it because he had already made his own picture, and what was his own was indisputable. This intermittent blindness was intensified by his pride in possessing: he could not endure the presence within his command of agencies whose responsibility did not run directly to himself. In this spirit he refused to allow OSS to operate within the South West Pacific theater and later, in 1944, he fought and lost a battle with General Marshall about the posting to his zone of Ultra advisers from the Special Branch, whose allegiance, defined by Marshall himself, was to the Pentagon in Washington.*

And there was another difficulty. At a time when Secretary Stimson and the War Department were writing off Australia as "a secondary theater," on April 18, 1942, it was announced that the Allied Supreme Commander in that theater would be a man who thought of himself as *nulli secundus,* second to none. Few studied MacArthur more closely than his British liaison officer, Lieutenant Colonel Wilkinson, who served at his side from the fall of the Philippines onward—but who also, through MI 6 channels, reported directly and without inhibition to Churchill. It was the long-suffering Wilkinson who, in late 1943, filed this vignette of the Supremo: "He is shrewd, selfish, proud, remote, highly-strung and *vastly vain.* He has imagination, self-confidence, physical courage and charm, but no humour about himself, *no regard for truth, and is unaware of these defects.*† He mistakes his emotions and ambitions for principles. With moral depth he would be a great man: as it is he is a near-miss, which may be worse than a mile . . . his main ambition would be to end the war as pan-American hero in the form of generalissimo of all Pacific Theatres."[3] *You are the hero.* Inevitably, and to his own detriment, such self-absorption was reflected in the publicity projected from SWPA, publicity used in calculated fashion by MacArthur to enhance, at all costs, his own image.

The inaccurate braggadocio of his communiqués, besides misleading the American public, poisoned the wells from which his intelligence was drawn. The vast flow of information which the Navy derived from its penetration of the Japanese codes, from traffic analysis and other sources, was filtered to SWPA, among other channels,

---

* For further details about MacArthur and the Special Branch, see p. 271.
† Author's italics.

through the Fleet Intelligence Officer of the Pacific Fleet. Men like Layton, or the staff of FRUPac, or the Belconnen unit in Australia knew too much of the truth to be taken in by the verbiage of publicity: their contempt for massive and demonstrable chicanery certainly did nothing to diminish the pervasive hostility and suspicion between Army and Navy which so unfortunately infected the atmosphere of the Pacific.*

Yet how could it be otherwise when, as Jasper Holmes sadly recalled, *Time* magazine on June 15, 1942, reported: "On a hugely swollen scale, the Battle of Midway was a repetition of the earlier rehearsal in the Coral Sea when Douglas MacArthur's bombers from Australia took the play from the Navy."[4] This nonsense, derived from MacArthur's publicity, "greeted the carrier pilots," as Holmes noted, "when they arrived at Pearl Harbor after sustaining grievous losses to win the Battle." Moreover, the inflated claims from "MacArthur's Headquarters" about the successes of his Army bombers in raids on Rabaul and elsewhere were immediately detected as false by FRUPac, whose cryptanalysts read the routine reports from Japanese bases about their actual losses. For all his loyal support of MacArthur, even the clear-sighted George Marshall was compelled, from time to time, to ask stern questions about the claims that emanated from SWPA.

There was another barrier interposed between the supreme commander and reality. It has been said of the staff system during Nixon's presidency that it represents "the most aberrant act of administrative insanity known to modern governments." From the military point of view, something similar might be observed about the way that MacArthur surrounded himself with a praetorian guard of deferential subordinates—"the Bataan gang," as his senior staff officers were bitterly christened. It was singularly dangerous for a man of so egocentric a temperament. Yet the arithmetic of his command structure, and the nature of the personalities involved, speak for themselves.

---

* The Australian press was similarly disillusioned. In September 1942 the general manager of the Melbourne *Herald* forwarded to General Rowell, then commanding in New Guinea, a protest from one of his war correspondents: "The fact is it is useless our writing anything unless it conforms to the communiqué though the communiqué be false." "It all boils down to the fact that MacArthur has ruled that all reports are subject to his communiqués," the manager added, "and so the whole business of deception goes on." (The *Herald*'s manager William Dunstan, it is relevant to note, won the Victoria Cross in the famous Lone Pine actions on Gallipoli in 1915.)

When MacArthur announced the staff for the new combined head-quarters of the South West Pacific Area—on April 19—the eleven senior positions at his command post all went to American officers, and of these no less than eight had been evacuated in the small group that accompanied him from Corregidor. In spite of the large respon-sibility he had now undertaken in respect of the defense of Australia and the direction of her forces, the only Australian with any significant authority at the top was General Blamey, his country's Commander in Chief, who also acted as Commander Allied Land Forces. The Bataan gang was strongly emplaced.

They closed ranks around MacArthur. Moreover, his standing in the eyes of the intelligence agencies, of the Navy and of his allies was further impaired by the fact that the two men on whom he most relied, Major General Richard Sutherland (his Chief of Staff) and Colonel Charles Willoughby (his Chief Intelligence Officer), were both soldiers cast in a hard, authoritarian, unattractive mold. In-dustrious and able, Sutherland was nevertheless a self-centered and arrogant autocrat with a brusque Prussian manner and an ugly temper.* Willoughby was flawed, as an intelligence officer, by the conviction that his avid reading of military history had made him an authority on strategy. Worse than that, he was jealous in his own domain and resented excessively the intrusion of others. MacArthur, aware of this quirk, nevertheless protected him—of all "the gang" he was the only one to serve his master without a break from 1941 to 1951 —and was prone to accept his appreciations as gospel,† particularly as Willoughby produced the intelligence estimates which were most likely to be palatable.

In the main it is damaging for commanders to adopt a staff which acts like a self-regarding coterie, an inner circle, and treats all other men, equal or subordinate, with a contemptuous disregard. When Sir Oliver Leese was appointed to command the Land Forces in South-

---

* He was also a Iago to MacArthur's Othello. Perhaps the best of the field commanders in SWPA, Major General Eichelberger, wrote of Sutherland that "he was a natural climber trying to advance his own interest at the expense of the other fellows . . . He knew how to work on General MacArthur like Paderewski playing the piano. He could bring out in MacArthur any latent envy and jealousy in his nature . . . Sutherland had a strange control over MacArthur." See Horner, *Crisis of Command: Australian Gen-eralship and the Japanese Threat*, p. 65.
† One must honestly add, not always. Some of MacArthur's more brilliant coups, as the campaign developed, were undertaken in defiance of Willoughby's intelligence estimates.

east Asia he did not further his cause by bringing with him from the Mediterranean a group of officers from the Eighth Army "with sand on their shoes." Haig in the First World War was weakened, where he should have found strength, by the effect on others of his opinionated Head of Operations, Brigadier Davidson. His intelligence chief, Charteris, notoriously—and at Cambrai disastrously—produced for Haig the picture he was thought to want rather than uncomfortable truths. As the Field Marshal's best biographer, John Terraine, remarked, "neither of these men, though both were talented, had the stature to argue with their C-in-C or change his opinions when they privately believed him to be in error."[5] In all the famous "marriages" between a general and his senior staff neither sycophancy nor self-interest has been the advisers' characteristic, but rather independence of mind and courage to stand up and be counted. From many important points of view, therefore, it looked from the beginning as though MacArthur, in spite of his panache, his considerable experience and his total self-confidence, might be at risk when it came to evaluating and applying intelligence and liable to take a wrong reading of the battlefield, of the enemy and even of his own troops. Of all the Allied theaters of war his is, perhaps, the one in which Ultra had the most checkered history.

Yet within a few days of his arrival in Australia MacArthur showed an awareness of the paramount importance of Sigint. As early as April 1 he signaled to the Adjutant General in Washington: "Investigation discloses that a central Allied signal intelligence section is required for the interception and cryptanalyzing of Japanese intelligence. The time delay and transmission uncertainties incident to sending intercepted material to Washington and elsewhere dictate that this work be handled locally. Allied forces here are organizing such a bureau." Indeed: but the unit thus established was the Central Bureau, run by the Chief Signals Officer, Brigadier General Spencer Akin, with Colonel Sherr as executive officer:* both were members of the Bataan gang. The naval Sigint unit, Belconnen (based on the 75 men from the Cast station in the Philippines who were evacuated with Commander Fabian), was not integrated into the so-called "*central* bureau,"

---

* It was Sherr who organized the Central Bureau at Brisbane in August 1942. Next month, unfortunately, he died in an aircraft accident while on a special mission to India and China.

but owed its allegiance directly to FRUPac in Hawaii and Op-20-G in Washington. Certainly Fabian serviced MacArthur's headquarters with intelligence (among other things, Belconnen, unlike the Central Bureau, possessed a Purple machine and could read the Magic cipher) but since the Bureau was Army-oriented, MacArthur-oriented, a futile friction and sense of apartheid between the two Sigint organizations was generated as the years went by.

This is not to say that during the early days MacArthur was starved of Sigint about Japanese intentions. On the contrary. On April 16 Sutherland warned MacArthur's air commander, General Brett, that "information obtained indicates hostile action by sea . . . will be made from Rabaul area about April 21 and that attack may be made on Port Moresby from SE about April 21." Six days later he modified this warning, advising the senior commanders in SWPA that the absence of any dangerous concentration of shipping, "together with *other information* available, points to a postponement of any enemy attack against Port Moresby until later in the month."* But on May 1 MacArthur wrote to Blamey that *information from many sources* suggested a Japanese drive southward "from Rabaul towards the islands and mainland in the northeastern sector of this area." The backing for these appreciations was, of course, signal intelligence: the evidence presented in Chapter 4 is a sufficient confirmation—confirmation, in particular, that Port Moresby was constantly in the Japanese sights.[6]

Nor was the seaward threat to Moresby the sole indication. On May 18 the Belconnen station intercepted a signal which mentioned a *land route* to Moresby—which could only be over the Owen Stanley Range, the spine of Papua (eastern New Guinea), from an area like Buna on the northern coast. The Navy's Signal Intelligence Summary records for this day that "problems of translation made it difficult to establish at that moment whether this road was to be used as an invasion route for the capture of Moresby, because a seaborne invasion was impossible in the face of Allied opposition, or whether it was to be used for supply purposes after the occupation. However, it was definitely

---

* On the 30th General Marshall signaled about a press dispatch in the Washington papers "under dateline Allied HQ Aust 27 Apr," which referred to a Japanese naval concentration in the Marshalls apparently preparing for a new operation. "Jap well aware that submarine scouting would be ineffective for obtaining information for such conclusions and justified in believing their codes broken—which would be disastrous." MacArthur patched up an explanation.

known that the Japanese were about to use the route for some important purpose." Adding all together, it is evident that the general drift of Japanese intentions—with Moresby as the objective—had been disclosed by intelligence sources well before the months-long campaign in Papua had even started.

If this view is correct, then MacArthur's initial reactions seem contradictory and incomprehensible. There is no significant evidence that he was (or needed to be) deeply concerned about a major invasion of the Australian continent. Indeed, by the time of his arrival or soon afterward the Australians' own desperate strategy, conceived in the aftermath of Pearl Harbor, was already fading: this was the notion of "the Brisbane line"—the abandonment of northern Australia to the enemy and a last-ditch defense of the mainland along the Tropic of Capricorn. During the first four months of 1942, moreover, over 50,000 American troops had arrived in Australia, as well as the battle-seasoned 7th and part of the 6th Australian divisions from the Middle East. Publicly, at least, MacArthur's intentions were outward-looking and aggressive from the start. After the U.S. Navy's victory at Midway they became grandiose.

On May 28 Nimitz proposed to MacArthur that they should cooperate in an attack on Tulagi, in the Solomons, but MacArthur turned the idea down on the grounds that SWPA was not strong enough for such an undertaking. Yet immediately after Midway, on June 8, he suggested to General Marshall that if he could be given two aircraft carriers and an amphibious division he could grab the main Japanese base at Rabaul! "I could retake that important area, forcing the enemy back 700 miles to his base at Truk with manifold strategic advantages . . ." Marshall, usually so levelheaded, liked and supported this impracticable proposition, but Admiral King sensibly stopped it dead in its tracks.

What is so extraordinary about this swing is that the vital central area, to which both signal intelligence and cool strategic judgment should have pointed, was first disregarded and then given only lax attention. Something so obviously had to be done about New Guinea before MacArthur could make any progress. It was equally obvious that the Japanese had their eyes on Port Moresby. Yet the suggestion for an amphibious assault on distant Rabaul simply ignored New Guinea's intervening land mass, and when that suggestion was rejected, MacArthur—it might be thought culpably—was slow to lay hands on those regions of New Guinea so close to Australia—Moresby in the south and Buna on the northern shore. And the Japanese got there first.

Few of the troops under MacArthur's command were filtered across the dividing strait. And yet, early in July, his staff was definitely warned by radio intelligence that the Japanese were likely to land at Buna and push south, over the Owen Stanleys, by the Kokoda trail to Moresby. Merely a battalion was then pushed up to Kokoda, and two divisions made a precautionary move from southern Australia to Queensland. But when, on July 15, MacArthur at last decided to capture a base at Buna (in August) and establish airfields there for attacks on Rabaul, it was already too late. On the night of July 21 a Japanese South Seas Force began to land at Buna and by the 29th its spearheads had reached Kokoda: within weeks the Australians were falling back over the mountains toward Port Moresby.

Superbly dogged fighting by the relatively raw Australians, back along the dreadful Kokoda trail and down at Milne Bay, restored the situation so that slowly, savagely but ultimately Buna could be re-covered and springboards set up in northern New Guinea for a forward leap. But that was not achieved *until the following January*, with 28,000 men the victims of malaria, and some miserable per-formances by American units which caused the heads of their com-manders to roll and General Eichelberger to emerge, at last, as a true leader in battle.* During these months the conventional picture of MacArthur as a farsighted, omnicompetent generalissimo collapses in the face of the facts. What is particularly disturbing is the cavalier attitude displayed toward sound intelligence sources—and the inabil-ity of MacArthur to visit the battleground and check up on the truth. The message was there, available—but the messengers were cold-shouldered.[7]

However, the basis was laid for a myth which still persists: Mac-Arthur was the general who won his battles with the fewest casualties. On January 28, 1943, his headquarters issued a triumphant com-muniqué which claimed that victory in the Papuan campaign had

---

* When inept leadership and inexperienced American troops created a shambles around Buna, and MacArthur told Eichelberger, "Go out there, Bob, and take Buna or don't come back alive," it is symptomatic that he drew the general to one side to say that if he was successful MacArthur would see that medals came his way and *would release his name for publication in the press!*

been achieved cheaply—because it had been conducted without the "necessity of a hurry attack": "the time element was in this case of little importance." Next day the communiqué appeared in the New York *Times* and a legend was born.

It was wholly untrue. When Samuel Milner was preparing his volume *Victory in Papua* for the official history of the U.S. Army in the Pacific, he received on March 8, 1954, a letter from General Eichelberger, who, more than any other man, was responsible for that victory. Eichelberger wrote that the communiqué was "one of the greatest surprises of my life. As you know, our Allied losses were heavy and, as commander in the field, I had been told many times of the necessity for speed." (The record shows signal after signal sent to Eichelberger, urging him on because time was short.) As to casualties (in a campaign in which the sick rate was appalling, and whose conclusion merely left MacArthur the positions he held—or should have held—six months earlier) it is sufficient to observe that losses in Papua were greater than those on Guadalcanal. The combined American/Australian figures are: dead 3,095, wounded 5,451, whereas on Guadalcanal the Americans lost 1,600 dead and 4,245 wounded. In Papua death, wounds and disease removed nearly 90 percent of the American 32nd Division. Such is the gap between propaganda and reality.

It is therefore refreshing to be able to turn to a genuine (and inexpensive) victory, famous as the Battle of the Bismarck Sea, which is a classic example of the effective application of Ultra. "As early as 19 February Allied intelligence, *which already had built up a reputation for accuracy in its predictions of enemy movements,* * had issued a warning of 'further troop movements to the Lae area.' By 28 February, G-2 talked in terms of a landing to be attempted at Lae on 5 March and at Madang on or about 12 March."[8] Translated, what this sentence from the official history of the Army Air Forces means is that signal intelligence had identified the presence at Rabaul of a large troop convoy (at about divisional strength—in fact, the Japanese 15th Infantry Division) which was due to sail for the northern coast of New Guinea, under heavy escort, to reinforce the Japanese presence there. At a time when SWPA was disorganized after the Papua campaign, this was a threat of a high order.

Fortunately the commander of the 5th Air Force, George C.

---

* Author's italics.

Kenney,* was a brilliant all-round airman who within a year had jumped from lieutenant colonel to major general. Inventive, authoritative and a good manager of men, he had all the qualities—including the ability to get on with MacArthur without losing his integrity—which were needed at this time in New Guinea. Both the aircraft and their crews were very tired. Many of each were survivors from the early days of the Japanese war. Maintained in the humid jungle, the battle-weary B-17 Fortresses suffered from an acute shortage of spares: fungus corroded the electrical equipment, lubricating oils would simply evaporate. Sometimes, to patch up bullet holes in a fuselage, mechanics were reduced to flattening a tin can and cutting out a piece to fit. The pilots of longer service were stale, enervated and losing heart. Between his arrival in August 1942 and the Bismarck Sea battle in the following spring, Kenney transformed the scene.[9]

In particular, two new methods for air attack on shipping were evolved and assiduously practiced. The first was "skip bombing," whereby a plane came in low and bounced its bomb off the surface of the sea into a ship's side: this was soon refined into precision bombing from masthead height, a dangerous art. The second was the coordinated attack. While the B-17's dropped their bombs from on high, beneath them medium bombers got to work while down on the deck specially modified B-25's,† with a powerful armament of forward-firing guns, would sweep the enemy convoy with bullets. By February 1942 the 5th Air Force had mastered these arts and for Kenney, alerted by signal intelligence about the Rabaul convoy, it was merely a matter of keeping them at high pitch and waiting for the kill.

It came during three days at the beginning of March 1943, when, as expected, the convoy arrived off the northern coast of New Guinea and all those careful rehearsals earned their reward. Destruction was total. In 400 sorties, and for the loss of five aircraft, the convoy was eliminated. Moreover, the Japanese never again attempted reinforcement on this part of their front by sizable shipping, and their troops

---

* Kenney had relieved the less competent General Brett in August 1942.
† The standard B-25 was a twin-engined medium bomber. In the modified B-25 C1, ten machine guns were fitted, a bombardier was omitted from the crew and only small demolition or fragmentation bombs were carried. The B-17 Fortress, with its four engines, was designed to operate as a heavy bomber at a considerable height.

now had to rely on support by submarine, air ferry or incidental barge traffic. They were like castaways.

It is thus unfortunate that over what MacArthur later called the decisive aerial engagement in his theater there should have been another controversy about fact and fiction. The immediate reports from SWPA described the convoy as consisting of 12 to 14 transports and 8 to 10 warships, including 3 cruisers: all sunk. But subsequent research, during and after the war, indicated that the correct figure for vessels sunk is 12 transports and only 4 destroyers. No matter. Thanks to the early warning supplied by Sigint the Japanese had suffered a defeat which proved to be irreversible. Still, it is worth noting that when the revised figures were produced in mid-1943 by the Historical Office of the Air Force, MacArthur sent to Washington a signal which "contained the remarkable suggestion that some action might be taken against those responsible for calling the claim into question"! Moreover (as a news release in the Washington *Post* of September 1945 reveals), he continued after the war to assert the larger, unsubstantiated claim.[10]

It was only a few weeks after this massacre in the Bismarck Sea that Ultra showed the way to the most dramatic single event in the Pacific war—the death of Admiral Yamamoto. On April 14 FRUPac decoded a signal sent out a few hours earlier from the headquarters of the Commander in Chief of the Japanese Southeastern Air Fleet. It revealed that on the 18th Yamamoto, in a plane escorted by six fighters, would be paying a rapid visit to locations in the Rabaul area. The time of his arrival at, and departure from, each of the specified points was given to the minute. And only a glance at the map was needed to realize that the whole of his tour would take place within the range of the South Pacific Air Force.

Intense discussion followed. When Layton took the signal in to Nimitz the possibilities were immediately obvious, though Nimitz's practical question was "whether they could find a more effective fleet commander." And this was a sensible thought. More than once in the history of war it has seemed preferable to allow an enemy commander to live whose method of conducting operations you have come to understand and whose overall competence you have come to doubt. Such, now, was Yamamoto's image at the headquarters of the Pacific Fleet in the Pearl Harbor he had sought to destroy. His old audacity and

~~IZ3S1Zx~~(wm)   (CY-1: #23916)

I KA MI (GUADALCANAL Oper. For.)
DE: SO SU FU (RABAUL Comm. Unit)
U TU 785 W 176
~~= = + = =~~ - - - - - - - - - - - -

From: ?
Action: RO HI 2   (SOLOMONS Defense Force)
           HO KO 8   ?
           KU TA 2   (Air Group #204)
           YU YO 2   (Air Flotilla #26)

           (Ballale Garrison Comdr.)
Info: NO KA 1   ?

4/131755/I &943   (TCI 4/140009/I on 4990 A kcs)bt

#7   From: CinC Southeastern Air Fleet.

          On 18 April CinC Combined Fleet will visit
RXZ, R___ and RXF in accordance following schedule:

          1. Depart RR at 0600 in a medium attack
plane escorted by 6 fighters. Arrive RXZ at 0800.
Proceed by minesweeper to R__ arriving at 0840.
(___have minesweeper ready at #1 Base). Depart R____
at 0945 in above minesweeper and arrive RXZ at 1030?
(- - - - - - -). Depart RXZ at 1100? ~~and~~ in medium
attack plane and arrive RXF at 1110. ~~xxxxxxx~~
- - - - - - -. Depart RXF at 1400 in medium attack
plane and arrive RR at ~~1##~~ 1540.

2. At each of the above places the Commander-in-Chief will make short tour of inspection and at _____ he will visit the sick and wounded, but current operations should continue. Each force commander - - - -·

JN-3: 2825 (MR) (Japanese) (S) Navy Trans. 4/141705/Q(?)

In case of bad weather the trip will be postponed one day. ---

Comment: Further details of trip first reported in HYPO _____. Translation of paragraph 2 is free one.

14.108

4P
COPEK OP
142157

JN-3: 2825 (MR) (Japanese) (S) Navy Trans. 4/141705/Q(?)

general ability were recognized and respected: yet again and again, at Midway, in the Solomons actions, he had seemed cautious and irresolute. All we now know about Yamamoto's pessimism strongly supports this view. Nevertheless, Nimitz concluded, "It's down in Halsey's bailiwick. If there's a way, he'll find it. All right, we'll try it." He then sent a signal to Halsey which spelled out Yamamoto's itinerary, and prudently recommended that to protect the security of the code breakers the intelligence should be ascribed to coast watchers in the Rabaul area. "If forces you command have capability shoot down Yamamoto and staff," he added, "you are hereby authorized initiate preliminary planning."

Planning could only be provisional because approval must be sought from Washington. The risks were enormous. According to Nimitz's biographer, for example, it was considered that "the assassination of so eminent a personage might have political repercussions": a curious reservation, in the midst of a world war. Infinitely more important was the possibility that accurate interception of a few aircraft, at a particular point in the vast Pacific and at precisely the right moment, might suggest to the Japanese something more than coincidence: might, indeed, "blow" the fact that the Americans were able to read their signals—even those relating to the secret journey of a commander in chief. So the agreement of the Secretary of the Navy and of the President himself was sought—and granted.[11]

The rest is history. Commander Air, Solomons, Admiral Mitscher on the morning of the 18th dispatched a strike force of long-range Lightning fighters which ambushed Yamamoto and his escort over the southern tip of Bougainville island. That afternoon a message came through to Nimitz from Halsey:

> P-38 led by Major John W. Mitchell, USA, visited Kahili area about 0930. Shot down two bombers escorted by Zeros flying formation. One shot down believed to be test flight. Three Zeros added to the score sum total six. One P-38 failed to return. April 18 seems to be our day.

Halsey, sending his congratulations via Mitscher to "Mitchell and his hunters," added, "Sounds as though one of the ducks in their bag was a peacock."

Though success was complete, the danger of compromising the

code breakers—much increased by inevitable speculation and loose talk—was frightful. The decision-makers, from Roosevelt and Nimitz downward, were indeed proved to be men of nerve and judgment, for the gamble paid off. Like all who play for high stakes in war, they would, nevertheless, have been exposed to passionate and justified criticism had the Japanese guessed the truth and radically altered their code system. In the event, all the investigations they conducted never seem to have led them to the central point—that the signal from the commander in chief of the Southeastern Air Fleet of April 14 had been broken. At most, they thought, some signals on local networks in the Rabaul area might have been penetrated. So the JN system continued as before. There had been little doubt as to the result of the strike, but confirmation came from the Japanese themselves when, on May 21, Yamamoto's ashes returned to his homeland on the battleship *Musashi* and Radio Tokyo announced his death while "engaged in combat with the enemy."[12]

The drama of the admiral's destruction was a symbolic episode in the history of the war in the Pacific: for both sides it marked, if not the beginning of the end, at least the end of the beginning. In the eyes of the Japanese Navy, Yamamoto seemed like the reincarnation of his great predecessor Togo, who some forty years earlier had shattered the Russians at sea: his successor, Admiral Mineichi Koga, lacked his panache, his intellectual drive, his charisma, and throughout the rest of the war no Japanese naval commander of equal distinction would emerge. The fire was guttering out.

In a larger sense, April 1943 approximately marks the beginning of a year during which the Americans turned with growing assurance from defense to counterattack. The matter took months of hectic debate to settle, but it was during this period that the Chiefs of Staff, Nimitz and MacArthur thrashed out an accepted strategy which would carry them first to the Philippines and finally to Tokyo. By the spring of 1944 they were poised for the great leap forward: and by then, moreover, the products of American industrial power were pouring forth in a volume which Japan could not hope to equal—*quantity* production of battleships, aircraft carriers, bombers and fighters in multitudes. There were more Marine units, more Army divisions—and a service of signal intelligence increasingly sophisticated and increasingly fruitful.

Yet it is important to maintain a perspective, and to understand that in the major American strategic decisions taken during this year, Ultra's role was not significant. Grand Strategy—the command decisions which determine the application of military power as between one major theater of war and another—is rarely dominated by considerations of intelligence. In relation to a particular battle, or even within a particular theater, Ultra was of infinite value. But those who ask—as many do—whether Ultra won the war should remember that at the very highest level of decision, where wars can be won or lost, other, more compelling factors come into play. It was not primarily on the strength of his intelligence sources that Hitler fatally invaded Russia. It was not, in any important sense, intelligence that led to the Anglo-American decision, at the Casablanca Conference, to undertake the combined bomber offensive on Germany, nor was intelligence the main ground on which the British argued for a Mediterranean strategy in 1943 rather than an invasion of Northwestern Europe.

In truth, the strategic decisions about the Pacific which the Americans took during that same year were affected more by the nature of the personalities involved than by anything as elegant as intelligence. The prime question was simple: whether to drive straight across the Central Pacific or whether to make the main advance on Japan more indirectly, via New Guinea and the Philippines. Naturally the latter was MacArthur's plan, which he argued with passion, cunning and hyperbole: seeming, at times, to demand that virtually all the American forces in the Pacific should be diverted to his front. The Navy, proud of its record, as inevitably demanded the direct approach. Since it would have been lunatic to transfer the great mass of brand-new warships down to the fringe area of the South West Pacific, the Navy was always liable to win the debate. Finally a working compromise was achieved, which sensibly permitted a forward move in both theaters and sufficiently silenced each vociferous prima donna. By the following spring, the Japanese had been so battered in SWPA, and lost so much ground, that MacArthur was now ready to hurtle ahead, while in the mid-Pacific amphibious operations under Nimitz, by seizing the Gilbert and Marshall island groups, had established launching pads for a devastating central thrust.

At the time of the Italian surrender in September 1943 a Magic intercept revealed a lugubrious signal to Tokyo from the Japanese Military Attaché in Lisbon. "It is generally considered here that the eventual outcome of the war is settled, and that it is now only a question of time. *This verdict, of course, includes the war in the Pacific.*" How right they had been in Lisbon: for the beginning of the end was in sight.

The separate assaults by Nimitz's Central Pacific forces* on the island complexes of the Gilberts and the Marshalls vividly demonstrated both the power and the limitations of Ultra. In the Gilberts the target was Tarawa, where the Marines struggled ashore on November 20, 1943: by the 23rd, after bitter fighting, all was over—at a cost of 1,090 killed and 2,311 wounded. For the American memory Tarawa is a name written in blood. A shocked public reacted with revulsion. Relatives of the dead wrote personally to Nimitz, one distraught mother beginning the letter: "You killed my son on Tarawa."[13] But the reason for the impact of Tarawa is like that on the British of the bombing of Coventry in November 1940: it was not the worst, it was the first. By comparison with the London Blitz, the ruination of the Ruhr, the fire storms in Hamburg and the flattening of Tokyo, Coventry is an episode small in scale. Similarly, by the later standards of loss in the Pacific and in Europe, Tarawa's thousand dead seem a small contingent. In late 1944, during the battle for the Hürtgen Forest and the Roer River, the American First and Ninth Armies in Germany "lost 57,000 men to enemy shells, bullets, and mines, plus another 70,000 to the devil's helpers—fatigue, exposure, disease."[14] During the Tarawa action, indeed, when the Japanese submarine I-175 torpedoed the carrier *Liscombe Bay* the ship exploded and sank with a loss of some 700, yet the sudden extinction of so many hundreds of men never had the emotional effect of the Marines' relatively equal casualties. There is not, and perhaps cannot be, a sense of proportion in these matters. The truth is that at Tarawa the American public, and the American command, first realized the cost of an assault landing on a strongly defended Pacific island.

And one hard lesson which Tarawa taught was this: decoded signals translated into Ultra could provide—and often provided abundantly —precise information concerning the enemy's capability on an island about to be assaulted. The name, the strength and the location of individual units, the amount of ammunition or rations available, the identity of the officer commanding—all these and many other invaluable details came to the Americans from the fountain of Ultra. But

---

* Now formally christened the Fifth Fleet.

what signal intelligence could not do was to provide topographical knowledge, nor could it penetrate the camouflage of those defensive positions so secretly and so skillfully devised by the Japanese. A machine-gun post concealed in a cave, a sunken bunker wrought from coconut logs, a cunning minefield—these were beyond the grasp of Sigint. You first made their acquaintance when you met them.* Now, one cause of the difficulties at Tarawa was that the Americans miscalculated the tide table: many landing craft grounded far from the beach, so that doomed Marines had to wade a long distance through a bullet-swept sea. And then, once ashore, the survivors were surprised and almost shattered by the enemy's concealed defensive positions. Throughout the Pacific campaign, in one island assault after another and culminating in the death struggle for Okinawa, this would be the pattern. Ultra was not a medium capable of supplying the answer.

Yet the landings on the Marshalls showed that Ultra could be decisive. The capture of this group of islands halfway across the Pacific meant that Operation Flintlock had been appropriately named, since its effect was like laying the muzzle of a gun against the flank of Japan's contracting defense line in the Pacific theater. And Flintlock was a visible expression of America's irrepressible industrial supremacy. When the Fifth Fleet set out under Admiral Spruance in January 1944 it consisted of 375 ships with 53,000 troops for the assault and a further 31,000 to furnish garrisons. Admiral Marc Mitscher's Fast Carrier Force, Task Force 58, alone contained 12 carriers, 8 battleships, 42 cruisers and destroyers and 700 aircraft. This was a far cry from the poverty-stricken days of Midway and the Solomons Slot. But the question was, which was the right nail to hit with so massive a hammer?

As usual in the Pacific, the Marshalls form a nest of islands in which Kwajalein atoll predominates—and air reconnaissance suggested that on Kwajalein the Japanese, present in strength, were actively constructing airfields. The consensus of Nimitz's commanders (certainly affected by what had happened at Tarawa) was that the secondary

---

* The problem was never-ending, and examples are infinite. In March 1945 the 1st Cavalry Division on Luzon in the Philippines, during forty-eight hours, tackled 137 caves and sealed 446 connecting tunnels. A little earlier, on Iwo Jima, 800 pillboxes (usually connected) and three miles of tunnels had to be neutralized within an area of eight square miles.

islands—Wotje, Maloelap—should be the target and that the apparently hard nut of Kwajalein should be cracked later. This issue was resolved dramatically. The biographer of Nimitz, Professor Potter, recorded the way things went.

At last, at a meeting on December 14, Admiral Nimitz polled the Fifth Fleet flag and general officers concerning where they should hit.

"Raymond," he asked, "what do you think now?"

"Outer islands," replied Spruance.

"Kelly?"

"Outer islands," replied Turner.

"Holland?"

"Outer islands," replied Smith.*

And so it went around the room, every one of the commanders recommending an initial assault on the outer islands of Wotje and Maloelap. When the poll was completed, there was a brief silence. Then Nimitz said quietly, "Well, gentlemen, our next objective will be Kwajalein."

Spruance and Turner stayed behind after the conference and protested so vigorously that Nimitz offered to relieve them if their hearts were not in the new Flintlock. Naturally, they carried on. But it was Ultra that persuaded Nimitz to take his subordinates by surprise, since Ultra had assured him that the revised plan would surprise the Japanese themselves.

The background to this assurance was a perception in JICPOA, the Joint Intelligence Center at Pearl Harbor, that the Japanese appeared to be moving reinforcements from Kwajalein to the perimeter islands. (They were indeed acting on the assumption that the blow they expected would fall on the fringe islands rather than on Kwajalein.) Nimitz therefore instructed Captain Layton to watch closely what looked like a developing pattern of redeployment. He wanted a daily picture of the buildup of naval, army and air units and of construction workers on the outer islands. It was Ultra intercepts of the routine

---

* For Flintlock, Admiral Kelly Turner (who had long emerged from the shadow cast by his handling of the initial operations at Guadalcanal) was in command of the amphibious element of the Fifth Fleet. General "Howling Mad" Holland M. Smith personified the Marines.

Japanese reports of ration strengths, sick returns and so on which enabled Layton to confirm the shift from Kwajalein outward in the enemy's order of battle. So fortified, Nimitz faced his commanders at that decisive conference—and they all looked at him as if he had gone mad. It was a rewarding madness, for the "stronghold" of Kwajalein was taken in a couple of days at a cost of 400 dead and 1,500 wounded.[15]

Ultra had proved to be an admirable navigator for Admiral Nimitz. It is ironical that just about this time MacArthur was screaming to Secretary of War Stimson, in a private letter:

> These frontal attacks by the Navy, as at Tarawa, are tragic and unnecessary massacres of American lives. . . . The Navy fails to understand the strategy of the Pacific, fails to recognize that the first phase is an Army phase to establish land-based air protection so the Navy can move in. . . . Give me central direction of the war in the Pacific, and I will be in the Philippines in ten months. . . . Don't let the Navy's pride of position and ignorance continue this great tragedy to our country.[16]

In fact, as a result of the double-thrust strategy enforced on MacArthur by the U.S. Chiefs of Staff, he was actually "in the Philippines" *nine* months after composing that mid-January letter! And it is instructive to compare the figures of the "massacre" at Tarawa with those for MacArthur's own campaign in Papua/New Guinea.

By a curious chance it is the subsequent operations along the coast of New Guinea during the winter of 1943–44, in which Australian troops had a leading role, which enable us to observe at first hand the quality and quantity of Ultra intelligence derived from a new source— the Japanese Army code. The Navy code, as has been seen, was a generous retailer of vital information at least since the spring of 1942, but the Army code proved to be more recalcitrant. During the thirties both British and American cryptanalysts had attacked and occasionally pierced this code system—a British officer broke it as early as 1933— but in its wartime form the Army code resisted all such attempts until the spring of 1943. Thereafter the output of information from this source became more and more abundant.[17]

The penetration of the code was piecemeal but progressive. In March 1943, the Wireless Experimental Centre in New Delhi made the first break into a high-level Army system—what was known as "the water transport code."* (Unlike the British, with their centralized control of merchant and passenger shipping, the Japanese allocated to its Army a substantial number of ships for use in its own right.) Then, in August, the "address code" was broken: this was the method for cryptographic concealment of the addressee of a signal, and to be able to interpret the "address" of a message meant that a vast amount of information could now be acquired about the name and location of individual Army units. At the turn of the year, an entry was made into the chief administrative code of the Japanese Army: a source, obviously, of a wealth of factual detail about the disposition of Japanese forces and the shipping organization which supplied them; and, for example, of invaluable statistics for monitoring the enemy's replenishment of its dwindling oil stocks. In February 1944 a copy of the code itself was captured, as well as some of the mechanical devices employed, "making available a tremendous volume of messages dealing with virtually every field of activity in the Japanese Army!" Finally, in the spring of 1944, a solution was achieved of one of the main code systems used by the Army Air Force, and from now on a river began to flow of translated signals dealing with the Army's air units: their strengths, their movements, their state of readiness. Within a year, in fact, American Sigint had established a comprehensive mastery over the enemy's military communications.

Nevertheless, it was a nightmare task. By comparison, the problem of deciphering the Japanese diplomatic traffic was child's play—once the Purple cipher was conquered—for it could normally be assumed that the intercepted signal on which the cryptanalysts got to work represented a complete text. But the cryptographic method of the Japanese Army was more complex. The signals themselves tended to be fragmentary rather than full, and the Japanese had a way of breaking a message into several parts so that an individual signal might contain only a portion of the message which, in its fragmentary state, might lack the context which could make it intelligible. The codes were in any case difficult to crack, and often some section of an intercept would either refuse to yield the original Japanese text or result in an erroneous interpretation. Moreover, even the readable messages consisted in the main of a miscellany of individual, localized orders

---

* Many thousands of "water code" signals were declassified in 1981 and are available in the National Archives.

and reports of the movement of individual units: very rarely did these Army messages contain a broad presentation of enemy intentions. Thus much of the work of the signal intelligence staff involved informed deduction from the particular to the general. Like the crafty fortune-teller who bases his predictions on scraps of information he has accumulated about his customer, so those who processed the Japanese Army signals had to leap from the known to the probable.

Much of the more routine work could, of course, be carried out within the Pacific theater—at the Central Bureau, for example, in Australia—but a metropolitan organization was unavoidable. As the History of the Operations of Special Security Officers Attached to Field Commands puts it: "The high level Japanese military cryptographic systems were of such difficulty that only a tremendous organization equipped with expensive and bulky electrical tabulating machinery could produce any results. Consequently, detailed items of immediate tactical significance to an Army commander in the field could be read at Arlington Hall, but could not be produced by an agency located in the theater and near the Army commander interested. Therefore 'combat intelligence' was being produced in Washington, some 15,000 miles away from the front lines." (The British experience in regard to the German Enigma cipher was precisely analogous. At Bletchley Park they deciphered the signals which produced battle intelligence for the commanders at the front.) But this centralization was only keeping in step with what was happening in the complementary field of traffic analysis. Although, once again, a tremendous amount of this work was done by special units in the forward areas, technology introduced sophistication. By the beginning of 1944 records were being kept on IBM machines of every individual radio contact between Japanese stations. Weekly and monthly tabulations showed the place of origin, the destination, the cryptographic system and the number of the messages intercepted. Here was a potent ally for the code breakers in the task of fixing the location and following the movements of, so far as possible, every unit in the Japanese Army.

Many thousands of signals were decoded: at first with difficulty and delay, but then with increasing speed.* Early in 1944, for example, the Special Branch unit in the Pentagon began to issue a "Japanese

---

* In July 1943, B Branch, the intelligence wing of the Army's Signal Security Agency, numbered 1,814. By July 1944 it had expanded to 2,574, of whom 82 percent worked on the signal traffic of the Japanese Army.

Army Supplement" as an addition to the regular Magic Diplomatic Summaries. Perhaps the significance of this development can be illustrated most authoritatively by a Memorandum for the President: Subject—"Magic," addressed to Roosevelt by General Marshall on February 12, 1944. "I have learned," Marshall wrote, "that you seldom see the Army summaries of 'Magic' material." He then described the arrangements whereby the Military Intelligence Service was extracting and summarizing essential information, and how he was having "these summaries bound in a Black Book both for convenience of reading and for greater security in handling." The importance of the 1943 breakthrough into the Japanese Army's signal traffic is then underlined. "The recent discovery of the Japanese Army machine code has added a tremendous amount of such material and will continue to give us a great deal from day to day. The problem is how to avoid being buried under *the mass of information,** and I think the present arrangement satisfactorily meets that difficulty." So, Marshall ended, "I should like to send these booklets each day direct to the White House."

If this Army Ultra was likely to be of interest to the President in a selective, condensed form, still more were the original decoded intercepts essential reading for General Blamey, the Australian Commander in Chief in the field.[18] After their outstanding performance in Papua his troops were now the sharp point of the spearhead that was being thrust steadily along the coast of New Guinea. Blamey himself would oscillate between Port Moresby and the Australian mainland, but wherever Blamey went Ultra was sure to go. A note to him of October 13, 1943, from his Director of Military Intelligence makes the point. "As discussed with you, sir, I will send to you direct under Most Secret cover such items from Ultra Secret sources as may have operational value or are of exceptional interest. In accordance with the promise given to overseas authorities, could such memoranda as the attached be destroyed after perusal?" Fortunately in this, as in many other respects, Thomas Albert Blamey took a very broad view about rules and regulations (especially when applied to himself). Among the Blamey Papers in the archives of the Australian War Memorial, therefore, may be found not only that cautionary memorandum but also a remarkable collection of the actual Ultra decodes

---

* Author's italics.

No. 72

By Auth. A. C. of S., G-2
Date 29 May 1944

War Department
Office of Assistant
Chief of Staff, G-2
Special Branch, M. I. D.

Total pages — 9
(Incl. TAB A) "MAGIC" SUMMARY

JAPANESE ARMY SUPPLEMENT

1. JAAF--Pilot Strength in China:

    a. Several reports on the number of flying personnel in JAAF units have been received. Most are fragmentary and scattered, but TAB A hereto tabulates a complete return of pilot strength by the Fifth Air Army on 16 Mar. In addition there is available an incomplete return by the 3rd Air Div which gives total figures for 11 Jan. The 3rd Air Div commanded all JAAF units in the

12 February 1944

Subject: "Magic"

I have learned that you seldom see the Army summaries of "Magic" material. For a long time, the last two months in particular, I have had our G-2 organization concentrating on a workable presentation on "Magic" for my use as well as for the other officials concerned, particularly yourself. A highly specialized organization is now engaged in the very necessary process of separating the wheat from the chaff and correlating the items with past information in order that I may be able quickly and intelligently to evaluate the importance of the product.

Recently I have had these summaries bound in a Black Book both for convenience of reading and for greater security in handling. Sometimes two or three of these booklets are gotten out in a single day. I think they contain all of the worthwhile information culled from the tremendous mass of intercepts now available and that are accumulated each twenty-four hours. The recent discovery of the Japanese Army machine code has added a tremendous amount of such material and will continue to give us a great deal from day to day. The problem is how to avoid being buried under the mass of information, and I think the present arrangement satisfactorily meets that difficulty.

I am attaching two of the current booklets which I hope you will glance through in order to familiarize yourself with the manner in which the information is presented. I should like to send these booklets each day direct to the White House and have them delivered to you by Admiral Brown.

(Sgd) G. C. MARSHALL

Chief of Staff.

which his obedient intelligence people forwarded to their insubordinate commander in chief.

Far too many to reproduce individually, these Japanese Army and Navy signals represent a fascinating cross section of the specific aid which Ultra could provide for a senior commander to whom exact and accurate knowledge of the enemy's strength, movements and intentions is his lifeblood. As convoys seek (or fail) to run reinforcements from Rabaul to New Guinea, Blamey has in front of him the name and size of the units aboard them. As the Japanese adjust the positions on their front, Ultra in minute detail betrays what is happening. We can even catch a glimpse of MacArthur and his staff reacting, as in this memorandum to Blamey of January 9, 1944, from his DMI:

> Whilst I was with Willoughby this afternoon at GHQ, Captain McCollum,* the head of US Navy Intelligence, brought in a message from most secret sources and of considerable interest.
>
> The message was from the Commander, Japanese Combined Fleet, and apparently sent to 8th Army Group at Rabaul. . . . It indicated that the Japanese garrison between Sio and Gali amounts now only to 1400 men and they are extremely short of rations and supplies. It further suggested that the combatant troops at Madang itself were composed only of *Nakai Shitai* [*Shitai,* a detachment, from the Japanese 20th Division known to be commanded by Major General Nakai].

The memorandum then explained that measures, apparently, were about to be taken to rescue these troops by sending them 500 tons of supplies by submarine and then withdrawing them. "General MacArthur," the DMI added, "has placed considerable significance on this message. I gathered, though I could not be sure of this, that he was calling together his Chiefs of Staff to study the situation with a view to determining whether or not the difficulties that the enemy is facing in the Madang-Rai Coast area present a favourable opportunity for some early action by US forces."

And so, by this steady accumulation of superiority in all respects— in manpower, in material strength, in territorial gains and in mercilessly accurate intelligence—by the spring of 1944 MacArthur and

---

* For McCollum's background, see p. 30.

Nimitz had truly reached a point in the Pacific war which can be defined as the beginning of the end.

The Japanese themselves were increasingly conscious of this shift in emphasis, as the boundaries of their Greater East Asia Co-Prosperity Sphere contracted. But by now they had other reasons for deep concern. Some were revealed to the Allies by Magic and Ultra; for others, Sigint was directly responsible. The Axis linkage between Germany and Japan was proving to be but a feeble connection. The Japanese merchant-shipping fleet, on which all the logistics and troop movements in the Pacific depended—as well as the supply of raw materials and oil—was rapidly disappearing beneath the waves as American submarine crews, now veterans at the game, were led to their prey by Ultra. And the declining fortunes of Germany, their partner in the West, were becoming starkly evident to the men in Tokyo, as Magic intercepts of their diplomatic messages unerringly revealed.

In the next three chapters, therefore, these three immensely important facets of Japanese disintegration will be examined more microscopically. For we have reached a phase in the Pacific war when, as those pessimists in Lisbon put it back in September 1943: "It is now only a question of time."

CHAPTER NINE

A Broken Axis: The Blockade-Runners' Ruin

They that sail on the sea tell of the danger thereof; And when we hear it with our ears, we marvel.
Ecclesiasticus 43:24

IN 1942 THE Second World War seemed to be living up to its name. As Japan pressed against the frontiers of India and sent her fleet into the Bay of Bengal, while German armor drove onward toward the Caucasus, many feared that the armies of these great powers might stretch out right across the globe and meet one another in triumph. It was never going to happen: it was never even intended to happen. But in that year, when the Russians were still semi-paralyzed, the Americans were only just beginning to get into the war and the British had been defeated both in Africa and in Asia, the idea that the East-West Axis might harden into a reality was not incredible. At the level of world strategy the Japanese and the Germans appeared to have much in common.

We now know that this was a fantasy. But we also know, in great detail, that at a more mundane level the interests of the two nations interlocked. Each entered the war in the expectation of quick and decisive results, consciously facing the risk of being crippled by shortages of vital materials; the Germans took longer than the Japanese to feel the pinch, but in 1942 the pressure was there, in both Berlin and Tokyo. However, the assets of one partner could do much to make up for the other's deficiencies, and it might have been expected that a supreme effort would have been made to achieve mutual support. Yet in practice the attempt was far less than supreme, its course was checkered and its conclusion abysmal. In clearing the seas of the Axis blockade-runners which sought to ferry their precious cargoes between Europe and Asia, the Anglo-American navies and air forces depended, as usual, on the trusted guidance of signal intelligence.

Germany's continental economy, even when it expanded into the Balkans and bit deep into Russia, could not furnish a sufficient supply of the very raw materials which were copiously available in Japan's vast new empire. To keep the Nazi war machine running, large stocks of rubber were required (urgently, until synthetic rubber could be churned out in quantity).* Tin was short—but plentiful in Malaysia. Items like wolfram and molybdenum, and even commonplace necessities like hides and hemp and vegetable oils were at a low level in the German inventory. To maintain their two-front engagement with the Americans in the Pacific and the British in Southeast Asia (as well as with their old opponent Chiang Kai-shek), the Japanese, for their part, had to overcome a perilous lack of essential metals. Their industrial base was incapable on its own of servicing the war effort. Moreover, in spite of her astonishing modernization, Japan was acutely weak in scientific know-how: Germany was far ahead in the technical evolution of new ideas and their practical application for military purposes. On paper, therefore, it seemed as though each partner in the East-West Axis could effectively buttress the other.

But even at the outset of her war with the Allies Japan suffered from another grave shortage: merchant shipping. Inevitably, therefore, the first attempts to transfer cargoes of necessaries between Europe and Japan were made in German surface vessels—or prizes of war. (There were also a few Italian ships.) Initiative and operational control of what were called the Yanagi transports were thus in the hands of the German Navy from the start, a fact which in practice imperiled the venture from its earliest days. For the ships were sailing, as it were, straight into the meshes of the Allied signal intelligence net. Magic (with its command of the diplomatic signals and the Japanese-German naval attaché code) and, most significantly, the British ability to read the German Enigma cipher contributed intelligence about the Yanagi operations which, cumulatively but decisively, aborted them.[1]

The need to exchange supplies by sea was further intensified by a

---

* By March 1943 it was calculated in Germany that only 30,000 tons of natural rubber remained in stock.

factor which is, perhaps, less generally appreciated. Until the invasion of Russia there was a viable overland route, along which the volume of traffic was certainly so large that it would not be easy to replace. From no less a source than the Chief Customs Bureau of the U.S.S.R. we know that during the first five months of 1941 the following commodities—212,366 tons in all—were transferred to Germany via the Trans-Siberian Railroad from Japan, Manchuria and occupied China: 14,270 tons of rubber and rubber wares, 180,187 tons of oils and fats, 9,361 tons of foodstuffs, 3,461 tons of minerals and 1,107 tons of chemicals and drugs. In return the Japanese had received many hundreds of wagonloads of heavy machinery, vehicles, locomotives, armor plate and aircraft. When Operation Barbarossa swept the German panzers into Russia's western provinces, one coincidental effect was to halt this invaluable traffic.

And yet, while economic necessity forced Japan and Germany to cooperate, it is important to remember that for Tokyo, at least, the relationship was that of a partner who seeks to extract what he can while continuously suspecting his opposite number. On July 9, 1942, for example, the Magic Summary showed that the Japanese were concerned about the way the Germans were building up stocks of tungsten, rubber and tin in Thailand and were showing signs of fear that the Germans would outbid them for further supplies because they seemed "to doubt whether the Germans perceive and recognize the true Japanese position in the Greater East Asia Co-Prosperity Sphere." (The Japanese themselves being busy setting up monopolies in Thailand for the export of rice, shellac, etc.) And similar Japanese suspicions were disclosed about German purchases of hides, rubber and tin in French Indochina.

In September 1942 the Magic intercepts showed that the Japanese were already dragging their heels: loitering over an agreement to supply rubber, and refusing to allow Germans to attend the loading of Yanagi transports at Singapore. The same month, nevertheless, they demanded from Germany an unattainable 1,000,000 tons of steel and quantities of scant aluminum, pressing the Germans also for more ships! There was a sense of discomfort and suspicion, with each side playing its own hand, which affected not merely the Yanagi scheme but the whole relationship and which it was certainly useful for the Allies to be able to monitor.

The winter months were always the most promising season for the blockade-runners. Ships leaving Bordeaux or other French Atlantic ports (the western bases for the traffic) or arriving after their dangerous voyage from the Far East obviously had a better chance of evading the surveillance of Allied aircraft and naval patrols amid the rough seas and long dark nights of "the furious winter's rages." Toward the end of 1942 it was known that about 26 ships, spread between Europe and the Japanese empire, were available for what was to be a major attempt by the Axis to break the Allied blockade by surface vessels.* But it was typical of the whole Yanagi operation that the majority of those ships that tried to make the passage, from either end of the world, were either scuttled or sunk. Many thousands of tons of the most desirable supplies and equipment were thus denied to the enemy: a benefit both to the Americans in the Pacific and to the Allied effort in Europe.

Four ships set out from France of which only one, *Karin*, survived (and *Karin* was also scuttled on March 10, 1943, after being stopped by the U.S.S. *Eberle* as she made her way back from Japanese waters). The loss rate daunted the Germans, who finally postponed further sailings until February 1943, when they intended to ship 75,000 tons of stocks accumulated on orders from Japan.† During the first two months of 1943 two more German ships were lost, coming from the East, and in March a Magic intercept revealed that the program had been cut to four ships with 20,000 tons of cargo. Of these one was sunk, one turned back and only two completed the voyage. During the whole winter operation 17 runners set out, 4 were sunk, 3 turned back, and of the 10 arriving *Uckermark* blew up in Yokohama. Nearly 34,000 tons of cargo were carried, but only 25,000 delivered.

The ships that sailed from Japanese bases during that winter of 1942–43 had an even more disastrous record. Seven attempted the trip, and six (including *Karin*) were lost. (One of the seven, *Dogger-bank*, carrying 3,200 tons of rubber from Saigon, was conveniently sunk in error by a German submarine, U-43.)

But it is another member of that ill-starred septet, *Hohenfriedberg*,

---

* There had been a first, successful phase between April 1941 and May 1942 during which 12 out of 16 ships made a safe voyage from the Far East to Europe and six months' harbor in the opposite direction. But during this phase signal intelligence was minimal and Anglo-American cooperation was, at best, embryonic.
† A sense of desperation is suggested by the discussions during that month about whether the aircraft carrier *Zeppelin* might be fitted with extra tanks for use as a blockade-runner.

which provides a perfect case history of the way that signal intelligence functioned in annihilating the German-Japanese blockade-runners. The history begins in 1942, throughout most of whose course the British cryptanalysts at Bletchley Park were unable to break the new Enigma cipher introduced for the Germans' Atlantic U-boat fleet at the beginning of the year.[2] In December, however, the breakthrough occurred and, by a curious coincidence, one of its invaluable consequences was its significance for the battle against the blockade-runners.

The reason was exquisitely simple. Admiral Doenitz's U-boat Command defined a strip of water about 200 miles wide, "Lane A," lying to the west of the French and African coasts, as a channel for the passage of blockade-runners. The strip was divided into four areas. Signals could thus be transmitted to U-boats "closing" any one of these areas, as a warning that a blockade-runner was either moving or about to move through it and should not be treated as hostile. During the months immediately following the break into the Atlantic U-boat cipher Bletchley was not always able to decipher intercepts immediately, but when one of these warning signals could be broken and translated quickly, it is obvious that the information gained, the knowledge about what was actually happening in "Lane A," was of critical importance. *Hohenfriedberg* was the victim of just such a break.

She departed from Batavia in December 1942. Two warning signals, of February 13 and 17, revealed that a ship was due to move northward through "Lane A" and forbade attacks on single ships in this area up to February 23. The second signal was explicit: the ship was *Hohenfriedberg*, formerly *Herborg*, disguised as *Herbrand*, call sign LIYG, and armed with one 7.5- and four 2-cm. guns and four machine guns. On February 20 further intercepts indicated that no less than four U-boats had been diverted to escort this important blockaderunner. They were told that she could be identified by the presence of scaffolding around her funnel. But the British got her. On February 26, U-264 signaled to U-boat Command:

> object-to-be-protected was sunk by a heavy cruiser, London class*
> . . . I have complete crew on board. Missed spread shot of four on
> heavy cruiser. Am starting return.

---

* Actually H.M.S. *Sussex*.

Bletchley's insight into the U-boat signal traffic accounted for yet another of the septet, *Regensburg:* a gallant trier, for she had already been torpedoed by U.S.S. *Searaven* in the Sunda Strait—between Java and Sumatra—in October 1942. After repair in Japan she set out again for Europe, but on the last lap an intercepted message to U-161 gave away her rendezvous and even her identification, for she was ordered to string up a line of laundry "from mizzenmast to stern," in good weather, and in bad to hang fire hoses from the mizzen. So the inevitable followed, and after being sighted on March 30 by the cruiser H.M.S. *Glasgow* she was scuttled.

During the whole period from August 1942 to March 1943, 15 ships sailed to the west, of which only 4 arrived. Over 93,000 tons of special cargo had been lost en route. The German Navy and Economic Ministry therefore decided that submarines rather than surface vessels would have to carry the main burden—already a major victory for the Allies, since this involved the diversion of U-boats from active operations and, moreover, one merchant ship could carry far more, and far more bulky, cargo than even a clutch of submarines. Still, the surface runs were not yet abandoned, as the story of the following winter demonstrates.

By the end of November 1943 it was known that several ships would be sailing westward from Japan via the Sunda Strait. Of the five that set out four were sunk, and though *Osorno* reached the estuary of the Gironde with her cargo she had to be beached after bombing by British aircraft. A comment in the American records on the fate of two of them, *Weserland* and *Burgenland,* illustrates the professional confidence of their adversaries: "They plotted nicely and appeared agreeably in the South Atlantic narrows approximately at the time anticipated."* And thereabouts U.S.S. *Somers* sank the former, while the latter was dispatched by two other American warships, *Omaha* and *Jouett.*

A new Sigint factor was responsible for the interception of *Burgenland,* on January 5, 1944. Toward the end of December it had been noted that when a blockade-runner was sighted signals were transmitted to U-boat Command with the prefix PPP. The result is clearly

---

* The record presumably means that the ships turned up at about the right point in the "narrows"—which must be about 2,000 miles wide!

set out in this after-action report from the U.S. South Atlantic
Strategic D/F Net.

> On 3 January 1944 Navy Department Communication Intelli-
> gence informed the C.O. South Atlantic Strategic D/F Net that
> the German blockade-runners when sighted had previously used
> a type of message commencing with the letters "PPP." These
> messages had been noticed one or two days prior to this, when a
> blockade-runner was sunk. Although the type of message was
> noticed and studied to a certain extent, the significance of it was
> not realized until the information was received from Washington.
>
> On 5 January the Fourth Fleet Operations Officer informed
> that a strange vessel, not on the merchant ship plot, had been
> sighted by a cruiser plane. A special extra watch was put on, with
> instructions to listen for this particular type of message, com-
> mencing with PPP, and to inform the watch officer or com-
> manding officer immediately if he received such a message.
> *Approximately twenty minutes later** this type of message was
> noticed being transmitted to Germany. The commanding officer
> immediately called the Fleet Operations Officer and informed him
> that in all probability the vessel sighted was a German blockade-
> runner. Acting on this information, orders were sent to a cruiser
> at sea to intercept the vessel.

Dispatch from the European ports was now hopeless. British air
reconnaissance and other sources indicated during the summer of
1943 that eight ships were possibly available and it was known that
the Germans hoped to send 50,000 tons to Japan. But Ambassador
Oshima's messages from Berlin revealed, through Magic, a justified
pessimism. British air patrols off the French coast maintained a
stranglehold. On November 10 Oshima did indeed go to Bordeaux
and inspect two vessels loaded with steel, aluminum and formic acid
for Japan. But his doubts about the possibility of the vessels reaching
his home waters—or even emerging from the Bay of Biscay—were
so serious that he made a proposal perhaps unprecedented in the
history of the war. He recommended to Tokyo that the ships' captains
should receive decorations even *before* the voyage began! The potential weight of cargo dropped steadily, as British mining and bomb-

---

* Author's italics.

ing took their toll of shipping still in port. By the end of 1943 only four vessels remained. On January 19, 1944, the Germans canceled the operation and ordered cargoes to be off-loaded. The Yanagi scheme was dead.

The practical significance of this victory can be stated in a single sentence. All the material transported by all the U-boats that successfully made their way from east to west, or vice versa, did not amount to more than the load that could have been carried by one of the surface blockade-runners. This was a particularly heavy blow for the Japanese: the evidence is plain, in the list of items which were waiting in Europe for delivery on their account but which, after surface blockade-running was abandoned, they decided to lease or to sell back to the Germans and Italians. Rolling-mill equipment, prototypes of large guns, samples of aircraft, heavy machine tools and presses were infinitely desirable for a nation like Japan, with its contracting industrial and technological base: but they were now beyond reach.*

To a limited degree quantity could be replaced by quality. If a submarine could not ferry material in bulk, it could at least transport brainpower. And, indeed, the list of U-boat passengers carried from Europe to Japan from 1943 onward shows that many technical experts, both German and Japanese, risked the dangerous voyage: radar technicians, engineers, medical people, ordnance and antiaircraft specialists, as well as ambassadorial staff from both countries. But this was the small change of a relationship which, theoretically, should have produced such enormous practical benefits for the two partners.

Indeed the problem—and the danger—of relying on U-boats to sustain a transport service was that a submarine on a long wartime voyage is as much at risk as a surface vessel, even though it can travel considerable distances submerged. For, sooner or later, it will be compelled to make signals: there was thus a chance that direction finding could pinpoint its position, while from 1943 onward the Allies' ability to read the U-boat cipher meant that any messages transmitted to or from a U-boat were liable to be translated. And

---

* Another perspective is provided by the fact that the three famous Atlantic convoys, SC122, HX229 and HX229A, which left America for Britain during March 1943, were carrying 600,000 tons of general cargo (from food to locomotives and from gunpowder to tanks and invasion barges) as well as 170,000 tons of fuel and 150,000 tons of frozen meat. Though over 20 ships went down, the actual deliveries were still enormous, by comparison with the meager traffic between Japan and Germany.

another limitation was at least as damaging. Many of the craft employed could not carry sufficient diesel for a complete voyage. Refueling was unavoidable: but refueling meant a rendezvous with a supplier, and a halt till the job was done—always a risky business. Too often, also, the fixing of a rendezvous meant further radio communications and a useful offering to the Allies' signal intelligence.

These two inherent weaknesses, compounded by experience gained during the Anglo-American defeat of the surface blockade-runners and the throttling effect of air and sea power, particularly in and over the Atlantic, were decisive. From 1942 onward 56 load-carrying submarines were dispatched to or from the Far East—29 were sunk in passage: 3 abandoned their missions: one was subsequently interned. Of the 23 that completed a full trip in one direction, only 5 voyaged back home, 9 being sunk, 2 interned, 6 (German or Italian) taken over by the Japanese, and one being given by Germany to Japan.

The Germans had been operating U-boats in eastern waters since 1942, particularly in the Indian Ocean, with their normal mission of commerce-destroying and convoy-disruption. A base was required, and in December 1942 Penang on the Malay Peninsula was selected, with Singapore for major repairs. But once again the Japanese turned sour—partly because they resented the presence of their partners in an exclusively Japanese theater. The situation is well illustrated in an American summary.

> Innumerable difficulties were placed in the way of the Germans. Services and supply were of poor quality; bases were never well equipped with personnel and supplies; and it was reported [as late as October 1944] that "everything must be begged in protracted discussion from the Japanese." U-boat and blockade-runner crews had to load, unload and repair their own vessels, while the few Japanese workers seemed to spend their time spying on new German equipment. No torpedo house was available. . . . U-boats had to go to Japan proper to change worn-out batteries.

And the fuel supplied was so unreliable that the Germans had to set up their own system of purification. The atmosphere is reminiscent of the cheerless reception accorded to British warships and Allied merchantmen after their Arctic convoys had fought a way through to the harbors of northern Russia: and, unfortunately, of the disgraceful treatment of U.S. Marines by the dockers of their allies when the Guadalcanal operation was being mounted.

Abraham Lincoln said of a certain engineer that he was capable of building a bridge from here to Hell, though he was a bit doubtful about the abutment at the other side. For those U-boats that managed to survive the voyage to the East "the abutment at the other side" was equally dubious. Still, they would have survived—though this was not the usual experience.

For the decision to shift the main burden of cargo-carrying from surface vessels to submarines was made at the worst possible time. By the end of 1942 the Germans had what amounted to a small fleet of tanker U-boats, adapted for refueling other craft—some 17 in all. But during the summer of 1943 increasing Allied dominance in the Atlantic, greater availability of escort carriers and, above all, the high quality of signal intelligence paid enormous dividends. The tankers, or "Milch Cows," were steadily obliterated, either in chance encounters or, more dramatically, in calculated searches by American hunter-killer groups enthusiastically (the British thought, over-enthusiastically) exploiting information provided by the cryptanalysts.

In the Indian Ocean, unlike the Atlantic, it still proved possible to use surface vessels for refueling until, in 1944, nemesis caught up with the two ships so employed, *Charlotte Schliemann* and *Brake*. After the former had been sunk in February as a result of signal intelligence, several U-boats were left thirsty, and it was due to the decryption of a signal giving them a rendezvous with *Brake* that she too was sunk on March 12, south of Mauritius. This ended the use of surface vessels as tankers in the Far East. But it is worth noting that while strikes at known rendezvous points were so often fatal to enemy shipping, their very precision—implying prior knowledge—was always liable to suggest that ciphers had been compromised.*

Shortly after *Brake* went down, for instance, the Admiralty's Submarine Tracking Room reported: "two rendezvous . . . between a supply U-boat and two outward-bound 740-tonners and a torpedo carrier [presumably a U-boat ferrying reserve armaments to Penang] were recorded by U-boat Control in a special cipher. Thus it is plain

---

* It was for this reason that the Admiralty's Operational Intelligence Centre was so alarmed by the Americans' sudden and concentrated attack on the Atlantic Milch Cow U-boats. It looked too perfect and too premeditated.

the enemy suspects, probably as the result of the sinking of a tanker in the Indian Ocean [i.e., *Brake*] and of a freighter U-boat off South Africa, both near a rendezvous, that we have gained physical possession of his current settings, perhaps by capture of a U-boat." "At present," the report continued, "the enemy traffic is being read despite the subterfuge employed":[3] but though neither the Germans nor the Japanese ever grasped how catastrophically their communication systems had been penetrated, the arrival out of the blue of an aircraft carrier or destroyer at the point of meeting between a U-boat and its supply vessel was always liable to raise suspicions. Still, war waged by signal intelligence is inherently, and more or less continually, a game in which both the stakes and the risks are high.

Nevertheless, this combination of adverse circumstances promised a rough ride for the freighter submarines. Indeed, Magic raised the alarm even before the venture started, for on March 31, 1943, one of Ambassador Oshima's messages to Tokyo revealed the plan to use U-boats for ferrying rubber and other materials.* Their first major effort was made between June 30 and July 8, when no less than eleven boats left France. But by the end of August five had been sunk in the Atlantic and one had abandoned its mission.

The reason for this immediate slaughter was the deadly consequence of accurate signal intelligence, the need to refuel and vulnerability at a rendezvous. It was known from decrypts that several submarines were about to sortie, probably for the Far East, and that it was customary for fuel to be taken aboard at an early stage—usually, at this period, to the southwest of the Azores. But this was an area where American escort carriers were active and tanker U-boats were being eliminated. Thus only one remained to service the freighters, some of which were also sunk, while others, only partly replenished, were compelled to refuel again in the Indian Ocean. And this time, thanks to more good signal intelligence, the tanker itself went down.

Fuel was a problem because these type 1X-C boats were not large enough: 750 tons, carrying a mere 110 tons of cargo. Their sorry story is a tale of wasted endeavor: of the 14 craft that left Europe between June 1943 and the following March, only one got to the Far East and

---

* Further intercepted signals from Oshima of April 14 and May 6 specifically confirmed the Germans' intention to "inaugurate a submarine transport service"—as opposed to casual voyages.

back, while 11 were sunk in passage and 2 captured. Only 750 tons of cargo reached Japan: only 110 were brought back to Germany.

So the Germans raised the ante. After March 1944 the type 1X-D was introduced, of 1,200 tons, capable of making the trip without refueling and of carrying up to 250 tons of freight. But the results were the same: of the 32 that sailed for Asia 15 were sunk, one damaged and withdrawn, and 3 seized by Japan after the German surrender. The 3 that returned to Europe delivered a meager gift of 83 tons of rubber, 67 tons of wolfram and 188 tons of tin: while all that the Japanese got as a result of this large-scale operation was some 600 tons. For the Allies, the comparative value of stopping the surface contraband-runners in their tracks is vividly illustrated by a single example. When *Weserland* was sunk she had 10,000 tons aboard. And now the Germans, always the dominant partner in these exchanges, lost heart and gradually abandoned the whole scheme. The Japanese, for their part, could hardly protest, since the minimal contribution of submarines which they made in the early stage had a disastrous record and by 1944 they had nothing further to offer.

What the Allied victory over the blockade-runners meant for Japan —and particularly, therefore, for the Americans in the Pacific war— may be deduced from an examination of the gross figures of various items known to have been sunk. A great proportion of the industrial diamonds: half the 325 tons of lead: most of the mercury: all of 3,700,000 steel balls: 4 out of 8 sets of the Würzburg ground radar and all the blueprints: virtually every other form of radar material: the single specimen of the British H2S blind-bombing device: all the 600,000 tablets and 8,000 ampules of the Atabrine drug: all the parts of a British Mosquito plane: every drawing of rocket and recoil-less guns, machine pistols, antitank guns and rifles: acoustic buoys and aerial cameras. While it would be absurd to pretend that, had these commodities arrived, they would have turned the tide in favor of an inevitably doomed Japan, it is equally evident that for a country fighting to the death in conditions of a siege economy, the loss, though not decisive, was more than trivial.

Sometimes the cargo was of a more curious character. A U-boat sunk off Manila on July 25, 1944, returning from Singapore, had safely transported thither from Lorient on the French coast a variety of radar devices, ten Enigma ciphering machines, acoustic and magnetic torpedoes and plans for a glider bomb. But what was the item "influenza virus" doing on its freight list? To produce protective cultures? Scarcely for a sudden essay in biological warfare. But there it was.

A remarkable case was that of the Bengali nationalist Subhas Chandra Bhose, who after being imprisoned in Calcutta as an agitator escaped in January 1941 and, with extraordinary persistence, made his way via Afghanistan and Russia to Germany.* Here he was instrumental in forming the embryo of an anti-British Indian Legion, as well as broadcasting sedition to India. Finally, on February 9, 1943, he embarked at Kiel on U-180, with the object of reaching Japan and organizing the Free India Movement, which the Japanese had initiated among the disaffected Indian prisoners in their hands—those taken captive during the Singapore debacle offering particularly promising material.[4]

But though he in fact reached Tokyo in thirteen weeks, having been taken over by a Japanese submarine off Madagascar, his trip was not so secret as was assumed. Special messages were transmitted to him by radio to keep him abreast of the nationalist situation. Intercepted and deciphered, these told the Allies not only about his presence aboard but also a great deal about the Free India Movement and its membership. Moreover, one of the officers on U-180, Lange, kept an account of the voyage and this was later acquired among documents seized from a U-boat under his command, U-505.† Once again, therefore, the signal intelligence net had prevented an interesting fish—indeed, a potentially dangerous fish—from slipping by undetected. In the event, the ultimate operations in Burma of Bhose and his Indian National Army proved to be as futile as, in any objective assessment, the endeavors of the blockade-runners must be judged to have been.

For the U-boat captains and crews the voyages were all in the day's work: a part of the trade for which they had been trained and to which they were accustomed. The statistics of their losses are indeed frightful, and the dangers to which they were exposed have been indicated. In 1943 and 1944, however, the likelihood of destruction was a fact of life with which U-boat crews were as familiar as the crews of Allied bomb-

---

* The Magic intercept of a signal from Bangkok to Tokyo on April 6, 1942, reported fully on Bhose. On May 28 Oshima in Berlin told Tokyo that Bhose had been received by Hitler, and described his plans for developing military action when he returned to the East.

† U-505 was captured off West Africa on July 13, 1944. The papers could therefore have only provided *retrospective* confirmation.

ers working over Germany or the ordinary infantryman in the field. And there cannot have been many in the U-boat fleet who counted blockade-running as more perilous than engagement in one of the great battles around the Russian or Atlantic convoys.

For the surface-runners conditions were entirely different. Merchant vessels of no great size or speed, thin-skinned and scarcely bristling with armaments, they had to make the whole trip above and not, like the U-boats, often under the waves. Signal intelligence, as has been seen, was the frequent agent of their destruction. They did not know this: but what they did know was that from the time that they set out from Bordeaux or Lorient until they docked in the Far East they were the prey, at any time on any day, of British or American aircraft or warships. It was a form of dicing with death, and their crews were brave men. They deserve a salute across the years, for courage is a human and not a national quality.

CHAPTER TEN

Massacre of the *Marus*

The steady development of the torpedo together with the gradual improvement in the size, motive power and speed of submarine craft of the near future will result in a most dangerous offensive weapon.
Lieutenant Chester Nimitz, U.S. Naval Institute
Proceedings, 1912

There were nights when nearly every American submarine on patrol in the central Pacific was working on the basis of information derived from cryptanalysis.
Captain W. J. Holmes, *Double-Edged Secrets*

THE FIRST JAPANESE ship was sunk by an American submarine a week or so after Pearl Harbor: the last, a coast-defense vessel, was sunk in the Sea of Japan on August 14, 1945, the day before the end of hostilities. During operations which thus spanned the whole of the Pacific war many of the enemy's fighting ships were destroyed by submarines, sometimes dramatically and often with important results. And yet, paradoxically, it is their obliteration of Japan's merchant navy which had the most decisive consequences. Through the sinking of the *marus*—as the merchant and transport ships were called—Japan gradually bled to death. The process started with occasional attacks on individual targets. It ended in a massacre.

Admiral Chester Nimitz, the Neptune of the Pacific, was an old submariner by trade and therefore supremely equipped to supervise this aspect of the many-sided war game played out in his theater. Long before 1914 he had been an instructor in the First Submarine Flotilla and commanded pioneer craft with evocative names like *Plunger*, *Snapper* and *Narwhal*. During the First World War he served as Chief of Staff to the Commander of the U.S. Atlantic Submarine Fleet.[1] So the man who, after Pearl Harbor, became Commander in Chief, Pacific Fleet and Pacific Ocean Area, was the appropriate Supremo for an onslaught which signally succeeded where the German U-boats failed —in an absolute elimination of the enemy's merchant shipping. Like the Germans, the Americans owed their astonishing (and largely unrecognized) success to the accurate guidance of their signal intelligence, but whereas the German Navy's cryptanalysts lost their grip on the Allied convoy codes in the middle of 1943 and never recovered their dominance, the men at FRUPac, Belconnen and OP-20-G continued to supply the American submarine fleet with critically accurate information right up to the end. So the young lieutenant's prophecy of 1912 was justified, for Admiral Nimitz increasingly wielded "a most dangerous offensive weapon."

But not at first. By the end of 1942, it is true, Japan had lost about one million tons of merchant shipping from all causes, American submarines having accounted for 142 *marus*. (By 1945 ten times that number would be sunk.) It is true, also, that though the Japanese command had anticipated a loss of about 800,000 tons in the first year of the war, actual sinkings were already more than could be endured. Indeed, the decision to evacuate Guadalcanal early in 1943 flowed directly from high-level and impassioned conferences in Tokyo at which the bitter fact had to be swallowed that the 300,000 extra tons of shipping required to service further aggressive action in the Solomons did not exist. Nevertheless, these truths should not be allowed to conceal the reality. For many reasons, as will be seen, American submarines were not yet achieving their full potential.

It is often forgotten, however, that of all the main belligerents America had the shortest war. The British and the Germans fought from start to finish. The Japanese had been in a state of war since the thirties, and their swift succession of victories from December 1941 onward owed much to their previous battle experience, their training and their readiness for action. Before Pearl Harbor even the Russians had soldiered their way through half a year of disasters. In their role of Johnny-come-lately the Americans had to move fast—and, indeed, their achievement in the Pacific as in Europe was due to an astonishing speed of adaptation, of developing new techniques, organizing mass production, creating vast forces and, above all, learning. For Chester Nimitz the question was, how soon would new skills and new technologies enable his submarine fleet to respond, as lethally as the Germans in the Atlantic, to the test and challenge of the Pacific war?

The first need was for improved intelligence. For most of 1942, as has been seen, the important JN25 code was largely unreadable and, in any case, the signals in this high-level system tended to refer to the movements of warships: breaking of the special *"maru* code" used by the Japanese for routing freighters, tankers, etc., only occurred later in the war. Moreover, the submarine service was not, as yet, considered secure as a recipient of Ultra intelligence. Jasper Holmes, who took over from Layton as the clandestine link between the Combat Intelligence Unit on Hawaii and the Pacific Submarine Command, has described how he would convey information at this time: "I went directly to the chief of staff of ComSubPac and delivered it orally. I did not tell him how the information was obtained, but he must have guessed. We kept no records. If I had a position in latitude and longitude, I wrote the figures in ink on the palm of my hand, and scrubbed my hands after I had delivered the message."[2] War, however, is a serious business, not likely to be won by compelling grown men to behave like schoolboys. Until an adult system was evolved for servicing the submarines with Ultra, their potential would inevitably be limited.

And, unfortunately, "moral fiber" and professional competence do not seem to have characterized every submarine commander in those early months. There are too many well-documented instances of a captain cracking under the tensions of a war patrol in distant enemy waters. At Midway, moreover, as Clay Blair puts it in his admirable *Silent Victory,* "the role played by U.S. submarines was one of confusion and error"; after the battle, heads rolled and, rightly or wrongly, several submarine commanders were rapidly transferred to staff appointments or otherwise removed from the scene of action. During the opening phase of both world wars most of the armed services, both American and British, had to hack out the dead wood: in this the U.S. submarine force was not exceptional.[3]

Indeed, the situation is reminiscent of an earlier war. By an odd coincidence, it was in 1942 that Douglas Southall Freeman published his magisterial *Lee's Lieutenants: A Study in Command.* In his foreword Freeman wrote: "If the recount of the change of officers in the first fifteen months of the war in Virginia seems discouraging, the events that followed the reorganization of July, 1862, are assurance that where the supreme command is capable, fair-minded and diligent, the search for competent executive officers is not in vain. The Lee and the 'Stonewall' Jackson of this war will emerge." *Mutatis mutandis,* this was now the challenge for the U.S. submarine service.

Yet it is difficult to be precise about the relative failure of the submariners during the operations of 1942, and surely it would be unjust to lay the whole burden on those young men who commanded the craft at sea. For not only were they inadequately supplied with intelligence about the enemy, and compelled to conduct their patrols according to peacetime tactical doctrines which war soon showed to be incorrect: they had not even got the right weapon with which to hit a hostile ship when one was observed through the periscope and all the complicated calculations for obtaining a strike appeared to have been carried out immaculately.

It is an extraordinary fact that the three great nations of the West who took so much pride in their technology, Germany, Great Britain and the United States, should all have entered the Second World War with stocks of torpedoes which functioned imperfectly, whereas the Japanese, long thought to be mere imitators of the "developed" West, possessed from the start a type of torpedo which was pre-eminent in range, in speed and in reliability. The technical deficiencies of the British and German weapons demand a complex explanation; here it is sufficient to say that the reasons for malfunction were identified and overcome with tolerable speed. In the Americans' case, however, what was blindingly obvious was allowed to persist for far too long. The background to this tragic delay is ugly and inexcusable.

The standard U.S. torpedo, the Mark 14, had two major defects. They were indicated in a letter to a senior officer on Admiral King's staff, written by Admiral Lockwood after he had arrived in Australia to take command of the submarines working out of Fremantle and sought to discover why the craft operating in Asiatic waters had met with so little success.

> The boys here have had a tough row to hoe in the last four months. Why they didn't get more enemy ships is a highly controversial point but my reading of all war diaries thus far submitted has convinced me that among the causes are: (a) bad choice of stations in that most likely invasion points were not covered soon enough nor heavily enough, (b) *bad torpedo performance, in that they evidently ran much too deep and had numerous pre-*

matures . . . , (c) buck fever—firing with ship swinging when he thought it was on a steady course; set up for one target and firing at a totally different one, (d) lack of or misunderstanding of aggressiveness; many evaded destroyers in the belief that they should save torpedoes for convoy following; one said he thought a sub should never "pick a fight with a destroyer."

But another, Coe of *Skipjack*, laid it on the line when he observed in his patrol report that "to make a round trip of 8,500 miles into enemy waters, to gain attack position undetected within 800 yards of enemy ships only to find that the torpedoes run deep and over half the time will fail to explode, seems to me to be an undesirable manner of gaining information which might be gained any morning within a few miles of a torpedo station in the presence of comparatively few hazards."[4]

The trouble was that it took too long for that morning to dawn. The torpedoes were the product and responsibility of the Bureau of Ordnance, and in spite of accumulating evidence to the contrary the Bureau of Ordnance continued to maintain that they were just fine. Yet the prescribed setting made the torpedoes run too deep, and the magnetic exploder at the torpedo's tip could not be relied on to detonate the warhead at the right, critical moment. Bitter experience made these defects familiar in the submarine fleet, but captains who set their torpedoes to run closer to the surface—and then fiddled their afteraction reports—tended to receive short shrift if their "insubordination" was discovered. In many an attack, moreover, skippers who followed the rule book thought that they had sunk their prey only to learn on return to harbor—often as a result of Ultra intercepts—that the ship had got away unharmed. One way and another, the early operations of the U.S. Navy's submarines were bedeviled. It was a situation that could not, and of course did not, last.[5]

It is self-evident, from the submarines' ultimate and decisive success, that competent commanders emerged in abundance; that effective tactics were evolved; and that in spite of bureaucratic obscurantism (and some pigheaded professionals) torpedoes were at last produced capable of ensuring a kill if the captain did his job and the submarine was in the right place to attack a target. But the remarkable achievement of signal intelligence in guiding craft to that right place, over and over again, is less immediately obvious although, without that guidance, the record would be very different.

It was early in 1943 that the necessary and fundamental change occurred in the application of Ultra to submarine warfare in the Pacific: a change which altered the tentative and almost amateur practices of 1942 into a system which, as it matured, can be fairly compared with the control of the Atlantic U-boats by the German U-boat Command (based on the cryptanalytical achievements of the B-Dienst), or with the deadly use of Ultra by the British in, for example, the interdiction of Axis transport shipping in the Mediterranean. Several convergent reasons account for this critical development.

Although the American submarine force had not yet reached its full potential, Japanese losses were already such that a decision had to be taken running counter to Japanese naval doctrine—which had always tended to despise the notion of convoys and the necessary diversion, for their protection, of warships whose "honorable" function was always visualized as aggressive. But a convoy system was now reluctantly introduced: and to organize convoys meant a network of radio signals assigning routes, issuing instructions to the escort and the port of destination—not to speak of any ports of call *en voyage*—arranging for air cover and so on. However, the code used for this purpose—the *maru* code—was also broken in early 1943: apparently, according to Captain Holmes, by FRUPac.[6] The submarine war thus entered a new dimension.

One of the reasons for caution in applying Ultra operationally to the submarines in 1942 had been the fact that the intelligence coming to hand (chiefly about Japanese warships) had been acquired from the main Japanese naval code, and there was a great and natural hesitancy about compromising a source of such wide and profound importance. But less reserve was reasonably felt about intelligence from the *maru* code: a compromise here, after all, would have been extremely inconvenient but not disastrous. As a result, the primitive arrangements which had existed in 1942 for applying Sigint operationally were put on a rational basis—the foundation for an ever-expanding system whose sophistication and efficiency moved steadily forward until 1945.

The intimate relationship now established between JICPOA's Combat Intelligence Unit and the Operations Officer of ComSubPac have been vividly described in *Double-Edged Secrets*. So close a connection was obviously not possible for the commander of the SWPA submarine force working from its bases in Australia. Still, it is evident, from the activities of the Australian craft, that the dissemination of Ultra intelligence bore fruit—even though the confidential report on the submarine service produced in December 1945 must have been overcalling its hand when it declared that "during the war submarine operational authorities were in constant communication by a direct telephone line with the United States Naval Communication Intelligence Organization"! But time and again we find the Australian-based submarines, even though they were on patrol at an immense distance from the Antipodes, striking with lethal assurance against targets whose precise location had been conveyed to them by radioed instructions derived from Ultra intelligence. Steadily and irreversibly, the net closed round the *marus*.

The terrible significance for Japan of the cumulative but remorseless erosion of her merchant navy can be illustrated by a single, striking statistic. From Midway onward, in the great fleet actions of the Solomons campaign and elsewhere, her fighting fleet had suffered shattering losses while the material strength of the U.S.A.—as Admiral Yamamoto had long ago predicted—was turning out new warships as if from the General Motors production line. And yet by 1944, of all the steel allocated in Japan for shipbuilding only one-sixth of the total was being diverted to reinforcements for the fleet: all the rest was absorbed in the effort to keep a merchant navy—above all, a tanker service—in being.[7]

As one reads the Ultra information about Japanese convoys—whether in particular signals or, as it so often appears, in the Magic Summaries—there is one recurrent and salient feature. With a regularity which might seem commonplace unless one remained alert to its priceless significance, the intelligence concerning a convoy presents not simply the number of ships, and often their names and individual cargoes, and the character of the escort, but also the route it is to take and *the noon position for some or all the days of its voyage*. Neither the German B-Dienst, in its accurate reporting of the Allied Atlantic convoys, nor the British service of Ultra, in its coverage of enemy shipping, supplied such precise and regular intelligence—certainly not on the scale that the breaking of the *maru* code made available in the Pacific.

Moreover, the area of that ocean, compared with the little inland sea of the Mediterranean or even the wide swathe of the Atlantic routinely used by convoys, is gargantuan, and the variety of islands and channels offers endless scope for alternative routing. To ensure a high rate of effective strikes against the Japanese convoys without the sure guidance of signal intelligence would therefore have involved an astronomical number of submarines to supply constant standing patrols. Even air reconnaissance, on the most lavish scale, could not have brought much alleviation. Ultra, and particularly its provision of "noon positions," offered immense economies. Instead of having to keep huge numbers of submarines at sea to patrol all possible routes (even if they had been available) the staffs in Hawaii and Australia, knowing a convoy's route and noon positions, had merely to direct one or more craft to a specific point—and there was the target. If life was not always like this—since the imponderables of sea warfare are manifold—the pattern recurred in so many operations that it may be considered to be roughly characteristic.*

As Clay Blair found when writing *Silent Victory,* the captains' war diaries and patrol reports, which provided him with a rich variety of action stories and human drama, rarely—and then only incidentally—reflect the inner truth of many a successful engagement. And the reason is simple: to maintain security, any reference to Ultra in such reports was rigorously forbidden. Admiral King stamped on the practice before it took root, as this COMINCH circular of May 18, 1943, indicates. SUPER SECRET X ULTRA X WAR DIARIES OF SUBMARINES BASING WEST AUSTRALIA FOR MONTHS NOVEMBER DECEMBER JANUARY CONTAIN NUMEROUS REFERENCES COMMUNICATION INTELLIGENCE X ALL MENTION THIS SOURCE MUST BE ELIMINATED FROM ORIGINAL AND ALL COPIES OF PAST AND FUTURE DIARIES. On July 13 ComSubPac in Hawaii reiterated the warning to the captains under his command. NEITHER ACTUALLY NOR BY IMPLICATION SHOULD REFERENCE BE MADE TO ULTRA MESSAGES SENT BY THIS COMMAND X SAME RULE APPLIES FOR WRITING UP PATROL REPORTS.

By a curious paradox, indeed, Ultra—as has already been pointed out—served on occasion as a corrective to the sincere but overoptimistic claims made by submarine commanders on their return from patrol. There is, as it happens, a classic example for which all the evidence is

---

* By the end of 1943, when 435 *marus* had already been sunk, there were only 73 submarines operating in the Central Pacific and less than 30 from Australia. The arithmetic is self-explanatory.[8]

available, and though the target in question was a warship rather than a *maru*, the case illustrates so many aspects of the Ultra story—and is inherently so dramatic—that it is worth describing in full detail.

Early in June 1943 the submarines *Trigger* and *Salmon* were on patrol within the Japanese Inland Sea, where, by good luck, the enemy carrier force was engaged in training exercises. At 0815 on June 9 an urgent OP OP OP, or highest priority signal, went out from ComSubPac.

ANOTHER HOT ULTRA COMSUBPAC SERIAL 27 X LARGEST AND NEWEST NIP CARRIER WITH TWO DESTROYERS DEPARTS YOKOSUKA AT 5 HOURS GCT 10 JUNE AND CRUISES AT 22 KNOTS ON COURSE 155 DEGREES UNTIL REACHING 33-55 NORTH 140 EAST WHERE THEY REDUCE SPEED TO 18 KNOTS AND CHANGE COURSE TO 230 DEGREES X SALMON AND TRIGGER INTERCEPT IF POSSIBLE AND WATCH OUT FOR EACH OTHER X WE HAVE ADDITIONAL DOPE ON THIS CARRIER FOR THE BOYS NEAR TRUK WHICH WE HOPE WE WON'T NEED SO LET US KNOW IF YOU GET HIM X . . .

And so it was that on the night of the 10th the aircraft carrier *Hiyo*, with a flank guard of a destroyer on each bow, came zigzagging down Tokyo Bay at 20 knots or so, the crisscrossing enabling Roy Benson in *Trigger* to work in to a range of 1,200 yards. He then fired a spread of six torpedoes—and dived deep and fast as a destroyer moved in for the kill.

We have his log. "Sighted what was reported as smoke on horizon. On the next observation it showed itself as the island of a huge aircraft carrier. She was totally unlike any other Japanese aircraft carrier seen: looked most like the U.S.S. *Saratoga* . . . 1955. Fired 6 bow torpedoes . . . went deep and stood by heading for the carrier. The target's screws had slowed and then stopped. 2013. Crackling and popping sound in the direction of the recent target. These were clearly audible through the hull." *Trigger* returned to Pearl Harbor on June 22 "elated in the conviction that she was the first submarine to sink a Japanese aircraft carrier."

But during her evasive actions she must have missed a signal from ComSubPac to *Salmon* and *Trigger* transmitted almost immediately after the operation. It read:

COMSUBPAC SENDS ULTRA TO SALMON OR TRIGGER X CONGRATU-
LATIONS TO WHICHEVER OF YOU DID THE BEAUTIFUL JOB X BOTH
NOTE THAT ABOUT HALF THE NIP NAVY IS NOW ENGAGED IN TRY-
ING TO TOW THE BIG FLAT TOP BACK TO YOKOSUKA FROM
APPROXIMATE VICINITY 34-14 NORTH 139-52 EAST X IF EITHER
OF YOU ARE IN POSITION TO DO SO THERE MIGHT STILL BE TIME
TO FINISH HER OFF X SHE IS UNABLE NAVIGATE BY HERSELF.

What in fact happened was an old, old story. Four of *Trigger*'s
torpedoes had exploded prematurely. But one had indeed struck home,
in *Hiyo*'s boiler room. She was towed back to Yokosuka and reached
dry dock with her decks awash: a temporary respite, since she would
be sunk in June 1944 during the Battle of the Philippine Sea. But the
significant fact is that all the Japanese signals relating to her recovery
were being read in Hawaii—including a sad instruction: "For the time
being, mail addressed to this ship will be sent to Yokosuka Post Office."

There was a sense in which the quality and accuracy of Ultra intelligence were sometimes more noteworthy than the ability of the submarine command to apply it in action. But things were on the mend.
In *Undersea Victory* Captain Holmes summarized the general situation
on New Year's Day, 1944, and noted that: "All U.S. submarines had
dependable radar. An answer to their torpedo exploder difficulties had
at last been found. A new explosive greatly increased the destructive
effect of torpedo warheads. The electric torpedo was in service." Moreover, although Japan had started the war with 6,000,000 tons of transport shipping, a figure which even then was dangerously low considering the vast spread of her commitments, by the beginning of 1944 that
figure had been reduced by no less than a million tons in spite of all
the output of Japanese shipyards. The balance sheet was certainly not
unfavorable: particularly since, during the two years after Pearl Harbor, the United States had only lost 25 submarines as against 47
Japanese.

By the spring of 1944, indeed, a tone of despair is beginning to
enter the enemy's signals. The Japanese Army Supplement to the
Magic Far Eastern Summary for March 6, for example, reproduces an
Army signal from Manila to Tokyo of March 1 which could hardly
have been transmitted a few months earlier. "While returning to
Japan," it stated, "a convoy of six tankers was attacked by enemy submarines on February 20 in the waters NW of the Philippines and five

tankers were sunk. . . . *The present situation is such that the majority of tankers returning to Japan are being lost."* And, significantly, an intercept of May 9 from Shipping Headquarters in Tokyo to Manila ascribed these losses to the difficulty of preventing espionage in Manila harbor!

Perhaps the most striking example of how the submarine force, guided by Ultra, was now capable of dealing clinically with a convoy of Japanese transports, and thus not only reducing the enemy's *maru* fleet but also having a direct effect on the land battle, is the case of the "Take" convoy (known to the Americans as Bamboo No. 1). Its function was to ferry from Shanghai to New Guinea the 32nd and 35th divisions as reinforcements to stem MacArthur's advance. On April 17 an escorted group of nine vessels (under the command of an admiral) started on its long voyage by way of Manila. In view of what was to happen, there was a certain irony in the fact that at the time of the Coral Sea action Admiral Kajioka, the convoy commander, was to have led the invasion force into Port Moresby.

For Bamboo No. 1 was doomed. In the habitual way, Ultra had identified its route and noon positions. Moreover, the wretched Kajioka had been furnished with an ancient coal-burning minelayer, the *Shirataka,* as his flagship, so that when the submarine *Jack* met the convoy north of Luzon its presence was announced by clouds of filthy smoke. Down went the freighter *Yoshida Maru,* taking with her a complete infantry regiment.

After a call at Manila the convoy moved on, only to be caught again in the Celebes Sea by the submarine *Gurnard.* At least three more ships were sunk and others damaged—the Magic Far Eastern Summary for August 1 recorded the precise details from Ultra intercepts. After desperate rescue operations had scraped the survivors together, Tokyo refused to risk any further convoying, and the broken remnants of two infantry divisions were ignominiously ferried to New Guinea by devious routes in landing barges. Here was a supreme example of how immaculate Sigint immaculately applied in action could produce a decisive result.

No wonder: for the accuracy of intelligence was now extraordinary. In the Magic Far Eastern Summary for August 18, 1944, details are given of a captured document known as "the X List." Issued by the Japanese Navy as "A List of Ship Names for Communication Security at Sea," it contained the radio call signs for all vessels listed as well as the name, speed and tonnage. It was a basic list of shipping registered up to July 1, 1943, updated by ten supplements to February 25, 1944. The impressive fact is this: of the 1,720 *marus* of 1,000 gross tons or over which had been identified by American intelligence (over half from Ultra) only 13 did not fit with "the X List."

It was this quality of precise Sigint which made possible a further and increasingly lethal development in American tactics—the use of the "wolf pack" technique. Only a brief reminder of the great wilderness of the Pacific is necessary to make it clear that without very specific locations of targets it would have been impossible to muster killer groups of submarines concentrated at the right place and at the right time. But Ultra made this feasible. As more submarines and trained crews became available, therefore, the Americans essayed—at first tentatively—a technique which the German U-boats had applied so murderously in the Atlantic battle under that great exponent of the art, Admiral Doenitz.

Not even the most ardent aficionado of the U.S. Navy would probably claim that the Americans ever reached an equivalent mastery. The German wolf pack was like a highly tuned machine, massive in its impact but flexible, adaptable and beautifully integrated. It was some time before the Americans even worked out a satisfactory method for controlling a submarine group: should it be by a supervising officer at sea, or should instructions be issued from ashore? Nevertheless—in their usual persistent way—by experiment, failure and fresh endeavor the means were evolved so that, in the end, we have instances of successful assaults not merely by a single pack but by several attacking an important target in sequence. Without Ultra, sophisticated operations of this character would have been no more practicable than, without the Sigint supplied to U-boat Command by B-Dienst, would it have been possible to orchestrate the maneuvers of those voracious Atlantic wolf packs.

Inevitably, the result of improved tactics and increasing strength was a one-way process. Between January and April 1944 U.S. submarines sank 179 ships of some 799,000 gross tons: between May and the end of August a further 219 ships had gone to the bottom, and their ton reckoning had passed the million mark. By the end of 1944 imports of oil, the vital essence of war, had almost entirely ceased and domestic stocks in Japan, as high as 43,000,000 barrels at the end of 1941, sank to less than 4,000,000 by March 1945.[9]

"Until late in the war," Craven and Cate observe in the final volume of their history of the Army Air Forces, "and for the whole of the war, the submarine was the chief killer, but it was ably seconded and made more effective by Navy, AAF, and Marine planes." This generous (though accurate) apportioning of the various contributions in the attack on Japanese shipping is, of course, a salutary reminder that other agencies were at work. With their range and their flexibility the air forces could seek targets beyond the reach of the submarines and then, as the throttling encirclement of Japan grew tighter and tighter, concentrated air strikes could be mounted from the neighboring islands on such shipping lanes as still remained open (fewer and fewer, since by the spring of 1945, 35 out of 47 regular convoy routes had been abandoned). This very diminution of viable seaways, plus the narrowing of the ring around the home islands of Japan, also provided the U.S. Air Force with opportunities that were fully grasped for sealing off harbors and infesting shipping routes with airborne mines. As abundant targets for submarines disappeared from the high seas and operations became more difficult and dangerous in the constricted waters still available to the enemy, air power—virtually unimpeded— was able to take over.

And yet, while this is true, the central fact is undeniable: until the fall of 1944 over 70 percent of Japan's shipping losses can be attributed to the U.S. submarines, apart from their incidental successes thereafter. When surrender came, the *marus* were mainly a memory and—thanks in large measure to Ultra—no major merchant fleet in history had been so mercilessly savaged.

It seems appropriate, therefore, to end this chapter with a kind of roll of honor: a list of the sinkings of Japanese merchant ships attributed to individual submarines by the Joint Army-Navy Assessment Committee which reported in 1947. The list is rigorously restricted to vessels under the headings Cargo, Passenger-Cargo, Transport and Tanker: it excludes warships large or small. It also excludes all sinkings assessed as "by combinations including U.S. submarines." As this book is not a technical history of submarine warfare the list has not been checked against later appraisals, and no doubt in this case or that the relevant figure should be larger or smaller. But as it stands, it provides a broad but graphic demonstration of the way things went, in a conflict during which the submarines of the United States accounted for some 4,780,000 tons of Japanese merchant shipping.

Attributions

Albacore 2:
Amberjack 2:
Angler 2:
Apogon 1:
Barbel 5:
Barbero 3:
Bashaw 3:
Batfish 2:
Baya 2:
Becuna 1:
Bergall 2:
Billfish 3:
Blackfish 1:
Blackfin 1:
Blenny 6:
Bluefish 8:
Bluegill 8:
Boarfish 1:
Bonefish 11:
Bowfin 15:
Bream 1:
Burrfish 1:
Bumper 1:
Cabezon 1:
Cabrilla 6:
Capelin 1:
Cavalla 1:
Cero 5:
Cobia 3:
Cod 4:
Crevalle 7:
Croaker 4:
Dace 5:
Darter 1:
Drum 14:
Finback 11:
Flasher 15:
Flier 1:
Flying Fish 15:
Gablian 1:
Gar 8:
Gato 8:

Grampus 1:
Grayback 10:
Grayling 5:
Greenling 13:
Grenadier 1:
Grouper 4:
Growler 6:
Guardfish 16:
Guavina 5:
Gudgeon 10:
Guitarro 6:
Gunnel 4:
Gurnard 10:
Haddo 5:
Haddock 8:
Hake 6:
Halibut 10:
Hammerhead 9:
Harder 9:
Hardhead 3:
Hawkhill 1:
Herring 5:
Hoe 2:
Icefish 2:
Jack 14:
Jallao 1:
Kete 3:
Kingfish 12:
Lagarto 2:
Lapon 11:
Mingo 1:
Muskellunge 1:
Narwhal 6:
Nautilus 5:
Paddle 4:
Pampanito 5:
Parch 6:
Pargo 5:
Permit 3:
Peto 7:
Pickerel 2:
Picuda 9:

Pike 1:
Pintado 5:
Pipefish 1:
Piranha 2:
Plunger 11:
Pogy 11:
Pollack 7:
Pomfret 4:
Pompano 5:
Pompon 3:
Porpoise 3:
Puffer 6:
Queenfish 6:
Rasher 16:
Raton 10:
Ray 9:
Redfin 5:
Redfish 4:
Rock 1:
Ronquil 2:
Runner 2:
U.S.S. S-36, 1:
S-31, 1:
S-35, 1:
S-37, 1:
S-38, 2:
S-39, 1:
S-41, 1:
Sailfish 6:
Salmon 2:
Sandlance 8:
Sargo 7:
Saury 5:
Sawfish 3:
Scabbardfish 1:
Scamp 3:
Scorpion 3:
Sculpin 3:
Sea Devil 6:
Sea Dog 8:
Sea Robin 5:
Seadragon 9:

Seahorse 17:
Seal 7:
Sealion II, 8:
Searaven 3:
Seawolf 15:
Segundo 2:
Sennet 5:
Shad 2:
Shark 4:
Silversides 21:
Skate 7:
Skipjack 4:
Snapper 2:
Snook 16:
Spadefish 17:
Spearfish 4:
Spot 1:
Steelhead 2:
Sterlet 4:
Stingray 3:
Sturgeon 8:
Sunfish 14:
Swordfish 9:
Tambar 10:
Tang 24:
Tarpon 2:
Tautog 19:
Tench 4:
Threadfin 1:
Thresher 16:
Tinosa 16:
Tirante 6:
Torsk 1:
Trepang 7:
Trigger 14:
Triton 8:
Trout 8:
Tullibee 2:
Tuna 4:
Tunny 4:
Wahoo 20:
Whale 8:

CHAPTER ELEVEN

Overhearing Oshima

Our main basis of information regarding Hitler's intentions in Europe is obtained from Baron Oshima's messages from Berlin reporting his interviews with Hitler and other officials to the Japanese Government.

General Marshall to Governor Dewey,
September 27, 1944

THE MASS OF Japanese diplomatic messages reproduced in the eight volumes of *The "Magic" Background of Pearl Harbor* is itself only a selection, albeit a substantial one, from the grand total of such communications deciphered by American cryptanalysts before December 1941. But just as the main flood of an incoming tide is preceded by smaller and less impressive waves, so the volume and significance of these intercepts can scarcely be compared with the intelligence supplied almost continuously by Magic between the day of Pearl Harbor and the Japanese capitulation in 1945. Even after that date a copious stream of vital information, about reactions in Tokyo and elsewhere, poured into Washington. A useful measuring rod is provided by the list of addressees of signals intercepted and deciphered during the very first year of the Pacific war. In 1942 these were messages exchanged between the Foreign Office in Tokyo and Japanese diplomatic posts in (among other cities) Berlin, Rome, Lisbon, Vichy, Madrid, Ankara, Stockholm, Buenos Aires, Hanoi, Helsinki, Sofia and Santiago.

Marshall's warning letter to Dewey of September 27, 1944, was unintentionally misleading in one small detail. From later Magic intercepts it is clear that after that date Oshima's privileged interviews with Hitler himself were rarely, if ever, repeated. In substance, however, the general's claim was correct: from this source alone Magic supplied the Allies with a unique insight—with intelligence about Germany's intentions, armaments and economic problems which, for a technical reason, the cryptanalysts at Bletchley Park were sometimes unable to provide by their breaking of the Enigma-enciphered signals. In one way or another, all these dealt with specific matters. What was missing was the play of mind, the character and quality of the thinking that had been finally distilled in the actual message. To a degree, of course, these could be deduced by experienced analysts. But the virtue of Oshima's communications was his firsthand reporting of private conversations with the Führer and his henchmen. That they often talked to impress or to conceal, to convey to Tokyo what they wanted the Japanese to believe, is self-evident. Nevertheless, much more was involved. Often, for example, an independent check reveals that Oshima was told the truth. Often, too, we find him reporting to Tokyo on situations which he had been permitted to investigate for himself: he was a perceptive eyewitness as well as a conveyor belt.

And this, it must be emphasized, was a wholly unexpected bonus— for the Americans themselves, and for the alliance of United Nations. When Friedman's team slaved away at cracking the Purple cipher, and even during the months before Pearl Harbor when Magic decrypts were abundantly available, the essential purpose of the cryptanalytical attack and subsequent study of the signals was to acquire information about Japan. Nobody conceived that Magic would turn out to be like the Roman god Janus, two-faced, capable of looking both to the east and to the west. In times of war, the temple of Janus was kept permanently open.

Its importance for the conflict with Japan has already been indicated, and will be enlarged on later. First, however, it will be useful to weigh the value of that incidental bonus, before examining the extent of the dividend that Magic was originally intended to deliver.

The early days were a halcyon time. In the spring of 1942 Hitler was brimming with confidence: the Japanese, for their part, had not only mauled the Americans—for whom the Führer felt a massive contempt*—but in capturing Singapore and reaching out to Burma had so damaged the British position in the Far East that troops and equipment which should have been used against Rommel in North Africa

---

* In 1938 Speer heard Hitler say about the Americans: "They would certainly not withstand a great trial by fire, for their fighting qualities are low." Even as late as April 1945, Speer noted: "Hitler went off into long explications of the notorious inability of American soldiers to accept defeats, although the Battle of the Bulge had just proved the opposite."

were being hastily transferred to India. The war was running well: the Japanese Axis was paying off, and in his present mood Hitler might well have repeated the famous capering dance which he performed after the French capitulation in 1940.

This euphoria was clearly revealed in the Magic intercepts. On March 24, 1942, for example, Oshima reported to Tokyo Hitler's reaction to the victories of his U-boats in the Caribbean and along the eastern shores of the United States. "I myself have been surprised at the successes we have met with along the American coast lately. The United States kept up the tall talk and left her coasts unguarded. Now I daresay that *she* is quite surprised." And well might Hitler register astonishment, for these were the dreadful months of Operation *Paukenschlag* (Drumbeat). Immediately after Pearl Harbor, Admiral Doenitz had switched the weight of his U-boat offensive from the North Atlantic to the shipping (mainly precious oil tankers) sailing from the Caribbean and the Gulf of Mexico. The slaughter was enormous. As Doenitz himself recalled, "Conditions were almost exactly those of normal peacetime. The coast was not blacked out, the towns were a blaze of bright lights. Shipping followed the normal peacetime routes and carried the normal lights."

Four days later there was another conversation and another outburst of confidence to report to Tokyo. "What we Germans are expecting," Hitler said, "is a landing attempt on the part of the British at Cherbourg or Le Havre. . . . You know they may attack in Norway, too, but *wherever it may be, Germany would rather welcome a landing attempt by the British.*" An invasion of Norway was never in the cards, for though Churchill yearned for one his Chiefs of Staff were adamant, but a constant feature of British deception schemes was the reiterated attempt to persuade the Germans that an invasion there was imminent, and such indications in Magic of Hitler's obsession with Norway (an obsession wholly irrational, for how could the British have assaulted Scandinavia in March 1942?) were important clues for the deceivers.

Germany's economic problems were well illustrated in the many exchanges between Berlin and Tokyo about shortages of essential raw materials. But a message from Oshima of April 13, 1942, in which he filed a careful estimate of German industrial mobilization, is a reminder that he was an unabashed and objective observer . . . in matters of detail. On the more general question of Germany's ultimate prospects it is probably true to say that Oshima—like many other ambassadors—took the color of his surroundings and tended toward overoptimism. But on particular points he recorded truths which, uncovered by Magic, should have given the Allies cause for thought at the time, and which have been verified by postwar investigation.

After the concentrated air raids on Hamburg, for example, Oshima had a look for himself and concluded that in spite of the holocaust industrial production had not been fundamentally affected. (Albert Speer, Hitler's industrial overlord, has testified that he feared this was about to happen but that, as in the case of other cities, relaxation of bombing allowed a breathing space for partial recovery.) Neither the British nor the American "bomber barons" would have accepted this proposition in 1943: yet Oshima supplied a hint. And after a long conversation with Hitler in January 1944 he informed Tokyo that "the Germans seem to have achieved a remarkable expansion in their production of essential weapons such as tanks and airplanes . . . war production is still gradually rising, as I believe. That upward trend will continue." We now know that even in that year of disasters German armament production, against all expectations, was sustained at an astonishingly high level. It was certainly worth overhearing Oshima: it is less certain that, in this respect at least, Allied intelligence got the message.

Of all the technical information which Magic produced from the signals of the Japanese Embassy in Berlin, perhaps none was more valuable than data concerning a weapon whose potentialities the Germans developed more effectively than the Allies. This was the jet-propelled aircraft, which, when it was first employed operationally by the Luftwaffe, looked as though it might provide the enemy with an advantage in the skies as significant as the Americans' earlier upgrading of the Mustang into a long-range fighter capable of escorting bombers to the far side of Germany. The Japanese were avid for information about jet propulsion. In consequence, the Berlin Embassy filed many reports which, as translated in the Magic intercepts, often have the same authority and exact description as a purloined blueprint might have provided.* (To read these reports, incidentally,

---

* An appendix to the Magic Far Eastern Summary of December 5, 1944, presents an assessment of Japanese progress in jet-propulsion up to that date. There is a full résumé of signals which indicate a continual pressure on Germany from Tokyo for information

makes one appreciate the flexibility of the Purple ciphersystem. Originated for purposes essentially diplomatic, it could cope with technicalities at the extreme range of contemporary scientific enterprise.)

Consider the case of the Arado 234. Apart from the Messerschmitt 262 this jet aircraft, capable of carrying a one-ton bomb, was the most efficient type the Germans produced, and no less than 527 were delivered to the Luftwaffe in 1944. But the Allies knew virtually everything about it. A Magic decrypt of a signal sent to Tokyo on October 31 by the Naval Attaché in Japan's Berlin Embassy supplied its dimensions, its maximum speed at varying altitudes and the reduction in speed caused by different bomb loads; the rate of climb, the optimum ceiling range and cruising range, the landing speed, the characteristics of its automatic pilot and details of the Luftwaffe units which specialized in operating the Arado.

Another but less successful type, the ME-163, had been described in a similar deciphered dispatch of September 6, and on October 19 the Attaché signaled an even more remarkable message—an account of an interview which he had been granted a week earlier with that ace of German designers, Professor Heinkel, who talked to him freely about the experimental Heinkel "rocket plane" and indicated that if all went well "as many as 1,000 of these aircraft should be produced by next spring." Heinkel was in fact chasing a will-o'-the-wisp: his plane never went into series production. But this sort of information, combined with the very precise data acquired at Bletchley Park from deciphering the Luftwaffe's Enigma signals, and from meticulous study by the British "Y Service" of the enemy's radio traffic, resulted in an almost encyclopedic awareness of what the Germans were doing with their jets. On November 17, 1944, the Magic European Summary issued by the German Military Reports Branch of MIS in Washington was amplified by an appendix on "Jet-propelled Aircraft" which, by summarizing the material obtained from all relevant sources, gave a striking demonstration of the intimate knowledge which signal

---

about jet aircraft, including demands for designs and detailed technical inquiries. Evidently, too, the Japanese tried hard to obtain priority for jet technicians on U-boats sailing from Germany, and probed for estimates of the probable date of their arrival. There is little evidence, however, that by the end of 1944 the Japanese themselves had made significant progress.

intelligence could supply about one of Hitler's most treasured secrets, another of the "wonder weapons" on which he was relying for survival.

In the end, however, it was probably what Oshima heard and saw for himself that was most rewarding. After the collapse of the Italians in the autumn of 1943, for example, intelligence officers might make their informed estimates about Hitler's intentions: and yet (bearing in mind the elaborate deceptive schemes that were mounted to persuade him that the Balkans were the prime target, thus compelling him to keep unnecessarily large forces there) how satisfactory it must have been to catch the flavor of his thinking from Oshima's signal to Tokyo of October 4, in which he reported that, in the Führer's view, the Allies would "either go north in Italy or they will try to land in the Balkans. I am inclined to believe that they will take the latter course." Moreover, Hitler added, he was holding twenty divisions in the Balkans as against eighteen on the Italian mainland. "I have finally had to adopt a defensive strategy," he significantly confessed, "although this is the very first time since the war began that we Germans had to do so." There was a real value in being able to hear him uttering such a *cri de coeur* to his only remaining major partner in the war.

Beyond price, however, was what Oshima revealed about the German defenses in the west, just at the time when Anglo-American plans for an invasion were at the highest pitch of preparation and every morsel of specific information was being assembled; often at the risk of death or torture for the men—and women—who worked within the German lines. It is difficult to assess the cost, in human terms, of the effort that would have been required to collect that mass of authentic, firsthand intelligence which merely a couple of Magic intercepts disclosed. On December 10, 1943, the Magic Summary reproduced a nine-page text of Oshima's description, for Tokyo, of his personal inspection of the Atlantic Wall. It contained an analysis of the German command structure for Northwestern Europe, a clear account of the defensive systems, a report on the number of divisions in the west and the pattern of rotation, as well as a dismissive estimate of the effectiveness of Allied bombing. A week later Magic produced a particularly detailed report from Berlin by Lieutenant Colonel Nishi, whose own eyewitness account examined the German preparations more professionally. He reviewed the defensive arrangements systematically, noting the types and quantities of artillery, the siting of machine guns to achieve an interweaving cross fire, the numbers and methods of emplacing antitank guns and the varying depths of the defense zones at danger points like Dieppe, Boulogne, Le Havre and La Rochelle. All this was manna from heaven.

And like the manna of the Bible, it was both providential and beyond reasonable expectation. Still more so, perhaps, was the insight that Magic occasionally provided into the activities of the Russians. Allies they too might be, but their stubborn and surly refusal to furnish information to their partners was rarely overcome, even by the visit of a Prime Minister or the presence in their midst of British and American Military Missions. It is a curious fact that the British probably learned more about the deployment of Soviet divisions, the nature of their operations and the scale of their losses from the content of intercepted radio signals, transmitted by the German armies on the Eastern Front and deciphered at Bletchley Park, than they ever did in formal communications from the Russians themselves.

The main contribution of Magic in this respect—as will be seen in the next chapter—was during the final phase of the Japanese war, when deciphered diplomatic signals to and from the Foreign Office in Tokyo told London and Washington much about Russian intentions in the Far East which would otherwise have been concealed by the inscrutable Stalin and his subordinates. But there were other occasions when Magic lifted the veil. A remarkable instance occurred in the spring of 1943. To get to Russia a Japanese representative, General Okamoto, traveled by train via Irkutsk, Alma Ata, Tashkent, Samarkand, Baku and Tiflis. With considerable ingenuity he contrived to spy out the land as he journeyed onward, making detailed notes of the social, economic and military situation in the Russian hinterland. He had a quick eye for signs of indifferent morale, material shortages and similar indices. All that he saw he radioed back to Tokyo, in a report which filled some thirty pages—and the Magic intercepts collared the lot. Everything is set out in a long appendix to the Magic Summary of May 14, 1943. By no conceivable covert operation could a British or American observer have made a similar journey, or, even if he had been allowed to do so, have been given the opportunity for so comprehensive a view. SOE and OSS were never privileged visitors in Tashkent or Samarkand.

Covert operations were, of course, a constant preoccupation of the Japanese themselves. Thanks to Magic, the Americans obtained detailed and specific information about the clandestine activities of Japanese agents during the run-up to Pearl Harbor: their ferrets were then identified both in the United States and in many areas of South America. After Germany and Japan became partners in the war these activities were naturally intensified. All the time, however, they were endangered by the camera eye—and sometimes, indeed, by the flashlight exposure—of Magic.

It became plain at an early stage that the Spanish and, to a degree, the Portuguese authorities were readily collaborating with the Japanese in the business of intelligence-gathering. On April 15, 1942, for example, Magic disclosed that the Spanish Foreign Minister, Suñer, was facilitating the passage of agents accredited to the Information Bureau of the Spanish Consul-General in San Francisco: another intercept, from Lisbon, contained information about an Allied convoy observed in the harbor of Lourenço Marques on June 19 . . . individual ships were named, and the nature of their cargoes.* (An earlier Lisbon-Tokyo signal, of April 13, reported Pan American Airways' transatlantic schedule and the staging posts which the Allies were developing for an air-ferry service across central Africa.) On May 8 Magic also produced a signal from Tokyo to Santiago, thanking the Chileans for their efforts in furthering the operations of Japanese intelligence within the United States.

The Military Intelligence Service in Washington had been quick to identify what it described as "a certain class of intelligence reports which purportedly originate in New York and Washington and which are forwarded by the Japanese from Madrid to Tokyo: originally collected by a Spanish intelligence net, and given to Japanese in Madrid." This assumption was amply confirmed by a Magic intercept of July 11, 1942, from the Japanese ambassador in Madrid. "In connection with the matter of the spy activities in the United States," he informed Tokyo, "through the good offices of Foreign Minister Suñer we are now, in strictest secrecy, in touch with the chief of the

---

* See also, for example, Magic Summary 371 of April 1, 1943, which contains the text of a very full Japanese report on the activity of the German Consulate-General in Lourenço Marques as the center of an "extensive and efficient espionage agency net" in Mozambique and South Africa, particularly in respect of intelligence about Allied shipping.

Falangist branches in New York and Washington. We are communicating through the telegrams and mail of the Spanish Embassy and Consulate-General."*

An important feature of miscellaneous intelligence-gathering is the way that, coincidentally, one piece of evidence can casually illuminate another area of operations. Here is a neat example. On July 24, 1942, the Magic Summary noted that what were called "TO Intelligence Reports" came from a Spanish network operating in Britain, and that they were passed straight to the "German Special Affairs Agency" (presumably the Abwehr). Moreover, the Summary indicated a confident Japanese belief that the German Agency "has a staff in Britain which has been constantly transmitting such information to Germany." Alas, since the earliest days of the war every German spy in Britain had been apprehended, and the "staff" whose radios fed the Abwehr with tidbits consisted either of double agents functioning under the control of MI 5, or fictional characters in whose real existence the Germans had been persuaded to place their trust. Magic thus made an important contribution by confirming, indirectly, that the Double-Cross System had not been blown.

The Japanese-German link in connection with intelligence from Britain had already resulted in what was surely one of the more ludicrous episodes of the war. In his 1945 confidential report on the Double-Cross System which Sir John Masterman finally published in 1972, he described graphically an episode involving the double agent code-named Tate.[1]

> The Germans instructed Tate to wait at 16.00 hours at the terminus of the Number 11 bus route at Victoria. He was there to enter a bus with a Japanese who would be carrying *The Times* and a book in his left hand. Tate was to wear a red tie and also to carry a newspaper and a book. After the fifth stop they would both alight and continue their journey by the next bus on the same route where, after an exchange of agreed remarks, the Japanese would hand the paper over to him. In it money would be found.

Unfortunately, Tate's Abwehr masters were unaware that the Number 11 bus was no longer running from Victoria Station! So, supposedly

---

* Appendix A to the Magic Summary of August 10, 1942, consists of a ten-page summary of Spanish participation in espionage in Britain and the United States.

desperate for the wherewithal to keep going, Tate signaled back to suggest the Number 16. Finally the transaction took place—observed, and photographed, by the Special Branch of Scotland Yard. The Japanese, who stupidly went straight back to his Embassy,* was recognized as an Assistant Naval Attaché, Lieutenant Commander Mitinory Yosii—and Tate (or MI5) was richer by £200. (But this was small beer. After a similar negotiation with the Abwehr in Lisbon, during July 1941, Tate extracted £20,000.) However, the faith of the Japanese in the Germans' ability to conduct covert operations was undiminished. On July 27, Magic picked up this message from Baron Oshima in Berlin: "In connection with my spying activities in America I would like to obtain some of the special secret ink used by the German Defense Bureau, together with instructions as to use."

Nevertheless, one had to be careful. There was the case, for example, of the Magic intercept of a message from Tokyo to Madrid on December 28, 1942. "When we evacuated our Embassy in Washington . . . we left 500,000 dollars in cash in a large safe in the Treasurer's office in the Chancery there." It had been left, the message explained, as a reserve for the Spanish government to draw on in its capacity as a protecting power. The combinations were given of the safe itself, and of a smaller internal safe. Could the Spanish ambassador go and collect? The Military Intelligence Service very wisely concluded that "though the Japanese seemed wholly confident in their cryptographic systems" the signal might be a plant, designed to test the systems' security: to take any form of action on this enticing communication might easily blow Magic to pieces. Surely a sensible conclusion, even though remarkable insights were available into the Japanese mind. Within a few weeks, for instance—on February 12, 1943—the Magic Summary was carrying the text of a ten-page report by Oshima to Tokyo on a conference held in Berlin the previous month for seventeen Japanese intelligence officers from Berlin itself, from Sweden, Spain, Portugal, Switzerland, Turkey, Bulgaria, Italy, Vichy, Paris and the Vatican. That certainly indicated a complete confidence in the cryptographic systems!

But the Spirit of Irony, which pervades all history, ensured that throughout the war the Americans, from Magic itself, could feel comfortable about Magic's integrity. Time and again the Japanese were

* The event occurred in 1941, before Pearl Harbor.

observed, in their intercepted signals, reflecting about the security of their codes and ciphers. The reason may have been arrogance or mere inefficiency, but the answer was ever the same: all is well.

There was the affair, for example, of the Mikimoto pearls. It was always difficult for the Japanese to keep up a cash flow for their clandestine operations: one trick, therefore, was to smuggle small but easily disposable objects whose sale could raise some funds. During the winter of 1942–43 the Americans discovered through Magic that a set of pearls was to be transferred to Europe via a Spanish diplomatic pouch. Without revealing the source of their intelligence they contrived to extract the pearls, which the State Department then formally delivered to the Spanish Embassy in Washington. As Ambassador Suma reported to Tokyo from Madrid on May 21, 1943, State used "very unpleasant language" and the Spaniards were much put out. "When I was talking to Ambassador Cardena the other day about the pearls and other matters," Suma continued, "twice his eyes narrowed and he said musingly, ponderingly and in a soft half-questioning voice: 'It is strange how quickly the United States finds out about matters such as these. I wonder if Japanese codes are safe.'" Almost immediately, on May 26, Foreign Minister Shigemitsu replied from Tokyo: "I have studied the matter from a number of angles, but I cannot believe it is the result of their having solved our codes."

There were times, indeed, when the Spirits of Irony and of Comedy worked in concert. On August 9, 1943, Tokyo signaled to Morishima, the Japanese representative in Portugal, to suggest that a certain class of intelligence known as the "Fuji" reports was possibly being fed to him by the enemy, so that they could keep a lookout for their appearance in the diplomatic signals and thus facilitate their cryptanalysis. Morishima was ordered to investigate. Magic then provided the delicious spectacle of a self-important functionary blowing his top. "Is this a civilized way to treat a man?" Morishima responded. "It reminds me of the hideous punishment of bygone ages and those damnable GPU agents. . . . I have never known another man to be treated as I have been treated. I know that codes are the very life of the Foreign Office and now that suspicion has been cast on me I can never live it down. People will always be whispering behind my back. It was a sneaking, dirty trick, if you ask me. Would you please condescend to consider that I herewith resign." From Madrid, Ambassador

Suma now poured oil on these troubled waters, and the storm only subsided when Tokyo instructed Morishima to "cut out worrying and rest easy." The curious feature of this episode is not so much its drollery as its implications, for amid the burlesque of hurt feelings nobody seems to have addressed himself to the central issue: were the diplomatic signals in fact being compromised? There is a blithe assumption that they were not.

It might indeed be claimed that Magic was often good for a laugh, whether in its revelation of individual attitudes or in its reflection of a more general trait, that dogged lack of a sense of humor which characterizes the Japanese mentality. What thoughts, for example, perturbed the Naval Attaché in Berlin before, on September 29, 1944, he summoned up the courage to suggest to Tokyo that his proposals should be considered for extricating himself and his colleagues in the event of a German collapse? What ponderous investigations lay behind the news—picked up by Magic in June 1942—that the question of adapting the Japanese to life in the tropics was being studied by the East Asia Research Institute, and that Drs. Ogura and Nakayama had come up with a solution? Contrary to Dutch practice, they said, they recommended a midday rest from 11 a.m. to 2 p.m., including a nap lasting from thirty minutes to an hour. That would have been helpful on Guadalcanal, where the prolonged death struggle was soon to begin!

And what solemn concern was behind the signal from Tokyo to their man in Peking on April 21, 1943, about an experimental importation of 1,000 laborers from northern China for use as miners or stevedores? "The original plan," so the message stated, "had been to send the workers without accompanying prostitutes. Subsequent developments have made it clear, however, that in the interest not only of the workers' efficiency but also of public welfare and morals it is necessary to import prostitutes at once." But there was a problem. How, Tokyo asked Peking, could these agreeable ladies be controlled "to avoid Japanese coming in contact with them"? It is improbable that intercepts like these struck a chime in the heads of the MIS officers responsible for processing them: still, perhaps there was somebody who remembered that, at the time of the Japanese failure in the Battle of the Coral Sea, Magic had reproduced the crass declaration by Vice-Admiral Takahashi that "the enemy's navy may be characterized as not merely incompetent but idiotic" . . . and then recalled, with satisfaction, a line in Shakespeare's *Twelfth Night*: "And thus the whirligig of time brings in his revenges."

But all this is trivial. Of far graver import was a notification in the Magic Summary of June 4, 1942, of the Japanese intention to construct "a Burma railroad"—followed, on January 4, 1943, by specific evidence that British prisoners of war were being employed for this purpose. The Summaries are rich, indeed, with material relating to the China/Burma/India theater—particularly on shifting Japanese attitudes toward their campaign in China and their political relationships with the Far Eastern countries. It is now evident that at the time of the 1944 Japanese offensive at Imphal, and the long-range penetration of Wingate's Chindits behind the enemy lines in Burma, Magic supplied precise intelligence about the reorganization of the Japanese command structure on the Burma front and critical information about the flow of Japanese reinforcing divisions from further east. The exact nature of this intelligence could not be deduced from the British Official History, nor was it available to the author when he was preparing *Slim the Standard-bearer*, the official biography of the commander of the Fourteenth Army, who, having led a defeated British force out of Burma in 1942, returned in triumph to Rangoon in 1945.

The Magic traffic on which this chapter is mainly based was, of course, deciphered more or less continuously and currently from 1940 onward. But there was another specific source, sometimes but not necessarily reflected in the Magic Summaries, which richly amplified the "main-line" Purple intelligence even though it only became available later in the war. This was the interchange of communications between the naval authorities in Tokyo and their naval attachés abroad.

Enciphered on the machine known as Coral, this traffic was peculiarly difficult to penetrate. Not only did Coral lack some of the technical vulnerability of its predecessors: the operational usage was more secure and sophisticated, so that far fewer errors were committed by which the Americans could make an entry. Also, all the posts using Coral came into action simultaneously, so that there were few if any cases of overlapping signals in another and already penetrated cipher, as happened in the case of Red and Purple. Commander Francis

Raven, who was closely involved in the attack on Coral, informed the author (letter of May 12, 1981) that the break-in actually occurred about April 1943, and soon afterward the naval attaché traffic was being read currently.* Gradually the previously intercepted but unintelligible material was "read back." In effect, therefore, the file now constitutes some 5,000 signals covering the whole war from the summer of 1940.[2]

Even the briefest summary of the range of items covered reveals the value of this intelligence, particularly after the break in 1943 made it immediately available. The Yanagi blockade-runners: the interchange of technical information: details of convoy movements: spy plots and other clandestine arrangements: U-boat operations in the Far East: reports on the techniques used by the Allies during the Normandy invasion—these are but a few of the themes which (although they are valuably reflected in the series of Magic Summaries) can often be studied in finer detail—and with a sense, perhaps, of closer intimacy— by working carefully over the actual signals in the Naval Attaché Series. As this file was only declassified in 1980, it certainly offers a field for more intensive research.

And so for the war against Germany,† for the destruction of the Japanese merchant navy and the thwarting of the contraband-runners, in its unveiling of Japanese covert operations and the intelligence it supplied about the enemy's political maneuvers and economic instability, Magic more than justified the claims made on its behalf by General Marshall, who of all people knew best its vital significance. But another role still remained. Apart from the anxious months which preceded the attack on Pearl Harbor, there was probably no period during the war when it was more important for the Allies to be sure about what was going on in the minds of the men in Tokyo than during those final weeks when a decision had to be taken about how

---

* In fact, Raven reported that once the technicalities of the system had been grasped the team working on it produced within twenty-four hours an analogue machine for reading the Coral traffic.

† In the personal "President–Former Naval Person" correspondence between Roosevelt and Churchill there are occasional references to "Magic" or "the Magics" in connection with events in the European Theater. Some are evidently based on the deciphered Japanese diplomatic traffic; in other cases it looks rather as though "Magic" was used as a general term for secret intelligence. Elucidation must await the edition of the correspondence by Professor Warren F. Kimball of Rutgers University.

to bring the whole business to an end. Must Japan be invaded, and if so at what cost? Should the atom bomb be used? What was Russia's posture? If Magic could not supply all the answers to these crucial questions, its reliable voice would nevertheless be heard once again: loud and clear.

CHAPTER TWELVE

A Scent in the Morning Air

Quelle est cette odeur agréable?
  Old French carol

A CRITICAL HISTORIAN is always in danger of appearing to pick at the clay feet of great men. In the case of MacArthur, the Mountbatten of the American scene, this risk is unavoidable, for like his fellow Supreme Commander in Southeast Asia, MacArthur was overwhelmed by an obsessive egomania which made him consistently claim too much for himself. False assertions which were sometimes intentional and sometimes bred of fantasy, ruthless depreciation of the work of others, a calculated exploitation of the delusive techniques of public relations, a considerable literature churned out by ignorant idolators or self-serving flatterers—all these form a cloud of unreality, distorting or concealing the actual man. To reach the heart of the matter involves a destructive process, which can too easily be taken for an attempt at a total demolition.

To establish the facts about a great commander's weakness in one or more areas of his operations, however, does not necessarily imply that, when all is said, he remains less than a great commander: only that he was not the miracle man, the acme of perfection that he claimed to be. If objective criticism indicates that MacArthur, like Mountbatten, was a flawed giant, it would nevertheless be unhistorical to suggest that his diminished stature is other than towering. For when one reviews the ranks of the American war leaders, who besides Marshall, Eisenhower, Nimitz and Spaatz seem to be of similar magnitude? Not Bradley, nor Patton, nor Stilwell, nor Clark—

for all their distinctiveness. The criticism leveled at MacArthur in this book, therefore, is not so much intended to eject him from his pedestal as somewhat to adjust his posture. And, unfortunately, such adjustments are necessary at almost every stage of the war in the Pacific.

In the spring of 1944, the Americans were on a launching pad. The significant date can be pinpointed. On March 12 the Chiefs of Staff issued a directive which instructed MacArthur to press on up the coast of New Guinea, establishing a forward base at Hollandia and by-passing the enemy's own main base at Rabaul,* and then to be ready to invade the southern Philippines in November, while Nimitz in the Central Pacific made another great island-hop—to Saipan and Guam in the Marianas (whence heavy bombers would be able to work over Japan), and further south to the Palaus, whence air cover could be supplied for the Philippine assault.[1] All the auguries of defeat indicated in the preceding three chapters were now converging. The creeping paralysis of their shipping losses would be compounded for the Japanese by the final neutralization and ultimate destruction of their enfeebled German ally: for in March 1944 the summer invasion of Fortress Europe was already planned and assured. While Japanese production waned, the vast industrial complex of the United States was pouring out fleets of aircraft and warships. On all sides, therefore, there was a scent in the morning air: an agreeable scent of decisive victory, as one success followed another.

And the successes were indubitable. MacArthur's swoop forward on Hollandia, a jump over several hundred miles,† was the largest amphibious operation so far attempted in SWPA: the logistics were formidable, the planning complicated[2] (80,000 men, 110 vessels, hundreds of aircraft). Yet Hollandia was seized almost overnight, to become the headquarters area from which the path to the Philippines was cleared and MacArthur's famous promise of "I shall return" was finally and fully implemented. General Marshall was naturally delighted. But he can scarcely have known all the facts when he immediately signaled to MacArthur that "the succession of surprises

---

* There was a domino effect, more evident in Washington than in SWPA. The Central Pacific air force was steadily neutralizing the more northerly Japanese base at Truk in the Carolines, which had so often acted as a staging post to, and backup for, Rabaul. Thus Rabaul itself was devitalized.

† The nearest position held by SWPA forces on April 22, when the assault occurred, was about 600 miles away.

effected and the small losses suffered, the great extent of territory conquered and the casualties inflicted on the enemy, together with the large Japanese forces which have been isolated, all combine *to make your operations of the past one and a half months models of strategical and tactical maneuvers.*"* (MacArthur himself was so pleased that after visiting the beachhead he treated his senior commanders to chocolate ice-cream sodas!)

Hollandia merits a close examination because the results achieved were directly attributable to accurate signal intelligence. Indeed General Willoughby, in his hagiographic book on MacArthur, claimed that Sigint had "proved as decisive at Hollandia as the German interception of the Russian General Samsonov's radio traffic had proved at the battle of Tannenberg in 1914." But this is less than the whole truth, for the salient point is that if MacArthur had had his way Hollandia would not have been his target—or, at best, no more than a secondary and subsequent objective. He wanted to smash his way into Rabaul, blind to the fact that it was now irrelevant. He argued his case vehemently, before the Chiefs of Staff decided to let Rabaul wither in isolation and instructed MacArthur to leave the great base alone; and he continued to argue even after those clear instructions had arrived. This is curiously at odds with the legend of "MacArthur the bypasser," "MacArthur who hits them where they ain't." The two dramatic bypasses of the Pacific war were that of Rabaul in the spring of 1944 and of Mindanao, the southern island of the Philippines. It was not at Mindanao that the landings occurred later in the year, but at Leyte Gulf. Each of these "hooks" was carried out by MacArthur under a directive from the Chiefs of Staff, not conceived by him.

Yet Rabaul's condition was grave, and the Japanese knew it—even though, for an attacker, it still remained a very hard nut to crack. On February 6, the Eighth Area Army at Rabaul signaled to Tokyo: "Complete suspension of shipping to Rabaul is something that units in this area cannot bear." A table in the Magic Summaries shows that of twenty ships sent to Rabaul in January seven were sunk en route, four in harbor, and three on the return trip. Another Ultra decode revealed that among Rabaul's urgent requirements were antiaircraft shells "of which we have a very small quantity in hand." By early March it was clear from Ultra that the Japanese had abandoned the

---

* Author's italics.

use of surface vessels to replenish or reinforce the base which once had been the pivot of all their operations from the Solomons to New Guinea. Since the Americans' strategic objective was to press on toward Japan as fast as possible, rather than to achieve local victories for their own sake, on the evidence of what was known about Rabaul it seems that the judgment of the Chiefs of Staff was shrewder than MacArthur's. The port was no longer a worthwhile target. But though its garrison was in some distress, past experience indicated that the Japanese would have fought desperately and to the last man: much American blood would have been spilled, therefore, to no great purpose.

So Hollandia it had to be, and the facts revealed by Ultra about the Japanese dispositions there were appetizing. The useful airstrip and its harbor of Humboldt Bay suggested that Hollandia ought to be the place where the defenses would be strongest, and yet as early as March 28 the Japanese Army Summary was reproducing the full Japanese plan for a main stand in the Wewak area, many miles nearer the SWPA's front line—on the assumption that the Americans would not risk a deeper thrust. Ultra made it clear that around Hollandia the troops were thinning out. (At the same time it produced much evidence of supply problems: between February 29 and March 20, for example, intercepts showed that convoys to Wewak lost twelve freighters.) On April 1 a decode of a Second Area Army situation report showed conclusively that this was how the Japanese were reading MacArthur's mind.

Very sensibly, therefore, he decided to feint where the enemy expected his heaviest assault, and to move on Hollandia in strength, with a secondary landing at Aitape (between Wewak and Hollandia) to capture the airstrips there. Nevertheless, in spite of Ultra, Willoughby overestimated the opposition (though in the Japanese Army Summary there is actually a map showing the enemy layout). But when Operation Reckless went in on April 22 it was not the enemy's machine guns which caused trouble: it was an appalling topographical miscalculation. Behind the thin strip of sand on one of the two landing beaches the jungle, it had been assumed, covered firm ground soon convertible into roads and marshaling areas. Alas, it was a swamp. A photograph in the Official History tells all: a model of how not to conduct amphibious operations. There are the huge landing ships with their noses nuzzling the shore: the narrow white slice of sand:

and then, just inland, a mass of heavy transport crammed immovably side by side. A human chain of sweating soldiers and a flotilla of small boats had to be used to shift as many stores as possible to the second beach, and it was a mercy that the intruding Japanese plane which later hit an ammunition dump at Humboldt Bay did not discover this profitable aiming point. There were many other delays and embarrassments, due to the unaccommodating terrain. Nevertheless, Hollandia was soon American—for the rest of the war.

Luck was surely with MacArthur—the good fairy of the fortunate general. For suppose the Japanese had been present in the larger numbers SWPA assumed, and suppose they had reacted with that ferocity which strewed the beaches of many Pacific islands with American corpses? On May 27 the island of Biak, over 300 miles farther to the west, was invaded in the expectation that its airfield could be grabbed quickly and cheaply, because Biak was lightly held. In fact over 11,000 men were on the island; commanded, coincidentally, by the visiting Lieutenant General Takuzo Numata, Chief of Staff of the Second Area Army.* But miscalculation about the defenses was even more disastrous. No one had foreseen that the ridges, terraces and caves of this coral outcrop would make marvelous firing positions, or that the Japanese would tunnel below ground to link one cavern with another. General Eichelberger had to be put in again—as at Buna in the early days—to retrieve the situation: but it was not until mid-August that resistance ended, with over 400 Americans killed and 2,000 wounded. Suppose sufficient Japanese had similarly stood firm on the beach at Hollandia, when the assault waves were nakedly vulnerable.

MacArthur might reasonably reply: "This is unfair. I used Ultra imaginatively, and after all I got the place. And sometimes things go right as well as wrong. Remember that when I took a chance and made a surprise attack on the Admiralties back in March, 300 miles away to the northeast, I snatched them quick and cheap and thus took Seeadler Harbor, a deep-water port where I acquired one of the largest fleet bases in the Pacific."[3] A fair comment: but when an amphibious assault is ill-planned and potentially catastrophic, we are entitled to say so!

For there is something else that takes the gloss off Operation

---

* Whose embarrassing presence was as unexpected as that of Field Marshal Model when the British airborne division landed at Arnhem.

Reckless. To supply extra air cover, Mitscher's Fast Carrier Task Force came down from the north. Yet in spite of all the Ultra intelligence available to SWPA, Mitscher found it quite impossible to obtain adequate information from the Army about the strength of the Japanese at Hollandia—other than the impression that the enemy was present in some force. His Chief of Staff, Arleigh Burke,* was so frustrated that he got into a dive bomber and flew over the beachhead area, where scarcely a Jap was to be seen. He and his pilot became so confident (he told the author) that they decided to touch down on an airstrip—but unfortunately a light aircraft gun hit them in the wing so effectively that they had to return at zero height over the sea for fear that it might fall off. When they at last landed on their carrier it did fall off—and Admiral Mitscher flashed a signal around the fleet to announce the safe return of his Chief of Staff. This, too, seems a curious way to mount an amphibious operation.[4]

Nevertheless, the capture of Hollandia meant that some 180,000 Japanese troops and 20,000 civilian workers had been cut off, along the coast to the eastward. Around Aitape was the Eighteenth Army under General Adachi, who with typical Japanese resolution preferred to hit back rather than give in. But Ultra, either in complete or fragmentary form, provided SWPA with a clear view of his capability and his intentions. On June 1, for example, a decode of a message to Tokyo from Southern Army at Manila showed how perilously Adachi was poised. "Due to the attack on Aitape by Mo [Eighteenth Army]," it read, "please rush to Wewak as absolutely necessary supplies by the end of June, the allotment [28 metric tons] of two RO submarines. If they don't get there, it is feared that there will be difficulties in carrying out Mo's plan of operations. Therefore please give this your special attention." An army offensive whose result depends on the load of two submarines is on its way to failure.

Even more disastrous for Adachi, however, was the decode which became available on June 25 of a signal sent out from his headquarters on the 20th, which announced that "an all-out attack on the enemy in the vicinity of Aitape" was in preparation for about July 10. It gave

---

* As a destroyer leader, particularly during the Solomons campaign, he was known as "31-knot Burke" because of his ardor in pushing his ships to the limit: units under his command were credited with one Japanese cruiser, nine destroyers, a submarine and several smaller fry. Admiral Burke was Chief of Naval Operations from August 1955 to August 1961, an unprecedented three terms in that post.

full details of the three divisions involved, the 20th, 41st and 51st, and specified the locations to which the Army Command Post and rear echelons would move before attack. It said that 20,000 men would be engaged. The records of the Combined Bureau, which handled this material, claim that "never has a commander gone into battle knowing so much about the enemy as did the Allied commander at Aitape on 10–11 July 1944."

The claim is just, for it is difficult to think of any other operation of the Pacific war—not even Midway—which demonstrates with a classic perfection the warning power of Ultra. When Adachi attacked on July 10 the passion of the assault along the Driniumor River at first made headway, but then was blunted and broken by counter-attacks, with a loss of 9,000 killed. In relation to the main war in the Pacific the Japanese remnants in eastern New Guinea were becoming a spent force. Yet they fought on, the final defeat at Wewak not occurring for nearly a year, on May 11, 1945. But all the residual fighting in this area was done by Australian troops, who lost 442 killed, 1,141 wounded and 16,203 sent to the hospital, mostly with malaria. That made nonsense of MacArthur's signal to Marshall of August 8, 1944, in which he stated of the bypassed enemy garrisons that "their capacity for organized offensive effort has passed. The various processes of attrition will eventually account for their final disposition." What he meant was that, having swept forward 1,000 miles with his American troops, he was marching on to glory while the Australians cleaned up the pigsty.

Meanwhile Ultra had also been coming to MacArthur's aid in the distant waters off the Philippines. Aroused by the threat of his thrust— for might it not reach westward into the Dutch East Indies and endanger their source of oil?—the Japanese began, for the first time, to pull troops out of Manchuria and shuttle them down to the South West Pacific. Early in April, Ultra revealed that a large shipment, the "Take" convoy of nine transports and a dozen escorts, would be sailing from Shanghai to New Guinea. By traffic analysis it was tracked to Manila, and before its departure on May 1 the following vital facts had been established by Ultra. (1) It was carrying 12,874 men of the 32nd Division and 8,170 of the 35th, with much equipment whose details were known. (2) The scheduled noon positions of the convoy for each day from May 2 to May 9 were identified. (3) The convoy had been supplied with an alternative route, to be followed only on special instructions. This also was known. (4) The precise point at which the convoy was to divide into two groups on May 7 and the destinations to which each would proceed were accurately established.

Commander Christie's submarines, which he deployed from Australia as ComSubPac directed his craft from Pearl Harbor, had ample warning.[5] The convoy lost one transport off Luzon in the Philippines on April 26, and three more in another submarine attack on May 8. Some 4,000 troops perished, including the commanding officer and virtually the whole of the 228th Infantry Regiment. Taking into account the simultaneous loss of equipment, no comment is necessary on the reduction in battle-worthiness of two fresh divisions. The "Take" convoy provides a clean-cut case of Sigint in action, yet it was not achieved easily. The report on this operation makes it evident that "preparation of the intelligence dispatched to the field commands required the examination and integration of a large number of separate and frequently fragmentary messages and traffic analysis."

But in fact anything attempted by the Japanese in the South West Pacific could only be a holding action. They sought still for a mortal blow—which could only be delivered by the Combined Fleet, against the rampaging Fifth Fleet of Admiral Nimitz. Admiral Koga, who succeeded Yamamoto, had a plan: work the bulk of his aircraft from shore bases, while using his empty carriers as a decoy to divert his enemy's powerful carrier groups—what Liddell Hart used to call an "offensive defensive." Unfortunately, two planes carrying Koga and some staff officers crashed in the Philippines during a storm on March 31. The plan was retrieved from the wreck, presumably by the resistance, and finally came into the hands of Holmes and Layton at Pearl Harbor. As it had been forwarded to them by SWPA and stamped "Secret. Not to be copied or reproduced without permission of General MacArthur," an urgent dispatch for clearance went out from Nimitz, and within a couple of days the text had been edited, duplicated and forwarded to the fleet commanders at sea.[6] The fact that it was already out of date does not diminish its importance. As will be seen, it almost certainly affected Spruance's judgment and, as certainly, ought to have affected Halsey's judgment during the two great naval engagements that were soon to follow.

The new Japanese commander, Admiral Toyoda, had more of Yamamoto's early aggressive spirit: with a new force and a new plan he sought a decisive action at sea. Under the veteran Ozawa he put together the Mobile Force, along the lines of Mitscher's Fast Carrier Task Force: and his plan, "A-Go," was to lure the American fleet into an area where land-based planes could combine with those of the Mobile Force in a shattering, decisive blow. "A-Go" was probably hopeless from the start: American superiority was now increasing remorselessly. But Toyoda emasculated the idea by a false strategic judgment. Thinking that MacArthur's was the main thrust, that the temporary diversion of Mitscher to SWPA confirmed this, and that the assault on Biak was unacceptable, he diverted many of his aircraft down to western New Guinea—thus wasting between a third and a half of his strike force. He was soon to be disabused.

For it must have been a thunderbolt-strike when he heard, on June 11 and 12, that fighters and bombers from the Fifth Fleet were ranging freely over the Mariana chain—Saipan, Tinian and Guam—and even 600 miles north over Iwo Jima, destroying aircraft and damaging airfields in an obvious bid for air superiority before an invasion, which indeed was launched on June 15, when, by the evening, 20,000 troops were ashore on Saipan. The Mobile Force was stationed far away, at Tawitawi off North Borneo, but Sigint had identified its location, so that when on the 15th Toyoda sent out the famous Nelsonian signal made by Admiral Togo on the eve of Tsushima, "The fate of the Empire rests on this one battle. Every man is expected to do his utmost," submarines were alert and in position—*Flying Fish, Seahorse*—to monitor and report as Ozawa made his way toward the Marianas through the San Bernardino Strait at the heart of the Philippines. "A-Go" seemed possible, since the Fifth Fleet had to maneuver within supporting distance of the Saipan landings, which meant that it was within range from many a shore-based airfield. What Ozawa did not take into account was the fact that most of these had already been maltreated.

Still less could he appreciate the quantity and quality of the opposition. The Fifth Fleet was now the most impressive in the world. A British naval historian, Captain Donald Macintyre, has summarized its strength and its proficiency at this moment when the great Battle of the Philippine Sea was impending.[7] "Operational efficiency had been raised to a pitch that would have been scarcely imaginable at the time of Midway, and now the whole vast array of 15 carriers, seven battleships, 13 cruisers and 58 destroyers covering hundreds of square miles was manoeuvred as one to turn into wind to fly aircraft on and off.

Aircraft direction, too, had achieved a scientifically controlled certainty far from the hit-and-miss muddles of the earlier carrier battles." Fast-moving, complicated, protracted, "the Great Marianas Turkey Shoot" has been analyzed in detail many times, but the final figures need no explanation: over 300 Japanese aircraft destroyed and three carriers sunk for the loss of some 30 American planes. (The sinking of *Shokaku* meant that only *Zuikaku,* damaged in the battle, was still afloat of the five carriers that attacked Pearl Harbor. And before the year's end *Zuikaku* would also have disappeared.)

Macintyre's reference to the quality of fighter direction is a reminder that in the Marianas battle there was an outstanding example of a technique the Americans gradually elaborated in the Pacific, as did the British and the Americans with great effect in the Mediterranean. This was the practice of carrying on board an officer highly skilled in the enemy's language, who could listen in to the voice exchanges between attacking aircraft and often provide last-minute intelligence of the greatest value. During the Turkey Shoot the Japanese used a master pilot, rather as the British used a master bomber to control their night bombers over German cities. On Mitscher's flagship was an able language officer, Lieutenant Sims, who got on to the net of the master pilot (and, when he was relieved, of his successor) and thus supplied the fighter-direction staff with a flow of up-to-the-minute information. Arleigh Burke felt it was like running an air battle from the bridge.* When it was all over Mitscher desperately desired to pursue the beaten enemy: but Spruance, whose orders had been "to capture, occupy and defend Saipan, Tinian and Guam," refused—to be bitterly criticized later by naval aviators. But he had his orders, and perhaps he remembered Admiral Koga's captured plan and the way the Japanese (as he had learned at Midway) built diversion and deception into their schemes. Anyway, Nimitz and the merciless King supported his judgment.

As usual, the coral formations and cave-indented hills of Saipan caused the struggle to be long and bloody. The Japanese knew that its fall would mean the first penetration of the final defensive perimeter surrounding their homeland. Fanaticism ran high, even to the

---

* At the end of the battle, when the Japanese master pilot was due to withdraw and it became a question of whether to finish him off, Burke announced: "You can't shoot that man down. He's done more good for the United States than any of us this day."[8]

extent of civilian men, women and children hurling themselves off the cliff to avoid capture. It took 67,000 troops to kill some 24,000 Japanese—though many more succumbed in the jungle or lurking in the caves. The military commander, General Saito, and Admiral Nagumo of Pearl Harbor fame both committed suicide. The significance of Saipan was clear when in Tokyo General Tojo and his cabinet resigned, to be succeeded by the more dove-like General Koiso: but that meant little, for the military hawks were unshaken.

From the intelligence point of view, the striking feature of victory in the Marianas was the arrival at JICPOA in Pearl Harbor of no less than 50 tons of captured documents.[9] Of immediate interest were those giving the disposition of the enemy in the Palau group, as of June 8: for the Palaus were next on the list. Ultra then took over, supporting and extending this information by the decode of a July 28 message to Tokyo from the staff of the Japanese 14th Division. Entitled "Disposition of Forces," it supplied all the details, unit by unit, of the garrisons on the main island of Palau and the four subsidiaries, Peleliu, Yap, Kotor and Angaur. Even the location of the mobile reserve was mentioned. When the 3rd U.S. Amphibious Corps launched its assault, therefore, the operational plan was based primarily on this intelligence, for the Japanese signal was partially broken by August 5 and available in full on the 17th. The attack began a month later, on September 15, with landings by the 1st Marine Division on Peleliu. When all was over, it turned out that with the exception of a single company no unit was encountered in the Palaus which was not identified in the Japanese message. Within its limits, therefore, Ultra had risen to the occasion.

It was not enough. The Marines expected to capture the island in four days, but the last pocket of resistance was not eliminated until November 26, by which time 1,792 Americans had died in the Palaus and 8,011 had been wounded, mainly on Peleliu. As at Tarawa and Biak, and as would be terribly the case on Iwo Jima and Okinawa, the secret defenses of the Japanese were strong beyond all expectation. A thousand mines sown offshore, and beach obstacles (as in Normandy) covered by machine guns and well-sited artillery: hidden bunkers and pillboxes constructed in depth from the beaches to the broken high ground inland—these were sufficient for an adamant opposition to the Marines, even when supported by tanks, naval and army artillery and bombardment from the air.

The real tragedy was that though the Ultra intelligence had been exceptionally good and the Marines had fought with their usual self-sacrificial devotion, the Peleliu landing might have been christened Operation Heartbreak, for that large sacrifice of brave men was unnecessary. Halsey had argued as far back as June that this was so, but Nimitz and MacArthur both felt that control of the Palaus was essential to cover the flank of an invasion of the Philippines. By September, Halsey had proved his point—and radically altered the plan for that invasion.

On September 11 Bull Halsey took over command of the Fifth Fleet—only it was now called the Third Fleet.[10] By a sensible and simple arrangement the ships kept station at sea while Spruance and his staff withdrew to Pearl Harbor for rest and to plan the next big operation: Halsey and his staff from the old Third Fleet, now redundant in the southern Pacific, moved in to carry on the battle—and carry with them the Third Fleet title and designations, which, for example, meant that Mitscher's Task Force 58 now became TF 38. Only a day after his arrival Halsey signaled to Nimitz an electrifying report. The aircraft of TF 38 had been ranging freely over Mindanao and even the central Philippines: Japanese air power there had been virtually destroyed and their oil stocks ravaged.

Halsey therefore proposed that the Palau assault should be abandoned, and that MacArthur's imminent invasion of the Philippines should bypass Mindanao and, supported by TF 38's aircraft, make straight for Leyte Gulf in the center of the islands. Nimitz dared not risk abandoning the Palaus—which, in retrospect, seems a misjudgment—but he immediately flashed the Leyte proposal to the American Chiefs of Staff, who were conveniently assembled in Canada for the Quebec Conference with their British counterparts. Marshall could not reach MacArthur, who was at sea and maintaining radio silence, but Sutherland at Hollandia accepted the proposition. The Chiefs of Staff were at a formal dinner party when the reply arrived. In his official report Marshall recorded:

Within 90 minutes after the signal had been received in Quebec, General MacArthur and Admiral Nimitz had received their instructions to execute the Leyte operation on the target date 20 October, abandoning the three previously approved intermediary landings. General MacArthur's acknowledgment of his new instructions* reached me while en route from the dinner to my quarters in Quebec.[11]

There are a number of occasions during the Pacific war about which it might be observed that the Americans had reached full maturity in the higher conduct of military operations. Perhaps nothing better expresses that sense of maturity than the decision to switch to Leyte: a correct decision, taken swiftly and without the opportunity of consultation with the commanders involved, but in complete confidence that they would prove capable—as the result demonstrated—of overcoming the immense problems of planning and logistic organization that now stared them in the face. Though MacArthur did not himself invent the idea of bypassing Mindanao, he deserves great credit for accepting it instantly since it meant, for SWPA, the swift reshuffle of their operational forecasts and the transport of a whole army 1,500 miles from its bases. Nerve was needed for the decision, and the polished skills of a competent staff for its execution.

The relevant figures speak louder than words. Admiral Kinkaid's Seventh Fleet, MacArthur's normal support, would be expanded by the loan of escort carriers, old battleships and amphibious vessels from the Third Fleet till it numbered no less than 738 ships. Then there was Task Force 38 with its 17 fast carriers, 6 fast battleships, 17 cruisers and 58 destroyers. And the War Department estimate of necessary supplies to be landed included 1,500,000 tons of general equipment, 235,000 tons of vehicles, 200,000 tons of ammunition and 200,000 tons of medical supplies. That was only the start. A further 332,000 tons of stores would be needed every month. In the opening phase 175,000 troops were to be employed. And all this mass of men, material and shipping had to be made to converge at the right time, in the right place, from nine different bases spread over the South West and Central Pacific within the enormous triangle roughly formed by Hawaii, Hollandia and Guam in the Marianas. Comparison with the Normandy invasion cannot be exact, since there the distances involved were much smaller and the strength of the enemy ashore much greater. Still—remembering the narrow width of the English Channel —it is instructive to note that during the eighty-seven days required to

---

* In fact this acknowledgment was also sent by Sutherland as from GHQ, SWPA. MacArthur only heard of it when he returned to Hollandia on September 17, but Sutherland had read his mind correctly: he was delighted.

expel the Germans beyond the Seine the amounts landed were some 3,000,000 tons of supplies, about 450,000 vehicles and 2,000,000 men. As an amphibious operation Leyte Gulf was certainly in the big leagues—quite apart from the fact that, coincidentally, it triggered off the biggest naval action of the Second World War.

To enter on a great engagement in the confident knowledge that the enemy is wildly underestimating your strength is a considerable benefit, and this, because of Ultra, was America's advantage on the eve of the Leyte battle. Pre-empting an air attack on the assault force, and the beachhead in its vulnerable early days, at the end of September and during the first week of October the 1,000 aircraft of TF 38 created mayhem over Okinawa, Formosa and Luzon, destroying around 500 planes at a cost of 79 from Mitscher's carriers. Two cruisers from the Third Fleet, *Canberra* and *Houston,* were torpedoed, but were towed away successfully to the fine natural harbor at Ulithi atoll.

However (in a fashion that Dr. Goebbels would have admired), the Japanese chose to convert this shattering defeat into a victory by propaganda double talk. Perhaps, too, they willingly swallowed the boasts of their airmen that 11 aircraft carriers and 2 battleships had been sunk, and another 8 aircraft carriers and 2 more battleships damaged: which would just about have eliminated Task Force 38! Tokyo Radio actually announced the destruction of 19 carriers, and the Emperor ordered a mass celebration. How sure could Nimitz and his commanders be that the Japanese High Command actually believed in this bombast?

Ultra provided the answer, most specifically by an intercept on October 17 from the Chief of the Japanese General Staff which more modestly—but seriously—recorded the destruction of 10 carriers and damage to 3 more. And then there were the signals sent out on the 12th and 13th to units of the Guards Division which garrisoned the outpost islands of Wake, Jaluit, Ponape and Nauru, telling them of the carrier sinkings as if to encourage these forlorn relics with "Now, here's the good news." Encouragement was certainly needed by those Japanese left high, dry and stranded; only that week, on the 13th, Ultra had produced one of the most significant intercepts of the Pacific campaigns, a signal from the Chief of Staff of the Japanese Fourth Fleet which baldly announced to the left-behind garrisons: "All personnel who have died of illness as a result of food situation since July 1 are to be considered as killed in action." In other words, though their situation was obviously crumbling daily, the Japanese were prisoners of their own wishful thinking and a racial inability to accept the dishonor of defeat. The American response was appropriately contemptuous—a communiqué from Pearl Harbor which read: "Admiral Nimitz has received from Admiral Halsey the comforting assurance that he is now retiring toward the enemy following the salvage of all the Third Fleet ships recently reported sunk by Radio Tokyo."

Yet the breezy confidence of Nimitz and Halsey could not blow away an uncomfortable fact which the Germans learned as they approached Moscow, and the Anglo-American armies as they fought their way over the borders of Hitler's Reich. However good the intelligence, however massive the superiority in numbers and equipment, any invader who is drawing close to the heartland of a fanatic, warrior nation must expect battles at least as bloody as those he has so far experienced —if not bloodier. This was a bitter truth which Ultra and Magic could alleviate but not dispel. There were no soft options in the Philippines, or at Iwo Jima or Okinawa, and the dread felt by the whole American administration and High Command about the unimaginable casualties that might be sustained in a final assault on Japan itself merely underlines the point. In October 1944, therefore, the question for MacArthur and Nimitz was never one of whether Sigint could open a clear road through Leyte to Manila and the liberation, so long promised, of the Philippine Islands. All they could expect, at best, was that it would ease their path.

And certainly the easement they received was considerable. By the summer of 1944 (when advance plans for the invasion of the Philippines were daily studied), the Japanese Order of Battle—that is to say, the structure and organization of the Army and the movement, location and strength of its individual units—was kept under the microscope by three main agencies: in the Pentagon by a special section of the Military Intelligence Service, at Pearl Harbor by the Joint Intelligence Center and by the intelligence staff of SWPA. It was virtually impossible for a division to be transferred from China or Manchuria, for a troop convoy to sail or for a major Japanese redeployment to be made in the field without the antennae of one of these agencies sensing the change. An incessant supply of Army and Navy Ultra, combined with the ancillaries of captured documents, aerial photo-

graphs, direction finding, traffic analysis and occasional prisoner interrogation, produced a sophisticated and centralized detecting machine such as any major military power ought to have evolved in the
latter stage of a long war—as the British, indeed, did, but the Germans
to a far lesser degree, at least on their western front. And whereas the
Japanese used few important deceptive measures to project a false
picture of their Order of Battle, British deception supplied the Germans with a vast amount of misinformation both in the Mediterranean
and in Northwestern Europe. The German intelligence maps were
thus marked up with details of many Allied divisions whose existence
was purely notional.[12] In the Pacific, by contrast, errors about the
state of the Japanese Army were most likely to occur if the Americans
themselves had miscalculated.

Thus when MacArthur issued his final invasion plan, King II, on
September 20, the layout of the Japanese Fourteenth Area Army and
its 224,000 troops scattered throughout the Philippine Islands was
known with some precision: constant monitoring is reflected in the
relevant issues of the Japanese Army Summaries. Only a small proportion was rightly thought to be on the island of Leyte, where the
assault was due to be made on October 20. There some 23,000 men
faced first the amphibious forces which, protected by Admiral Kinkaid's Seventh Fleet, would make the initial landings, and then the
200,000 troops of General Krueger's Sixth Army whose mission was to
press inland from the beachheads. By the 22nd all seemed well in hand.
MacArthur made a much-publicized trip ashore and a florid broadcast
to the Philippine people. Congratulatory messages arrived from
Churchill and Roosevelt. The next day MacArthur presented a Distinguished Service Cross to the guerrilla leader Colonel Ruperto
Kangleon, who now became acting governor of Leyte.

British writers about resistance movements have tended to concentrate on European examples: yet immediately after the fall of
Corregidor and Bataan the basis was laid for resistance in the Philippines. Indeed, the movement had so steadily expanded that by the
end of 1944 Colonel Fertig was commanding 38,000 guerrillas down
in Mindanao while in northern Luzon Colonel Volckmann had another 18,000. At first the leaders were few—small groups of Americans,
or even individuals, who had resolutely refused to obey the surrender
order and took to the hills with the local *maquis*. During the next two
years a section of SWPA's Allied Intelligence Bureau (which was

responsible for all forms of clandestine activity) nurtured the spontaneous reaction of the Filipinos themselves against their oppressive Japanese overlords by sending in (usually by submarine) more and better-trained officers to act as nuclei for the resistance. The risks were great, for the Japanese practiced torture and execution as liberally as the Gestapo. Nevertheless, a comprehensive net of radio communication was gradually established between Australia and the emerging guerrilla groups. The system of coast watchers which had proved so fertile during the Solomons campaign was established on a large scale. Characteristically—as in France or Yugoslavia—a powerful Marxist element in the form of the Hukbalahaps held sway in Luzon, as ruthless against former landlords and tenant farmers as they undoubtedly were against the Japanese.

Undoubtedly, too, many private scores were settled and even vigorous banditry committed under the cover of national resistance. Collaboration was certainly rife. All the same, the elaborate records now available show that the resistance movement in the Philippines was a substantial and effective organization well worthy of comparison with its European equivalents. And, as happened in Europe before and after D Day 1944, it proved capable of supplying MacArthur with detailed intelligence about the Japanese garrison before he launched his invasion,* as well as of assisting his troops, once ashore, by sabotaging enemy communications, supplying guides and local information, and generally—in the best traditions of resistance—creating a sea in which the liberators could swim.[13]

Well primed by intelligence, therefore, and perhaps better conceived than any of his previous amphibious landings, MacArthur's King II operation went so smoothly on October 20 that Admiral Kinkaid observed, "The execution of the plan was as nearly perfect as any commander could desire." On A Day, the 20th, more than 107,000 tons of material were landed on the beachhead through which Krueger's Sixth Army was to advance, for the loss of a mere 49 American lives. Yet soon the unexpected, and what might be called the ferocious death-wish of the Japanese, dispelled an initial euphoria.

---

* This liaison worked in reverse. On October 10 two officers flew in by night to the landing beaches and, through the local guerrillas, warned the Filipinos so effectively that on the 20th no civilian was hurt by the massive preliminary bombardment. A useful reference on Filipino resistance is Colonel Allison Ind, "Allied Intelligence Bureau" (David McKay, 1958). Ind was one of the group that flew out from the Philippines with MacArthur in 1942: he became Deputy Controller of the Allied Intelligence Bureau.

There would be a day when the mass of troops ashore would seem in as grave jeopardy as the Marines on Guadalcanal after the first flush of their own easy landing. And when that threat was overcome, the fighting would drag on long after December 20, the date when the Chiefs of Staff, on MacArthur's advice, had prescribed a final assault on the northernmost island of Luzon and the capture of the Philippines' capital, Manila.

Not till December 26 did MacArthur transfer from Krueger to Eichelberger's Eighth Army the "mopping up" of Leyte, and not till January 9 did some 1,000 ships enter the Lingayen Gulf for the invasion of Luzon—thus postponing the planned assaults on Iwo Jima and Okinawa. Even then, MacArthur's boasts were premature. When he congratulated Krueger on December 26 he announced: "This closes a campaign that has had few counterparts in the utter destruction of the enemy's forces with the maximum conservation of our own." But the Leyte campaign was still wide open. The crack 11th Airborne Division reckoned that the so-called mopping up was "bitter, exhausted, ragged fighting—physically, the most terrible we were ever to know." In a sardonic reflection Eichelberger noted that "between Christmas Day and the end of the campaign we killed more than 27,000 Japs. . . . The phrase 'mopping up' had no particular appeal for a haggard, muddy sergeant of the Americal Division whose platoon had just been wiped out in west Leyte." On October 20 the landings seemed rich in promise. That day there was truly a scent of victory in the morning air. Why, then, was the immediate consequence a near-disaster, and the ultimate result so long delayed?

The answer to the first question is to be found at sea and in a plan called Sho—the Japanese word for "victory," which, ironically, stands in retrospect for the death-ride of the arrogant and once all-powerful Combined Fleet. Many naval historians, from Samuel Eliot Morison with his broad, colorful brush to Paul Dull in his clinically exact study, *The Imperial Japanese Navy,* have described in minute detail how the Japanese High Command decided that, since to lose the Philippines would be intolerable, the fleet must sally forth against the invaders in a spirit of all-or-nothing, to provoke one final, decisive, cataclysmic action. As soon as it was certain that Leyte was the target, therefore, Sho was activated—a typically complicated Japanese scheme whereby the Southern Force was to pass through the Surigao Strait south of Leyte and, after sweeping northward, meet off the invasion beaches the Center Force, whose task was to work its way through the San Bernardino Strait (at the southern tip of Luzon) and then, wheeling right, to form the other half of the pincers intended to crush Kinkaid's transports and escort craft as they lay offshore from Leyte.

What injected some credibility into this desperate foray (reminiscent of Scheer's heroic order to his battle cruisers at Jutland: *Ran an den Feind, voll einsetzen*—"Charge the enemy, make straight for him") was a reversion to Admiral Koga's original deception-trick. Ozawa, with a Northern Force consisting of half a dozen carriers virtually stripped of aircraft, was to trail his coat far to the north of Leyte in the reasonable expectation that Halsey the impetuous would hurl his Third Fleet in pursuit: a suicidal maneuver which Ozawa loyally undertook, knowing that Kinkaid's huge but weakly protected amphibious force would thus be exposed to the converging claws of the pincers. Halsey swallowed the bait, forgetting what the captured Koga plan had taught about how the Japanese had it in mind to use their carriers as decoys—and ignoring the protests of some of his subordinates. And thus, though the Southern Force was eliminated in a brilliant night engagement, Admiral Kurita's Center Force was allowed to reach the waters off the beachhead, where, by one of the finest naval actions of the Second World War, Kinkaid's light escort carriers and puny destroyers held off an enormous battle army until, unaccountably, Kurita's nerve broke, the Center Force withdrew and disaster was averted. In war there is no entitlement to such miracles, and neither Nimitz nor posterity has been able to condone Halsey's absence at what the Commander in Chief, a charitable man, described in his book *The Great Sea War* as "the most crucial hours of the battle."[14]

So luck was once again with MacArthur. In the event, the naval Battle of Leyte finished the old Combined Fleet, for there was no way of replacing those sunken battleships, 4 carriers, 10 cruisers and 9 destroyers. Yet when Kurita's battle line swept down toward the invasion beaches, by any normal standards of sea warfare he should have brushed aside the thin screen of destroyers and light carriers, thus opening up the delectable prospect of obliterating with his powerful armament a defenseless huddle of transport shipping and the hopeless troops ashore. Sho could never have achieved, and perhaps was not expected to achieve, an absolute victory, for the American Third and Seventh fleets would surely have combined to take a crushing revenge.

But by that time MacArthur, who had once been humiliated at Cor-regidor, would have suffered another major reverse at the hands of the Japanese—and the American Navy would have an ineffaceable stain on its record.

The sea fight is reckoned to have been the largest of its kind in the war. It is curious, therefore (if one looks back to Midway and sub-sequent engagements), that signal intelligence seems to have made so small a contribution. We know, on the authority of Captain Holmes, that when the main Japanese fleet sailed from Singapore down to Borneo on the first leg of its venture, the movement was detected by radio intelligence and a warning was issued.[15] But though the many U.S. submarines deployed sank several warships and sent up-to-the-minute reports on the Japanese advance, this seems to have been the result of chance contacts rather than of precise guidance from Ultra. The positioning of the Seventh Fleet to block, successfully, the Surigao Strait and of the Third Fleet (until Halsey went off at a tangent) to block San Bernardino may be said to have happened be-cause of a logical deduction that, since the Japanese were known to be out in strength, this was the way they must come. Yet in the main the conflict has all the characteristics of an "encounter battle": air re-connaissance, or the mere sight of the enemy looming on the horizon, brought more useful information to anxious admirals on the bridge than the tried and tested source of Sigint.

As the battle on land developed, far more Ultra was available—yet the development was disappointingly slow. And there is disconcerting evidence that the intelligence was not adequately applied on the battlefield.*

First, however, we may note the more tangible obstacles: human, geographical, climatic. Initially the Japanese intended to fight the main defensive battle on Luzon, where the bulk of the Fourteenth Area Army was stationed under General Tomoyuki Yamashita, the

---

* Curious insensitivities about the value of special intelligence occurred in SWPA. There is the Mutsupina incident. He was a Japanese weather reporter in the Solomons who had a false idea of the exact point when midnight occurs: in consequence he habitually sent out his signals too early *with the next day's settings.* This enabled the Americans to break very early the next day's circuits and keep "all informed" of the new settings. But in spite of warnings to SWPA the Mutsupina location was "taken out" and an in-valuable source lost. On another occasion SWPA announced in advance a Japanese landing at a place and a time known ahead from Sigint. Unfortunately a typhoon aborted the landing—which left the Japanese perplexed about an announcement con-cerning plans they had devised but not implemented.

captor of Singapore. But at Manila was Yamashita's superior, Count Terauchi, commander of the Second Army, whose writ ran from Burma to the Pacific: and on October 23 Terauchi, against American expectation or Yamashita's judgment, ordered that all possible strength should be mustered "to totally destroy the enemy on Leyte." Heavy reinforcements were therefore rushed toward the beachhead over which, by October, more than 2,000 aircraft were operating. As in the Marianas Turkey Shoot the Fourth Air Army suffered huge and irreplaceable losses, while of nine reinforcement convoys dispatched between October 23 and December 11 about 80 percent was sunk. Nevertheless, something like four or more divisions joined the 16th, and the Battle of Leyte was still raging fiercely when on November 17 Terauchi transferred his headquarters to Singapore. Such was the scale of the human obstacle that unexpectedly impeded Krueger's Sixth Army.

Terauchi's departure, incidentally, is worth a comment, for by the ingenious use of signal intelligence it was predicted three weeks earlier. From intercept stations in India the Combined Bureau learned that Saigon was beginning to signal direct to Tokyo instead of via Manila. A deduction then that Terauchi was therefore about to move was confirmed on November 16, when an Ultra translation of a Southern Army message disclosed that the transfer would occur the next day.

But the obstacles were material as well as human, and the question is whether they too should have been predicted. In ten days, beginning on October 28, four separate typhoons swirled over the island and during the first forty days of the operation 35 inches of rain fell. Airfields could not be perfected, and thus MacArthur lost the use of the ground-based squadrons on which he was relying. Indeed, the soil and its drainage proved unsuitable, and no heavy bombers were based on Leyte throughout the campaign. Could rain be a legitimate excuse— any more than at Passchendaele? Or should MacArthur and his "Bataan gang," with their intimate knowledge of Philippine conditions from the days before Pearl Harbor, have anticipated those natural phenomena and made allowances for them?

Should they, indeed, have been so taken by surprise when Kurita's battle fleet loomed on the horizon off Leyte? Signal intelligence had revealed that the Mobile Fleet was at sea, and it could only have one objective. Moreover, Kinkaid's Seventh Fleet was on the radio net by which Ultra and other special intelligence were circulated. If it be argued that Kinkaid was justified in wrongly assuming that the San Bernardino Strait would be blocked by Halsey's Third Fleet, yet another question arises. According to MacArthur's objective biographer, Clayton James, two months before the Leyte operation Admiral Raymond Tarbuck, who for a year had been MacArthur's naval adviser and naval liaison officer at GHQ, "did some intensive intelligence work" and calculated the main bases of the Japanese fleet. By plotting circles—derived from factors of speed and distance—he found that their common intersection was at Leyte Gulf. He accurately prophesied, moreover, the movements of the Southern and Center Forces through the Surigao and San Bernardino straits. But Willoughby and the chief operations officer, General Chamberlin, discounted the proposition and did not even see fit to forward it to Admiral Kinkaid. Once, reflecting on his experiences at SWPA, Tarbuck wrote that "it was surprising how little the Army officers at GHQ knew about water."[16]

Far more disquieting, however, is the firsthand and indisputable evidence that throughout the Leyte campaign Ultra was handled by MacArthur's command with an astonishing degree of negligent indifference. The evidence is to be found in a file entitled Reports by U.S. Army Ultra Representatives with Field Commands in the South West Pacific, Pacific Ocean and China/Burma/India Theaters of Operations, 1944–1945. These were reports on their personal experience written at the end of, or immediately after, the war with Japan by the Special Branch officers who were attached to the higher headquarters in the field with the responsibility for receiving and distributing Ultra intelligence.

Three features notably distinguish these reports. First, they were written frankly and without reservation, since they were submitted directly to Carter Clarke and the Military Intelligence Service in Washington without passing through normal service channels—so that the commanders and staffs these Special Branch officers had serviced were prevented from reading, objecting to or even withholding what had been written. Second, the reports from officers who had carried out their task in MacArthur's SWPA are suffused by a sense of frustration which is supported by many concrete examples. And thirdly, this tone of dissatisfaction—in a set of papers submitted independently by a number of highly intelligent and deeply motivated officers—contrasts very markedly with the flavor of the similar reports produced by those Special Branch representatives who served in the European theater from Normandy until the end in Germany, for here one is impressed by the sense of fulfillment, of satisfaction with a job well done, of men working in an atmosphere of trust, of confidence, and of a prevailing respect for their unique contribution.[17]

In regard to Leyte, however, such an atmosphere seems to have been missing from the start. Major John Thompson, who with other Special Branch officers (and some British) was assigned to the Central Bureau in Australia in the latter half of 1944, recorded: "It was hoped that the presence of these officers in Central Bureau would insure that operational Ultra reached the commands who needed it in the fastest possible time, contribute to an improvement in the quality of Central Bureau decodes, and also carry with it all the benefits of closer liaison in a field where linguistic personnel in the various intelligence agencies were daily duplicating each other's efforts or producing conflicting results."

However, Thompson added, "upon the urging of the Chief Signal Officer, the Chief of Staff of SWPA cancelled this arrangement while the personnel were en route to Australia." Sutherland then summoned Thompson to Leyte for an interview. The gist of his instructions was that General Marshall's directive to MacArthur about the handling of Ultra was to be interpreted, so far as the Special Branch representatives were concerned, in the narrowest and most restrictive manner possible. The old hands of Central Bureau were still to call the tune and, in particular, would decide for themselves in Brisbane which Ultra decodes were to be forwarded to commanders at the front. Thompson then described how, by personal relations and the demonstration of their evident ability, the Special Branch men gradually established a more liberal and productive mode of working with the Central Bureau, referring scathingly to "the extra latitude both we and the Central Bureau had as a result of the absence from Australia of those officers who might otherwise have insisted that their conceptual framework be adhered to in more detail." What he is saying is that Sutherland, Willoughby and company were too far away, in the Philippines, and too preoccupied to prevent Thompson and his colleagues from properly executing their mission back at base.

Major John Gunn was supposed to sail from Hollandia with the intelligence echelon of MacArthur's headquarters. He was left behind, and compelled to "hitchhike" to Leyte on one of the Sixth

Army's convoys, aboard "a vessel whose Commanding Officer kept 18 quarts of bourbon whiskey in his safe and his top secret battle plans for several operations on the top of his desk in his sleeping quarters." When he arrived, MacArthur received him cordially but "it is a matter of record that the same observation cannot be made of a number of his immediate subordinates." "As for the handling of Ultra," Gunn discovered, "complete insecurity was a recurrent malignancy. . . . One fact was obvious—the main factor contributing to such incidents was a basic lack of appreciation of the value of our material."

The Navy shared this guilt about security. Gunn noted that Navy furniture shipped from Hollandia to Leyte was addressed to "The Ultra section" and mess bills were inscribed to "Lt. X., c/o The Ultra section." Captain James Sargent, who also served at Leyte, records that the sign outside the Ultra Intelligence Office read "ULTRA personnel only." Messages were frequently distributed with "ULTRA" clearly stamped on the outside envelope. Sargent was attached to the headquarters of the Fifth Air Force, who relied on material from their own local signal intelligence squadron rather than the Ultra forwarded by the Central Bureau. In the SWPA theater, Sargent concluded, the Special Branch detachment was unable to operate as "more than a quasi-administrative-signals-corps outfit." "It is unfortunate," he acidly observed, "that personnel within the theater are permitted to guard their own inadequate functions jealously at the expense of gaining better intelligence from War Department sources, which are often considered as mere undesirable encroachments."

Major Easley, attached to the headquarters of Krueger's Sixth Army, had to travel on a separate ship. On D Day he himself was disembarked at Leyte while Krueger and his staff stayed aboard their own craft until D + 4. During that time Easley, completely separated from the headquarters he was supposed to serve, "was reduced to wandering up and down the beach, obtaining food and shelter from whatever unit was at hand."

But perhaps the most damning evidence is supplied by Colonel Heckemeyer, attached to Eichelberger's Eighth Army, which, as has been seen, fought those prolonged and bloody "mopping up" battles. "GHQ policy," he said, "operated to send to the individual armies only such Ultra cables as were considered pertinent to their immediate field of operations. This resulted in an almost complete lack of Ultra information being received at Eighth Army . . . it became quickly apparent that General Eichelberger was keeping himself informed on the Ultra level through naval sources, and it was an extremely awkward position for a Special Security Officer. It was possible to make clear to General Eichelberger that the restrictions on the dissemination of the information originated at GHQ and not at the War Department. Even so, General Eichelberger made it clear that while he knew the writer had 'done all that could be done' the General resented the position in which he had been placed."

The Americans were not unique in this. The officer in charge of the Ultra Special Liaison Unit attached to the British Eighth Army headquarters in North Africa in the autumn of 1941 has informed the author that the staff was "so unco-operative, indeed so hostile" that he was compelled to transfer his unit to the headquarters of the Desert Air Force, "and we firmly stayed there." But these were early days, when the desert army had as yet acquired little experience of the quality of Ultra and had not yet learned how to handle it properly. MacArthur's staff at Leyte Gulf had been intimately acquainted with the quality and authenticity of Japanese Ultra for over two years, and its attitude toward this intelligence—and the Special Branch officers to whom General Marshall had specifically delegated responsibility for its handling—is unacceptable.

Since MacArthur himself could charm birds off trees—even Nimitz and Halsey warmed toward him in his presence—it is difficult to assess whether his "cordial reception" of Special Branch officers like Major Gunn was conveniently cosmetic, or whether it represented a genuine recognition that their arrival ought to accelerate and improve his supply of Ultra. If the latter was the case, the lax and even hostile attitude toward the Special Branch system—which existed more obnoxiously in SWPA than in any other theater—must be attributed to his staff: to Sutherland, Willoughby, Akin and others, carrying on a private war against newcomers personifying the Washington whose overriding authority they deeply resented—against men whose posting to SWPA seemed that of rivals encroaching on the arrangements for intelligence which the staff themselves had originated and which they considered immaculate. That looks like too easy an explanation. MacArthur must have known—as Supreme Commander he certainly ought to have known—what was going on. Nor is it irrelevant to remember that it was MacArthur, in the first place, who resisted Marshall's instructions that Special Branch was to operate in the South West Pacific on the same terms as in the other theaters of war.

Whatever the explanation, the facts remain. At this period, and during this vitally important battle, the treatment of Ultra by those in authority appears to have been dismissive and suspicious rather than welcoming and open-minded. Which is not to say that the amount of Ultra actually available was slight. As the fighting on land intensified— the same feature may be observed during the Normandy campaign— the number of Japanese Army signals increased and were decoded with increasing speed.[18] A report prepared for the Military Intelligence Service in Washington on March 27, 1945, headed "Examples of Operational Value of Information Derived from Cryptanalysis of Japanese Army Systems," states specifically: "Since 13 Nov. 1944 current Japanese situation reports for operations on Leyte and Samar have been available. These reports are for the most part general situation summaries, including precise information as to the location, composition and activities of Japanese forces, both in front line positions and in rear areas. They also include information about the arrival of reinforcements, casualties, and statements as to U.S. activities, dispositions and intentions, as well as of Japanese intentions."

On the air side, the material was equally abundant. Consider the sources on which the Far Eastern Air Force drew. Information of immediate tactical use was drawn primarily from the raw, undigested Ultra intelligence on the Navy's radio circuit: this was handled by the Special Branch man with the Seventh Fleet, who processed it and passed it directly to his opposite number with FEAF. The Military Intelligence Service in the Pentagon relayed a large volume of intelligence items, particularly of strategic or long-range interest. Washington's particular value, it was felt at FEAF, was as a source of finished intelligence, as a research center and as a place where queries could be answered. The Central Bureau in Brisbane radioed major items of information and forwarded its entire output of relevant but less urgent Ultra in a special pouch, which would reach FEAF two to four days later. A limited amount of material arrived from GCCS in England, passed on via Washington or Brisbane—the two major points where the American and British communication links for Ultra were interconnected. Over the Americans' own network came occasional Ultra items originated in Delhi, and from Guam after

Nimitz's headquarters and the Combat Intelligence Center had been transferred there from Pearl Harbor.[19]

As the Philippines were gradually dominated, therefore, and in early 1945 the war against the Japanese entered its final phase, a situation report on the condition of American signal intelligence would have to record that in spite of local aberrations in handling the traffic, the actual flow of information was strong and continuous, and that although the channels through which the intelligence passed had increased and ramified, they had at last been integrated into a comprehensive and well-ordered structure. In this, as in other respects, the Japanese had been outclassed. During the last few months before they were compelled to surrender, both Ultra and—even to a greater degree—Magic would continue to furnish the "Open Sesame" which unlocked the enemy's secrets.

CHAPTER THIRTEEN

The Mastiffs
and the Spaniel

*Sato's account of the interview with Molotov leaves a mental
picture of a spaniel in the presence of a mastiff who also knows
where the bone is hidden.*
     Russo-Japanese Relations, a survey by the Pacific
     Strategic Intelligence Section, June 18, 1945

*To be defeated in the air is finally to be defeated and to be at the
mercy of the enemy, with no chance at all of defending oneself,
compelled to accept whatever terms he sees fit to dictate. That is
the meaning of the "command in the air."*
     General Giulio Douhet, *The Command of the
     Air,* 1921

FOR THOSE WHO have to plan the conduct of a war—still more for
those who have to fight, suffer and see their comrades die—the cold
objectivity of subsequent historians can seem like an insult. What can
they really know about the way things were? How can they dare to
comment on terrible events and agonizing decisions in which they
personally played no part? Who are they to judge about what went
wrong? The historian can only reply, with humility, that war is a
muddle: that even those directly involved in it rarely see the whole
picture: and that a postwar study of what happened at the time, and
of the contemporary documents, can sometimes clarify what the cloud
of war itself concealed.

With this proviso, it may be claimed that during the last months
of the Pacific war the main strategic ideas by which the Americans had
hoped to bring it to an end—to end it, at least, without an ultimate

Armageddon and the loss, perhaps, of millions of lives on both sides—
had only led them into an impasse. In spite of all the blood that had
been shed and the billions of dollars that had been spent, by the
summer of 1945 the island-fortress of Japan still loomed ahead, battered, besieged, but defiant. And this was not exactly what had been
intended.

Even the official historians of the USAAF are compelled to admit
that the first method by which it had been hoped to debilitate, if not
to reduce, the fortress had resulted in undeniable failure. This was the
buildup of a heavy bomber force which, operating primarily from
Chinese bases, was to have had a major role in destroying Japan's will
to resist. For a variety of reasons, technical, political and geographical,
it proved impossible to sustain or even develop in strength an assault
to which great hopes and immense resources had been committed. The
verdict of the official historians, Craven and Cate, is merciless.

> The title for the MATTERHORN plan was "Early Sustained
> Bombing of Japan." The bombing was neither early nor sustained.
> It achieved no significant results of a tangible sort and the in-
> tangible effects were obtained at a dear price.[1]

The whole weight of the B-29 Superfortresses was therefore shifted
to islands in the Pacific whose capture, often at great cost, was mainly
undertaken so that huge airfield complexes could be constructed
within a sufficient range from Japan: airfields so capacious that from
these secure platforms fleets of B-29's could drench Japanese into
submission. To establish a base for what General Marshall called "a
new type of offensive" involved the seizure of Saipan in the Marianas
(June 15, 1944: 17,000 casualties). When better fighter support and
bases closer to Japan proved to be essential, the dreadful battle for
Iwo Jima had to be fought (February 1945: 5,931 Marines killed,
17,272 wounded as well as over 2,500 naval casualties).* Then came
the bloodbath of Okinawa (April–July: 12,520 dead, 36,631 wounded,
other casualties 16,211, with 36 ships sunk and 368 damaged). But, as
Field Marshal Wavell once dared to point out to Churchill, "a big
butcher's bill is not necessarily evidence of good tactics."

---

* Apart from its value as a base, Iwo Jima provided emergency landing fields for B-29's
in trouble, and no less than 2,400 Superfortresses (crewed by some 27,000 men) were
saved by this facility.

And the tactics had failed—in the opening phase at least. Between the first major B-29 raid on Tokyo on November 24, 1944, and the radical change in techniques which General LeMay introduced during the following March, results were so meager that the end-product was a crisis for the USAAF. The B-29 Superfort had been designed to undertake precision bombing from high altitudes. During those winter months a combination of factors—particularly the cloud cover that blanketed so many targets in Japan—demonstrated that persistence in the sacred doctrine of precision bombing had no hope of being cost-effective. In Europe the USAAF's fanatical belief that masses of B-17 Fortresses could fly over Germany protected merely by the firepower of their own guns had produced a near-disaster in 1943. Now, in the spring of 1945, the majestic B-29's seemed like the by-product of another fallacy.

Crisis was averted by adapting the Superfortresses to a role for which they had not been designed or intended: area bombing (not precision bombing) with incendiaries (rather than explosives) which were scattered on Japanese cities from relatively low altitudes. The result was a morbid triumph: fire storms worse than those that raged through Hamburg, and damage to centers of population so awe-inspiring that the cumulative effect was perhaps more ghastly than the scenes at Hiroshima and Nagasaki combined.

We know now that the effect of this B-29 offensive, as well as an ever-tightening blockade, the end of the German war and other adverse factors, began to generate a sense of despair in Japan, reaching upward from the man in the street to the Emperor himself. But even that despair was not universal. In any case, the historian has to shed hindsight, and consider what the situation looked like *at the time* to the statesmen and the Chiefs of Staff in Washington. With Germany eliminated, they yearned to finish the Japanese war as soon as possible. And since all their strategies had so far failed to bring the enemy to the conference table, they took the only realistic course that seemed open to them. On May 25, 1945, the Joint Chiefs of Staff issued a directive for Operation Olympic, an invasion of the great southern island of Japan, Kyushu, with a target date of November 1. A landing on the heartland of Honshu was to follow some months later, and operations were to continue until resistance in the Japanese archipelago had ended. It was a decision born of desperation, for the butcher's bill this time would have been enormous. Churchill in his memoirs estimated "the loss of a million American lives and half that number of British—or more if we could get them there." The British, of course, had their own Olympic (the plan code-named Zipper, whose object was an invasion of Malaysia and the recovery of Singapore), as well as their fleet now operating in the Pacific.[2]

Thus the dream which Roosevelt and his Chief of Staff, Admiral Leahy, had shared with other senior Navy and Air Force officers, that Japan might be brought to her knees merely by air bombardment and blockade, seemed to be fading.[3] In those summer months, moreover, the inner circle of men who knew the secret of the atom bomb had no grounds, as yet, for expecting a miracle from that quarter, since the weapon had not even been tested. There was, indeed, still a lingering hope that the B-29 would fulfill its promise, for when all the heavy bomber units in the Pacific were brought together under the experienced General Spaatz as "the U.S. Army Strategic Air Forces in the Pacific," the Joint Chiefs on July 1 gave the USASTAF the mission of "accomplishing the progressive destruction and dislocation of Japan's military, industrial and economic systems to a point where her capacity for armed resistance is fatally weakened." But in July 1945 this was unhappily reminiscent of the prince in the poem.

> Too late for love, too late for joy,
> Too late, too late!
> You loitered on the road too long,
> You trifled at the gate.
>
> The enchanted princess in her tower
> Slept, died behind the grate.
> Her heart was starving all this while
> You made it wait.

But in this case the prisoners starved of hope were those members of the peace movement in Japan who knew that in spite of all the damage that had been—and still might be—wreaked by the weapons of conventional warfare, so long as the Allies insisted on Unconditional Surrender, the war party, strongly entrenched, would carry on the fight until the last Japanese general had committed hara-kiri on the top of Fujiyama.

During these days of dilemma, therefore, it was crucial for the decision-makers in Washington to know as much as possible about what was passing through the minds of their opposite numbers in Tokyo. Moreover, since the Allies had a firm promise from Stalin that the Russians would enter the war against Japan about three months after Germany's capitulation, it was equally important for Washington and London to know the current state of play between Japan and the U.S.S.R. Some in Britain and America eagerly awaited Russian intervention, on the grounds that it would hasten the end of the war. Others, perhaps more farsighted, feared that Stalin would seize the opportunity for further territorial expansion. Whatever Moscow's aims and attitudes, it was certain that little would be learned from the Russians themselves. But onto this whole great area of darkness Magic cast the illumination of a searchlight's beam.

It was a scene of constant flux. During the last year of the war Japan's posture toward Russia went through many permutations. Yet it would not be an exaggeration to say that from the lavish intelligence supplied by the Magic intercepts not only the major shifts of emphasis but even the more subtle nuances of Japan's day-by-day policies were known and understood in Washington. Of no less importance— certainly of growing importance during the tense final months—was the fact that from Magic the Americans also acquired a deep insight into the Far Eastern policies of the U.S.S.R.

After the German withdrawal from Normandy, Japan's intercepted diplomatic traffic showed that the representatives in Europe, particularly Oshima, were making an intensive effort to provide the Foreign Office in Tokyo with a factual basis for assessing Germany's prospects. Such symptoms as the assassination plot of July 20, for example, were investigated and analyzed by Oshima with great care and surprising accuracy. As the months ran on, the intercepts showed first an increasing pessimism and then, as the Allied drive slackened, and the Wehrmacht achieved a sort of stability within the frontiers of the Reich, the mood changed to one of relief. But the Japanese had already decided to take out an insurance policy. A group of no less than forty-four Magic decrypts of messages passed between Shigemitsu, the Foreign Minister in Tokyo, and Ambassador Sato in Moscow show that during the winter months of 1944 Japanese diplomacy was hectically devoted to terminating the German war—with Russia. In other words, if a formula could be found whereby the Germans and the Soviets could come to terms, then Japan's own desperate situation would be greatly relieved, since Hitler would be free to concentrate on the Anglo-American armies in the west, and Allied resources which might otherwise have gone to the Pacific would be sucked into the European maelstrom.

Poor Japan! The only result was the first in a series of Russian rebuffs. It is all in the intercepts. Molotov stonewalls. The Kremlin is not interested. When Sato tried at least to obtain for Japan the position in Moscow of "protecting power" for Germany's interests, he reported to Tokyo on November 18 Molotov's sardonic response: "That's a job that won't make your fortune." By the end of the year it was evident that the Foreign Office in Tokyo had settled, realistically, for maintaining a delicate balance in a situation where "Japan's friends are Russia's enemies and Russia's friends are Japan's enemies." How little Moscow was prepared to give was revealed to Washington after the Yalta Conference in early February 1945, for the Magic intercepts showed the Japanese desperately attempting, at first, to deduce from the Yalta communiqué what twist, if any, had been given to Russo-Japanese relations and then endeavoring to get an answer from the Russians themselves. On February 22 Sato sent to Tokyo his report on an interview with Molotov during which, he said, he had pressed as hard as possible. But the stone wall was still impenetrable.

By the spring of 1945 there was a severe change of climate. The Pacific Strategic Intelligence Section, which monitored the Magic intelligence meticulously, noted that the spaniel-mastiff relationship was already acute and that Shigemitsu and the Foreign Office were adopting toward Russia "a policy of obsequiousness based on fear." Ever since 1941 the Non-Aggression Treaty between Japan and Russia—which (as Magic revealed at the time) the then Foreign Minister, Matsuoka, had negotiated—remained intact and by its mere existence offered a shred of hope that Russia might, in the end, accept a closer partnership with Japan. But on April 5, 1945, Moscow gave notice that when the Treaty ran out, in a year's time, it would not be renewed. Once again the Magic intercepts revealed to the Americans Tokyo's frantic attempts to obtain a renewal of the pact, and Moscow's stern, unbending rejection of every overture.

What had always been possible now began to seem probable, and a new note of fearful expectancy appears in the diplomatic signals: a note struck loudly and clearly in a message of May 26 from the Japanese Military Attaché in Moscow, who pointed out that Russia might "enter the war against Japan at the same time as the United

States launches its all-out attack on the Japanese mainland . . ." A little earlier another realist, Lieutenant Colonel Hamada (the intelligence officer in the Kwantung Army, who had worked in the Military Attaché's office in Moscow), had turned up in another Magic intercept, suggesting to Tokyo that though Russia would leave strong forces in the West, many troops could be transferred to the East. "Assuming that the Russians do intend to attack Manchukuo they will probably gain a quick victory by using overwhelming force, at least double the strength of ours." At the same time Magic made plain to the administration in Washington that the Japanese were acutely conscious of an unrelenting barrage of criticism in the Soviet press and in radio broadcasts: each of Japan's "political sins" was being hauled into view—Manchuria, the controversy over Sakhalin and Port Arthur, the undeniable aid to Germany.

The Pacific Strategic Intelligence Section, weighing up the evidence supplied by Magic, came to the conclusion that in the summer of 1945 Russia could strike at her own convenience, with no need to search for a *casus belli*. "All that is needed is the igniting spark, and these can be drawn at will from the arrogant Japanese Army, the unyielding Navy and the officious and truculent police, all of whom have been the despair of the Japanese Foreign Office in its efforts to propitiate Russia."

By a curious twist, it was the Japanese themselves who kept the Americans abreast of the extent to which those efforts were failing: and not merely from the intelligence Magic supplied about diplomatic endeavors. It was from these intercepts that hard facts also emerged (which could scarcely have been obtained from any other source) about the rate and scale of Russia's redeployment. Their suspicions fully aroused, the Japanese were now carefully noting every indication of Russian troop movements, and many details surfaced in the Magic traffic which were invaluable for those in Washington who needed to keep up to date on Soviet policy. After earlier evidence of such movements in April and May, a Japanese courier who had reached Moscow on June 1 after a cross-country journey filed a report which Ambassador Sato sent by radio to Tokyo on the 4th. It stated that "the Red Army seems to be continuing mass shipments to the Far East." In a sixty-eight-hour period between May 26 and 29, the observer reported, some 200 "transport trains" had been noted, laden with tanks, guns, aircraft and trucks. All trains moving eastward appeared to carry military material. This continuing train-watch was maintained, for example, by another courier, who traveled on the Trans-Siberian Railroad in early June, and by the Japanese Consulate in Manchukuo, which kept up a daily surveillance over a period of fourteen days. No wonder that Sato's frequent situation reports became increasingly pessimistic, so that on May 20, after describing another fruitless session with Molotov, he affirmed that "by July or August Russia would have completed her military preparations in the Far East."

Indeed, as he studied the situation from day to day in Moscow, Sato's despondency increased to a point at which, on June 8, he signaled to Tokyo that if Russia entered the war against Japan there would be no hope of "saving" the Emperor. Should Russia attack "we would have no choice but to reach a decision quietly and, resolving to eat dirt and put up with all sacrifices, fly into her arms in order to save our national structure." A cry from the heart: it was a confession of despair to which Sato would refer back again on July 20, after the spaniel had once more—and this time finally—cowered before the mastiff.

The form of this self-abasement can be summarized in an excerpt from the "extremely urgent" message which Togo, now Foreign Minister, sent to Sato on July 11: "Since we are secretly giving consideration to termination of the war in view of the pressing situation confronting Japan both at home and abroad, you are not to confine yourself [in talking to Molotov] to the objective of a rapprochement between Russia and Japan but are to sound out the extent to which it is possible to make use of Russia with regard to ending the war as well." A day later Togo pushed the proposition further: "His Majesty is deeply reluctant to have any further blood lost among people on both sides and it is his desire, for the welfare of humanity, to restore peace with all possible speed. . . . It is his private intention to send Prince Konoye to your place as Special Envoy and have him take with him a letter from the Emperor containing the above statements. Please inform Molotov of this and get the consent of the Russians to having the party enter the country."

Unfortunately, like some character in a Chekhovian tragicomedy, Prince Konoye never "got to Moscow." It must have been with an extreme fascination that the intelligence officers and their superiors in Washington read the prolonged exchanges between Sato and Tokyo, and observed the withering of Japan's hopes as Molotov and his colleagues blandly blocked every avenue of approach until Stalin had left for Potsdam and the Japanese were brought to their senses by the double shock of the atom bomb and a Russian invasion. That his people must come to their senses was clear enough to the wretched Sato. "If the Japanese Empire is really faced with the necessity of terminating the war," he declared, "we must first of all make up our minds to terminate the war."

As this drama was played out Magic settled the Americans, as it were, in the front row, enabling them to assess every subtle modulation of the actors' thoughts and emotions. The high value placed at the time on this remarkable signal intelligence may be judged from a single file (SRH-040) in the National Archives in Washington. It is headed: Magic Diplomatic Extracts, July 1945: selected items prepared by MIS, War Department, for the attention of General George C. Marshall. The extracts consist of no less than 78 pages: they laid before the Army Chief of Staff the full texts of all the prolix and anguished messages from which brief quotations appear earlier in this chapter. If one remembers that during the transitional phase after Roosevelt's death, when Truman was no more than a novice, Marshall above all those who had conducted the war to its final crisis was left holding the torch, one sees that Magic, the aid on which he had always relied, now mattered to him more, perhaps, than ever before.

The urgency with which the Magic intercepts were handled during these decisive days is well illustrated by a footnote appended to the transcript of Togo's signal to Moscow of July 17, in which he rejected Sato's conclusion that Japan had no choice, in view of Russia's intransigence, "but to accept unconditional surrender or terms closely approximating thereto." Togo laid it on the line. "If today America and England were to recognize Japan's honor and existence, they would put an end to the war and save humanity from participation in the war, but if they insist unrelentingly upon unconditional surrender, Japan is unanimous in its resolve to wage a thoroughgoing war. The Emperor himself has deigned to express his determination. Hence we have made this request of the Russians, but we are not seeking their mediation for anything like an unconditional surrender." The footnote to this decrypt reads: "The above was received direct from Arlington Hall, rather than from MIS as is customary, to avoid the delay inherent in that procedure."

There was a particular reason why that mid-July signal from Togo, apparently defining the attitude of Tokyo toward unconditional surrender, had a special relevance. For the question raised by the various Japanese overtures to Moscow was central to the whole situation: If Japan was the spaniel, who in fact was the more menacing mastiff? Was it actually Russia? Were the Americans, in spite of their years of war and their notable triumphs, unable to deliver the *coup de grâce* without Stalin sending in his troops at the last minute like a Blücher at some eastern Waterloo? These uncertainties gained in force as opinion hardened in Washington against the earlier policy of enticing Russia into the Japanese war, an objective for which Roosevelt had been prepared to match offer with price as Stalin steadily raised the ante. But "instinctively, Truman was thinking in terms of the containment of Russia, and was anxious that, in the Far East, Russia should make as little headway as possible . . . he was more available than Roosevelt had been to advisers who suggested a frankly anti-Russian policy."[4]

It was thus essential to know as much as possible not simply about the Russo-Japanese relationship but also about the dominant issue to which Tokyo's attempted rapprochement with Moscow was, after all, subordinate. For to what had that diplomatic effort been mainly directed? To finding a way out of the war which the Americans and the British—not the Russians—were still relentlessly waging. Thus the outstanding "need to know" in Washington was about how the men in Tokyo were reacting, from day to day, to the problem posed by their burning cities, their dwindling imports, their etiolated air force, their sunken warships: the problem, in fact, of whether and when to surrender, conditionally or unconditionally, in the face of an Anglo-American combination which was already throttling Japan. Here, too, Magic supplied a revealing spyglass.

Perhaps the most moving expression of despair by a patriotic but intelligent Japanese came from Kase, the Minister in Berne. Magic picked up his long report to Tokyo of May 14 in which, after submitting a detailed argument in favor of peace, he ended: "There will be those who will point out that rather than bow the knee to the enemy we shall fight on and offer inspiration to our future generations, but I say that our heroic blood which has been shed on Tarawa, Makin, Saipan, etc., and spread over the face of the Pacific is already a sufficient inspiration. I am far away in Switzerland, far from the shells and the bullets, unable to see the sufferings of our forces, and therefore I feel as if my words were those of a mere bystander." But

Kase was not speaking for himself alone. As Magic also disclosed, leading Swiss bankers were recommending peace and on May 4 the German consul-general in Zurich told his Japanese counterpart that, in the opinion of himself and the German minister in Berne, "Japan should end the war while she still had a chance."

Sato voiced Kase's thoughts in very similar terms when he signaled to Togo on July 20: "Japan may be said to be standing literally at the crossroads of destiny and—although the people who have continued to fight can close their eyes in good conscience, having given of their patriotism in full measure—our country is on the verge of ruin. While it is a good thing to be loyal to the obligations of honor up to the very end of the Greater East Asia War, it is meaningless to prove one's devotion by wrecking the state. I must therefore insist that we are required to bear every sacrifice for the existence of the state." The next day Okamoto, the minister in Stockholm, chimed in with the views to which, as he put it, he had been "inexorably led." "We miscalculated and belittled the enemy's actual strength," he declared, "and . . . are now in the midst of an impossible, unreasonable war which has made practically the whole world our enemy."

Such was the broad tenor of the diplomatic signals, of which far more are available than can be quoted: peace, it might be said, was literally in the air. On July 21 Togo had again seemed wholly unresponsive to this barrage of advice from his consulates and embassies, for he told Sato: "With regard to unconditional surrender, we are unable to consent to it under any circumstances whatever. Even if the war drags on and it becomes clear that it will take much more than bloodshed, the whole country as one mass will pit itself against the enemy in accordance with the Imperial Will so long as the enemy demands unconditional surrender." Yet even Togo continued to clutch at straws. The Potsdam Conference opened on July 17: on the 25th Togo sent another "extremely urgent" signal to Sato, pointing out that between the departure of Churchill (just unseated in the general election) and the arrival of the new Prime Minister, Attlee, there would be a gap which could be used to the advantage of the Japanese.

Sato was to "proceed, if necessary, to a place of the Russians' choosing in order to obtain an interview with Molotov." (There is something almost pathetic in Togo's comment that if a meeting cannot be arranged "your request for an interview will at least go a long way to impress upon him our determination in this matter.") If Molotov proved amenable, Sato was to say to him that if the Russians would receive Prince Konoye as a Special Envoy this "would permit Stalin to acquire the reputation of an advocate of world peace, and, further, that we are prepared fully to meet the Russian demands in the Far East." It was all, of course, a waste of time.

But had the cryptanalysts whose skills made available the full texts of all these, and many other, Japanese communications through the medium of Magic—had they, too, wasted their time? Wasted it in the sense that in spite of the abundant evidence they provided about a will for peace in Japanese circles, the two bombs were nevertheless dropped on Hiroshima and Nagasaki, raising clouds which still over-shadow the human race?

We are entering a realm of argument where it is vital to keep a firm grip on the facts and not to make a blur of what should be clearly distinguished. The first point is semantic. Much confusion has been caused by general statements such as "the Japanese really wanted peace." It is untrue that the Japanese nation *as a whole* was so minded. In the countryside, certainly, and amid the ashes of ravaged cities there were many who had had enough. But it would be wrong to assume that the armed services, by and large, were ready to haul down the flag except on terms of strictly "honorable conditions": the spirit of the kamikaze pilots, of the men who had driven the Combined Fleet on its death-ride to Leyte and the monster battleship *Yamato* to its doom off Okinawa, indeed of the soldiers who had fought to the last on Okinawa itself, on Iwo Jima and in the Marianas, was still ablaze. In any case, broad references to "the Japanese" carry the implication that a political structure existed in Japan,* as in the British or American democracies, whereby grass-roots sentiment could directly and powerfully affect judgment at the top. In 1945 this was no more the situation in Japan than it was in Hitler's Germany. Vital decisions were made by a small dominant group at the peak of the national pyramid: and on the issue of peace that group was absolutely divided.

---

* "Only the Japanese failed to rise up, overthrow the war leadership with their own hands and restore peace as an act of sovereign will. The Japanese people were passive recipients of a 'termination of hostilities' bestowed by the ruling elite. This remarkable docility contrasts with the spirited dynamic resistance in other countries." *Japan's Last War* (p. 223), by Saburo Ienaga, professor emeritus of the Tokyo University of Education.

Within the Supreme War Council, Togo as Foreign Minister was ready to make peace—but only on terms which preserved the hallowed position of the Emperor. The Prime Minister, Baron Suzuki, was with him, as, it seems, was the Navy Minister, Admiral Yonai. Above them the Emperor Hirohito and his chief henchman, the Lord Keeper of the Privy Seal, Marquis Koishi Kido, saw clearly that Japan was finished. But the War Minister, General Anami, and the Chiefs of Staff of the Army and Navy—General Umezu and Admiral Toyoda— vigorously and even viciously opposed the very concept of surrender. "You ask, what is our aim?" the trio might have said, drawing on Churchill's "blood, toil, tears and sweat" speech in 1940. "I can answer in one word: Victory—victory at all costs, victory in spite of all terror, victory however long and hard the road may be: for without victory there is no survival." All that has been subsequently learned about the attitudes of this implacable hard core—including its attempt to frustrate the final surrender by a military coup—is a reminder that in Japan's last councils there were two distinct voices and that one of them, nihilistic in its clamor for a Japanese *Götterdämmerung*, was opposed to peace at any price.*

Once this split at the very heart of the Japanese High Command is understood, the problem for the Americans of making a correct deduction from the Magic intercepts can be perceived in its true proportions. For while, as has been seen, they volubly and even passionately presented a desire for peace, the interchange of signals was wholly on the diplomatic network and the attitudes expressed were no more than those of the Japanese Foreign Office and its representatives abroad: evidently a more sophisticated, liberal and worldly-wise group than the military junta in Tokyo. But the voice of the junta itself was inaudible (in the intercepts, that is to say) except insofar as Togo's suddenly emphatic rejection of Unconditional Surrender might have been taken to be the sign of a man under pressure from his colleagues. There is a curious analogy here, from the American point of view, with the period immediately before Pearl Harbor, during which

---

* As late as May and June 1945 captured B-29 airmen were used for vivisection experiments at Kyushu Imperial University under orders of the Western Japan Military Command. The experiments involved removing the prisoner's lung or stomach and were, of course, fatal. The implication is not of an intent to surrender to a victor liable to punish war crimes. Saburo Ienaga, *op. cit.*, p. 189.

Magic produced that wealth of diplomatic traffic but no evidence of
Admiral Yamamoto's assault plan, because the military and naval
staffs in Tokyo were simply keeping the diplomats in the dark about
their real intentions. And so, as we recall the countdown, day by day,
to the point of no return when a decision had to be taken as to
whether or not an atom bomb should be dropped to prevent a bloody
invasion of the Japanese islands, we are bound to ask whether the
Magic material, for all its wealth of information, supplied Truman
and his military and political advisers with a firm base of fact on which
that decision could be made.

The answer must surely be this: that Magic alone was not enough.
For though the voice of the Japanese war party was not heard in the
Magic intercepts, from other signal intelligence sources a frightening
amount of evidence had come to hand which indicated the determination of the military to fight on and registered the scale of their preparations. The collection of Magic material for July 1945 which was
assembled for General Marshall, for example, contained an up-to-date
assessment of the presence of Army divisions on the Japanese home
islands—evidently acquired, in the main, from decoded Army signal
traffic. It showed a figure of 36 active divisions, including one armored
division. The total of troops in eight identified Army Areas amounted
to 2,110,000. Fifteen of the divisions were reckoned to be of veteran
quality: the rest probably of lower grade. Still, as the Allies had
learned in Germany, when a nation is fighting in the last ditch even
old men and boys with bazookas or automatic weapons, and even
units formed from the sick, the halt and the maimed can maintain
a fanatical defense. Two million soldiers with their backs to the wall:
a formidable prospect.

Nor was there much comfort to be gleaned from the 40-page document entitled: Estimated Unit Locations of Japanese Navy and Army
Air Forces, 20 July 1945 (File SRH-055 in the National Archives).
In spite of many appalling losses of pilots and aircraft, this very detailed Order of Battle (which was now being updated every week)
shows a substantial number of squadrons on hand for home defense.
And there is one disquieting feature. "Training of all kinds," it states,
"other than suicide training in tactical units, is believed to have been
abandoned in view of the expected imminent invasion." As the eye
runs over the descriptive notes about individual units it detects with

sinister frequency the word "suicide."* Ever since Leyte the kamikaze had been a threat, even though methods of destroying them improved. At Okinawa on April 6, 200 out of a force of 355 had got through to the assault area and done much damage. In May a new form of suicide operation occurred: five aircraft carrying commandos attempted to land on the American field at Yontan. Four were shot down, but the fifth landed and decanted a group of commandos who, before they were all killed, by hurling grenades and incendiaries destroyed 7 aircraft, damaged 26 more, and ignited 70,000 gallons of fuel. It could certainly be expected that these self-sacrificial young men, with their Samurai spirit, would have still less compunction about offering up their lives in defense of the homeland.†

In a study of signal intelligence, it would not be appropriate to discuss all the complicated and controversial issues raised by the dropping of the bombs. But if one sets the evidence supplied by Magic about a peace mood against the intelligence, furnished mainly by Army and Navy Ultra, about Japan's defensive preparations, it is at least understandable why Truman took his decision. In 1953 he wrote to the air historian Professor Cate and described how, on the day after a message reached him at Potsdam that the trial explosion in New Mexico had been successful, he summoned a meeting of his advisers —Byrnes, Stimson, Leahy, Marshall, Eisenhower, King, etc. "I asked General Marshall," Truman wrote, "what it would cost in lives to land on the Tokyo plain and other places in Japan. It was his opinion that such an invasion would cost at a minimum one quarter of a million casualties, and might cost as much as a million, on the American side alone, with an equal number of the enemy. The other military and naval men present agreed. . . . We sent an ultimatum to Japan. It was rejected. I ordered atomic bombs dropped on the two cities named . . ."[5]

The pioneer theorist of air warfare, General Douhet, might have found in this event the supreme justification of his concept, for the Japanese did indeed learn that "to be defeated in the air is finally to

---

* File SRH-103—Suicide Attack Squadron Organization, July 1945—contains a virtually complete breakdown of the naval organization, with the serial number and exact location of dozens of units: the whole force comprising "suicide" motor torpedo boats, the *Kaiten* one-man submarines and the *Kooryu* midget submarines.
† Even at the end, when the U.S.S. *Missouri* was entering Tokyo Bay for the formal ceremony of surrender, there was a plot to attack her by kamikaze bombers.

be defeated and to be at the mercy of the enemy . . . compelled to accept whatever terms he sees fit to dictate." Yet critics have pointed out that the first terms offered were not in fact accepted, for the bomb on Hiroshima was not followed immediately by an unconditional surrender as demanded in the Potsdam Declaration: it took the Nagasaki bomb, the Emperor's personal decision, the adjustment of terms whereby the imperial status was preserved and perhaps the Russian declaration of war (on August 9, between the two bombs) to extract a capitulation from Tokyo.[6]

In this sense, therefore, the Magic intercepts whose value was both significant and questionable at the time of Pearl Harbor leave us, at the end of the war, with questions about their significance which are valid, though probably unanswerable. It is argued, for example, that in dropping the bombs the Americans were seeking to forestall a Russian declaration of war on Japan, or at least to prevent it from giving the U.S.S.R. much by way of territorial gains. Now that we know how clearly Magic revealed Russia's disdain for Japan's overtures, and her obviously aggressive intentions, can it be believed that this was not a factor in the final and lethal decision? Magic certainly disclosed the pacific mood of the Emperor, and in Togo's signals it is evident that terms of unconditional surrender were unacceptable chiefly because they did not guarantee the Emperor's historic position. With these indicators available, why—it may be asked—did Truman not pay more heed to Stimson and Grew, and the argument that an escape clause should be offered which would enable the Japanese to save "face": why was it only at the last that Hirohito was offered an olive branch and enabled, at the climacteric meeting with his Cabinet on August 14, to utter words which ended the war, "the unendurable must be endured"? It does not seem improper to recall, at this point, Professor Trevor-Roper's observation that "history is not merely what happened: it is what happened in the context of what might have happened."

Amid this tangle of uncertainties one fact is indisputable. Up to the very last minute the Japanese failed to appreciate that the Americans had mastered their codes and ciphers, so that Magic and Ultra continued to operate in tandem, more efficiently than any secret agent because of their ability to provide with so little delay complete transcripts of the most intimate messages sent out by the enemy during this time of high crisis. There was always the possibility of irony, and even of comedy, in this situation, as earlier instances have demonstrated. It is singularly appropriate, therefore, that even after the surrender Magic should have produced an intercept whose implications, farcical from one point of view, nevertheless illustrate in a flash how impeccable signal intelligence can lay bare and frustrate even an enemy's most secret schemes.

The scene was set by a memorandum of August 11 to General Marshall from the Assistant Chief of Staff responsible for the G-2 or Intelligence branch, Major General Clayton Bissell. It is entitled: Ultra Intelligence during and after Arrangements to Terminate the Japanese War. Bissell first pointed out, shrewdly, that while some Japanese Army Ultra was being read within a few hours, some of the Army code systems involved longer delays and some had not even been solved. To guard against the possibility of Japanese Army orders "for general or isolated repudiation of the surrender" escaping detection, Bissell suggested that the terms for the cessation of hostilities should provide for the transmission of all Japanese Army communications in the clear. But, he went on:

> Cryptographic systems used for communication by the Japanese Foreign Office with its diplomatic officials in neutral countries (Sweden, Switzerland, Portugal, Vatican, Afghanistan) are being fully read with speed. If the Japanese are given no reason to suspect those systems are compromised, and communications to those diplomats continue, intelligence of importance may be obtained. . . . The United States and Great Britain would also obtain substantial long-term benefits from . . . the continued use by the Japanese of the systems in the post-war period, especially their machine system.

In other words, Bissell was arguing that it would be absurd to throw away all the advantages that had accrued since the Purple diplomatic cipher was first penetrated in 1940. And then—hey, presto! On September 6 Foreign Minister Shigemitsu signaled to the legations in Berne, Lisbon and Stockholm that "since we have received no orders whatsoever from the Allied Supreme Command regarding code communications, it will be our policy to continue to use the remaining cipher machines and code books. (We are making preparations so that we can dispose of the cipher machines and code books at any time.)" Of course Magic picked up the signal, and in consequence

Washington was kept aware by the intercepts, almost hour by hour, of every Japanese scheme to ignore or evade the surrender terms, to use the horrors of Hiroshima and Nagasaki as propaganda weapons for traducing a barbaric enemy and, in sum, to diminish the shock of defeat by acting as though it had never occurred or, alternatively, was in some sense reversible.

> But this rough magic
> I here abjure . . .

How wise Bissell had been in advising General Marshall not to end a tempestuous war with Prospero's words in the last act of Shakespeare's play!

Notes

Unless otherwise indicated, references are to files in the Modern Military Section of the National Archives in Washington.

CHAPTER ONE

1. The basic source is file SRH-043, Statement for Record of Participation of Brigadier General Carter W. Clarke, GSC, in the Transmittal of Letters from General George C. Marshall to Gov. Thomas E. Dewey, the Latter Part of September 1944. (This was not declassified until November 30, 1979.) See also Forrest C. Pogue, *George C. Marshall*, Vol. II.

2. This paragraph is disputed, particularly by former members of the OSS. It certainly sits rather uncomfortably in the text. Carter Clarke presumably drafted the letter for Marshall and may have inserted this item for extra emphasis.

   However, there are now two relevant files available: SRH-066, Examples of Intelligence obtained from Cryptanalysis, and SRH-113, Selected Documents concerning OSS Operations in Lisbon, MIS War Department, 5 May–13 July '43. The latter file was lodged too late for consultation. From SRH-066, however, it seems that the affair started with a report from the Italian General Staff (Rome/Tokyo, June 29, 1943) that "American espionage agency in Lisbon knows minute details of Japanese ministry there and also has the Japanese code book." Morishima, the Lisbon minister, was particularly sensitive about security and was outraged at the suggestion. The source of the Italian allegation was never established by the Japanese, but an inspector was sent to Lisbon to investigate, where he was "resented and ill-treated" (Madrid/Tokyo, July 12, 1943). Morishima in his usual way offered to resign.

   In fact the code was not changed, but on September 18, 1943, a new and more complicated system of super-enciphering the code was introduced. By the beginning of December, however, the problem had been solved and messages continued to be read. "The OSS," observes the file, "though misguided, carried out their operations with some skill."

3. For German Ultra and the Northwestern Europe campaign, see Ralph Bennett, *Ultra in the West*, and Ronald Lewin, *Ultra Goes to War*.

CHAPTER TWO

1. For Yardley see the files: William F. Friedman, A Brief History of the Signal Intelligence Service, and Anon., The Need for New Legislation Against Unauthorized Disclosure of Communications Activities. See also SRH-038, A Selection of Papers Pertaining to Herbert O. Yardley: 1918–1950. This important file contains the War Department documents which reflect the authorities' concern about Yardley's disclosures and the administrative complications involved in getting rid of him.

2. See Barbara W. Tuchman, *The Zimmermann Telegram*, Constable, 1959. Patrick Beesly has in preparation a history of Room 40 based on papers recently available in

the Public Record Office. See also Christopher Andrews, "The Mobilisation of British Intelligence for the Two World Wars," Working Paper No. 12 of the International Security Studies Program, the Wilson Center, Smithsonian Institution, Washington.

3. See Stephen W. Roskill, *Hankey*, Vol. II, Ch. 9.
4. Donald McLachlan, *Room 39*.
5. Ladislas Farrago, *The Broken Seal*, p. 36.
6. Foster, Oral History (Naval Archives).
7. David Kahn, *The Codebreakers*, p. 387.
8. Farrago, *op. cit.*, Ch. 4.
9. Smith-Hutton, Oral History (Naval Archives).
10. Friedman, *op. cit.*
11. For Redl see Fitzroy Maclean, *Take Nine Spies*, Ch. 2.
12. Had Yardley not been dismissed, the Canadians would have been denied any association with Bletchley Park and "the Ultra secret" (private information).
13. For Enigma, see Peter Calvocoressi, *Top Secret Ultra*, Cassell, 1980, and Ronald Lewin, *Ultra Goes to War.*
14. Further details of this early American intelligence about Enigma are in Lewin, *op. cit.*
15. For Friedman's career see Ronald W. Clark, *The Man Who Broke Purple*, which is unreliable on his cryptanalysis.
16. See Note on Sources (p. xiii) for files on SIS.
17. For the Polish effort, see Jozef Garlinski, *Intercept*, Dent, 1979, and Lewin *op. cit.*
18. See Ralph W. Baldwin, *The Deadly Fuze*, Jane's, 1980.
19. Private information.
20. Private information.
21. See Patrick Beesly, *Very Special Intelligence*, for Anglo-American cooperation in this field.

CHAPTER THREE

1. See footnote, "Cloud of Suspicion," in *Proceedings* of U.S. Naval Institute, July 1980, p. 39.
2. Private communication from Miss Kay Halle.
3. For Tricycle see Sir John Masterman, *The Double-Cross System*, and Ewen Montagu, *Beyond Top Secret U.* Montagu, who was naval representative on the Twenty Committee, which supervised the "Double-Cross System," makes the valid point (p. 74) that through Ultra it was known that the Abwehr at this time had assisted a senior Japanese official to visit Italy from Berlin in order to obtain details about the British aircraft-carrier raid on Taranto. (Montagu was sent to Washington to pick up the pieces after J. Edgar Hoover's mishandling of Tricycle.) Lieutenant Colonel T. A. Robertson, who was in charge of B1A, has confirmed the relevant details in correspondence with the author.
4. Roberta Wohlstetter, *Pearl Harbor: Warning and Decision*, p. 211.
5. See Paul Kramer, "Nelson Rockefeller and British Security Coordination," *Journal of Contemporary History*, Vol. XVI, No. 1 (January 1981).
6. Wohlstetter, *op. cit.*
7. *Ibid.*, p. 3 and *passim*.
8. F. H. Hinsley, (ed.), *British Intelligence in the Second World War*, Vol. I, Ch. 14, "Barbarossa."
9. *Ibid.*, Appendix 13, "The Special Signals Service from GC and CS to the Middle East." The PRO file ADM/223/88, however (p. 320), states that Ultra was sent direct from Bletchley to Middle East Command "by SLU Link established at Cairo on 20th July 1941, and at Alexandria on 14th August 1941—and later extended to Malta." The discrepancy is presumably accounted for by improvements in handling the traffic in the Middle East.
10. Wohlstetter, *op. cit.*, pp. 44 ff. and *passim*.

11. Forrest C. Pogue, *George C. Marshall,* Vol. II, Appendix One, "Marshall and Pearl Harbor."
12. *Ibid.*
13. Dyer, Oral History (Naval Archives).

CHAPTER FOUR

For the relevant signal traffic the basic source is the file: The Role of Radio Intelligence in the American-Japanese Naval War, August 1941–December 1942.

1. Privately printed record of NSA seminar. See also David Kahn, *The Codebreakers,* pp. 863 ff.
2. The chapter in ADM/223/88 on *Bismarck* is authoritative. This little-known extensive postwar analysis of "Admiralty Use of Special Intelligence in Naval Operations" correlates Ultra and other Sigint with what actually occurred in operations. See also Patrick Beesly, *Very Special Intelligence,* and Ronald Lewin, *Ultra Goes to War.*
3. W. J. Holmes, *Double-Edged Secrets.*
4. Edward Van Der Rhoer, *Deadly Magic.*
5. Walter Lord kindly made available to the author the notes of his interrogation of Rochefort when he was writing *Incredible Victory.* They usefully confirm other sources.
6. But see Aileen Clayton, *The Enemy Is Listening,* for the first thoroughgoing record of "Y Service" in action, written by a senior participant.
7. Holmes, *op. cit.*
8. Private information from one of the unit.
9. It has always to be remembered that in the command structure of the Pacific Fleet Layton was the filter—or the coordinator—through whom intelligence from a variety of sources, including FRUPac, reached Nimitz.
10. A clear analysis of the Coral Sea action is in Paul Dull, *The Imperial Japanese Navy,* Ch. 8. Samuel Eliot Morison's history, Vol. IV, has an account in his inimitable style.
11. Holmes, *op. cit.*
12. See relevant chapter in ADM/223/88, which supports Beesly, *op. cit.,* and Lewin, *op. cit.*
13. Walter Lord, *Incredible Victory.*
14. It is not always possible to establish the date on which a signal was decoded and translated and distributed (even though the transmission date is given) from the Role of Radio Intelligence file; and it should *never* be assumed, without specific evidence, that a break occurred soon after transmission. This is the classic danger against which the historian has to guard in using decodes and decrypts. In this case the timing seems definite.
15. See E. B. Potter, *Nimitz,* for Theobald's subsequent decline. He was incapable of maintaining good relations with the Army in what was a Combined Operations Theater.
16. Holmes, *op. cit.*

CHAPTER FIVE

1. The Need for New Legislation Against Unauthorized Disclosure of Communications Activities covers the *Tribune* affair and is the basic file for this chapter. See also Thomas B. Buell, *Master of Sea Power,* p. 203. The article by Ruth R. Harris, "The Magic Leak of 1941 and Japanese-American Relations," *Pacific Historical Review,* Vol. L, No. 1 (February 1981), is a most stimulating analysis of the whole subject in its broader implications.
2. McCollum, Oral History (Naval Archives).

3. Foster, Oral History (Naval Archives).
4. Laski also wrote of Roosevelt (p. 754): "A large part of his approach to the problems of his time was conditioned by his belief that the pathology of American life, especially of its economic life, was occasioned by the malpractices of evil men; and from this he drew the inference that it is in the power of legislation, within the existing legal framework, to correct those malpractices, if it is wisely administered." But here was a case when the existing legal framework was inadequate to check the malpractice.
5. Translated as *Journey for Our Time*, Arthur Barker, 1953.
6. Edward Van Der Rhoer, *Deadly Magic*.
7. W. J. Holmes, *Double-Edged Secrets*.

CHAPTER SIX

1. Reminiscences of Lieutenant Colonel Howard W. Brown, prepared under the direction of the Chief Signal Officer.
2. *The Signal Corps: The Outcome*, pp. 338–42.
3. *Ibid.*, p. 346.
4. W. J. Holmes, *Double-Edged Secrets*.
5. A communication from Professor McVittie, who discussed the problems of Anglo-American cooperation further in conversation and correspondence.
6. Holmes, *op. cit.*
7. History of the Special Branch, MIS.
8. This section is based on conversation and correspondence with Edwin Huddleson, who generously communicated his unique experience.
9. Major General C. A. Willoughby, affidavit of May 8, 1945, in Hearings before the Joint Committee, Part 35, p. 87.
10. MacArthur to the Adjutant General, quoted in D. M. Horner, "Special Intelligence in the South West Pacific Area in World War II," in *Australian Outlook 32*, 1978.
11. *Ibid.*
12. Marshall letter to MacArthur on the use of Ultra intelligence, 23 May 1944.
13. List of Special Security Representatives and Special Security Officers, 15 February 1945.

CHAPTER SEVEN

For signal traffic the relevant files are: The Role of Radio Intelligence in the American-Japanese Naval War, August 1941–December 1942, and Radio Intelligence in World War Two: Tactical Operations in the Pacific Ocean Areas, January 1943. Paul S. Dull, *The Imperial Japanese Navy*, provides succinct analyses of individual operations.

1. *The War Against Japan (History of the Second World War)*, Vol. II, p. 273. HMSO, 1959.
2. See E. B. Potter, *Nimitz*, pp. 177 ff.
3. Walter Lord, *Lonely Vigil*. Subsequent references to coast watchers are drawn from this source.
4. Taken from The Role of Radio Intelligence, these examples are subject to the general caveat that it is not always clear when the signals were broken or to whom they were distributed. Still, the drift is evident.
5. The drama of these engagements is best conveyed by Morison.
6. See Ronald Lewin, *Slim the Standard-bearer*.
7. See Potter, *op. cit.*, p. 185. "Fletcher left sea duty with a reputation for hard luck, which some observers, but not Nimitz, regarded as partly the result of ineptitude."

See also p. 200 for Nimitz's endorsement of Fletcher's return to sea duty. Turner survived, to undertake higher commands.

8. See Ronald Lewin, *The Chief*, p. 134.
9. Dull, *op. cit.*, p. 203.
10. See note 4: in this case the timings are more specific.

CHAPTER EIGHT

1. Clayton D. James, *The Years of MacArthur*, Vol. II, p. 104.
2. *Ibid.*, p. 111.
3. Christopher Thorne, *Allies of a Kind*, p. 370, note 39.
4. W. J. Holmes, *Double-Edged Secrets.*
5. John Terraine, *Douglas Haig: The Educated Soldier.*
6. Horner, *op. cit.*
7. D. M. Horner, *Crisis of Command: Australian Generalship and the Japanese Threat,* provides a particularly clear analysis of MacArthur's attitude.
8. Craven and Cate, Vol. IV.
9. *Ibid.*, where a full account of Kenney's revival of the SWPA air force may be found. See also *General Kenney Reports.*
10. Craven and Cate, *op. cit.* See also Clayton D. James, *op. cit.*, Vol. II, pp. 301 ff.
11. The high-level policy discussions are described in E. B. Potter, *Nimitz.*
12. The whole episode, including Yamamoto's fatalism and Japanese scrutiny of their signal traffic after his death, is examined in Hiroyuki Agawa, *The Reluctant Admiral.*
13. Quoted in Potter, *op. cit.*
14. Charles B. MacDonald, *The Mighty Endeavor: American Armed Forces in the European Theater in World War II.*
15. Layton, Oral History (Naval Archives).
16. Quoted in Potter, *op. cit.*, p. 280.
17. The British break: private information.
18. Blamey Papers: Australian War Memorial, Canberra. Quotation from these papers is by permission of the authorities.

CHAPTER NINE

The basic file is: Blockade-running Between Europe and the Far East by submarine, 1942–December 1944. For German Ultra and blockade-running the best authority is Patrick Beesly, *Very Special Intelligence*. ADM/223/88 contains a short but informative section.

1. It is important to distinguish between the general intelligence about the German Navy's coastal and harbor traffic, obtained from the Hydra cipher, and the specific intelligence acquired from the Atlantic U-boat cipher, Triton. See Beesly, *op. cit.*
2. Beesly, *op. cit.*, and Ronald Lewin, *Ultra Goes to War*. The Triton cipher, introduced early in 1942, was broken on December 13 of that year.
3. Quoted by Beesly, *op. cit.*, p. 248.
4. See Peter Calvocoressi and Guy Wint, *Total War*, Ch. 18, for an admirable account of Bhose and his operations.

CHAPTER TEN

The basic source is SRH-011 (8 vols.): The Role of Communications Intelligence in Submarine Warfare in the Pacific, Jan. 1943–Oct. 1943.

For the broad picture and individual actions the essential references are W. J. Holmes,

Undersea Victory, and Clay Blair, *Silent Victory.* But Captain Holmes published in 1966, before it was permissible to reveal his intimate firsthand knowledge of the use of Ultra, and Clay Blair did not have access to much recently declassified material. The human realities of submarine warfare are well depicted in the novels of Harry Homewood, a regular submariner who survived eleven Pacific patrols.

1. For Nimitz's early career, see E. B. Potter, *Nimitz.*
2. W. J. Holmes, *Double-Edged Secrets,* p. 125.
3. Blair supplies a number of specific examples.
4. Lockwood and Coe are quoted in Blair.
5. See Appendix IV, "Torpedoes," in Donald Macintyre, *The Battle for the Pacific.* The Mark 13 airborne torpedo had similar deficiencies. According to Macintyre, "analysis of 105 drops at more than 150 knots in mid-1943 revealed that 36% ran cold, 20% sank, 20% had a faulty deflection, 18% unsatisfactory depth, while only 31% ran satisfactorily." The malfunctioning and gradual improvement of the submarine torpedo are discussed *passim* in Holmes, *Undersea Victory,* and in Morison.
6. Holmes, *Double-Edged Secrets,* p. 126.
7. W. N. Medlicott, *The Economic Blockade (History of the Second World War),* Vol. II. HMSO, 1959.
8. Holmes, *Undersea Victory,* p. 281.
9. The disastrous decline in Japan's domestic oil stocks was considerably accelerated by the intensive bombing campaign against oil targets carried out in 1945 under General Spaatz, the famous exponent in 1944 of a strategic offensive against oil targets in Germany. This campaign and the parallel campaign of airborne mining are described in great detail in Craven and Cate, Vol. V.

CHAPTER ELEVEN

Apart from the eight volumes of *The "Magic" Background of Pearl Harbor* the source for this chapter is the series of Magic Summaries.

1. J. C. Masterman, *The Double-Cross System,* p. 93.
2. This is the SRNA Series (see list of documentary sources).

CHAPTER TWELVE

1. Robert R. Smith, *Approach to the Philippines (U.S. Army in World War II).*
2. *Ibid.*
3. But only after a prolonged high-level dispute. Nimitz proposed to the Chiefs of Staff that the base should be handed over to Halsey. See Clayton D. James, *The Years of MacArthur,* Vol. II, p. 387.
4. Personal to author from Admiral Burke. See also Burke, Oral History (Naval Archives).
5. For Christie and submarine operations from Australia see W. J. Holmes, *Undersea Victory,* and Clay Blair, *Silent Victory.*
6. W. J. Holmes, *Double-Edged Secrets.*
7. Donald Macintyre, *The Battle for the Pacific.*
8. As note 4.
9. Holmes, *Double-Edged Secrets.*
10. See E. B. Potter, *Nimitz,* p. 322.
11. Quoted in *ibid.,* p. 323.
12. A useful reference is Charles Cruickshank, *Deception in World War II,* Oxford University Press, 1979.

13. General Willoughby's *The Guerrilla Resistance in the Philippines* contains much contemporary information.
14. Chester W. Nimitz and E. B. Potter, *The Great Sea War,* Harrap.
15. Holmes, *Double-Edged Secrets.*
16. Clayton D. James, *op. cit.,* p. 358.
17. See Reports by U.S. Army Ultra Representatives with Field Commands in the South West Pacific, Pacific Ocean and China/Burma/India Theaters of Operations, 1944–1945, and the equivalent series of reports by Ultra representatives in the European theater. See also A. G. Rosengarten, "With Ultra from Omaha to Weimar, a Personal View," in *Military Affairs,* October 1978.
18. For the escalation of radio signals in the Normandy campaign, see Ralph Bennett, *Ultra in the West,* and Ronald Lewin, *Ultra Goes to War.*
19. CINPAC's advanced HQ on Guam was established on January 2, 1945. For the move of part of JICPOA, and readjustments of the intelligence organization at Pearl Harbor, see Holmes, *Double-Edged Secrets,* p. 197. Further information from Commander Francis Raven, who served on Admiral Layton's staff at Nimitz's advance HQ on Guam.

CHAPTER THIRTEEN

Prime sources: The Magic Summaries; Magic Diplomatic Extracts, July 1945: selected items prepared by MIS, War Department, for the attention of General George C. Marshall; and Publications of the Pacific Strategic Intelligence Section.

1. Craven and Cate, Vol. X, p. 175.
2. For Zipper, see *The War against Japan,* Vol. V, *passim.*
3. Craven and Cate, Vol. V, p. 711.
4. Peter Calvocoressi and Guy Wint, *Total War,* p. 857.
5. There is a photocopy of Truman's complete letter in Craven and Cate, Vol. V, between p. 712 and p. 713.
6. See the animated exchange on the theme of "Was the Hiroshima Bomb Necessary?" between Joseph Alsop and David Joravsky in *The New York Review of Books,* October 23, 1980, and subsequent correspondence in the issue of February 19, 1981.

Appendices

APPENDIX I: "AMERICA DECIPHERED OUR CODE"

(This section of Chapter 14 of Volume 43 in the War History series issued by the Japanese Defense Agency, which is entitled "Examination of the Failure of Our Operations," was translated by Rear Admiral E. T. Layton, USN, and first published in the *Proceedings* of the U.S. Naval Institute. It is reprinted by kind permission of Admiral Layton and the editor of the *Proceedings*. Dates and times are Tokyo Standard Time Zone.)

Our Navy used many different codes/ciphers but an examination of their message texts indicates that the system most certainly broken was in all probability the Navy Code "D." Of all our regular codes, it was the one used principally for strategic matters. It was a five-digit mixed code made up in two volumes, one for sending and one for receiving, and was also provided with a separate table of five-digit random additives which, when applied in accordance with special rules for use with Code "D," completely altered the original code text. Navy Code "D" was first placed in effect on 1 December 1940; Random Additive Table #8 was put into use just before the start of the war, 4 December 1941.

Three other separate tables were also in use in conjunction with Code "D": (1) a Table of Grid Positions (in latitude and longitude), (2) a Table of Geographic Designators, and (3) a Table for Enciphering Dates (of events). The first of these used three Kana [a syllabary representing the 50 basic sounds in the Japanese language: essentially the vowels A, I, U, E, and O alone or in combination following the consonants K, S, T, N, M, Y, R, and W] plus two numerals. The initial Kana designated the selected 15 degree by 15 degree square (of the earth) of latitude and longitude, while the second and third Kana (using the 50 Kana) indicated the selected latitude and longitude within the above square, to the nearest 20 minutes; the two numerals further refined the designated position in the above 20-minute square to the nearest two minutes of latitude and longitude [less than a two-mile square in the middle of the ocean].

The second table, for geographic designators, consisted of two or three Roman letters, which were used to indicate a specific place, geographically; the first letter represented a common geographic entity (for example, "A" represented America, "P" stood for Japan's Mandated Islands [which they called their South Sea Islands]; the second letter stood for a specific geographic place name; and if there was a third letter, that place was near the geographic place designated by the second letter (for example "PS" stood for Saipan, "PST" represented Tinian).

The third table was a different-type, three-Kana table and was used for enciphering the date of an event or action; this table was arranged in Kana sequence [analogous to our a, b, c . . . etc.]. Both these latter tables were used, without change, from the beginning of the war.

After the plain text of a message was written out, all the dates, grid locations, and geographic place names were then enciphered by using the respective tables, and this modified text of the message was then encoded into a series of five-digit code groups taken from the transmission volume of Code "D." Now, following the special rules for the use of the Random Additive Table with Code "D," another series of five-digit code groups were selected from the Random Additive Table and placed in sequence under each corresponding five-digit code group, and, using false addition —i.e., without carrying forward 10's—the final code text was arrived at, e.g.:

A. Assume the text begins:	"Enemy"	"Sighted"	etc.
B. Code Text from Code "D":	52194	73442	etc.
C. Random Additives from Table:	39682	44189	etc.
Coded and Enciphered Message:	81776	17521	etc.

Since the Random Additive Table consisted of 500 pages, each containing 100 random five-digit groups, the (false) addition of these additives to the code groups completely altered the original/modified code text of the original text, making it extremely complicated and very difficult to "break." It is said that our experts in cryptanalysis, and others connected with code and cipher matters, were unable to "break" it.

The Japanese Navy issued orders to replace Code Book "D" with Code Book "D-1" and to replace Random Additives Tables #7 and #8 with new Table #9 on 1 May 1942, although it is said that this had been originally planned for 1 April. According to the postwar statement of the officer in charge of code changes, this change in code could not be carried out because of the delays in distribution of the new code books, and was made just before the sortie of the fleet for the Midway operation [27 May 1942— Japanese "Navy Day"—the anniversary of Admiral Togo's victory in the

Battle of Tsushima Straits, and the date the Japanese Carrier Striking Force sortied from the Inland Sea for Midway]. . . .

Breaking our code, even partially, undoubtedly increased the reliability of America's strategic estimates and gave them some definitive intelligence on our concepts of operations and furnished them with a substantial outline of our plans for operations in the future. There is no doubt that from early May onward a great many of our radio messages dealt with operational matters. As there is very little of that material now available, it is not possible to speculate as to which of those messages were broken, but subordinate forces undoubtedly communicated their intended movements to other forces concerned, based on the overall plan. There is no doubt that there were many radio messages concerning the "M1" (Midway) operation during the early days of May, but we have no reference material containing the geographic designators "AF" (Midway), "AO" (Aleutians), or "AOB" (Kiska); undoubtedly, there were radio messages concerning future reconnaissance operations by the [auxiliary seaplane carrier/tender] *Kimikawa Maru* and Submarine Squadron 1 that contained the geographic designators "AO" and "AOB." We have no radio files to show how the enemy confirmed "AF" to be Midway, but the diary of Commander Sanagi of the Naval General Staff contains the entry "MIDWAY IS SHORT OF FRESH WATER," and a radio message to that effect was indeed transmitted.

Our Navy was not able to break the American military's code(s); our intelligence appreciations and strategic estimates were primarily based on communications intelligence which was derived from enemy traffic analysis, call-sign identification, direction-finder bearings, and the interception of plain-language transmissions [particularly those of aviators when airborne]. As an example, we could estimate when a strong American force sortied from port or was operating, because their air patrols in that area became intensified and expanded and many patrol planes' messages then came up on the air; we could also ascertain the general area of the enemy's intended attack because of their custom of stationing submarines in that general area, in advance of the planned attack.

However, it is said that since the beginning of the war, only a few of our many intelligence estimates based on communications intelligence really "hit the mark," and our Navy's confidence in them was, therefore, relatively low.

APPENDIX II

AG 312.1 (13 Oct 43) OB-S-B   bsk 2B-939 Pentagon
14 October 1943

SUBJECT: Special Security Officer for the
              South West Pacific Theater.

TO: Commander-in-Chief, South West Pacific Area.

1. The Special Security Officer for the South West Pacific Area is the representative of the War Department on the staff of the Commander-in-Chief, South West Pacific Area, in sole charge of the receipt and transmission of all Ultra Dexter intelligence and in sole charge of bringing such intelligence to the attention of the Commander-in-Chief and those senior intelligence and operations staff officers designated by the Commander-in-Chief. He will advise the Commander-in-Chief as to all problems of security in connection with the receipt, transmission, handling and use of Ultra Dexter intelligence.

2. The Special Security Officer for the South West Pacific Area will be designated by the Assistant Chief of Staff, G-2, War Department General Staff, who will transmit to him directly all orders necessary to insure the security of Ultra Dexter intelligence and the transmission to and from the South West Pacific Area of all Ultra Dexter intelligence required. He will be attached for administration and discipline to the staff of the Commander-in-Chief, South West Pacific Area.

3. *Mission:* As a representative of the War Department, the Special Security Officer for the South West Pacific Area will:

   a. Be in sole charge of the receipt of all Ultra Dexter intelligence and the transmission of all such intelligence to and from the South West Pacific Area.

   b. Be equipped with special cryptographic systems which shall be available solely to him and to subordinate officers and non-commissioned officers reporting to him, for the receipt and transmission of Ultra Dexter intelligence and related information. No other channels or ciphers or personnel shall be used to transmit Ultra Dexter intelligence or comments or questions in connection with such intelligence, except by specific authority of the Assistant Chief of Staff, G-2, War Department General Staff.

   c. Be in sole charge of furnishing Ultra Dexter intelligence to the Commander-in-Chief and to those senior intelligence and operations staff officers designated by the Commander-in-Chief.

d. Advise the Commander-in-Chief with respect to establishing and enforcing security policies and practices concerning the production, receipt, transmission, dissemination and use of Ultra Dexter intelligence.

e. Advise the Commander-in-Chief with respect to the expeditious collection and transmission to the War Department of collateral information required for the production or evaluation of Ultra Dexter intelligence.

f. Maintain liaison with Signal Intelligence Service and with all others having access to Ultra Dexter or Rabid or T/A intelligence in the South West Pacific Theater.

g. Provide the War Department with Ultra Dexter or Rabid or T/A intelligence available in the South West Pacific Theater.

h. Maintain direct communication at all times with the Assistant Chief of Staff, G-2, War Department General Staff, with respect to all matters concerning Ultra Dexter intelligence.

4. Communications between the Special Security Officer for the South West Pacific Theater and the War Department will not be discussed with nor made available to any person except by authority of the Assistant Chief of Staff, G-2, War Department General Staff. This applies to all communications whether by means of special cryptographic systems or by courier pouch or otherwise.

5. The Commander-in-Chief, South West Pacific Area, will provide the Special Security Officer with a suitable office for the secure receipt, handling and storage of Ultra Dexter intelligence and related material and of his special cryptographic material and will make available communication facilities and channels for the receipt and transmission by the Special Security Officer of Ultra Dexter intelligence and related information by means of his special cryptographic systems.

6. The Commander-in-Chief, South West Pacific Area, will issue such directives and assist in establishing such liaisons as may be necessary to enable the Special Security Officer to accomplish his mission.

By order of the Secretary of War:

J. A. ULIO
Major General,
The Adjutant General.

APPENDIX III: SPECIAL SECURITY REPRESENTATIVES AND SPECIAL SECURITY OFFICERS

15 February 1945

Southwest Pacific Area

HECKEMEYER, Benjamin W.	Lt. Col.	SSR, SWPA, GHQ Leyte
MOUNTAIN, Maurice J.	Major	GHQ Leyte
GUNN, John H.	Major	GHQ Leyte
FLORY, Harry D.	Captain	GHQ Leyte
HAYES, Norman T.	1st Lt.	GHQ Leyte
OLSEN, Russell	1st Lt.	GHQ Leyte (Liaison 7th Fleet)
BAKER, George H.	1st Lt.	GHQ Leyte
MCCARTHY, William H.	Major	GHQ Luzon
CRIMMINS, John H.	Major	8th Army
MCKEE, James H., Jr.	Captain	1st Corps
ARMSTRONG, James I.	Captain	24th Corps
GRAHAM, Philip L.	Captain	FEAF
STERLING, Thomas M.	Captain	FEAF
SARGENT, James C.	Captain	FEAF
WASHBURN, Edward S.	1st Lt.	FEAF (en route)
PARDOE, William E.	1st Lt.	FEAF (en route)
SOGARD, Jefferson D.	Captain	5th AF
VAUGHAN, James R.	Captain	13th AF
THOMPSON, John R.	Major	Deputy SSR, Brisbane, GHQ, Rear Echelon
MERRIAM, Brewer J.	1st Lt.	Brisbane, GHQ, Rear Echelon
HALL, Edward T.	1st Lt.	Brisbane, GHQ, Rear Echelon
MCMILLAN, Cyrus J.	2nd Lt.	Brisbane, GHQ, Rear Echelon

Feb. 1945

India-Burma and China Theaters

WYATT, Inzer B.	Lt. Col.	SSR, India-Burma and China Theaters, New Delhi
DAY, Pomeroy	Major	Deputy SSR, India-Burma Theater, New Delhi
COLCLOUGH, William F., Jr.	Major	Deputy SSR, China Theater, Chungking
DILLER, George E.	Major	HQ, USF, New Delhi
KILLICK, John A.	1st Lt.	HQ, USF, New Delhi
LEE, Wayne A.	1st Lt.	HQ, USF, New Delhi
FLOWER, Edwin G., Jr.	1st Lt.	HQ, USF, New Delhi
HALE, Edward B.	1st Lt.	HQ, USF, New Delhi
WOOD, Franklin	Captain	HQ, USF, New Delhi
CRAIGE, Archibald	Captain	Eastern Air Command
LORD, Edmund P.	Captain	20th Bomber Command

POWELL, Richard G.	Captain	10th AF
CUMPSTON, Sam E.	Major	SACSEA, Kandy
HARR, Karl G., Jr.	1st Lt.	14th AF
AUGENBLICK, Robert L.	Major	Northern Combat Area Command

Feb. 1945

Pacific Ocean Areas

ERVIN, Thomas E.	Major	SSR POA
WOOLSEY, Ross A., Jr.	Captain	USAR POA
DELL, Sam T.	Major	10th Army
GOODYEAR, Lawrence R.	1st Lt.	CINC POA (en route 10th Army)
MILLER, Alfred A.	Major	AAR POA
KINGSTON, Charles T.	Captain	21st Bomber Command
POMEROY, William H.	Captain	CINC POA
ORRICK, William H., Jr.	1st Lt.	CINC POA
HAMILTON, Gordon C.	1st Lt.	CINC POA
PRITCHARD, Lawrence D.	1st Lt.	CINC POA (en route RAGFOR)
LEATHERS, Harlan F.	1st Lt.	CINC POA (Forward)
GAILLARD, John P.	Captain	CINC POA (en route 24th Corps)

Bibliography

I have drawn extensively on the Official History of the U.S. Army in World War II: particularly on the volumes in the *Pacific Series* and, in the *Technical Series*, on *The Signal Corps: The Outcome*. The magisterial 15 volumes of Samuel Eliot Morison's *History of United States Naval Operations in World War II* were inevitably consulted, as were the relevant volumes in the British Official History. The series of histories edited by W. F. Craven and J. L. Cate, *Army Air Forces in World War II*, was also indispensable. Other books to which I referred include:

Agawa, Hiroyuki. *The Reluctant Admiral: Yamamoto and the Imperial Navy*. Kodansha International Ltd., 1980.

Baldwin, Ralph B. *The Deadly Fuze*. Jane's, 1980.

Bateson, Charles. *The War with Japan*. Barrie and Rockliff, 1968.

Beesly, Patrick. *Very Special Intelligence*. Hamish Hamilton, 1977.

———. *Very Special Admiral*. Hamish Hamilton, 1980.

Bennett, Ralph. *Ultra in the West*. Hutchinson, 1979.

Blair, Clay. *Silent Victory*. Lippincott, 1975.

Brooks, Lester. *Behind Japan's Surrender*. McGraw-Hill, 1968.

Buell, Thomas B. *Master of Sea Power: A Biography of Fleet Admiral Ernest J. King*. Little, Brown, 1980.

Calvocoressi, Peter, and Wint, Guy. *Total War*. Allen Lane, The Penguin Press, 1972.

Carver, Field Marshal Lord (ed.). *The War Lords*. Weidenfeld and Nicolson, 1976.

Clark, Ronald W. *The Man Who Broke Purple*. Weidenfeld and Nicolson, 1977.

Clayton, Aileen. *The Enemy Is Listening*. Hutchinson, 1980.

Craig, William. *The Fall of Japan*. The Dial Press, 1967.

Dixon, Norman F. *On the Psychology of Military Incompetence*. Jonathan Cape, 1976.

Dull, Paul S. *The Imperial Japanese Navy*. U.S. Naval Institute Press, 1978.

Farrago, Ladislas. *The Broken Seal*. Arthur Barker, 1967.

Hashimoto, Mochitsura. *Sunk: The Story of the Japanese Submarine Fleet.* Cassell, 1954.

Hetherington, John. *Blamey: Controversial Soldier.* The Australian War Memorial and Australian Government Printing Service, 1973.

Hinsley, F. H., *et al. British Intelligence in the Second World War.* HMSO, 1979. Vol. II, 1981.

Holmes, W. J. *Undersea Victory.* Doubleday, 1966.

————. *Double-Edged Secrets.* U.S. Naval Institute Press, 1979.

Homewood, Harry. *Final Harbor.* McGraw-Hill, 1980.

Horner, D. M. "Special Intelligence in the South West Pacific Area in World War II," in *Australian Outlook,* 1978.

————. *Crisis of Command: Australian Generalship and the Japanese Threat, 1941–1943.* Australian National University Press, 1978.

Hoyt, Edwin P. *The Battle of Leyte Gulf.* Playboy Press, 1979.

Ienaga, Saburō. *Japan's Last War.* Blackwell, 1979.

Kahn, David. *The Codebreakers.* Weidenfeld and Nicolson, 1966.

Kenny, George C. *General Kenny Reports.* Duell, Sloan and Pearce, 1949.

King, Ernest J., and Whitehill, Walter Muir. *Fleet Admiral King.* Eyre and Spottiswoode, 1953.

Lewin, Ronald. *Slim the Standard-bearer.* Leo Cooper, 1976.

————. *Ultra Goes to War.* Hutchinson, 1978.

————. *The Chief: Field Marshal Lord Wavell.* Hutchinson, 1980.

Long, Gavin. *MacArthur as Military Commander.* Batsford, 1969.

Lord, Walter. *Day of Infamy.* Harper & Row, 1967.

————. *Incredible Victory.* Hamish Hamilton, 1968.

————. *Lonely Vigil: Coastwatchers of the Solomons.* Viking Press, 1977.

Lundstrom, John B. *The First South Pacific Campaign.* U.S. Naval Institute Press, 1976.

MacArthur, Douglas. *Reminiscences.* McGraw-Hill, 1964.

MacDonald, Charles B. *The Mighty Endeavor: American Armed Forces in the European Theater in World War II.* Oxford University Press, 1969.

Macintyre, Donald. *The Battle for the Pacific.* Batsford, 1966.

Manchester, William. *American Caesar: Douglas MacArthur.* Hutchinson, 1979.

Marder, Arthur. "Bravery Is Not Enough: The Rise and Fall of the Imperial Japanese Navy, 1941–1945." Distinguished Faculty Lecture, University of California, February 7, 1978.

Masterman, J. C. *The Double-Cross System.* Yale University Press, 1972.

Mayo, Lida. *Bloody Buna.* David and Charles, 1974.

McLachlan, Donald. *Room 39: Naval Intelligence in Action.* Weidenfeld and Nicolson, 1968.

Mee, Charles L. *Meeting at Potsdam*. André Deutsch, 1975.

Melosi, Martin V. *The Shadow of Pearl Harbor*. Texas University Press, 1977.

Montagu, Ewen. *Beyond Top Secret U*. Peter Davies, 1977.

Pogue, Forrest C. *George C. Marshall,* Vols. II & III. Viking Press, 1966 and 1973.

Potter, E. B. *Nimitz*. U.S. Naval Institute Press, 1976.

Rohwer, Jürgen. "Ultra, B-Dienst und Magic," in *Marine-Rundschau,* No. 76, 1979.

——, and Hümmelchen, G. *Chronology of the War at Sea*. 2 vols. Ian Allan, 1974.

Roskill, Stephen W. *Hankey,* Vol. II. Collins, 1972.

Slim, Field Marshal Lord. *Defeat into Victory*. Cassell, 1956.

Thorne, Christopher. *Allies of a Kind*. Hamish Hamilton, 1978.

Van Der Rhoer, Edward. *Deadly Magic*. Scribner's, 1978.

Willoughby, Chas. A. (and Chamberlin, John). *MacArthur, 1941–1951*. McGraw-Hill, 1954.

——. *The Guerrilla Resistance in the Philippines*. Vantage Press, 1972.

Winterbotham, F. W. *The Ultra Secret*. Weidenfeld and Nicolson, 1974.

Wohlstetter, Roberta. *Pearl Harbor: Warning and Decision*. Stanford University Press, 1962.

Zimmerman, John L. *The Guadalcanal Campaign*. Historical Division, HQ, U.S. Marine Corps, 1949.

Index

Abwehr, 52–3, 125, 241; questionnaire of, 53–5, 63
Adachi, Lieutenant General Hatazo, and Aitape, 252–3
Adak, planned Japanese landings at, 100
Admiralties, MacArthur attack on, 251
Admiralty's Operational Intelligence Centre, 135
AF, *see* Midway
A-Go plan, 255
air reconnaissance, and Solomons, 164, 167; and Guadalcanal, 172–3; and Japan and Kwajalein, 194; British, and German ships, 210; and Japanese convoys, 225; and Leyte, 266
aircraft, jet-propelled, Germany and, 235–6, 235–6n, 237
aircraft carrier, 93–4
Aitape, 250, 252–3
Akagi, 96, 105, 110
Akin, Brigadier General Spencer B., 181, 271
Aleutians, Japanese code and, 10; Japan and, 84–5, 100–1, 104, 114–15; decoding of date for, 106; Roosevelt's worries about, 115
Alexander, General Harold, 166
Alice Springs, MacArthur at, 176
"Alice Springs Stakes, The," 176n
Allied Intelligence Bureau, 263n
Allies, and reading of enemy codes, 12; and Magic, 18; and cooperation, 135–7, 207n; and enciphering machines, 153; intelligence units of, 160; intelligence of, and Lae, 184; and blockade runners, 205, 207; intelligence of, and German armament production, 235; invasion

plans of, 237; decisions of, re Japan, 245–6; *see also* Britain and United States
Alphabetical Typewriter, 36; *see also* Purple
American Black Chamber, The, 33, 33n
American Democracy, The, 118
Anami, General Korechika, 286
Angaur, Ultra and, 257
Annual Report Submitted to the Governments of the American Republics, 125–6
Arado, 234; Magic and, 236
Arctic convoys, Russians and, 212
Ardennes, Germans and, 61
Arlington Hall, 127, 132–3, 135, 198
Army, *see under names of countries*
Army Pearl Harbor Board, 14
Astrolabe, 97
Atlanta, Scott on, 162
atom bomb, 277, 282, 285, 287–9
Attlee, Clement, to Potsdam, 284
Attu, Japanese and, 10, 100
Australia, 23, 91, 91n; U.S. and, 83; and Central Bureau, 149; and coast watchers, 156, 159–60, 172; and New Guinea, 175, 196; MacArthur in, 176–92; War Department and, 178; American troops to, 183; strategy of, 183; and Philippine guerrilla groups, 263
Australian Mandated Territory, 156
Axis, blockade runners of, 205, 207, 207n, 208–12, 215–17

B-17s, 186, 186n
B-25s, modification of, 186, 186n

B-29s, change of role of, and result,
    275–7; captured airmen of, 286n
Balfour, Lord Arthur James, 23
Balkans, 237
Ballard, to French Frigate Shoals, 98
Bamboo No. L, *see* Take
Barkley, Alben W., 15
Barnett, Johnston on, 113–14
Bataan, 131, 262
"Bataan gang," 179–81, 267
Battle of the Bulge, 233n
Battle of the Fourth of June, *see* Midway
battleship, replaced by aircraft carrier, 93
Beesly, Patrick, 135
Belconnen group, 85, 87, 98, 99n, 106,
    179, 181–2, 219; Purple machine of, 182
Bell, Alexander Graham, daughter of,
    133n
Bell, Elliot V., and Dewey and Clarke,
    7–8, 12–13
Benson, Roy, and *Hiyo*, 226
Bertrand, General Gustave, 16n
Bhose, Subhai Chandra, 216, 216n
Biak, 251, 255, 257
Bismarck, 82, 88
Bismarck Archipelago, 156
Bismarck Sea, Battle of, 185–7; *see also*
    New Guinea
Bissell, Major General Clayton, 13, 14,
    151n, 290–1
Black Chamber, The, 20–3, 31–3, 126
Blair, Clay, 220, 225
Blake, George, 126n
Blamey, General Sir Thomas, and
    MacArthur, 177, 180, 182, 202; and
    Army Ultra, 199, 202
Bletchley Park, 68, 121, 126, 132–3, 142,
    233; and Enigma, 12, 16, 16n, 17, 21,
    26, 35, 46, 117, 121, 125, 144, 198, 208–9,
    233, 236; staff at, 16, 19–21, 29, 126;
    precedents of, 20–1; and cooperation
    with U.S., 46, 135, 144, 144n; and
    German naval cipher, 82; compared
    with FRUPac, 86; and battle of Mata-
    pan, 95; and *Scharnhorst*, 96; Special
    Liaison Units of, 122; Japanese crash
    course at, 134; and low- and high-grade
    codes, 136; reference index at, 143;
    atmosphere of, 143; and Russia, 238;
    see also Britain

Blitzkrieg, 61
blockade runners, 205, 207, 207n, 208–12,
    215–17
Blunt, Anthony, 54, 126n
Bolero, 177
Booth, Wing-Commander Roy, 149
Bougainville, 124, 156; coast watchers and,
    159, 165, 171
Boussole, 97
Bradley, General Omar N., 247
Brake, sinking of, 213–14
Bratton, Rufus S., 76
Brett, General George Howard, 182, 186n
Brewster, Kingman, quote from, 112
Brewster, Senator Owen, 3
Briggs, Ralph T., interview with, 74–5
Brisbane line, 183
Britain, and signal intelligence, 6, 39–40,
    see also Bletchley Park; secret sources
    of information of, 11; and U.S. and
    sharing of intelligence, 11, 44–7, 46n,
    47n, 120, 135–7, 144, 153; and Ultra, 16,
    16n, 19, 64, 144, 151, 223–4; alliance
    of, with Japan, 21–2; and Four Power
    Pact, 22, 22n, 23; and Washington
    Naval Conference, 22–3; navy of, in
    Pacific, 23; and Yardley, 33; and Purple,
    36, 45; and Japanese, German, Italian,
    and Russian signal systems, 44–5; and
    Tricycle, 52–3; and necessities of war,
    68; in spring, 1942, 82–3; at Singapore,
    collaboration of, with FRUPac, 86; and
    direction-finding, 90n; signal-intelligence
    unit of, and Nagumo, 92; and low-grade
    signals, 105–6; security measures in, and
    concern re those of U.S., 116–17, 119–21,
    121n, 123, 123n, 144; and enemy radio
    traffic, 122; and *Abwehr* signals, 125;
    post-war history and security, 126n;
    Royal Navy of, in two wars, 162–3; and
    Mediterranean strategy and intelligence,
    192; and Enigma, and Yanagi opera-
    tions, 205; and *Hohenfriedberg*, 208;
    and Axis shipping, 210, 223–4; and
    Milch Cows, 213, 213n; length of time
    of, in war, 219; torpedoes of, 221; Japan
    and, in Far East, 233–4; and Norway,
    234; Double-Cross system of, 240; and
    Japanese-German intelligence link,
    240–1; and Burma, 244; and language

officers, 256; deception of Germans by, 262; and *Zipper*, 277; and Japan and Russia, 278; post-war benefits to, from Japanese systems, 290; and Enigma, *see under* Bletchley Park; *see also* Allies *and* GCCS

British Naval Intelligence, 24, 26

British Solomon Islands Protectorate, 156, 156n

Broken Seal, The, 36

Brown, Lieutenant Howard E., 129–31

Buka, Japanese airstrip at, 171

Buna, 182, 184, 184n, 251

Bundy, McGeorge, 32n

Bunyan, John, 153

Burgenland, sinking of, 209

Burgess, Guy, 126n

Burgscheidungen Castle, capture of, 40n

Burke, Admiral Arleigh, 252, 252n, 256, 256n

Burma, Indian National Army and, 216; intelligence about, 244

Byrnes, James F., and atom bomb, 288

Cactus, *see* Guadalcanal

Caesar, Julius, and ciphers, 4

Callaghan, Admiral Daniel J., 162

Canada, 33, 136–7

Canberra, MacArthur in, 177

Canberra, torpedoing of, 260

Cape Esperance, 164, 166, 173

Cardena, Ambassador, 242

Cardivs, 92, 96, 99, 108

Carlyle, Thomas, 153

Carroll, Lewis, quote from, 39

Casablanca, decisions at, and intelligence, 192

Cast, 83n, 87; and Japanese diplomatic traffic, 129–30; transfer of, 138, 148, 181; Belconnen and, 181

Cate, J. L., 230, 275; Truman to, 288

Central Bureau, MacArthur and, 149; establishment of, 181, 181n; and Belconnen, 182; and Japanese Army code, 198; Special Branch officers at, 269; and intelligence, 272

Central Pacific, Special Branch and, 144–8, 151

Chamberlin, General Stephen J., 268

Charlotte Schliemann, sinking of, 213

Charteris, General John, 181

Chennault, Claire, 152

Chiang Kai Shek, 115, 176, 205

Chicago, damaging of, 166

Chicago Tribune, and article on Midway, 113–15, 117, 117n, 118–20, 125, 127; and Roosevelt "war plans," 114; U.S. Navy action against, 116–17

Chiffriermaschinen Aktiengesellschaft, and enciphering machine, 35

Chile, and Japanese intelligence, 239

China, Japanese assault on, 49

China/Burma/India theater, Magic Summaries and, 244

Choiseul, 156, 164, 172

Chokai, 161, 166–7; end of, 168n

Christie, Commander Ralph W., 254

Churchill, Winston, 11–12, 83, 157, 178, 245n, 276–7, 284, 286; and Norway, 234; and Philippine invasion, 262; Wavell to, 275

cipher, meaning of, vs code, 3–4; requirements for breaking of, 26; *see also* codes, enciphering machines, *and names of*

Clark, General Mark W., 247

Clark, Ronald, 37, 40n

Clarke, Colonel Carter, and Dewey, 5–9, 12–13; and Clarke Inquiry, 14; and joint committee, 121; and Special Security Officers, 150–1; and Special Branch reports, 268

Clausen Investigation, 14

Clausewitz, Karl von, 157

coast watchers, 156, 159–60, 164–5, 171–3

Code Compilation Company, 20n

codes, and ciphers, 3–4; requirements for breaking of, 26; identifying mistakes and operators of, 87–8, 88n; distribution of changes in, 89, 89n, 99; complexity of solutions of, 126; water transport and address, 197, 197n; breaking and changing of Japanese, *see under* Japan; maru, *see* marus; *see also names of and under* Japan

Coe, and U.S. torpedoes, 222

Combat Intelligence Center, 147–7

Combat Intelligence Unit, 139–40

Combined Bureau, 45–6, 253
Combined Fleet (Japanese), 84, 173, 285;
    and Midway, 96, 99–100, 108; and JN
    25b, 105; lack of future of, 110; and
    Guadalcanal, 170; message from, 202;
    and Nimitz, 254; end of, at Leyte,
    264–5
Command of the Air, The, quote from,
    274
Congressional Inquiry into Pearl Harbor,
    see Joint Committee, etc.
convoys, Japanese, 223–5, 227–8, 230;
    see also Take
coordinated attack, 186
Coral, and Naval Attaché series, 244–5,
    245n
Coral Sea, battle of, 10, 79, 91–6; John-
    ston and, 114; MacArthur claims re
    battle of, 179; Takahashi and, 243–4
Corderman, Lieutenant Preston, 40
Corregidor, Radio Intelligence office in,
    131; MacArthur and, 266; fall of, and
    Philippines, 262
Cory, Lieutenant Ralph, 123
Coventry, British and, 193
Craven, W. F., 230, 275
Crisis of Command, etc., 180n
Cromwell, Captain John P., 121n
Crudiv 5, Inouye instructions to, 92
Crudivs, in Rabaul and Solomons, 166–7
cryptanalysis (ysts), 16, 88; and World
    War II, 17; American, British, German,
    and Japanese, 19; and internecine
    struggles, 24; difficulties of, 28, 106;
    U.S. Army, in peacetime, 36; and
    Voynich manuscript, 81–2; Washington
    and Hawaii units of, 83; review of, for
    security, 119–20; Joint Committee for
    surveillance of, 121; U.S. Army and
    Navy and, 122; challenges to, 128; train-
    ing for, 134–5; and meteorological data,
    136; German, and breaking of Enigma,
    153; temporary blindness of, 157–8;
    American and British, and Japanese
    Army code, 196; American submarines
    and, 218; German, and Atlantic U-boats,
    223; and Japanese diplomatic messages,
    232; report on, for MIS, 272; see also
    code names and signal intelligence
Cryptographic School, opening of, 134

Cunningham, Admiral Andrew, 95–6,
    117, 168
Custine, Marquis de, 118

Darwin, 176, 176n
Davidson, Brigadier J. H., 181
Day the Dam Burst, The, 176n
Deadly Magic, 133
de Gaulle, Charles, and Orient, 157
Denniston, Alastair, 21
Depression, U.S. and, 118
Dewey, Thomas E., and Clarke and
    Marshall, 5–8, 12–13, 18, 112; letters
    to, from Marshall, see under Marshall
Dickens, Charles, and London fog, 16
Diplomatic Summaries, 143
direction finding, U.S. Navy and, 27;
    importance of, 89–90, 90n, 158–9; and
    MI, 97; and battles of the Slot, 164; and
    Guadalcanal, 169; and submarines, 211;
    and Philippines plans, 262
Doenitz, Admiral Karl, 56, 208, 229, 234
Doggerbank, sinking of, 207
Donovan, William, 11, 33
Doolittle, James Harold, 93, 96
Double-Edged Secrets, 139, 218, 223
Douhet, General Giulio, 274, 288–9
Driscoll, Agnes, 29, 34
Dull, Paul, 170, 264
Dunstan, William, 179n
Dutch, in spring, 1942, 82
Dutch Harbour, 100–1
Dyer, George C., and Pearl Harbor, 78
Dyer, Thomas, description of, 107, 107n

early warning system, 171
Easley, Major, 270
Eberle and Karin, 207
Eichelberger, Major General Robert, 180n,
    184, 184n, 251; and Papua, 185; and
    Leyte, 264; and Ultra, 271
Einstein, Albert, 37
Eisenhower, Dwight D., 6, 11, 12, 120, 247;
    and intelligence staffs, 150; and Ultra,
    150–1; and atom bomb, 288
Emerson, Ralph Waldo, quote from, 118
enciphering, machines for, 34–7, 42, 153;
    see also names of

Enigma, 16n
Enigma, 36–7; Poles and, 16, 16n, 35, 40,
    45–6; and capture of U 110, 26, 26n;
    machine, description of, 34–5; Ameri-
    cans and, 35; Purple and, 36, 42–3;
    Japanese and, 43; breaking of, 56, 68,
    153; and Yanagi operations, 205; for
    Atlantic U-boat fleet, 208, 211; and
    German jets, 236; Britain and, *see*
    Bletchley Park
Enterprise, 93, 108, 162, 170
"Estimate of Enemy Intentions," 155
Evans, Major F. W., and Enigma, 35
"execute," 71, 73–5

Fabian, Commander Rudolph J., at
    Hewitt Inquiry, 47n; and Cast, 85, 148;
    and SWPa, 181–2
Fabyan, Colonel George, 38
Far Eastern Air Force, 272
Farago, Ladislas, 36
Federal Bureau of Investigation (FBI),
    recruitment for, 119; and signal intelli-
    gence, 121; and South and Latin
    America, 125; *see also* Hoover
Fertig, Colonel Wendell, 262
Fiji-Samoa-New Caledonia line, 84
Finnegan, Joseph, 87
Finschhafen, in Japanese hands, 156
First South Pacific Campaign, The, 109n
Fitzgerald, F. Scott, quote from, 49
Fleet Radio Unit, Pacific, *see* FRUPac
Fletcher, Admiral Frank, 81, 94, 99, 103,
    110, 162, 167, 169
Flying Fish, and A-Go, 255
Formosa, TF 38 and, 260
Forrestal, James, 14
Foster, Vice Admiral Paul Frederick,
    115–16
Four Power Pact, 22–3
Fourth Air Attack Force (Japan), message
    from, 98
Fourth Fleet (Japan), 92, 95
France, and Four Power Pact, 22n
Frances the First, quote from, 83
Free India Movement, 216
Freedom of Information Act, 112
Freeman, Douglas Southall, 220–1
French Frigate Shoals, 97–8, 110

Friedman, William F., 233; background,
    career, and personality of, 37–41, 39n,
    40n; collapse of, 41, 46; and Voynich
    manuscript, 81–2; and Joint Committee,
    121; to Britain, 143; *see also* Purple
FRUPac (Hypo), and Japanese codes,
    83, 83n, 85–7, 90–1; collaboration of,
    with other signal intelligence teams,
    85–6; and Japanese signal traffic, 90;
    strengthened credibility of, 91–3; and
    Japanese aviation buildup in South
    Pacific, 92; and Midway, 93, 104, 106;
    and Coral Sea battle, 94–5; and Yama-
    moto, 99, 99n, 109, 187; and French
    Frigate Shoals, 110; and Johnston case,
    117; fears of, re security, 122, 127;
    Huddleson and, 145; Special Branch
    link at, 146; and Cast, 148; and JN 25
    change, 155; and traffic volume and
    direction finding at Guadalcanal, 169;
    and MacArthur publicity, 179; Bel-
    connen and, 182; and American sub-
    marines, 219; breaking of maru code
    by, 223; *see also* Hypo *and* signal
    intelligence
Fuchida, Captain Mitsuo, 52

Gasa, Biuku, 159
George II, King, 39
Germans (y), codes of, 5–6, 10, 12, 16–17,
    214, *see also* Bletchley Park *and*
    Enigma; and cryptanalysis, 24; prin-
    ciples of cipher system of, 26; and
    Purple and Enigma, 35–6; coordination
    of communications systems of, with
    Japan, 43; pact of, with Italy and
    Japan, 44; Britain and signal system of,
    44–5, 121; intelligence of, and Japa-
    nese, 53, 53n, 54, 59, *see also* Abwehr;
    and Japanese codes, 55; and breaking
    of Enigma cipher, 56, 153; Roosevelt
    and activities of, 59; and Ardennes, 61;
    signals from, and *Bismarck*, 82; and
    breaking of codes, 117, 214; and enemy
    radio traffic, 122; B-Dienst of, 132,
    223–4, 229; lack of independence of
    signal intelligence of, 142; and Japan,
    203–7, 209–11, 211n, 212–15; Navy of,
    and Yanagi transports, 205; shortages

Germans (y), codes of (*cont.*)
   in, 205–6, 205n, 234; Navy cryptanalysts of, and Allied codes, 209; replacing of U-boats by, 209, 211–13;
   Navy intelligence of, and Allied convoy
   codes, 219; length of time of, in war,
   219; torpedoes of, 221; industrial production in, 234–5; jet-propelled aircraft
   of, 235–6, 235–6n, 237; spies of, in
   Britain, 240–1; deception of, by Britain,
   262; B-17s and, 276; and Russia, Japan
   and, 278–9; recommendation of, to
   Japan, re peace, 284; lack of political
   structure in, 285; fanaticism in, re
   continued fighting, 287; Magic and, *see*
   Magic; *see also* Hitler, *and under*
   Oshima
Ghormley, Admiral Robert L., 168, 172
Gibbs, General, 38
Gilbert Islands, 161, 192–3
Gillis, J., 136–7
Glasgow, and *Regensburg*, 209
Godfrey, Rear Admiral John, 24–5
Government Code and Cypher School
   (GCCS), 21, 45–6; harmony within,
   24; peacetime resources of, 45; and
   Ultra, 272; *see also* Bletchley Park
Grampus, coast watchers on, 172
Grand Strategy, and intelligence, 192
"Great Marianas Turkey Shoot," 256,
   267
Great Sea War, The, 265
Greater East Asia Co-Prosperity Sphere,
   62, 83, 203, 206
Grew, Joseph Clark, 289
Grey, Sir Edward, and World War I, 155
Grey, Nigel de, 21
Guadalcanal, 155–6, 213; Cory and, 123;
   press leak about, 124; U.S. and Japa-
   nese struggle for, 156, 160–75, 177;
   losses at, 156, 163, 165–6, 173; and
   coast watchers, 159, 165n, hasty prep-
   arations for, 160–2; as hallowed ground,
   162; denominator for, 167; Japanese
   evacuation of, 172, 174–5, 219; combination of intelligence methods and,
   172–3; *see also* Henderson Field,
   Solomons, *and* U.S. Marines
Guadalcanal Campaign, The, 160n
Guam, 28, 255–6

Guderian, Heinz, 61
Gunn, Major John, 269–71
Gurnard, and Take convoy, 228

Hagelin machines, 36
Haig, Field Marshal Douglas, 181
Halle, Kay, 51
Halsey, Admiral William Frederick,
   raids of, 11; to Coral Sea, 93–4; and
   Midway, 99; ordered to Pearl Harbor,
   108–9, 109n; relieved by Spruance, 109;
   and Leyte, 109, 258–9, 265–6; Ultra
   intelligence to, 146; replaces Ghormley,
   168, 170; praise of coast watchers by,
   172; and Yamamoto assassination, 190;
   and Koga plan, 254; and Mindanao, 258;
   and Third Fleet, 258, 261; and San
   Bernardino Strait, 268; and MacArthur,
   271
Hamada, Lieutenant Colonel, 280
Hankey, Sir Maurice, 22–3
Harding, Warren G., 21
Harness, Representative, speech of, 11
Hart, Liddell, 254
Hart, Admiral Thomas C., Pearl Harbor
   inquiry of, 14–15
Hawaii, 97, 103–4; *see also* Pearl Harbor
Hebern, Edward, 34
Hechler, Ted, Jr., 78–9
Heckemyer, Colonel Benjamin W., 270
Heinkel, Ernst, rocket plane of, 236
Henderson Field, 155, 163, 170–1, 173,
   175; *see also* Guadalcanal
Hepburn, Admiral Arthur J., 167n
Hewitt, Admiral Henry Kent, inquiry of,
   47n, 66
Hirohito, Emperor, 276, 281–2, 286, 289
Hiroshima, 276; bombing of, and contro-
   versy re, 44, 64, 285, 288–9; Captain
   Fuchida and, 52; and unconditional
   surrender, 289, 291
Hiryu, 96, 105, 110
*History of the Operations of Special
   Security Officers*, etc., 150, 198
History of the Special Branch, MIS, The,
   141–2, 144
Hitler, Adolf, 61, 233–4; intentions of,
   in Europe, 10, 13; conduct of struggle
   against, 17; and Enigma, 35; and war

with U.S., 44; and Japan, 59; and
intelligence, 177, 192; and invasion of
Russia, 192; and Bhose, 216n; opinion
of Americans, 233, 233n; and British,
234; and jets, 237; and Balkans, 13;
Magic and, *see* Germany; Oshima and,
see under Oshima; *see also* Germany

Hiyo, Trigger and, 226–7

Hohenfriedberg, 207–8

Holland, Elmer J., quote from, 112

Hollandia, 248–52; *see also* Operation
Reckless

Holmes, Captain Jasper (W. J.), 83, 86–7,
95, 139–40; and second bombing of
Pearl Harbor, 97; device of, re Midway, 105–6; and *Yorktown* officer, 106–
7; and Yamamoto's death, 124; and
Rochefort, 138–9; report of, 139, 141,
146–7; Huddleson and, 145; on *Time*
report re MacArthur, 179; and cryptanalysis and submarines, 218; and
breaking of maru code, 223; and
delivery of information, 220; re U.S.
submarines, 227; and Koga plan, 254;
and intelligence re Leyte, 266

Holtwick, Lieutenant Commander Jack S.,
and messages re Coral Sea, 95, 95n

Honshu, planned landing in, 276

Hoover, J. Edgar, 53–4, 63, 119, 125

Hopkins, Harry, 76

Horner, D. M., 180n

Hornet, 93, 108

Houston, torpedoing of, 260

Howse, Philip, and meteorological cipher,
136–7

Huddleson, Edwin E., Jr., 145–6

Hughes, Charles Evans, 22–3

Hukbalahaps, in Luzon, 263

Hull, Cordell, and Nomura, 58–60

Hurley, Patrick, 176

Hürtgen Forest, losses at, 193

Hydra, penetration of, 26

Hypo, 83n, 85–7, 138–40; *see also*
FRUPac

ICPOA, *see* JICPOA

Ienaga, Saburo, 285n, 286n

Ikki, Colonel, at Tenaru River, 169

Imperial Japanese Navy, The, 170, 264

Incredible Victory, 110

Ind, Colonel Allison, 263n

Indian Ocean, German surface vessels in,
212–14

Indianapolis, at Pearl Harbor, 78

Inouye, Vice Admiral Shigeyoshi, 92

Institute of Pacific Relations, 51

interpretation, problem of, 63–4

Italy, 22n, 44–5, 54, 59; and broken
codes, 122; surrender of, 192; and
transfer of cargo, 205

Ito, Captain Jinsaburo, 34, 36

Iwo Jima, 194n, 261, 285; Fifth Fleet
and, 255; Japanese defenses at, 257;
planned assault on, 264; battle for,
275; as emergency landing field,
275n

J machine, 36; *see also* Purple

J19 code, "Winds" signals and, 70–1

JN25, 85–8, 99; breaking of, 93, 99, 159;
changes in, deferred, 99; altering and
replacement of, 105, 127–8, 155, 161;
U.S. Navy and, 116–17; and Grand Jury
trial, 119; OP-20-G and, 137, 155;
resistance to attack, 161n, 167, 220;
continuation of, after Yamamoto's
death, 191

Jack, and Japanese convoy, 228

Jaluit, Japanese signals to, 260

James, Clayton, and Tarbuck, 268

Jane's Fighting Ships, Johnston's use of,
115, 115n

Japan(ese), breaking of codes of, 5–6, 8,
10–12, 14, 55–7, 121, 124, 129, 153,
161, 161n, 164, 172, 176, 178, 182n,
190–1, 196–9, 198n, 202, 213–14, 241–3;
suspicions about breaking of codes and
belief in security of, 10–11, 55–6, 56n,
153, 191, 241–3, 289–90; search of
Portuguese Embassy of, 11; and altering
of codes, 11, 56, 56n, 85, 116–17, 127–8,
169, *see also* JN-25; diplomatic, naval
and military codes of, 18, 19, 21, 28n,
33, 41, 47, 65, 121, 129, 148, 196–9, 198n,
202, 223; early confrontation of, with
U.S., 19; alliance of, with Britain, 21;
and Washington Naval Conference,
21–3, 33; and World War I and Four

Japan (ese), breaking of codes of (*cont.*)
Power Pact, 22, 22n; theft and capture
of code books of, 25, 25n, 131; study
of, 25, 27, 29–30, 133–4; Yardley and,
33; and signal intelligence, 33–4, 55;
and enciphering machine, 34–7; Navy
of, and ciphering machines, 35–6; and
Red, Purple, and Enigma, 36–7, 43,
56n; Army of, and signal traffic, 38;
and German cipher machines, 43;
Britain and signal system of, 44–5; and
Germany and Italy, 44, 53, 59, *see also
under* Germany; Roosevelt policy
toward, 57; Magic, and plans and
preparations of, 57–60, 64–6, 68; and
Russia, 59, 64, 278–83, 285, 289; and
Netherlands Indies and Singapore, 60;
rivalry and disagreement in armed
services of, 61–2, 84, 91n; U.S. assumption of targets of, 64, 64n; final 13-part
and 14th part signal of, 73–7; in spring,
1942, 82–3; and Victory Disease, 83, 88,
96; objectives of, 84; Navy, analysis of
radio traffic of, 90; King and Rochefort
and plans of, 91; training programs of,
104; and Aleutian diversion, 114–15;
change of codes by, and *Tribune*, 116–
17; and enemy radio traffic, 122; supplements re Army and Navy of, 143,
143n; observers of, compared with
Allies, 160; losses of, on Guadalcanal,
163; soldiers of, and Guadalcanal,
173–4; superior equipment of, 174;
Navy of, and Yamamoto, 191; and
Kwajalein, 194; causes of concern to,
203; erosion of merchant navy of, 203,
218–19, 223–4, 248, 256; shortages and
weaknesses in, 205–6; ships of, and
American submarines, 218–19, 227–31;
length of time of, in war, 219; torpedoes
of, 221; convoys of, 223–5, 227–8, 230;
transport shipping of, from start of
war to early 1944, 227; Navy of, and
X-list, 228–9; and jet propulsion, 235–6,
235–6n; and naval attachés' communications, 236, 244–5; covert operations
of, 239; Spanish and Portuguese collaboration with, 239–40, 240n; and German
covert operations, 240–1; and Burma
railroad, 244; Allies' decisions about,

245–6; auguries of defeat for, 248; and
Aitape, 252–3; troops of, to South West
Pacific, 253; and SWPA, 254; deception
in schemes of, 256, 290–1; propaganda
of, re Leyte, 260–1; fanaticism and
death wish of, 261, 263, 287; torture and
execution by, 263; final phase of war
with, 273; in summer of 1945, 275;
bombing of, 275–6, 282, 288–9, *see also*
Hiroshima *and* Nagasaki; despair in,
276, 283; peace movement in, 277, 285,
285n, 286; war party of, 277, 285–6; lack
of political structure in, 285; split in
High Command of, 285–6; and vivisection experiments, 286n; Truman and
Marshall and invasion of, 288; U.S.
ultimatum to, 288–9; events required
for unconditional surrender, 289;
merchant navy of, *see* marus; and
Midway, *see under* Midway; *see also
names of codes*
Japanese Coast Pilot, translation of, 30
Japanese Diplomatic Secrets, 33
Japanese Imperial Railway, 25
Japanese Order of Battle, 86, 89, 114,
261–2, 287–8
Japanese War Ministry, circular of,
50–1
Japan's Last War, 285n
JICPOA, 139–40, 145, 147, 223; and
Kwajalein, 195; and Marianas documents, 257
Johnston, Stanley, and article re Midway,
113–15, 115n, 117, 117n; and Coral Sea,
114; U.S. Navy action against, 116
Joint Committee on the Investigation of
the Pearl Harbor Attack, 54; hearings
before, 3, 13, 15, 19, 47n, 52, 62–3, 67–8;
quote from report of, 49; and Roosevelt,
50n; and "execute" signal, 71–2; verdict
of, 75; and Kramer testimony re Cory,
123
Joint Intelligence Committee, 119
Jouett, sinking of *Burgenland* by, 209

K campaigns, 97n, 98, 103
Kaga, 96, 105, 110
Kaiten, and suicide operations, 288n
Kajioka, Admiral Sadamichi, 228

Kakuta, Rear Admiral Kakuji, 103
kamikaze, 285, 288, 288n
Kanglion, Colonel Ruperto, DSC to, 262
Karin, scuttling of, 207
Kase, Minister, 283–4
Kavieng, Japanese base at, 156
Kennedy, John F., rescue of, 159
Kenney, Major General George C., 185–
    6, 186n
Kido, Marquis Koishi, and peace, 286
Kimball, Professor Warren F., 245n
Kimmel, Admiral Husband Edward, and
    intercepts, Magic, and "execute," 55,
    62–3, 67, 69, 71, 75; and Pearl Harbor,
    68–70, 69n, 75, 77–9
King, Admiral Ernest Joseph, 7, 7n, 9;
    and strength of Navy, 23n; message of,
    to Rochefort, 91; and Midway, 97, 103;
    105; and signal intelligence re K cam-
    paigns, 98; and Yamamoto's plans, 99;
    to Nimitz, re publishing of message,
    113–14; Cunningham warning to, 117;
    and "control of dissemination and use
    of radio intelligence," 120–3; daughter's
    description of, 121; and JN37, 137; and
    transfer of cryptanalytical units, 138;
    and Holmes's report, 139; and Mac-
    Arthur and Rabaul, 183; Lockwood to
    staff of, on torpedoes, 221–2; and
    references to Ultra, 225; support of
    Spruance by, 256; and atom bomb, 288
King II, MacArthur invasion plans, 262–3
Kinkaid, Admiral Thomas, and Leyte,
    168, 259, 262, 264–5, 267–8
Kirishima, and Guadalcanal, 169
Kiska, Japanese and, 10, 100
Knowles, Commander K. A., 47
Knox, Dillwyn, 21
Knox, Frank, 14, 116
Koga, Admiral Mineichi, 191, 254, 256,
    265
Koiso, General Kuniaki, 257
Kokoda trail, 184
Kolambangara Island, battle of, 164
Kondo, Admiral Nobutake, 103, 170
Konoye, Prince Fumimaro, 281, 285
Kooryu, and suicide operations, 288n
Kotor, Ultra and, 257
Kramer, Lieutenant Commander Alvin D.,
    30, 30n, 63, 71, 76, 121, 123

Krueger, General Walter, and Leyte,
    262–4, 267, 270
Kullback, Solomon, 40
Kumana, Eroni, 159
Kurita, Admiral Takeo, 168, 265, 267
Kwajalein, 98, 194–6; losses at, 196
Kyushu, planned invasion of, 276

Lae, 156, 185
La Pérouse, Comte de, 97
Laski, Harold, 118
Lasswell, Alva, 30, 86–7
Layton, Admiral Edwin, 140, 220; and
    Naval Intelligence, 30; and Anglo-
    American cooperation, 47n; and Hewitt
    inquiry, 66; and traffic analysis and
    direction finding, 90; sound judgment
    of, 93; and second bombing of Pearl
    Harbor, 97; article of, 97n; letter from,
    re Sigint and Midway, 107–8; Huddle-
    son and, 145; and MacArthur publicity,
    179; and signal re Yamamoto, 187;
    Nimitz instructions to, re Kwajalein,
    195–6; and Koga plan, 254
Leahy, Admiral William O., 277, 288
Leary, H. Fairfax, 79
Lee's Lieutenants: A Study in Command,
    220–1
Leese, Sir Oliver, 180–1
LeMay, General Curtis, 276
Lewin, Ronald, 144n, 244
Lexington, 94, 96; Johnston on, 114
Leyte, 260, 285; Japanese and, 99, 166,
    262–8, 272; Halsey and, 109, 258–9,
    265–6; Kinkaid and Kurita and, 168;
    landings at, 249; and Sutherland, 258,
    258n; men, material, and shipping for,
    259; Ultra and, 260, 266, 268–9, 272;
    battle at, and mopping up after, 262,
    264–8; *see also* Philippines
Liddell, Guy, and Tricycle, 54, 54n
Lincoln, Abraham, and engineer, 213
Lingayen Gulf, and Luzon, 264
Linn, George W., and "execute," 73, 73n,
    74–5
Liscombe Bay, torpedoing of, 193
Lloyd George, David, Hankey to, 23
Lockwood, Admiral Charles A., 221–2
Lonely Vigil, 172

Long, Captain Andrew, 24–5
Long, Gavin, 176
Lord, Walter, 110, 137, 156–7, 172
Lourenco, Marques, 239, 239n
loyalty, 19
Luftwaffe, 235–6
Lundstrom, John B., 109n
Lunga Point, battle of, 164
Luzon, 194n, 260, 262–4, 266

M 16, see Bletchley Park
MacArthur, General Douglas, 176–80,
    180n, 181–4, 184n, 185–7, 191–2, 196,
    202; and intelligence materials and
    officers, 67, 130, 145, 148–50, 150n,
    151, 177–8, 180, 180n, 181–4, 202, 268–
    71; and news of Pearl Harbor attack,
    77; and Port Moresby, 94; control of
    aircraft by, 94; and shooting down of
    Yamamota, 124; and Brown, 131; and
    SWPA, 140, see also SWPA; directive
    to, re Tulagi, etc., 157; and Papua and
    New Guinea, 175, 196; as hero, in
    Australia, 176; and Congressional Medal
    of Honor, 177; plea of, for reinforce-
    ments, 177, 183; and Philippines, 177,
    191–2, 196, 248, 258, 261–4; descrip-
    tions, character, and excessive claims
    of, 179, 184, 184n, 187, 247; staff of, 179–
    81; and Sutherland, 180, 180n; and
    press dispatch re Marshalls, 182n; and
    Tulagi and Rabaul, 183; myth about,
    184–5; and Nimitz and strategy, 191–2;
    to Stimson, re Navy in Pacific, 196;
    criticism of, 247–8; Chiefs of Staff
    directive to, 248–9; and Hollandia,
    248–51; and Aitape, 250; Ultra and,
    253; and Koga plan, 254; Toyoda and,
    255; and Palaus, 258; and Mindanao,
    258–9; and Leyte, 258, 258n, 264–7; and
    Luzon and Manila, 264; and Corregidor,
    255; and Halsey, 271; Marshall and,
    see under Marshall
MacArthur as Military Commander, 176
McCallum, Daniel, 30
Maclean, Donald, 126n
McCollum, Commander Arthur, 30, 30n,
    77, 114
McCollum, Captain, 30, 202

McCormack, Alfred, 141–5, 152
McCormick, and mobile monitoring, 28
McCormick, Colonel Robert, and Chicago
    Tribune report on Midway, 114, 120;
    and Roosevelt, 114, 117
Macintyre, Captain Donald, 255–6
Mackenzie, Hugh, 171–2
McVittie, G. C., 135, 135n, 136–7
Madang, 185, 202
Magic, 17–18, 21, 26, 48, 50, 121, 143, 206,
    237; birth pangs of, 33; and Abwehr
    questionnaire, 54–5; and Roosevelt's
    attitude toward Japan, 57; and Japanese
    plans and preparations, 57–60, 64–6, 68;
    and Nomura, 58; and Pearl Harbor,
    60–9, 76–7, 286–7, 289; restriction of
    intelligence of, 67, 69–70; U.S. and
    before Pearl Harbor, 67–9; and Roberts
    Commission, 69n; and 13-part signal,
    76–7; failure of, 90; compromising of,
    122; intercept, re leakage, 125; and war
    operations, 129; and Fabian and Cast,
    148; men involved in work of, 153;
    Belconnen and, 182; and Japanese
    military attaché in Lisbon, 192–3;
    Marshall to Roosevelt re, 199; and
    Japanese concerns, 203; and Yanagi
    operations, 205–7; and Ambassador
    Oshima's messages, 210; and Axis
    freighter submarines, 214, 214n; and
    Bhose, 216n; and Japanese convoys,
    224, 227–8; intelligence supplied by,
    through and after Pacific war, 230, 273,
    278–91; and Germany, 232–5, 237–8;
    and Japan, 233, 239; and Hitler and
    Norway, 234; and German jet-propelled
    aircraft, 235–7, 235–6n; and Russian
    activities and intentions, 238; and
    Lourence Marques, 239n; and Japanese
    clandestine activities, 239–40, 240n; and
    Double Cross System, 250; and safe in
    Japanese Embassy, 241; and Mikimoto
    pearls, 242; and Morishima, 242; and
    trivialities, 243; and China/Burma/
    India theater, 244; and Roosevelt-
    Churchill correspondence, 245n; reli-
    ability and importance of, 245–6, 289;
    and Rabaul, 249; and enemy fanaticism,
    261; and Russian Far Eastern policies,
    278; footnote to intercept of, of Togo

signal to Sato, 282; and Marshall, in
July, 1945, 282, 287; and Tokyo, re
surrender, 283, 288; and American
deductions and decisions from, 286–7;
and Yamamoto's plan, 287
*"Magic" Background of Pearl Harbor,
The*, 44, 60, 62–3, 232
Magic Summary, start of, 143; *see also*
Magic
Malaysia, plan for invasion of, 277
Maloelap, as target, 195
Man Who Broke Purple, The, 37, 40n
Manila, planned capture of, 264
Manila Bay, Halsey raids on, 11
Manstein, General Erich von, 61
Marblehead, and mobile monitoring, 28
Marianas, 255–7, 285
Mark XIV, defects of, 221–2
Marshall, General George, 14, 50, 50n,
76, 151, 247; and Dewey, 5–8, 7n, 12–13;
letter to Dewey from, 6–12, 18, 112,
232; character of, 50; and Congres-
sional inquiry, 50, 50n; and Magic, 67,
245, 282, 287; and "execute," 71, 73;
and 13-part signal, 76–7; instructions
from, on intelligence, 120, 122; and
MacArthur, 120, 151, 178–9, 182n, 183,
253, 269, 271; and JN 37, 137; and
Special Branch, 142, 178, 269, 271; and
Anglo-American accord, 151n; and
Bolero, 177; to Roosevelt re Magic and
Black Book, 199; and Hollandia, 248–9;
and Leyte, 258–8; and "new type of
offensive," 275; and atom bomb, 288;
Bissell to, re Japanese communications,
290–1
Marshall Islands, 192–4; Japanese and,
161; MacArthur and press despatch re,
182n; *see also individual names of*
marus, result of sinking of, 218–19, 223–
4; losses of, 219, 223, 225n, 228, 230–1;
breaking of code of, 220, 223–4; allocation of steel for, 224; X List and, 229;
U.S. Navy, Air Force and Marines and,
230; list of sinkings of, 230–1
Mason, Paul, 165, 165n, 171
Mason, Commander Redfield (Rosey), 30,
87
Masterman, Sir John, 240
Matapan, battle of, 95–6

Matsuoka, Yosuke, 58–9, 279
Mauborgne, General Joseph, 40
Melbourne *Herald*, re MacArthur, 179n
Menzies, Major General Stewart, 151n
meteorological information, 135–7
MI, 84–5, 86–100, 105–6
Middle East, British concern about, 64
Midway, 79, 91, 137, 155; and Japanese
naval code, 8, 10; and Magic, 68; and
Japan, 84, 97, 99–100, 109, 110n, 156–7;
FRUPac and, 93; Army bombers and,
94; cryptanalysis and, 99; Americans
and Japanese plans for, 103–10; decoding of date for, 106; and fresh water,
106, 106n; Spruance and, 109; impres-
sions of battle at, 110–11, 110n; and
newspaper articles, 113–14; aftermath
of, 113–14, 156–7; losses at, 174; *Time*
article on, 179; MacArthur's intentions
after, 183; submarines and, 220; Yamamoto and, *see under* Yamamoto; *see
also* MI
Mikawa, Admiral Gunichi, 161, 165–7
Mikimoto pearls, 242
Mikuma, sunk at Midway, 115n
Military Intelligence Service (MIS), 241,
268, 272; *see also* Special Branch
Milne Bay, 184
Milner, Samuel, letter to, 185
Mindanao, 249, 258–9, 262
Mindanao, off Canton, 49
Missouri, kamikaze plot against, 288n
Mitchell, Major John W., 190
Mitscher, Admiral Marc, and Yamamoto
assassination, 190; Fast Carrier Force
of, 194, 255, 258; and Hollandia, 252; to
SWPA, 255; and language officer, 256;
Task Force of, 260
MO, 84–5, 91–3, 96, 157; *see also* Port
Moresby
Mobile Force, Japanese, 255
Model, Field Marshal Walther, 251n
Mogami, guns of, 115n
Molotov, Vyacheslav, and Sato, 274, 279,
281, 284–5
Montgomery, Field Marshal Sir Bernard
Law, 150
Morishima, orders to, re codes, 242–3
Morison, Samuel Eliot, 93–5, 264
Mount Tantalus, bombs on, 97n

Mount Vernon Academy, 133, 133n, 135
Mountbatten, Admiral Louis, 247; and
    Special Security Officers, 150, 152
Musashi, and Yamamoto ashes, 191
Mussolini, Benito, Matsuoka and, 59
Mustang, upgrading of, 235
Mutsupina, 266n

Nagano, Admiral Osami, 61
Nagasaki, 276; bombing of and contro-
    versy re, 44, 285, 288; and uncondi-
    tional surrender, 289, 291
Nagumo, Admiral Chuichi, 91–2, 97, 257
Nakai, Major General, 202
Nakayama, Doctor, 243
"Narrative of the Combat Intelligence
    Center," etc., 139
National Security Agency (NSA), 20, 82,
    139
Nauru, Japanese signals to, 260
Navy, *see under names of countries*
"Need for New Legislation Against Un-
    authorized Disclosures," etc., 126
Netherland Indies, 60
New Britain, 156, 161
New Georgia, 156
New Guinea, 156–7, 161, 184, 192, 202;
    U.S. and Japan and, 157, 161, 186–7;
    Japan and, 157, 171, 175, 181, 253, 255;
    coast watchers and, 159; western, enemy
    designators for, 161; MacArthur and,
    183–4, 187; and Japanese convoy, 185–6;
    Kenney and problems in, 186; losses at,
    196; Australians and, 196, 199
New Hebrides, coast watchers and, 159
New Ireland, 156
"New Order," recognition of, 44
New York *Daily News,* and Midway re-
    port, 114
New York Times, The, and MacArthur
    communiqué, 185
New Zealand, 23, 83
Nimitz, Admiral Chester William, 30,
    203, 247; and Japanese code, 56; Com-
    mand Summary from headquarters of,
    81; and intelligence, 91–3, 96–8, 103,
    105n, 108, 115, 145, 160, 196; and MO,
    93–4; and Coral Sea, 96; and Midway,
    96–8, 100, 103, 106–10, 110n; and
    Yamamoto, 99, 187, 190–1; and Halsey,
    108–9, 109n, 258, 265; King to, re signal,
    113–15, 117; and Japanese Order of
    Battle and Aleutian plan, 114; and
    Rochefort award, 138; and Holmes's
    report, 139; Twitty and, 140; and
    Special Branch, 147, 152; and JN 25,
    155; directive to, re Tulagi, etc., 157;
    and Guadalcanal, 166–7, 169; and
    Ghormley and Guadalcanal, 168; and
    MacArthur, 183, 191–2, 271; and Gilbert
    and Marshall islands, 192–6; letters to,
    re Tarawa, 193; and Kwajalein, 194–6;
    and elimination of marus, 218–19; and
    submarines, 218–20; island hop of, 248;
    Japanese hoped-for blow to, 254; Koga
    and, 254; support of Spruance by, 256,
    and Palaus and Leyte, 258; and Sigint
    and Philippines, 261
97-shiki O-bun In-ji-ki, 36; *see also*
    Purple
Nishi, Lieutenant Colonel Takeichi, and
    German defenses, 237–8
Nixon, Richard M., and staff system, 179
noise, 63–5
Nomura, Kichisaburo, 55, 58–60
Normandy, invasion of, 259–60
Norway, Britain and, 234
Numata, Lieutenant General Takuzo, 251

Office of Naval Intelligence, *see* U.S.
    Naval Intelligence
Office of Strategic Services (OSS),
    MacArthur and, 178
Ogura, Doctor, 243
Okamoto, General Seigo, 238
Okamoto, Suemasa, and ending of war,
    284
Okinawa, 194, 261, 285; Japanese defenses
    at, 257; TF 38 and, 260; planned
    assault on, 264; bloodbath of, 275;
    kamikaze and, 288
Omaha, sinking of *Burgenland* by, 209
On Active Service in Peace and War, 32n
Op Nav, 97–8
OP-20-G, 27, 30, 30n; and "winds" signal,
    74; collaboration of, with FRUPac, 85;

and Japanese codes, 85, 87; and Yamamoto's plans, 99, 99n; and King, 105; and Johnston case, 117; concern of, re breaking of codes, 122, 127; protest from, re *Time*, 125; memorandum from, re clandestine operations, 125; move and expansion of, 133; and JN 25, 137, 155; and Cast, 148; and traffic volume and direction finding at Guadalcanal, 169; Belconnen and, 182; and American submarines, 219

Operation Barbarossa, 206

Operation Flintlock, 194–5, 195n

Operation Olympic, 276–7

Operation *Paukenschlag* (Drumbeat), 234

Operation Reckless, 250–2

Oshima, Baron Hiroshi, messages of, from Berlin, 10, 210, 241; and Japanese codes, 55; and U-boats and submarines, 214, 214n; and Bhose, 216n; Marshall to Dewey re, 232; and Hitler and Germany, 232–5, 237, 278

Osorno, bombing and beaching of, 209

Ozawa, Vice Admiral Jisaburo, 254–5, 265

Pacific, Japanese moves in, information about, 10–11, 18; U.S. operations and war in, 10–11, 18, 50, 50n, 63–4, 112; war in, and breaking of codes, 17; defenses of, 23; responsibility for, 83; war in, and American cryptanalysts, 128; American strategic decisions re, 191–2; verdict of Japanese Lisbon attaché about, 192–3; U.S. superiority in, 202–3; B-29s and, 275; *see also* South West Pacific

Pacific Strategic Intelligence Section, re Japan and Russia, 274, 279–80

Palaus, 257–8

Panama Canal Zone, 115

Pan-American Union, 125–6

Papua, 182–5, 196, 199

Patterson, Eleanor and Joseph, 114

Patton, General George S., Jr., 150, 247

Pearce, Eddie, and Naval Intelligence, 30

Pearl Harbor, 10–11, 11n, 23, 47–8, 64, 67, 109; Dewey and, 5–7; U.S. shock, suspicion, and shame about, 17, 49, 51–2, 57, 62; conspiracy theory about, 50, 50n, 51, 57; and *Abwehr* questionnaire, 53–5; lack of preparedness at, 53–5, 61, 68–70, 76–9; questions about, 60–3, 65–9, 71, 73, 75; warning to, 76–7; U.S. sham attack on, 77; results of attack on, 78–80, 82, 90; FRUPac at, 83; second bombing of, 97; planned final return visit to, 99; broadcast during attack on, 104; fear of fresh assault on, 105; casualties at, 124; intelligence center at, 139–40, 146; signal intelligence after, 141; affidavit in Inquiry file of, re Special Branch, 147–8; investigations into, *see under names of committees and inquiries*; Magic and, *see* Magic

Peleliu, 257–8

Penang, as U-boat base, 212

Pershing, John J., 38

Pestilence, code name, 157

Philby, Kim, 126n

Philippine Sea, battle of, 255

Philippines, 253; radio surveillance posts at, 28; and signal intelligence, 83n, 129, 160, 273; monitoring of Japanese units in, 131; and coast watchers, 160, 263; MacArthur and, 177, 191–2, 196, 248, 258, 261–4; planned invasion of, 258, 261–3; U.S. concern re liberation of, 261; resistance movement in, 262–3, 263n; gradual domination of, 273; *see also* Leyte

Phoenix, 79

Pilgrim's Progress, 153

Pogue, Forrest, 50n, 77

Poles, and Enigma, 16, 16n, 35, 40, 45–6

Ponape, Japanese signals to, 260

Popov, Dusko, 52–5

Port Moresby, Japanese and, 84, 91–2, 94, 182–4, *see also* MO; MacArthur plan for, 94

Portugal, 239

Potsdam, conference in, 282, 284

Potter, E. B., 195

PPP, German signals and, 209–10

press, and leaks and security, 112–14, 116, 117n, 118, 124–5, 128; *see also names of papers and magazines*

Prince of Wales, 79, 93
Purple, 17, 36–44, 44n, 45–6, 51, 56n, 197,
   233, 244; and Japanese diplomatic signals, 17; and Enigma, 36, 42–3; Britain
   and, 36, 45–6; penetration of, 37–41,
   43–5, 51, 60, 67, 129; and Red Machine,
   42–3; security of, 56n; and SWPA, 158;
   Belconnen and, 182; flexibility of, 236

Rabaul, 157, 202; Japanese and, 91, 156–
   7, 160–1, 185–7, 248–50; U.S. and, 157,
   186, 190, 248, 248n; MacArthur and,
   179, 183–4, 248, 248n, 249–50; warning
   re, 182
radio intelligence, *see* signal intelligence
Rainbow Five, 64, 67, 69
Ralston, James Layton, 136
Rangoon, Japanese and, 166
Raven, Commander Francis, 244–5, 245n
Read, Jack, 165, 171
Red Book, Japanese, 27–8
Red Machine, 36, 41, 244; and Purple,
   42–3
Redl, Colonel Alfred, 32
Redman, John, 138
Redman, Joseph, 138
Regensburg, and Enigma, 209
Rejewski, Marian, 40
"Rendezvous in Reverse," 97n
Rendova, battle of, 164
Rennell Island, battle of, 164
Repulse, 79, 93
Richardson, General Robert C., 145
Roberts, Justice Owen J., Pearl Harbor
   Commission and report of, 11, 11n, 14,
   69n
Rochefort, Captain Joseph, and ciphers
   and codes, 3–4; and cryptanalysis, 29,
   29n; and Japanese language, 29–30;
   monitoring of Japanese radio transmis-
   sions by, 65; and Purple and Magic, 67;
   and "execute," 71, 73; and Japanese
   codes, 85–6, 89; Holmes's description
   of, 86–7; and messages from and to
   Admiral King, 91–3; and dates for
   Aleutians and Midway, 106; Holmes's
   suggestion to, 106; Layton letter re
   work with, 107–8; to Lord, re Naval
   Intelligence, 137–8; as victim, and

proposed award to, 138–9; and ICPOa
   and Hypo, 140
Rockefeller, Nelson, 59
*Role of Radio Intelligence in the
   American-Japanese War, The*, 89n,
   157n
Rommel, Field Marshal Erwin, 61,
   233–4
Roosevelt, Franklin D., Dewey and 5–7, 9,
   13; and Pearl Harbor, 5, 7, 14, 50, 68,
   76; and Roberts Commission, 14; and
   fear, 48; Congressional inquiry and, 50n;
   and Japan, 57, 64, 277; Nomura and,
   58, 60; and South American undercover
   group, 59; and 13-part signal, 76; and
   intelligence, 83; and Pacific situation,
   83; McCormick and, 114, 117; and Foster
   mission, 115–16; and press leaks, 118;
   Diktat of, re cryptanalytical units,
   119–20; and MacArthur, 176–7; and
   Bolero, 177; and Yamamoto assassination, 190–1; and Magic and Black Book,
   199; correspondence of, with Churchill,
   and Magic, 245n; re Philippine invasion, 262; Marshall, after death of,
   282; and Stalin, re Japanese war, 283
Rowell, General, protest to, 179n
Rowlett, Frank, 40
Rózycki, Jerzy, 40
Russia, 44, 44n; and Japan, 59, 64, 278–83,
   285, 289; effect of invasion of, 206; and
   Arctic convoys, 212; length of time of,
   in war, 219; Magic and, 238; and shar-
   ing of information, 238; and Germany,
   Japan, and, 278–9
Russie en 1839, La, 118
Russo-Japanese Relations, quote from,
   274
Ryujo, and Guadalcanal, 169–70
Ryukaku, *Shoho* mistaken for, 86, 92

Safford, Laurence L., 27–9, 34, 41, 47n,
   71, 73–5
Saipan, 255–7
Saipan-Guam area, Japanese to, 104
Saito, General Yoshitsugu, 257
Saku, Constable, report of, 160n
Sakuma, Shin, 34
Salamaua, in Japanese hands, 156

Salmon, and Japanese carrier, 226–7

Samar, 168, 272

Samsonov, General Aleksandr V., 249

San Bernardino Strait, 265, 268

San Francisco, Callaghan on, 162

Sandford, Major A. W., 149

Santa Cruz Islands, battle of, 164

Saratoga, and Solomons, 162, 170

Sargent, Captain James, and Ultra, 270

Sato, Naotake, 278–82, 284; and Molotov, 274, 279, 281, 284–5; to and from Togo re termination of war, 281–2, 284

Saturday Evening Post, The, Yardley articles in, 33

Savo Island, 164, 166–7, 173–4

Scharnhorst, sinking of, 96

Scheer, Reinhard, at Jutland, 265

Scott, Admiral Norman, 162

Sculpin, sinking of, 121n

Seahorse, and A-Go, 255

Searaven, and *Regensburg*, 209

security, 113–28, 130, 140–1

Seeadler Harbor, MacArthur and, 251

Shakespeare, William, 244

Shanghai, surveillance post in, 28, 32n

Sherr, Colonel Joe, 129–30, 181, 181n

Sherwood, Robert, and Stimson, 32

Shigemitsu, Mamoru, 242, 278–9, 290

Shirataka, and *Jack*, 228

Sho, 264

Shoho, 86, 92–5

Shokaku, 92–5, 169, 256

Short, Walter Campbell, and intercepts, Magic, and "execute," 62–3, 67, 69–70, 70n, 71, 75; and Pearl Harbor, 68–70, 69n, 75, 77

Shortlands Islands, 170

Sigaba, 36, 153

Sigint, *see* signal intelligence

Signal Corps Unit Training Centers, 134

signal intelligence, 47–8, 63, 69; U.S. preparation for, 19; before Pearl Harbor, 54–5; difficulties created by, 65; many pieces of, 66; units of, 83, 83n; credibility, quality, and accuracy of, 90–3, 105, 105n, 115, 129–30, 191, 194, 223, 227–9, 236–7; and King and Rochefort and Japanese plans, 91; and battle of the Coral Sea, 93–6; and Matapan, 95–6; and MI, 96; and Nimitz, 98; and

Aleutians, 100; and Midway, 103, 107–8; early warning system supplied by, 107; newspaper reports derived from, 113–15; dangers of leaks in, risks and stakes of, 113, 128, 214; in Pacific, 126–7; expansion of, 128–9, 131–2; main developments in, between 1942 and 1945, 129–54; delays in delivery of, 130; American preeminence in, 132, 132n; Stimson and, 141; McCormack report on, 141–2; and Solomons, 157–8, 160–1, 164–7, 169, 174–5; and battles of the Slot, 164–5; failure to profit from, 164, 166–7, 167n; record of, and change of Japanese call signs, 169; and Guadalcanal, 172–3; and Tokyo Express, 173; SWPA and, 178–9; and Rabaul, New Guinea, and Port Moresby, 182–3, 185–6; and Japanese defeat at New Guinea, 187; inability of, 194; and Japanese Army code, 196–9, 202; and Japanese military communications, 197; and Japanese concerns, 203; and Yanagi operations, 205–7; and Axis blockade runners and cargo-carrying vessels, 205, 207, 207n, 208–14, 217; new factor of, and *Burgenland*, 209; and Bhose, 216; and Japanese merchant shipping and convoys, 219, 224–5; and American submarines, 220–3, 225, 225n; and X-list, 228; and Hollandia, 249; and Take convoy, 254; and Mobile Force, 255; and Philippines, 261; and Leyte, 266–7; and Terauchi departure, 267; integration of, 273; and Japanese determination to keep fighting, 287; MacArthur and, *see* MacArthur, and intelligence; *see also all units of, such as* FRUPac *and* Cast, *and names of codes:* Purple, Enigma, *etc.*, cryptanalysis, direction finding, *and* traffic analysis

Signal Intelligence Service (SIS), 19n, 38–41, 132

Signals Intelligence Board (Britain), 121n

Silent Victory, 220, 225

Sims, Lieutenant, 256

Singapore, 45, 60, 79–80, 233; and U-boats, 212; and Indian prisoners, 216; plan for recovery of, 277

Sinkov, Colonel Abraham, 40, 149

Skelly, William, Clarke and, 6
skip-bombing, 186
Slim the Standard-bearer, 244
Slot, 177; importance of, 155; British and,
    156; coast watchers and, 159–60, 171;
    "Tokyo Express" and, 163, 170–2;
    various names for battles of, 164; Sigint
    and, 164–5; Japanese and, 166–7,
    170–2
Smith, General Holland M., 195, 195n
Smith-Hutton, Captain Henri, 30–1, 31n,
    115n
Solomons, 155–61; U.S. and Japanese
    struggle for, 156, 160–75; coast watchers
    and, 159, 171; signators, 161, 167; losses
    at, 162, 165–6, 170, 173; Northern, battle
    of, 164; Eastern, battle of, 164, 169–70;
    U.S. aircraft at, 169; see also Guadal-
    canal
Somers, sinking of *Weserland* by, 209
Soryu, 96, 105, 110
South America, 59, 124–5
South West Pacific Area (SWPA), 140;
    MacArthur and, 145, 148; and intelli-
    gence, 145, 147–52, 178–9, 266n, 268,
    270–1; Cast and, 148; meager achieve-
    ments of, 177–8; publicity from, 178–9,
    179n, 184–5; and OSS, 178; staff of,
    179–80; disorganization of, after Papua,
    185; reports from on New Guinea, 187;
    Japan and, 192, 254; submarine force
    of, 223–4; and Hollandia, 248, 248n,
    252; and Adachi, 252; and Mindanao
    bypass, 259; Allied Intelligence Bureau
    of, and Philippines, 263, 263n; and
    Special Branch, 268–72
Spaatz, General Carl, 247, 277
Spain, collaboration of, with Japan, on
    intelligence, 239–40, 240n, 241; and
    Mikimoto pearls, 242
Special Branch of Military Intelligence
    Service, 141–3, 143n, 144–7, 153, 268–9,
    271–2; staff and atmosphere of, 142–3;
    Ultra Advisers of, 144n, 178; Special
    Security officers of, 146–7, 150–3; and
    Japanese Army Supplement, 198–9
Special Liaison Units, British and
    Americans and, 144, 146, 151, 271; and
    success of signal intelligence, 153
Speer, Albert, 233n, 235

Spruance, Admiral Raymond, 109–10,
    146, 194–5, 258; and Koga plan, 254,
    256
Stalin, Joseph, and intelligence, 177; and
    sharing of information, 238; and war
    against Japan, 278, 283, 285; see also
    Russia
Stark, Admiral Harold Raynsford, 50,
    50n, 55, 67, 69, 74–6
State Department, information to, on
    Japanese moves, 10; and Black Cham-
    ber, 20, 24; and Japanese authorities,
    60
Stilwell, General Joseph, 150, 152, 247
Stimson, Henry L., 14, 32, 32n, 141, 178;
    and deciphering of Japanese, 32, 32n,
    38; MacArthur letter to, 196; and atom
    bomb, 288–9
submarines, American, and Japanese
    merchant navy, 218–19, 227–31; ineffi-
    ciency of, 219, 221–2; competence of
    commanders of, 220–2; torpedoes of,
    221–2, 227; and signal intelligence,
    220–3, 225, 225n; claims of commanders
    of, 225–6; loss of, 227; and wolf pack,
    229; air power replaces, 230; and
    Japanese A-Go plan, 255; and Leyte,
    255
submarines, German, replacing U-boats,
    209, 211–13; passengers on, 211; casual-
    ties to, 212; Magic and, 214; as transport
    service, 214n; abandoning of, 215; see
    also U-boats
submarines, Japanese, 227–8, 288n
Suicide Attack Squadron Organization,
    288n
suicide operations, Japanese and, 287–8,
    288n; see also kamikaze
Suma, Ambassador, 242–3
Sunda Strait, 209
Suñer, Ramón Serrano, 239–40
Sutherland, Major General Richard K.,
    130, 180, 180n, 182, 269, 271; and Leyte,
    258, 258n
Suzuki, Baron Kantaro, and peace,
    286

Takahashi, Vice Admiral Ibo, 243–4
Take convoy, 228, 253–4

Tarawa, 110n, 161; battle and losses at, 193–4, 196; MacArthur and, 196; secret Japanese defenses at, 257

Tarbuck, Admiral Raymond, 268

Tate, double agent, 240–1

Taylor, Rufus L., 30

Taylor, Telford, to England, 143, 143n

Tenaru River, battle of, 169

Terauchi, Count Hisaichi, 267

Terraine, John, and Chareris and Davidson, 181

Thailand, Germany and Japan and, 206

Theobald, Rear Admiral Robert A., 100–1

Thompson, Major John, and SWPA, 269

Thornton, to French Frigate Shoals, 98

Thucydides, quote from, 128

Thurber, James, 176n

Tiltman, Brigadier John H., 82, 136, 136n, 137

Time magazine, disclosure of breaking of code by, 124–5; and MacArthur publicity, 179

Times Literary Supplement, The, review in, 33n

Times, London, and leakage, 125

TINA, British and, 88

Tinian, 255–6

Tizard Mission, 45

Togo, Admiral Heihachiro, 191, 255; to Sato, 281–2, 284–5; and terms for peace, 282–4, 286, 289

Tojo, General Hideki, 51, 257

Tokyo, U.S. Embassy in, 25; raid on, 93, 96, 276; Japanese return to, 175; MacArthur–Nimitz strategy and, 191; *see also* Japan

Tokyo Express, 163, 170–4

torpedoes, 218, 221–2, 227

Toyoda, Admiral Soemu, 254–5, 286

Toyoda, Admiral Teijiro, replaces Matsuoka, 59

traffic analysis, 65, 198; importance of, dependence on, and intelligence produced by, 89, 89n, 90, 155, 160–1; and Japanese carriers, 92; and MI, 97; training for, 134; and Solomons, 157–9; and battles of the Slot, 164; and Mikawa's cruisers, 166; and Tokyo Express, 171–3; and Guadalcanal, 172–

3; and SWPA, 178; and Take convoy, 253–4; and Philippines plans, 262

Trans-Siberian railway, 206

Travis, Sir Edward, 121n; and meteorological data, 137

Trevor-Roper, H. R., 49, 80, 289

Tricycle questionnaire, 53–5, 63; *see also* Popov, Dusko

Trigger, and Japanese carrier, 226–7

Tropic of Capricorn, 183

Truk, 93–4, 103–4, 161, 169, 248n

Truman, Harry S., and Friedman, 38; as President, 282; and anti-Russian policy, 283; and atom bomb, 287–9

Tulagi, 156, 156n, 157, 160; Japanese and, 84, 96, 157, 157n, 160–1; struggle for, and securing of, 162; MacArthur and Nimitz and, 183

Turner, Admiral Richmond Kelly, 64, 162, 165–7, 195, 195n

Twelfth Night, Takahashi and, 244

Twitty, Colonel Joseph, and JICPOA, 140

Typex, 36, 153

U 110, capture of, 26, 26n

U-boats, 69, 211–17, 229; Allied intelligence and, 135; and new Enigma cipher, 208–9; Milch Cow, 213, 213n; failure of, 219; cryptanalysis and, 223; Hitler and victories of, 234; *see also* submarines

Uckermark, blowing up of, 207

Ueno, Commander Toshitake, 98

Ultra, 16, 16n, 18–19, 21, 26, 46, 46n, 64, 68, 151, 270, 272–3; British and, 90–1, 121, 271; and *Scharnhorst*, 96; Cromwell and, 121n; use of, and compromising of, 121–2; handlers of, and capture by the enemy, 123, 123n; security and lack of, 124, 150, 270; and war operations, 129; and Japanese language, 134; Anglo-American cooperation and, 135, 144, 151; and submarine force, 139–40, 140n; intelligence from, to Halsey and Spruance, 146; and Special Branch, 146–7, 178, 269, 271; Fabian's team and, 148; men involved in work of, 152–3; enciphering machine and, 153; and

Ultra (cont.)
  SWPA, 181; and Battle of Bismarck
  Sea, 185; and death of Yamamoto, 187;
  and 1943 decisions, 192; and Fifth
  Fleet assaults, 193; capability and
  inability of, 193–4, 202; and Kwajalein,
  195–6; and Japanese Army code, 196,
  199; and Blamey, 199, 202; and Japanese concerns, 203; and submarine and
  transport shipping, 220, 222–5, 228–30;
  references to forbidden in reports, 225;
  and claims of submarine commanders,
  225–6; and X-list, 229; and Rabaul,
  249–50; and Hollandia, 250–2; and
  Aitape, 252–3; and Philippines and
  Take convoy, 253–4; Palaus and, 257–8;
  and Leyte, 260, 266, 268–9, 272; and
  enemy fanaticism, 261; and plans for
  Philippines, 261–2; and Terauchi departure, 267; improper handling of,
  268–72; and Samar, 272; and Japanese
  defensive preparations, 288
Ultra Advisers, 122, 144n, 178
Ultra Goes to War, 36n, 126, 144n
Ultra Secret, The, 16, 16n
Umezu, General Yoshijiro, 286
Undersea Victory, 227
United Nations, Magic and, 233
United States, and intelligence gathering,
  6; and Japanese codes and ciphers,
  17–19, 132, 132n, see also Magic; early
  confrontation of, with Japan, 19; route
  of, to Magic and Ultra, 19–21, 24, 26;
  and Four Power Pact, 22, 22n, 23; and
  two-ocean struggle, 23, 23n; divisions
  within, on cryptanalysis, 24; and Enigma, 35; and Japanese machines, 35–6;
  Hitler and war with, 44; and intelligence cooperation with Britain, 44–7,
  46n, 47n, 120; and Purple, 46, see also
  Purple; and Ultra, 46n, see also Ultra;
  and signal intelligence, 47–8; and Pearl
  Harbor, 49–50, 50n, 51–5, 57, 60, 62–3;
  and value of deciphering, 57; and
  Japanese war plans, 64, 64n; and necessities of war, 68; and Pacific responsibility, 83; increased production and
  sophistication of, and industrial improvement and supremacy, 110, 174,
  191, 194, 202, 219, 224, 248, 255; irresponsibility and nonconformity of
  people and press of, 112–13, 118, 128;
  and signal-intelligence security system
  of, 113, 115, 117, 117n, 118–21, 121n,
  122–7; monitoring of enemy wireless
  traffic by, 122; post-war history, and
  security, 126; wartime response in, 132;
  and Special Liaison Units, 146–7, 151;
  and Tulagi, Solomons, and Rabaul, 157;
  aircraft of, in Solomons, 169; change
  of, from defense to counterattack, 191;
  convoys of, to Britain, 211n; and Milch
  Cow U-boats, 213, 213n; length of time
  of, in war, 219; upgrading of Mustang
  by, 234; and language officers, 256;
  worry of, about assault on Japan, 261;
  plans of, for Japan, 274–7; post-war
  benefits to, from Japanese systems, 290;
  see also Allies, Departments of
U.S. Air Force, and Sigint, 131; and
  Japanese shipping, 230; plans of, for
  defeating Japan, 275–7
U.S. Army Strategic Air Forces, 277
U.S. Army, antagonism between Navy
  and, 24, 140–1, 144, 179; and cryptanalysis, 28n, 122; and Japanese language, 29–31; secret communication
  record of, 31; Yardley and Black
  Chamber and, 31; and pooling of
  intelligence with Navy, 41, 122–3, 141,
  144–7; fears of, of California invasion,
  105; and Ultra Advisers, 122; and signal
  intelligence, 129; growth of cryptographic services in, 132–3; Cryptographic School of, 134; and JN37, 137;
  difficulty of distributing intelligence to,
  and maintaining security of, 140; and
  security, 144; and Central Bureau, 149n;
  hardships of, at Guadalcanal, 174;
  increase in, 191
U.S. Army Air Force, and Ultra Advisers,
  122
U.S. Army Intelligence, and Magic and
  Pearl Harbor, 67
U.S. Army–Navy Intelligence Committee,
  authorization of, 67
U.S. Marines, and Japanese language,
  29–30; and Guadalcanal, 123, 156, 160,
  164–8, 171, 174, 213; and Solomons, 158,
  162; history of, and coast watchers,

159–60; and Tulagi, 160; Turner and, 162; increase in, 191; and Tarawa, 193; dockers' treatment of, 213; and Japanese shipping, 230; and Peleliu, 257–8

U.S. Naval Institute, *Proceeding* of, and Pearl Harbor, 78–9

U.S. Naval Intelligence, acceleration of, 24–5; and language students, 30; and Magic and Pearl Harbor, 67; Midway report of, 111

U.S. Navy, Court of Inquiry of, 14; and cryptanalysis, 24–5, 27, 122, *see also* Op-20-G; and Japanese language, 25, 27, 29–31, 134–5; and signal intelligence, 41, 129, 132–3, 137, *see also* U.S. Naval Intelligence; and U-boats, 69; in spring of 1942, 82; and Johnston article, 116; and JN 25, 116–17; and *Tribune* affair, 119; War Department, and joint committee of FBI, 121; and meteorological ciphers, 136–7; internecine conflict in, 137–9; and Guadalcanal and Solomons, 162–7, 167n, 168–71, 173; and intelligence to SWPA, 178–9; Signal Intelligence Summary of, and Moresby, 182–3; and Midway, 183; and Pacific plans, 192; MacArthur letter re, 196; and Japanese shipping, 230; and Leyte, 266; and Ultra security, 270; and Army, *see under* U.S. Army; Code and Signal Section of, *see* Op-20-G

U.S. Office of Naval Operations, 60

U.S. Pacific Fleet, 69, 84

U.S. Signal Corps, official history of, 19n; investigation of Black Chamber by, 32; and Enigma, 35; and radio intelligence, 141–2

U.S. South Atlantic Strategic D/F Net, report from, 210

Vandegrift, General Alexander A., 124, 167, 171–2; and Guadalcanal, 162, 165–6

Van Der Rhoer, Edward, 87, 123, 133–4

Vella Lavella, coast watchers on, 172

Very Special Intelligence, 135

Victory Disease, 83, 88, 96

Victory in Papua, 185

vivisection, Japanese experiments with, 286n

Volckmann, Colonel Russell W., 262

Vouza, Sergeant Major Jacob, 159–60

Voynich, William, manuscript of, 81–2

Wainwright, General Jonathan M., 131

Wake Island, 97, 106, 106n; Japanese signals to, 260

Walrus and the Carpenter, The, quote from, 39

War College Theories, 137–8

War Department, and Black Chamber, 20, 24; Navy and FBI joint committee of, 121; and Ultra, 150; Australia and, 178

Washington, D.C., and combat intelligence, 198; and Japan and Russia, 277–8, 280, 283

Washington Naval Conference, 19, 21–3, 33, 58

Washington Post, The, and Foster mission, 116; and Japanese code, 124; and MacArthur claim re New Guinea, 187

Washington Times Herald, and Midway, 114

Wasp, and Solomons, 162, 169–70

Watchtower, 157

Wavell, General Archibald, 168, 275

Wenger, Joseph N., 31, 31n, 121, 125

Weserland, sinking of, 209, 215

Wewak, 250, 252–3

White House Papers, The, 32

Whitehill, Walter, 133

Wilde, Oscar, and London fog, 16

Wilkinson, Lieutenant Colonel Theodore S., 75–6, 178

Willoughby, General Charles, and intelligence, 147–9, 180, 180n, 202, 268–9, 271; and MacArthur, 180, 180n, 249; and Hollandia, 250

"Winds" signals, 70–1, 73–5, 123; *see also* "execute"

Wingate, Brigadier Orde Charles, 244

Winterbotham, F. W., 16, 16n

Wireless Experimental Centre, 196–7

Wohlstetter, Roberta, 63

wolf pack, 229

Wolfe, General James, 39, 64–5

World War I, Japan and, 22, 22n
Wotje, as target, 195

X List, 228–9

Y Service, British, 90, 236
Y Subcommittee, 121n
Yalta, Japanese and, 279
Yamamoto, Admiral Isoroku, 84; death
    of, 30, 124, 187, 190–1; and Pearl Har-
    bor, 53, 61–2, 79, 82; and Midway, 96,
    99–101, 103–4, 109–110, 113, 170; plans
    of, 98–9, 138, 155, 170, 187, 190, 287;
    and battle of Eastern Solomons, 169–
    70; Japanese Navy and, 191; and in-
    creasing U.S. strength, 224
Yamashita, General Tomoyuki, 266–7
Yamato, 169–70, 285

Yanagi operation, 205–7; end of, 211
Yap, Ultra and, 257
Yardley, Herbert, 19–23, 31–4, 38–9, 58,
    126
Yokohama Flying Boat Squadron, 161
Yonai, Admiral Mitsumasa, and peace,
    286
Yontan, and suicide operation, 288
Yorktown, 94, 96, 106–7, 109–10
Yoshida Maru, sinking of, 228
Yosii, Lieutenant Commander Mitinory,
    and Tate episode, 241

Zacharias, Ellis, 25, 27–8, 30–1, 36
Zeppelin, as blockade runner, 207n
Zimmerman, John L., 160n
Zipper, 277
Zuikaku, 92–4, 169, 256
Zygalski, Henryk, 40